Transportation

Fourth Edition

Robert C. Lieb
Northeastern University

1994

DAME
PUBLICATIONS, INC.
7800 Bissonnet– Suite 420
Houston, TX 77074

Desktop Publishing: Joseph J. Marquez, III

Cover Photograph: Santa Fe Railway Double Stack Train at Cajone Pass, California *Courtesy of Santa Fe Railway*

© **DAME PUBLICATIONS. INC. — 1994**
7800 Bissonnet–Suite 420
Houston, TX 77074

ISBN 0-87393-227-7
Library of Congress Catalog Card No. 93-74191
Printed in the United States of America

Table of Contents

Preface

It is difficult to believe that seventeen years have passed since I began the research which led to the first edition of this book. Since that time the structure of the transportation industries has changed dramatically and the marketplace has become far more competitive. These changes have been driven not only by regulatory reforms but also by new approaches to management thinking. The pace of change has quickened and carriers, shippers, travelers, and public policy makers now interact in a very dynamic environment. Public awareness of transportation issues has also increased as media coverage of such topics as deregulation, carrier bankruptcies, highway safety, air quality, and energy conservation has expanded.

It has become increasingly obvious that transportation planning cannot occur in isolation, but rather must be integrated with the planning process of other economic sectors. While integration is desirable, it increases the complexity of transportation issues. This book has been written to assist students and practitioners in comprehending this complexity.

The book doesn't attempt to provide final answers to the diverse transportation problems facing the nation. Instead, it seeks to identify those problems while providing background information to assist the reader in analyzing the issues and alternatives involved. Hopefully, the book will stimulate the reader to pursue further study in this field. It is only through such study that the practitioners and policy makers of tomorrow will be able to cope effectively with the future transportation challenges that are certain to confront our nation.

I have attempted to offer a readable and comprehensive treatment of transportation topics which might be useful to people with a variety of backgrounds, including business, economics, and government. While the primary focus of the book is intercity transportation, some attention is also devoted to international and metropolitan transportation issues. In examining such issues, the book considers not only the views of carrier management, but also those of public officials and consumers of transportation services.

To facilitate the development and flow of material, the book is organized into six parts. Part I identifies the significance and role of transportation in our society and also defines the perspective of the shipping public as it views transportation alternatives. Part II concentrates on the development, structure, and cost and service characteristics of the intercity modes, and also examines the international airline and maritime industries. Those chapters serve as the foundation for the public policy and carrier management discussions of subsequent chapters. Part III focuses on the interaction of cost and demand considerations in the transportation pricing process. It also gives attention to the ratemaking procedures employed by carriers and ratemaking innovations. Part IV examines the role of various government units in the regulation and promotion of intercity carriage. The development of the extensive government involvement in transportation is traced, and the difficulties inherent in such a complex private-public interrelationship are discussed. Part V provides a review of a number of carrier management problems and public policy issues. The book concludes with Part VI, which devotes attention to transportation within our metropolitan areas. The institutions, problems, and government policies that relate to metropolitan transportation are examined, as is the interface that exists between the intercity and metropolitan transportation systems.

I would like to express my thanks to Nick Luise of UPS Worldwide Logistics and Clement Hanrihan of the UPS Foundation for their support in development of the fourth edition of this book. Their belief in the significance of the project was very important to me.

The contributions of many people have been vital to the development of all four editions of this book. Among the foremost contributors to this effort have been my past and present students at Northeastern University. Their enthusiasm for transportation has made our interaction most enjoyable, and has proven quite inspirational. Similarly, my contacts with representatives of carriers, shippers, industrial associations, and government agencies have proven invaluable.

I also greatly appreciate the contributions of my colleagues at Northeastern to this revision. I'm especially indebted to Rae Andre for her encouragement and support throughout this process. My interaction with fellow faculty members Jim Molloy and Bob Millen provided important feedback which helped shape the book. My research assistants during the past several years, Laurent Bazini, Yves Zuber, Jean Francoise Coste, Beatrice Lambert, provided invaluable assistance in researching related topics and reviewing preliminary materials. They spent many long hours at the library searching for relevant material. I'd also like to thank my secretary, Gladys Saheed, for her assistance. My colleague Steve DeRosier also played a very important role in convincing the college's computers to accept my often ill-prepared offerings. Tom Harvey, of Harvey Consultants, also helped immensely by volunteering to read early versions of the manuscript.

Thanks also to Frank Quinn, Editor of *Traffic Management* for his willingness to discuss various aspects of the book with me, and Janice Murad of BMW for the materials which she shared with me. Jack Harman and Larry Phillips of the Federal Department of Transportation helped me identify people and materials which were very important in addressing the public policy making process in transportation.

I worked closely with Joe Marquez of Dame Publications in developing the manuscript. It was a pleasure to work with him.

Finally, a special note of appreciation is due to my daughter and friend, Kristin. You have also been through this process four times! I clearly remember telling you, while writing the third edition of this book, to give me a solid kick in the posterior if I ever considered doing a fourth edition. Thank you for not exercising that option.

Robert C. Lieb
Northeastern University

Part One

TRANSPORTATION: ITS SCOPE AND FUNCTION

Aircraft Operations Boston Logan Airport *Courtesy Massachusetts Port Authority*

Chapter One

TRANSPORTATION AND ITS ROLE IN SOCIETY

Our nation's transportation system has a pervasive impact on each of us. It not only influences our personal mobility and the prices that we pay for goods and services, but it also is a major determinant of where we choose to live and work. At the same time, individuals affect the transportation system through such actions as their purchase of transportation services and their commitment to the automobile. In turn, automobile use has significant implications with respect to contemporary concerns involving pollution, congestion, and energy conservation.

Although this two-directional pattern of influence is quite meaningful in terms of the realization of both personal and national goals, the transportation system and its operations are little understood by the general public. Historically, the public has tended to take the existence of transportation services for granted, and public interest has only been stimulated by such incidents as carrier bankruptcies, strikes, or accidents. However, in recent years public awareness of transportation issues has increased as our national transportation problems have been more widely publicized. One often hears such questions as: Why doesn't the federal government build a high speed rail passenger network linking our major cities. Or, why doesn't the local transit company buy some new equipment, increase service, and lower fares to attract additional passengers?

Superficially there is great appeal in such suggestions. However, because of the complexity of our nation's transportation system, and due to public dependence upon it, there are no simple solutions to these problems. The basic purpose of this book is to illustrate this complexity and to provide sufficient background to allow the reader to become conversant with the issues involved.

ECONOMIC SIGNIFICANCE OF TRANSPORTATION

Development of an adequate transportation system is essential to a nation's economic progress. As an integral part of national production and distribution systems, an adequate transportation network is necessary to provide a means of servicing domestic and international markets. This is of primary importance in the early stages of economic development because it promotes an accumulation of capital, which allows the economy to progress from the subsistence level at which most production is consumed locally. Transportation and other government programs, such as education and health care, necessarily compete for public expenditures, particularly in developing countries. There are indications, however, that a balanced approach to expenditures in these areas, rather than a disproportionate concentration of government outlays in one area, leads to a more desirable growth pattern.[1]

Naturally, as an economy expands, its demand for transportation facilities and services increases. This typically leads to an increasing flow of capital from both the public and private sectors into transportation.

Federal, state, and local government transportation expenditures have grown steadily in the United States and have played a major role in fostering development of the country's extensive transportation system. In recent years such outlays have averaged more than $100 billion per year (see Table 1-1).

The extent of the federal commitment to such development was illustrated by congressional passage of the Intermodal Surface Transportation Efficiency Act of 1991. The legislation called for federal outlays of $151 billion during the subsequent six years. Of that amount, approximately $119.5 billion was to be spent on highway improvements and $31.5 billion was to be used on mass transit projects.[2]

The combination of public and private transportation expenditures helps promote regional specialization and division of labor, which in turn fosters large-scale production. These factors combine to lower raw material and finished goods prices in the economy and to increase the availability of goods throughout the nation. National commodity flows necessitate the emergence of large-scale distribution patterns, with market areas for specific commodities being at least partially determined by transportation prices. In developing countries the emergence of national trade patterns is critical in triggering the movement from regional self-sufficiency to a national economy.

The availability and prices of transportation services in an economy has a decided impact on overall price levels, because transportation costs comprise part of the total market price of any item. This cost component reflects both the movement of raw materials to a point of production and the flow of finished products to consumers. On an annual basis, Americans spend nearly one trillion

TABLE 1-1

Summary of 1992 Government Spending for
Transportation Facilities and Services (in billions)

	Federal	*State and Local*	*Total*
Highway System	$16.3	$62.8	$79.1
Air Transportation	8.2	8.0	16.2
Rail Transportation	1.2	1.3	2.5
Water Transportation	1.5	2.0	3.5
Transit	1.8	9.0	10.8
Total	$29.0	$83.1	$112.1

SOURCE: Eno Transportation Foundation, Inc., *Transportation in America*, 11th edition (Lansdowne, VA: the Foundation, 1993), p. 73.

dollars on passenger and freight transportation. This equals nearly 18 percent of Gross National Product.[3]

The significance of transportation costs, as related to the wholesale prices of products, varies considerably among commodities. For some bulk commodities, such as sand and gravel, transportation outlays comprise more than half the wholesale price; on other items, such as high technology products, the ratio is less than one percent. The price (rate) charged for moving a particular commodity from origin to destination is a function of several factors, including the value of the commodity, its handling characteristics, the distance of the shipment, and the quantity of the commodity to be moved.

While transportation influences the overall price level as an input in practically every economic activity, it also has a positive effect on prices due to the regional specialization and division of labor that it fosters. These factors tend to lower the prices of goods in the economy, as does the fact that a well-developed transportation system opens distant markets for producers, thereby promoting greater competition and broader consumer choice.

Additionally, the improved access and greater alternative use that result from expansion of the transportation network can have a positive effect on land values. For example, this is often observed in the suburbs of metropolitan areas following expansion of a freeway or transit system that provides improved access to the core city. Conversely, transportation can have a negative impact on property values. The environmental degradation which affects properties that abut freeways and airports and the adverse effects automobile congestion and emissions on the quality of urban life are contemporary illustrations of such problems.

SOCIAL, POLITICAL AND MILITARY SIGNIFICANCE OF TRANSPORTATION

A nation's transportation system is not only shaped by economic considerations but by social, political and military issues as well. Thus, transportation policy cannot be formulated or critiqued in a purely economic context. Several such social and political considerations are examined in the following discussion.

Social Significance

A viable transportation network contributes to improved living standards through promotion of regional specialization and tends to broaden the perspectives of the nations and individuals involved. This cultural diffusion, fostered at the national or international level, is desirable because it works toward promotion of mutual understanding.

At the local level, the social impact of transportation is more obvious. For example, freeway systems and mass transit have permitted many people to enjoy suburban living while still having access to the educational, cultural, and social attractions of the core city. Similarly, many of these people are employed in the city, yet reside in the suburbs. However, the separation of home and work locations is a mixed blessing. In many cities this necessitates massive commutation, which intensifies the pollution and congestion problems of the core area. Extensive highway building programs in urban areas have also led to neighborhood disruption and the dislocation of many businesses and families.

As implied in the preceding discussion, the existence of transportation facilities plays a major role in the determination of industrial and residential location patterns. Consequently, considerable attention is being devoted by all levels of government to the patterns of development that result from government expenditures for particular forms of transportation facilities. The intention of such analysis is to integrate transportation programs into broader plans for community and regional development so that development can be managed in an orderly fashion.

Several aspects of transportation's negative impact on society have already been discussed. Two additional negative factors deserve mention.

Transportation accounts for approximately two-thirds of the volume of petroleum products consumed in the United States.[4] This issue has attracted growing attention as concern with energy conservation has escalated. Also, accidents in the various forms of transportation annually generate an awesome toll in property damage, injuries, and death. Transportation accidents resulted in more than 40,000 deaths in 1992.[5] In response to these problems, growing national attention has been focused on the promotion of transportation safety. The scope of governmental involvement in safety and environmental issues is discussed in considerable detail in subsequent chapters.

Political and Military Significance

Because of the importance of transportation in realization of governmental goals, it has always attracted considerable political attention. The significance accorded transportation at the national level was illustrated by the establishment of the cabinet-level Department of Transportation (DOT) in 1966. Similarly, nearly all states have organized departments of transportation.

Government involvement has often been precipitated by the inability of the private sector to finance an adequate rate of transportation system growth. Additionally, government powers must frequently be exercised to secure feasible routes or to provide facilities, such as waterways, that would not generate sufficient rates of return to attract private capital.

Government outlays for transportation facilities have often been used to promote national unity. In the United States during the 1860s, the financial assistance and land grants provided by various governmental units facilitated construction of a transcontinental railroad system, which was specifically aimed at promotion of closer ties between the western area of this country and the rest of the nation. The Canadian national government was similarly motivated in building railroad facilities into it's western provinces.

Another major reason for governmental involvement in transportation is its military significance. Centuries ago, military considerations played a major role in development of the highway system of ancient Europe. More recently, the construction of the Interstate Highway System was partially motivated by a congressional desire to improve our national defense capabilities. Similarly, much of the federal expenditure for waterway development has been related to defense concerns. In fact, the federal Statement of National Transportation Policy clearly specifies the importance to be given to national defense considerations in formulating transportation policy. The value of military expenditures for transportation capability was clearly shown in the convincing victory of the Allied forces in the Gulf War of 1990-1991. Many attributed the speed with which that conflict was resolved to the superior transportation and logistics capabilities of the Allied forces.[6]

THE U.S. GOVERNMENT ROLE IN TRANSPORTATION

As outlined in the preceding discussion, the multi-dimensional significance of transportation has prompted considerable government involvement in development of transportation in the United States and its regulation. The following discussion briefly examines the role which the Federal Department of Transportation (DOT) and various regulatory agencies play in this field.

The Department of Transportation

The DOT was established in 1966. The objectives that Congress set for the organization were stated in the act which created the agency:

> To assure the coordinated, effective administration of the transportation programs of the Federal Government; to facilitate the development and improvement of coordinated transportation service, to be provided by private enterprise to the maximum extent feasible; to encourage cooperation of federal, state, and local governments, carriers, labor, and other interested parties toward the achievement of national transportation objectives; to stimulate technological advances in transportation; to provide general leadership; to develop and recommend to the President and Congress for approval of national transportation policies and programs to accomplish these objectives with full and appropriate consideration of the needs of the public, users, carriers, industry, labor, and the national defense.[7]

Figure 1-1 provides an organization chart of the Department. The agency has more than 113,000 full-time permanent employees and maintains in excess of 3,000 field offices in the United States and foreign countries. The responsibilities of the major operating units of the agency are outlined briefly in the following discussion. Each of these units and their programs and policies are examined in considerable detail in subsequent chapters.

Office of the Secretary (OST). The Secretary of Transportation is a cabinet member appointed by the President with the advice and consent of the Senate. The secretary acts as assistant to the President in all matters related to

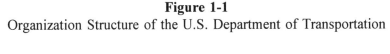

Figure 1-1
Organization Structure of the U.S. Department of Transportation

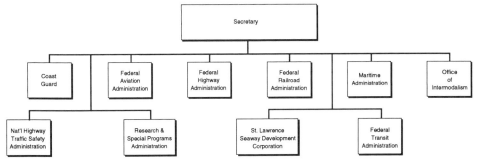

SOURCE: U.S. Department of Transportation, Washinton, D.C.

federal transportation programs. In 1993, President Clinton's selection for Secretary was Federico Pena, former mayor of Denver, Colorado.

The Secretary works through a number of assistant secretaries and is supported by the OST (Office of the Secretary of Transportation) which gives overall direction and leadership to the Department. The Secretary has primary responsibility for formulation and implementation of national transportation policies.

The Coast Guard. The Coast Guard, which is not only a component of the DOT but also a branch of the armed forces, was incorporated into the DOT when the agency was established in 1966. Its basic mission is enforcement of federal laws on the high seas and waterways subject to U.S. jurisdiction. Those laws govern such matters as navigation, vessel inspection, port safety and security, and marine environmental protection. The Coast Guard also sets ship construction and safety standards. It maintains a network of rescue vessels, aircraft and communications facilities to carry out its responsibilities.

In recent years the agency's most visible activities have included active participation in our country's attempts to limit drug trafficking and illegal immigration by sea, and participation in the cleanup of the 1989 Exxon Valdez oil spill in Prince William Sound, Alaska.

The Federal Aviation Administration (FAA). The FAA's primary responsibility is management of the nation's airspace in a safe and efficient manner. This involves development and enforcement of safety regulations and operation of the nation's airway system. The controllers who operate the national airway system are employees of the FAA.

The agency is charged with promotion of civil aeronautics and air commerce both within the United States and abroad. It also manages extensive research and development programs. In addition it administers the federal airport program and certifies and registers aircraft and commercial/private pilots.

As the financial condition of the U.S. airline industry has deteriorated during the past several years, the FAA has become quite aggressive in not only policing airline safety practices but also in inspecting commercial aircraft. The agency attracted considerable attention in early 1993 by banning the aircraft of several countries from U.S. airports due to the poor safety practices and records of those countries.

The Federal Highway Administration (FHWA). The primary responsibility of the FHWA is management of the Federal-aid highway program in conjunction with the states and to assist them in construction of the Interstate, primary, secondary, and urban road systems. It administers the federal program of financial aid to states for highway construction and rehabilitation, and develops and administers federal highway safety programs. Its Office of Motor Carrier Safety regulates the safety performance of interstate commercial motor carriers while focusing on such issues as driver qualification, hours-of-service standards for workers, hazardous materials movements and noise abatement. The agency also funds highway research and development programs

The Federal Railroad Administration (FRA). The FRA is responsible for federal support and promotion of the railroad industry, including administration of subsidies to Amtrak. The agency develops and administers railroad safety regulations covering such matters as maintenance of equipment, equipment standards and operating practices within the industry. It also conducts research and development programs to improve railroad service and safety. A major research focus of the FRA during the past several years has been investigation of various forms of high speed rail passenger service

The Federal Maritime Administration (MARAD). The agency is essentially involved in promotion of the country's merchant marine. It determines the need for operating subsidies for the industry and administers those subsidies. It also sponsors research and development for ship design, propulsion and operations. MARAD is also responsible for maintenance of the National Defense Reserve Fleet of government owned ships which can be mobilized during times of national emergency.

National Highway Traffic Safety Administration (NHTSA). The mission of NHTSA is to reduce the deaths, injuries, and economic losses which result from motor vehicle accidents. This involves prescription and implementation of motor vehicle safety standards. The agency provides funds for state and local highway safety programs, and through such funding is able to influence state-level guidelines concerning such issues as mandatory seatbelt use laws and speed limits. In conjunction with the Environmental Protection Agency and the Department of Energy NHTSA sets fuel economy standards for the automotive and light truck industries.

Research and Special Programs Administration. The agency acts as the Department's primary research, analysis and technical development unit. Its Office of Hazardous Materials Transportation formulates regulations governing the movement of hazardous materials by all modes of carriage. Its responsibilities also include pipeline safety and development of emergency preparedness programs.

Federal Transit Administration. The Federal Transit Administration is responsible for development of comprehensive, coordinated mass transportation systems for urban areas. It provides financial assistance to state and local governments for transit equipment, facilities and operational improvements. It also conducts research and development activities related to mass transportation and provides assistance for technical studies, planning, engineering and design of transit systems.

Office of Intermodalism. Among the provisions of the previously mentioned 1991 highway legislation was establishment of an Office of Intermodalism within the DOT. This recognized the growth of intermodal traffic (freight that is transferred between modes while moving between origin and destination) in the transportation marketplace. The new office was created to facilitate projects that cross modal lines, and to bring about a dialogue between various interest groups representing the several modes of carriage.

THE REGULATORY AGENCIES

The federal regulatory agencies in transportation, including the Interstate Commerce Commission (ICC), the Federal Maritime Commission (FMC), and the Federal Energy Regulatory Commission (FERC) are expert bodies primarily involved in administration of the regulatory statutes in transportation. They were created by Congress, and their authority is broadly prescribed by law. The regulatory agencies are integrally related to the legislative, executive and judicial branches of the federal government in the development and administration of transportation policy.

An important feature of the regulatory agencies is their independent status. This independence from the other branches of the federal government minimizes the likelihood of political interference in their activities. Each of the agencies has five commissioners who are appointed by the President, with the advice and consent of the Senate. The appointments of the regulators expire in a staggered fashion so that a single-term President cannot, except under unusual circumstances, appoint a majority of the members of a particular regulatory agency. No more than a simple majority of the members of each agency may be from one political party, and they can only be removed from office due to inefficiency, neglect of duty, or malfeasance in office. When their terms expire, commissioners can be reappointed.

The regulatory bodies have been given broad transportation policy guidelines by Congress, and they are charged with the development of specific regulations and procedures within these limits. Consequently, the agencies not only serve in an administrative capacity, but also act to formulate policies in those areas in which the law in nonspecific.

The Interstate Commerce Commission

The ICC is the federal regulatory agency that controls many of the economic aspects of interstate surface transportation. With some exceptions, the interstate operations of railroads, motor carriers, water carriers, surface freight forwarders and brokers are included in the agency's domain. In carrying out its responsibilities, the ICC is actively involved in such matters as control of entry and abandonment of service, ratemaking, consolidations, mergers and acquisition of control.

The regulatory reform movement has reduced the workload and employment base of the Commission. By 1993 the agency had approximately 600 employees, less than half the number it employed a decade earlier.[8] During the same ten year period its annual budget was reduced by congress from $66 million to $44 million.

Federal Maritime Commission

The FMC began operating in 1961, when it assumed the regulatory responsibilities of the Federal Maritime Board, which was abolished that year through a government reorganization. The regulatory responsibilities of the agency include oversight of the services, rates, practices, and agreement of carriers involved in the foreign and domestic offshore water commerce of the United States. It may review rates filed by carriers and ensures that carriers adhere to the rates on file with the commission. The FMC also investigates charges of discriminatory practices in the maritime industry and licenses ocean freight forwarders.

The Federal Energy Regulatory Commission

FERC was created through the Department of Energy Organization Act of 1977. The agency administers a wide variety of regulations involving energy issues. In a transportation context, the agency regulates the interstate movement of oil and natural gas by pipeline. Prior to the agency's creation, the ICC had regulated oil pipeline operations. The primary focus of the agency's transportation responsibilities is carrier ratemaking and financial reporting.

TRANSPORTATION POLICY DEVELOPMENT

At this point, attention should also be given to the process by which national transportation policy is formulated. Figure 1-2 illustrates this process with respect to regulatory policies. In enacting the laws that serve as the foundation for economic and safety regulation of transportation, Congress acts as the basic formulator of national transportation policy. Inputs to this lawmaking process are provided by many parties, including the DOT, the President, and various lobby groups representing such interests as shippers, carriers, environmentalists, and consumers. The final output of this interaction may be the passage of a statute that in some way influences our national transportation system. If the law pertains to an aspect of economic regulation, it is likely that it will require administration by a federal regulatory agency, such as the ICC, the FMC, or the FERC.

Essentially, the regulatory agencies administer the economic aspects of transportation law on case-by-case basis. However, this role does not have to be a passive one based primarily on agency precedent. Because many provisions of transportation law have been drafted by Congress in rather vague terms, they provide considerable latitude for regulatory agency interpretation. Consequently, as was clearly demonstrated during the late 1970s and early 1980s, the agencies can exert considerable influence on the policy-making process. During that period, the CAB (which was eliminated in 1985) and ICC promoted substantial deregulation of air and motor carriage by liberally interpreting the governing statutes and reflecting these views in agency decisions. These actions gave impetus to congressional reconsideration of regulatory policies in transportation and ultimately led to passage of several regulatory reform statutes.

For many years the regulatory agencies played a parallel role in administering safety regulations. However, these responsibilities were transferred to the DOT following its creation in 1966.

Figure 1-2
The Process of Formulating and Implementing Regulatory Policies in
Transportation

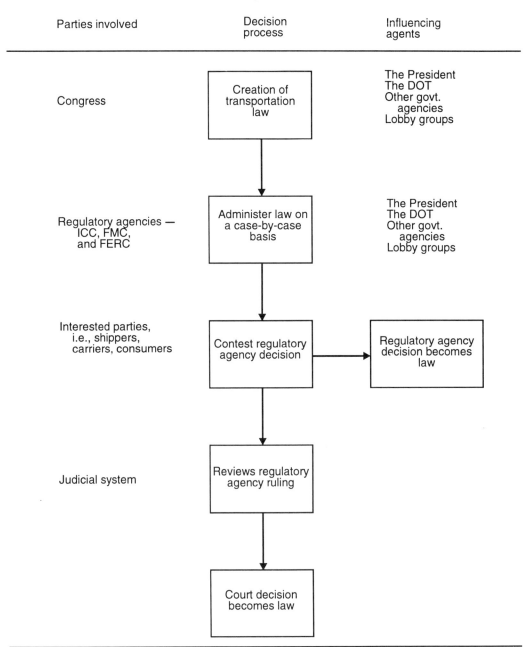

When individual cases are being considered by the regulatory agencies, shippers, carriers, and other interested parties may provide formal inputs to the agency by filing position papers or appearing at hearings. In certain instances the agency's decisions may be appealed on legal grounds in the court system. Some cases pertaining to transportation matters are ultimately heard by the Supreme Court. For example, during 1992 the Court dealt with such transportation issues as Amtrak's ability to use the power of eminent domain to seize the track of other railroads and the liability of a formerly bankrupt transportation company to environmental claims filed years after it reorganized.[9]

A parallel transportation policy development process also occurs at the state level, with state legislative bodies, regulatory agencies, and courts interacting in a pattern similar to that of their federal counterparts.

The preceding discussion of the transportation policy formulation process was by no means comprehensive. In fact, this subject is discussed extensively in later chapters. However, the brief introduction which has been provided should allow the reader to quickly comprehend the significance of contemporary transportation issues.

DOMESTIC TRANSPORTATION SYSTEM

The United States benefits from the existence of a highly developed and extensive transportation network. In most instances we have a choice of several different modes (or forms) of transportation to serve our needs. The business traveler contemplating a trip from New York to Boston may choose between airline, railroad, bus, or private automobile as a means of intercity travel. Each mode has distinctive cost and service characteristics; for example, air travel is typically faster than bus or rail passenger service, but it also tends to be more expensive. Consequently, the traveler is faced with a series of tradeoffs. The traveler must decide the relative importance of such factors as speed, convenience, and cost in making a modal selection. The choice will be influenced by such factors as the perceived value of the individual's time and the size of the person's expense account.

Similarly, those wishing to ship freight, whether industrial or governmental shippers or individuals concerned with moving their personal belongings to a new home, are generally faced with several different modal alternatives. Additionally, in both freight and passenger movements the individual may also typically choose among several companies in a given mode of carriage. Or the shipper may decide to personally provide the service by, for example, leasing or purchasing a truck rather than using a for-hire carrier (a company which is in the business of selling transportation services in the marketplace). The individual who chooses to provide the service, rather than buy it, is said to be engaged in private carriage. That is, the person's primary business is not selling transportation services. Rather, the shipper has decided, after making the kinds of tradeoffs discussed above, that he can better meet needs by providing the service himself. The farmer moving his produce to the market in his own truck and the local department store making deliveries in its own vehicles provide illustrations of private carriage. In a noncommercial context, each of us engages in private carriage when we choose to drive to work or to the shopping center rather than take a bus.

Market Share of Intercity Carriers

The several basic modes of carriage that play prominent roles in the intercity movement of passengers and freight are highway carriage (buses, trucks, and automobiles on public highways), railroads, airlines, water carriers, oil pipelines, and freight forwarders. Forwarders function in a middleman capacity, linking shippers and companies that provide for-hire services in the other modes. The role of freight forwarders in the contemporary transportation system is discussed in Chapters 4 and 6.

The market shares of both freight and passenger traffic handled by the several modes of intercity carriage have shifted dramatically throughout the years as a result of a number of factors, including technological changes, regulation, and government financing of expansion of our national transportation system. The causes and effects of these shifts are discussed in detail in Chapters 3 through 6.

In the freight sector (see Table-1-2), the railroad industry's market share declined from 61.3 percent of intercity ton mileage (one ton mile is one ton of freight moved one mile) in 1940 to 37.4 percent in 1991. During the same period, the market share controlled by the oil pipeline industry nearly doubled. This fact surprises many people, due to the limited range of commodities that are suited to pipeline movement. However, the volume of traffic handle by oil pipelines is merely reflective of the tremendous utilization rate of petroleum products in the United States. The speed and flexibility of the trucking industry have contributed to the expansion of its share of the intercity freight market from 10 percent in 1940 to 26.3 percent in 1991. The market share of domestic water carriage, which is primarily composed of bulk and liquid commodity movements, has stayed relatively constant since 1940. At the same time, air freight has expanded greatly in terms of absolute ton mileage, but still comprises less than one percent of intercity ton mileage.

Significant modal shifts have also occurred in intercity passenger travel. Increased automobile ownership coupled with the expansion and upgrading of our national highway system has led to the emergence of the automobile as the dominant mode of intercity passenger carriage; in recent years it has annually

TABLE 1-2

Intercity Freight Market Share by Mode
(percent of freight ton miles)[a]

	1940	1950	1960	1970	1980	1985	1992[d]
Railroads	61.3[c]	56.1	44.1	39.8	37.5	36.4	37.0
Trucking	10.0	16.3	21.7	21.3	22.3	24.8	27.2
Oil Pipeline	9.5	12.1	17.4	22.3	23.6	22.9	19.5
Water[b]	19.1	15.4	16.7	16.5	16.4	15.5	15.9
Air		0.03	0.07	0.17	0.21	0.27	0.37

[a] Includes both for-hire and private carriers, mail and express.
[b] Includes Great Lakes and rivers and canals.
[c] Percentages do not total 100 percent due to rounding.
[d] Preliminary.

SOURCE: Eno Transportation Foundation, Inc., *Transportation in America*, 11th ed.
(Lansdowne, VA.: the Foundation, 1993), p. 44.

accounted for more than 80 percent of intercity passenger mileage. The balance of intercity passenger movements are handled by the commercial airlines, railroads, and bus companies. Table 1-3 traces the market-share changes experienced by intercity commercial passenger carriers between 1940 and 1991. The dominance of air passenger carriage in this field is obvious, as is the precipitous decline of rail and bus passenger traffic.

Scope of the System

One measure of the scope of the domestic transportation system is the intercity route mileage of the various modes (see Table 1-4). The causes of the expansion or contraction of the intercity route mileage of the individual modes are examined in Chapters 3 through 6.

Our nation also possesses an extensive urban transportation network. In addition to the route mileage specified in Table 1-4, approximately 112,000 route miles of transit operations exist in urban areas.[10] This includes bus, trolley, commuter rail, and subway operations. The urban transportation system also

TABLE 1-3

Intercity Passenger Market Share by Mode
(percent of passenger miles)

	1940	1950	1960	1970	1980	1985	1992
Automobile	89.0	87.0	90.4	86.9	82.5	80.1	80.5
Airlines	0.4	1.8	4.1	9.3	13.9	17.0	17.1
Private Air	0.1	0.2	0.3	0.8	1.0	0.8	0.6
Bus	3.1	4.5	2.5	2.1	1.9	1.4	1.1
Rail	7.5	6.5	2.8	0.9	0.7	0.7	0.7

SOURCE: Eno Transportation Foundation Inc., *Transportation in America*, 11th ed. (Lansdowne, VA.: the Foundation, 1993), p. 47.

includes approximately 624,000 miles of urban streets that serve the transportation needs of metropolitan residents.

Another measure of the scope of the domestic transportation system is the vehicle stock of the various modes. The highway system of the United States is traveled by approximately 143.5 million automobiles, 44.5 million trucks, 512,800 school and non-commercial buses, and 114,200 commercial buses. The railroad system has an equipment stock of approximately 1.2 million freight cars, 6,400 passenger cars, and 23,200 locomotives. There are roughly 212,000 aircraft in this country. Finally, more than 36,000 barges and towboats travel our waterway system and more than 450 ships ply deepwater routes.[11]

In utilizing this extensive transportation system, Americans spent more than $357 billion for freight transportation services and nearly $619 billion for passenger travel in 1991. Each year such transportation outlays are approximately 18 percent of our Gross National Product.[12]

SUMMARY

The transportation system of the United States is an important component of the nation's economic, social, and political structure and thus influences many aspects of our daily lives. Conversely, individual decisions concerning such matters as the purchase of transportation services from for-hire carriers and the use of private automobiles affect the development of the transportation system.

TABLE 1-4

Intercity Route Mileage Within the
Continental United States, 1960 and 1990 (statute miles)

	1960	1990
Highways [a]	557,729	753,626
Airways	293,003	388,000
Railroads [b]	217,552	145,979
Oil Pipelines	190,944	213,535
Inland Waterways	25,253	25,777

[a] Does not include more than 2 million miles of rural roads.
[b] Includes crude and products pipelines.

SOURCE: Eno Transportation Foundation, Inc., *Transportation in America*, 11th ed. (Lansdowne, VA.: the Foundation, 1993), p. 64.

The United States has an extensive transportation network that has evolved through a joint system of public and private expenditures. Due to transportation's importance in the realization of personal, business and governmental goals, extensive governmental involvement has emerged in both the promotion and regulation of transportation. The promotional expenditures of various government units play a major role in financing the growth and maintenance of the national transportation network. Further, the economic and safety regulations that have been applied to transportation have had a pervasive impact on the structure and performance of the transportation industry.

DISCUSSION QUESTIONS

1. Why have federal, state, and local government units played such an active funding role in transportation development?
2. Discuss briefly the relative roles played by Congress, the Department of Transportation, and the regulatory agencies in formulating and administering national transportation policy.
3. Distinguish between the promotional and regulatory roles that the federal government plays in transportation.
4. What are the most important transportation problems facing your community? Explain why they are important.
5. Briefly explain the importance of transportation to our national economy.

NOTES

1.   Wilfred Owen, *Strategy for Mobility* (Washington, D.C.: Brookings Institution, 1964), pp. 191-94.
2.   Mitchell E. MacDonald, "Congress Passes Highway Bill With a $151 Billion Price Tag," *Traffic Management* (January, 1992), p. 13.
3.   Eno Transportation Foundation, *Transportation in America*, 10th ed. (Lansdowne, VA: the Foundation, 1992), p. 4.
4.   Ibid., p. 20.
5.   ` Ibid., p. 35.
6.   "Half Audie Murphy, Half Jack Welch," *Business Week* (March 4, 1991), pp. 42-3.
7.   Public Law 89-670, Section 2 (1970).
8.   Information supplied by the Interstate Commerce Commission.
9.   See "Amtrak's Big Victory," *Journal of Commerce*, March 31, 1992, p. 6A; also, Mark B. Solomon, "Supreme Court Upholds Ruling On Penn Central Pollution Claims," *Journal of Commerce*, March 3, 1992, p. 3B.
10. Data supplied by the American Public Transit Association, Washington, D.C.
11. Eno Transportation Foundation, Inc., p. 63
12. Ibid., pp. 8-9.

SELECTED REFERENCES

Coyle, John J., Edward J. Bardi, and Joseph L. Cavinato. *Transportation* 3rd ed. St. Paul, Minnesota: West Publishing Company, 1992. Chapter 1. "Transportation and the Economy," pp. 3-24.

Eno Transportation Foundation, Inc. *Transportation in America*. 10th ed. Waldorf, MD: the Foundation, 1992.

Owen, Wilfred. The Accessible City. Washington D.C.: Brookings Institution, 1972. Chapter 5. "Combining Transportation and Community Development," pp. 114-35.

Owen, Wilfred. Strategy and Mobility. Washington, D.C.: Brookings Institution, 1964. Chapter 3. "Transportation Requirements for Development," pp. 44-85.

U.S. Bureau of Census. *Statistical Abstract of the United States: 1991* 111th ed. Washington, D.C.: U.S. Government Printing Office, 1991.

U.S. Congress. Office of Technology Assessment. *Moving Ahead, 1991 Surface Transportation Legislation*. Washington, D.C.: U.S. Government Printing Office, 1991.

U.S. Department of Transportation. *Moving America-New Direction New Opportunities: A Statement of National Transportation Policy*. Washington, D.C.: the Department, 1990.

Chapter Two

TRANSPORTATION: THE PERSPECTIVE OF THE INDUSTRIAL SHIPPER

Although this book focuses primarily on the structure, regulation and performance of the domestic transportation industries, it is important that the perspective of the shipping public be included. Each of us, at various times, acts as a shipper. We may contact a household goods carrier to move our belongings to a new home or send a trunk full of books and clothing to a family member who is away at school. However, the scope of our individual transactions is greatly overshadowed by the shipping activities of large corporations. For example, National Semiconductor annually ships more than ten billion parts around the world.[1] Sears Roebuck and Company moves more than five billion pounds of freight each year.[2] It is important that the significance of transportation to shippers, both large and small, be understood, not only in dollar terms but also as a means of realizing company objectives. This understanding will make later chapters concerning carrier and governmental actions more meaningful. Consequently, this chapter concentrates on the industrial shipper.

LOGISTICS MANAGEMENT IN MANUFACTURING

In the typical manufacturing firm, transportation planning is viewed as a component of logistics management. The Council of Logistics Management has defined logistics as:

> ...the process of planning, implementing and controlling the efficient, cost effective flow and storage of raw materials, in-process inventory, finished goods and related information from point of origin to point of consumption for the purpose of conforming with customer requirements.

As shown in Figure 2-1, the task of managing logistics in the corporate manufacturing setting is a complex one, which is managed by a logistics group

Figure 2-1

The Logistic Network of a Typical Manufacturer

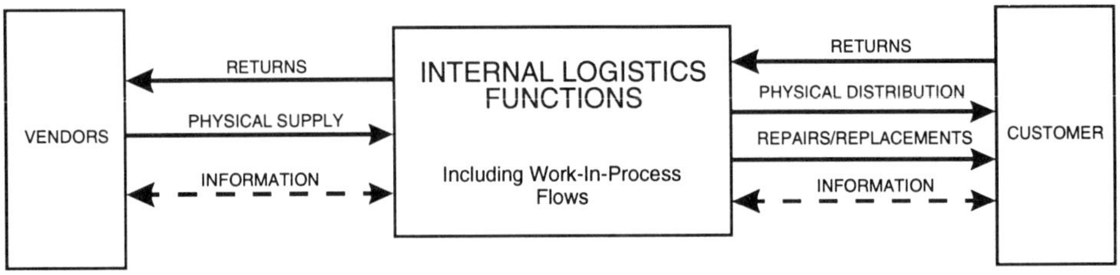

or department that is often headed by a vice president or director of logistics. Logistics professionals attempt to manage the flows of materials, products and information in a "seamless" fashion from the company's vendors (suppliers) through the company's manufacturing process, to customers. Instead of looking at this process as a series of separate components, many companies view the entire process as a "supply chain" which links vendors, their company, and customers. As illustrated by the figure, there are several types of flows which must be managed. While storage is clearly a component of this process, there is considerable pressure on manufacturing firms to minimize inventory levels thereby cutting costs and releasing capital for other uses. Many companies have moved to Just-in-Time (JIT) manufacturing which involves scheduling receipt of supplies from vendors so that deliveries occur just as the supplies are needed in the production process. These companies attempt to produce just as the customer needs the product. Such diverse companies as McDonnell Douglas, Digital Equipment Corporation, and Haggar Apparel Company have benefited from these changes.[3] The extent to which large American manufacturers have embraced the JIT concept was demonstrated by a survey of the 500 largest American manufacturers which found that nearly one-third of them had established some form of JIT program.[4] While savings in inventory costs are important, companies seeking to create a JIT environment must be careful to assure production lines are supplied adequately while maintaining competitive customer service levels.

Logistics Activities of Manufacturers

A broad range of activities is typically included in corporate logistics management. Several of the most important of these are examined briefly in the following discussion.

Transportation. Transportation management, which will be explored in much greater detail later in this chapter tends to be the most expensive element of corporate logistics costs and also the most time consuming function. It includes such activities as selecting the mode of transportation to be used, rate negotiations with carriers, and choosing the proper service to be used in moving a particular shipment.

Inventory Management. To satisfy internal groups such as manufacturing and marketing and external customers a company must aggressively manage inventory levels. As noted above, there is growing pressure on companies to minimize inventory levels, but in doing so there are a number of inventory issues to be addressed. For example, when dealing with physical supply inventory, management must decide what mix of supplies is needed from vendors, when the supplies are needed, and in what quantity individual items should be ordered. It must also be decided which vendors are to be used and where supplies are to be shipped. Further, if storage is to take place, a decision must be made in terms of where storage is to occur. This process may not sound that complicated, but it should be noted that many manufacturers rely upon numerous suppliers, many of them in foreign countries, for literally thousands of items which will be used in their production processes.

In addition to managing physical supply inventory, logistics professionals must also, in conjunction with manufacturing managers, plan work-in-process inventory flows. Such flows, which entail movement from one stage of production to the next, and often from one location to another, are critical in meeting the company's manufacturing schedule. In many companies, the volume of work-in-process flows exceeds the total volume of physical supply and physical distribution flows.

At the end of the production process the company must also manage finished goods or physical distribution inventory to meet customer service level targets while effectively controlling finished goods inventory costs.

Inventory management concerns do not end with delivery of the finished product to the customer. Companies must also maintain inventory for repairs and replacement of defective products. This can be enormously expensive, and is a chronic problem in the high technology industry which is faced with the pressures of both extensive new product introduction and products which continue to function years after their purchase. All of those products need to be supported and require inventory commitments.

Because inventory management is so important in a competitive environment, not only in terms of cost control, but also in terms of maintaining customer service levels, considerable management attention has been devoted to developing inventory control systems. Such systems, which are typically driven by computer software, range in complexity from a simple ordering system which can be bought at a local software store for several hundred dollars to multi-million dollar systems which are specifically designed to monitor a broad range of inventory issues for a large corporation. Several hundred inventory control software packages are available to logistics managers. They must decide if any of those are suited to the company's needs or if the potential benefits of a customized inventory control system justify the costs of having such a system developed for the firm.

Industrial Packaging. Logistics professionals must also be concerned with industrial packaging issues. In contrast to customer packaging, which is often used to enhance the attractiveness of the product, industrial packaging is primarily concerned with such issues as protection of the product as it moves through logistics channels, ease of handling of the package, and effective use of the cubic capacity of transportation vehicles.

Logistics managers must anticipate some degree of loss and damage in the shipment of products. To aggressively address this issue managers must consider one of the many "tradeoffs" which exist in this field. By adding more packaging materials to a product, loss and damage may be reduced. However, as a result of doing so, packaging costs rise and shipment weight increases, thereby increasing transportation costs. As package size increases, it also tends to become more difficult to handle, and uses more space in a carrier's vehicle. This means that less of the product will fit in the vehicle. These added costs must be weighed against the higher product survival rate which results and its impact on customer service.

In many cases, logistics managers work with the company's industrial engineers to evaluate packaging possibilities. Some carriers, including United Parcel Service, also have packaging specialists who can work with shippers to identify problems which may be contributing to loss and damage claims.

Material Handling. In logistics management, attention must also be given to how materials are to physically move within a company's facilities. There are literally hundreds of types of material handling equipment, including such diverse options as forklifts, overhead conveyor systems and robotic storage and retrieval systems, which might be employed. They range from labor intensive to capital intensive systems.

There are many factors which enter into the decision making process. These include the nature of the items to be moved, the diversity in size and weight of those items, the flow patterns desired, and the speed at which those items have to be moved. Further, capital availability may limit the options considered. Again, collaboration of logistics professionals with industrial engineers or material handling consultants is often required to effectively assess the options.

Warehousing. Some storage is inevitable, and a company must decide where it is to take place. This can be a very complicated decision, particularly for a company which serves a broad area from geographically dispersed manufacturing plants. From a location standpoint, potential strategies can range from centralized to decentralized storage. In the former, items are held in a centralized facility and shipped in small quantities to customers. In the latter, decentralized stocking locations are established, large quantities shipped to those locations, and final delivery to customers moves short distances. Centralized stocking systems tend to generate lower facility costs and higher transportation costs, while the situation is reversed in the decentralized scenario.

Another important warehousing issue to be addressed is the use of private versus public warehousing space. In a private, company-owned or leased facility, the company may be able to design the facility specifically to its needs, but the capital commitment is likely to be high. By using public warehouses for storage, the company is able to limit its capital commitment to a particular location and maintain flexibility. Again, the decision-making process involves many tradeoffs reflecting such issues as the potential impact on customer service, capital availability, the range of services offered by public warehouses in a particular markets, tax implications, and the size and stability of the market being examined.

Most large manufacturers use a combination of private and public warehousing space. Reflecting competitive pressures, many companies have shifted from private to public warehousing in recent years, generating a return of capital to the company through elimination of company owned facilities. Further, when expanding into new markets, few companies establish their own warehousing facilities until the long-term dimensions of the market are established.

Location Issues. Company decisions concerning the location of facilities, whether manufacturing plants, warehouses, or distribution points, play an important role in determining a company's logistics cost structure and its ability to serve its customers. Inappropriate location decisions are costly to reverse, particularly if a company has chosen to build rather than lease facilities. If a facility is to be closed, additional costs are generated by such matters as labor turnover, hiring and training of new personnel at a different location, and moving expenses. Consequently, location decisions cannot be treated casually. Analysis of company location decisions should be a continuing process due to the dynamic nature of the markets served by many companies.

Location decisions are typically approached at two levels: (1) the selection of a general geographic area and (2) the choice of a site within a particular community. Proceeding on this basis, the decision makers must consider a variety of factors, which often vary by location. Among these are the comparative cost and availability of labor, energy, raw materials, capital, property, and transportation. Additional attention must be given to matters such as access to markets, living conditions, tax rates, and community services offered in various locations.

The relative significance of the various location selection variables differs across industries. For example, manufacturing locations of some industries, such as steel and paper, have tended to be drawn toward the source of raw materials, which lose a considerable portion of their weight in the manufacturing process.[5] However, transportation system improvements have tended to make many such industries more flexible in terms of location.

Logistics managers are often heavily involved in company decisions concerning the location of facilities. Their insight into such issues as the potential impact of a location change on transportation costs and customer service standards are often critical to the decision making process.

Other Logistics Management Functions. While the functions discussed above are almost universally included in the realm of logistics management in manufacturing firms, many other functions are included in some firms.

Order processing is often controlled by a company's logistics organization. Orders are received, cleared, compared with inventory levels and production plans, forwarded to the appropriate organizational unit, and fulfilled.

While purchasing has traditionally been organized by many companies as a stand-alone function, increasingly it is being incorporated into logistics units of manufacturing firms. When this occurs, logistics is responsible for such matters as identifying potential vendors, placing orders, monitoring the markets for the materials being used, and evaluating vendor performance.

After sales service is also frequently considered a logistics responsibility. The function is often called "field service" and may include such activities as installation of products in customer facilities, handling product returns and replacements, management of inventory for returns and replacements, and maintenance of communications linkages with customers following sales.

Logistics Interaction with Other Functions

In view of the range of activities managed by the logistics group in the typical manufacturing firm and the impact of those activities on other organizational units, it is very important for logistics managers to work closely with their counterparts in other functional areas. Unless manufacturing and logistics managers interact effectively the company may waste resources on unnecessary physical supply and work-in-process inventory. At the other extreme, poor planning may produce inventory shortages which interrupt production schedules. In today's competitive marketplace, neither of those options is acceptable.

Similarly, a company's marketing plans cannot be realized without close cooperation between logistics and marketing managers. Finished products must be available at the right time, in the right place, without the company carrying unnecessarily high levels of finished goods inventory. The same philosophy should be applied to replacement and repair parts to serve the after sale market. The interaction with marketing should also include an ongoing dialogue about the physical design of new products. Logistics managers can provide valuable insight into the transportation cost implications of various product designs. Industrial engineers should also be included in those discussions to take advantage of their technical expertise with respect to such issues as alternative materials which might be used in new product design.

The interaction between logistics managers and industrial engineers is not limited to new product design. As noted earlier, they often provide valuable input into decisions related to such matters as industrial packaging, plant layout, and material handling equipment.

Logistics managers also routinely interact with those involved in corporate finance. The logistics process is expensive and necessarily competes for capital budget funds. At the same time, through thorough analysis of options, logistics managers can often identify new ways of cutting costs, thereby improving the company's working capital status and competitiveness.

As more companies have come to understand the significance of logistics from both a cost and customer service standpoint, the interaction of logistics managers and those involved in the company's strategic planning process has increased. Many companies now view logistics as an important differentiating factor, particularly in industries which produce homogeneous products. If the company's physical product is very similar to that offered by competitors, a more effectively managed logistics function may provide the necessary competitive edge through lower costs or more rapid response to customer needs.

TRANSPORTATION'S ROLE IN LOGISTICS

As noted earlier, transportation is often the most costly and time consuming component of corporate logistics management. Its planning is also critical in meeting production schedules and customer requirements. It involves facilitating the movements of supplies from vendors to the company, work-in-process inventory to the next stage of production, finished goods to customers, and repair and replacement items to customers.

Managing the corporate transportation function is multi-dimensional. The following discussion briefly reviews the types of decisions which have to be made in this area and the activities which must be managed.

Modal Selection

One of the basic decisions that must be made is selection of the mode of transportation to be used for a specific shipment. As will be discussed in Chapters 3-7, each of the modes have specific operating and cost characteristics, and managers must weigh them in selecting a mode. In some instances, managers must consider the tradeoff between speed and cost. Typically, a faster mode of transportation will be more expensive. In situations in which speed is critical, the more expensive mode may be justified. In other situations, service considerations such as the mode's record for on-time deliveries, consistency of service, or equipment availability may be more important in influencing the mode selected.

Most manufacturers, and other large consumers of freight transportation services, use the services of several different modes of carriage in meeting their aggregate transportation needs. The "modal split" is determined by many factors including the mix of items to be shipped, the origin-destination combinations involved, and the time pressure related to individual shipments.

Carrier Selection

In addition to selecting the mode to be used for a particular shipment, logistics managers must also select the specific carriers to be used. In a particular market, there may be many carriers (in some cases hundreds) which might be used. Again, price and service considerations come into play. There may be substantial variation not only in the prices offered by individual carriers but also the level of service which they are capable of delivering.

Shippers moving items over broad geographic areas, of necessity, use multiple carriers. However, there is a clear trend among large shippers to limit the number of carriers which are used. This not only gives the shipper more leverage with the carriers that are used, but also reduces the time involved in the carrier selection and evaluation process. An illustration of this is provided by Reynolds Metal Company, which has reduced the number of carriers it uses from 750 to 15.[6]

Carrier Evaluation

Once a carrier is selected and used, logistics managers should routinely evaluate the carrier's performance. The shipper must decide what the most appropriate measures or "metrics" are, then monitor the carrier's performance. Such issues as on-time deliveries, loss and damage claims, and billing accuracy are often included in such metrics. Carriers failing to meet those performance standards should be warned, and if improvement doesn't follow they should be terminated.

Rate Negotiation

As a result of the movement toward transportation deregulation, carriers have considerably more pricing freedom. Consequently, shippers can attempt to negotiate rate reductions or discounts with carriers. This has become quite common, particularly with respect to large shippers, who because of their market power, have considerable bargaining leverage. Those involved in corporate logistics management often conduct these negotiations with the carriers. The process by which these rate negotiations occur is discussed in detail in Chapter 9.

Freight Consolidation

Generally speaking, in transportation as the size of a shipment increases, the transportation charge per unit of weight tends to fall. That is, there is a "rate taper" as shipment size increases. To take advantage of this taper, logistics managers often attempt to consolidate company shipments. For example, instead of shipping each day's production to a distribution center, a company may hold its production for several days and ship it in consolidated form at lower per unit transportation costs. In this instance, logistics managers must weigh such factors as the possible need for additional storage space at the plant to accumulate several days' production prior to its shipment against potential transportation cost savings. Another illustration of the concept might involve convincing several of the company's separate business units to "pool" their freight and ship in consolidated form to a common destination.

Service Selection

In attempting to meet corporate transportation requirements, logistics managers must also decide what level of service is necessary for a particular shipment. It is not uncommon for carriers such as United Parcel Service (UPS) to offer several options to shippers. Shippers may select between overnight, second day, third day or deferred delivery. Obviously, the faster the service, the higher the transportation charges, and the time-cost tradeoff comes into play.

It is important that logistics managers use their transportation budgets effectively. Service levels must be matched with the needs of the particular shipment, and those needs vary substantially within a company. Some shipments, such as the movement of raw materials into a traditional production operation, may not require fast, expensive transportation service. In contrast, the movement of replacement parts to customers is likely to require expedited, expensive movement.

Documentation/Tracing/Claims

Managers of corporate transportation are also typically involved in preparation of shipping documentation, tracing of shipments, and filing of loss and damage claims with carriers.

Shipping documentation such as the "bill of lading" must be prepared. This serves as the basic contract between carrier and shipper and specifies such factors as the names of the parties involved, commodities and quantities shipped, routing, rates, and carrier liability.

There are also instances in which shipments must be traced with the carrier. For example, this may occur if a shipment which is critical to an important customer has failed to arrive on time. It is important that the status of the shipment be determined quickly and a new arrival time quoted to the customer. By supplying shipment details to the carrier the logistics manager can initiate the tracing process which should yield that information. In recent years many transportation companies have sought to differentiate their services from those of their competitors by enhancing their tracing capabilities. The use of "bar coding" on packages, scanners in terminals and other more exotic technologies have permitted such differentiation.

Loss and damage claims are a reality of life, even when dealing with highly efficient carriers. Those involved in corporate logistics management are generally responsible for filing related claims with carriers. This process tends to be very labor intensive and time consuming, and many companies establish a dollar standard below which claims will not be filed. For example, a company might decide that due to processing costs, claims which will generate less than $100 when paid will not be filed. It should also be noted that the nature of a carrier's response to claims filed by a shipper will often influence the shipper's future use of that carrier.

Freight Payment

After having provided transportation service, a carrier sends a freight bill to the shipper. In some instances, these bills are inaccurate. It has been estimated that 5-6 percent of the bills sent by motor carriers are incorrect.[7] They may be too high or too low. This generally results from listing the wrong commodity on the freight bill, recording the wrong shipment weight, or applying the wrong rate.

Many shippers audit freight bills for accuracy. In many cases, only those bills in excess of a specified dollar amount are audited. If mistakes are found, overcharge claims may be filed with the carrier. The auditing may be done internally, or by outside companies including several dozen large banks such as Chase Manhattan and Bank of Boston which offer freight payment services.

The importance of freight bill auditing has increased during the past several years as reports of failing carriers sending bogus bills to shippers as a means of generating short-term cash flow have surfaced. In some cases, these abuses were not uncovered until the carriers were in the process of being liquidated.

Private Carriage Options

Corporate transportation managers are often involved in private carriage. That is, their companies have instituted private transportation operations, typically in trucking. Many are of limited scope, such as delivery operations for local dairies and department stores, but some are both extensive and interstate in nature. One such fleet is maintained by West Point-Pepperell, Incorporated. It consists of 168 tractors, 850 trailers and employs 184 drivers.[8]

Private carriage frequently offers potential savings in transportation costs, but the conversion to private carriage is often precipitated by service considerations. Potentially, it offers better service because of flexibility of routes and schedules, greater speed, and reduction of loss and damage. It also provides a company with access to transportation equipment when it needs it. This access is not automatic when dealing with for-hire carriers, particularly if the shipper needs specialized equipment.

Shippers that generate small volumes are unable to utilize privately owned vehicles intensely enough to justify the equipment investment. Larger shippers, due to their buying power, often are able to use this leverage with carriers to obtain the rates and services which they desire. In most instances, companies that have moved into private carriage still use for-hire carriers, particularly to meet peak volume requirement.

In addition to assessing the desirability of moving into private carriage, logistics managers are likely to be involved in management of the private carrier operation if one is established. Numerous decisions must be made including those related to the ownership or leasing of vehicles, scheduling of operations, and maintenance of the vehicle fleet.

One issue which historically limited the attractiveness of private trucking operations was the fact that most such operations were only loaded in one direction. For example, a manufacturer might have used its private fleet to move finished products from its manufacturing facility to a distribution center. Generally, this led to an empty "backhaul" since there was nothing to bring back to the manufacturing plant from the distribution center. In some instances, stops at vendor locations were planned, but that was unusual. However, the deregulation movement addressed this issue and improved the situation. Private trucking fleets are now permitted to obtain for-hire operating certificates which permit them to carry goods for other companies as backhauls. As a result, in many companies the private trucking fleet is also a revenue generator.

Corporate Travel

Corporate transportation management also often includes management of corporate travel. In the typical large company employees travel extensively on corporate business. In some instances companies establish the equivalent of an in-house travel agency which has the ability to write tickets for employees. Based on the extent of employee travel, it may also be possible to negotiate discounted rates with carriers.

Many companies also have extensive employee relocation programs which are managed by the company's transportation group. To ease the strain of relocation on employees these groups often handle all of the details of employee moves. Quite frequently the moves are handled under contracts which have been negotiated with household goods carriers.

THE CARRIER'S PERSPECTIVE-IS THIS A GOOD ACCOUNT?

It is very important that shippers understand what constitutes a good account to a carrier. In some instances, carriers are rather selective with respect to the accounts they pursue. Carriers typically look at a potential account according to several dimensions. These include:

1.   What is being shipped? If it is high in value, the "value of service" to the shipper is likely to be high.

2.   What quantity is being shipped? Generally carriers prefer larger shipments which give them better equipment utilization. If the shipper is currently a small account, what are its prospects for growth? A carrier may be willing to service small accounts if the prospects for growth in the account are good.

3.   Does the shipper originate traffic on a regular basis? If so, the carrier is better able to schedule equipment and personnel.

4.   What are the origins and destinations between which the shipper moves freight? Ideally, shipments originate in major markets and

move to major markets, thereby increasing the likelihood of a carrier back-haul.

5.   Does the shipper place any special demands on the carrier? Is specialized equipment necessary to serve the account? Does the shipper require special pickup and/or delivery schedules? The more specialized the demands are, the less attractive the account is, unless the shipper is willing to defray the additional costs incurred by the carrier in meeting those demands.

6.   What is the financial condition of the shipper? Is it solvent and does it pay its bills on time?

A thorough understanding of such issues contributes to effective negotiations with carriers. This matter is discussed more extensively in Chapter 9.

CHANGES AFFECTING CORPORATE TRANSPORTATION

A number of significant developments have increasingly affected those involved in corporate transportation management. Each of these matters is examined briefly in the following discussion.

Deregulation

The movement toward transportation deregulation in the United States has had a major impact on those involved in corporate transportation management. The carrier marketplace has become very dynamic and competitive intensity has increased. The number of carriers and service options have expanded dramatically, requiring more managerial analysis. As previously discussed, many shippers are now able to aggressively negotiate contracts with carriers. In many cases these contracts have yielded lower rates and higher service levels to shippers.

Increased Industrial Competition

As American corporations have encountered greater competition both domestically and internationally pressure has increased to control costs to maintain competitiveness. Since transportation outlays are often substantial, they have received increasing management scrutiny in this environment. This has focused managerial attention on getting more for each transportation dollar spent and led to increasing shipper pressure on carriers to discount their rates.

At the same time, many shippers have come to understand that a properly designed corporate transportation program can yield service improvements which might be valued by customers. This has also led to pressure on carriers to constantly improve the quality of service offered to shippers.

Internationalization of Business

Many American companies rely heavily upon foreign suppliers. They also generate an increasing percentage of their sales and profits in foreign markets. As their businesses become more international in nature, logistics managers find that their responsibilities become more complex. Much of their knowledge concerning domestic operations does not apply in the international setting. For example, business practices, regulations and documentation requirements are often quite different. Managers are also confronted with customs clearance, and duty payment issues for the first time. However, transportation differences often cause the most significant problems. The modes available are often different as are the carriers serving international markets. The transportation infrastructure of foreign countries is often inferior to that which exists in the United States. The regulatory agencies and the regulations which they enforce tend to vary significantly from those which exist in the home market. Understanding these differences, coping with them, and building an international transportation network to serve the needs of the company presents a very challenging task for corporate transportation managers.

Third Party Logistics

During the past several years there has been a proliferation of "third party logistics" companies. These companies offer to manage logistics functions for firms which have traditionally managed those functions "in house." Generally they offer to perform those functions more cost effectively or in a manner which yields higher levels of customer service. A 1991 study of the 500 largest manufacturers in the United States found that 37 percent of those companies used third party logistics services.[9] The most frequently "outsourced" logistics functions are shown in Table 2-1.

Many of the companies offering third party logistics services are subsidiaries of large transportation companies. Such companies as Federal Express Corporation, Consolidated Freightways, Yellow Freight Systems, Roadway Express, and United Parcel Service have entered this market in an attempt to broaden the services offered to customers.

An interesting illustration of how a third party relationship works is provided by a contract between Roadway Logistics Services (ROLS) and Ford

TABLE 2-1

The Most Frequently Used Third Party Logistics Services

Logistics Function	% of Fortune 500 Companies Citing Use of Third Party Logistics Company for that Service
Warehouse Management	45%
Shipment Consolidation	45
Logistics Information Systems	32
Fleet Management/Operations	28
Order Fulfillment	26
Carrier Selection	21
Rate Negotiation	21
Order Processing	6
Product Assembly/Installation	6
Product Returns	2

SOURCE: Robert C. Lieb, "The Use of Third Party Logistics Services by Large American Manufacturers," *Journal of Business Logistics*, Vol. 13, No. 2 (1992), p. 34.

Motor Company. Under the terms of the contract, ROLS is responsible for meeting the inbound and outbound transportation needs of the company's Cleveland, Ohio engine plant. ROLS determines the plant's transportation requirements, selects the carriers to be used, negotiates freight rates with the carriers, schedules pick ups and deliveries, and monitors carrier performance. The arrangement has reduced Ford's operating costs and improved the quality of transportation service which the plant receives.[10] General Motors and Chrysler have also signed third party logistics contracts covering transportation requirements at a number of their plants.

The use of third party logistics services is expanding rapidly and this is fundamentally changing the way in which logistics activities are managed in many corporations.

Just-in-Time Manufacturing

As noted earlier in the chapter, there has been an important shift to JIT manufacturing by many American manufacturers. This shift has had major effects on logistics requirements and activities, ranging from the need to redesign facilities to elimination of storage space. It also impacts on a company's transportation requirements. A plant operating on a JIT basis will require more frequent, smaller deliveries than a plant operating on a traditional manufacturing basis. Since there is limited room for error, the most important carrier selection criteria become on-time performance and flexibility.[11] While it is generally believed that moving to a JIT manufacturing system will result in higher transportation costs, research has indicated that this is not necessarily true. One study found that nearly one-third of the companies operating on a JIT basis actually experienced reduced transportation costs.[12] In some cases this has been accomplished by arranging for a carrier to conduct "vendor sweeps" on the way to the manufacturing plant. This involves the carrier making multiple stops at different vendor locations on the way to the plant. While the carrier charges for the stops, the resulting consolidated truckload rates more than offset those charges.

Computers and Information Technology

Computers and information technology have come to play very important roles in logistics management. Personal computers, linked to company networks, have become common in corporate logistics. They, in conjunction with literally thousands of software packages, are routinely used in analyzing the many tradeoffs which exist in this field. In addition, they are increasingly tied to the computers of vendors and carriers to provide real time linkages to facilitate such things as order processing and scheduling.[13] Electronic data interchange (EDI) has become so common that some shippers now require carriers to have such capabilities before they are considered for possible freight movements. In some cases these linkages are used to transmit a variety of information including freight bills and loss and damage claims.

Green Logistics

The strong contemporary focus on environmental protection has had an impact on corporate logistics and transportation requirements. The "green movement," particularly in Europe, has fostered a reassessment of such logistics issues as the nature of packaging materials used in shipping a company's products to the marketplace. For example, Germany's recycling law stipulates that the manufacturer is responsible for taking back all of the packaging used in protecting goods during shipment. This has forced companies to develop "reverse logistics" programs for the flow of materials in the return direction. Bills providing for similar regulations in the United States have been introduced into the U.S. Congress.[14] Such regulations are likely to become more common and will generate additional transportation costs and a more complex logistics planning process.

LOGISTICS MANAGEMENT IN NON-MANUFACTURING SETTINGS

While this chapter has devoted primary attention to the logistics management activities of manufacturers, it should be noted that logistics activities are also very important in non-manufacturing settings. For example, retailers such as WalMart, KMart and L.L. Bean not only face many of the same logistics problems as manufacturers, but also engage in what many believe to be leading-edge logistics practices. Some large retailers have established "quick response" replenishment programs with suppliers which allow the retailers to maintain minimum inventories to meet customer demand because their suppliers ship on a Just-in-Time basis. KMart has estimated that its quick response program has fostered a 15 percent increase in annual sales while trimming inventories by 20 percent.[15] The application of logistics management practices in such non-manufacturing settings continues to grow and is the subject of substantial research.[16]

SUMMARY

This chapter has focused on the perspective of the industrial shipper. Shippers view management of a company's transportation requirements as part of logistics management. Meeting a shipper's transportation needs is often a quite complex task involving many responsibilities. Predominant among these are modal and carrier selection, shipment consolidation, rate negotiations, and carrier evaluation. In many companies the responsibilities also include management of the firm's private carriage operations and participation in industrial location decisions. The transportation expenditures of many companies are substantial, and knowledge of the available options can have considerable dollar and service significance.

Those involved in corporate transportation management are increasingly being influenced by changes in regulation, technology and management practice. Transportation deregulation has generated a more competitive marketplace in which the number of options has increased greatly. As many companies have entered foreign markets and begun to use foreign suppliers, those involved in corporate transportation management have had to design and manage international transportation networks which have little in common with domestic systems. Computers and information systems have produced real benefits by serving not only as tools of analysis and control, but also in facilitating improved communications between shippers and carriers. The emergence of third party logistics services, which are being widely utilized, has provided an alternative means of managing logistics activities.

DISCUSSION QUESTIONS

1. What are the primary benefits generated by a Just-in-Time manufacturing program?
2. What factors should be considered in choosing between the modes of transportation for a particular shipment?
3. What is "reverse logistics?"
4. What is the meaning of the term "freight consolidation" and what is its relevance to corporate transportation managers?
5. From a carrier's standpoint, what are the factors which determine if a particular account is attractive or not?
6. How has the movement toward transportation deregulation affected logistics managers?

NOTES

1. Helen L. Richardson, "Get More Than You Pay For," *Transportation and Distribution* (February, 1993), p. 30.
2. James Aaron Cooke, "Why Sears Turned Logistics Inside Out," *Traffic Management* (May, 1992), p. 30.
3. James Aaron Cooke, "How Quick Response Works at Haggar," *Traffic Management* (November, 1991), pp. 30-2; also, "Bringing JIT Benefits to the Bottom Line," *Traffic Management* (November, 1991), pp. 57-8, 60-1.
4. Robert C. Lieb and Robert A. Millen, "JIT and Corporate Transportation Requirements," *Transportation Journal* (Spring, 1988), Vol. 27, No. 3, pp. 5-10.
5. For an extensive discussion of location issues, see Walter Isard, *Location and Space Economy* (Cambridge, MA: The MIT Press, 1956), especially pp. 24-54.
6. Mitchell E. MacDonald, "Partners in Quality," *Traffic Management* (May, 1991), p. 40.
7. Information provided by trucking executives.
8. Mitchell E. MacDonald, "How to Run a Profitable Private Fleet," *Traffic Management* (December, 1992), pp. 27-8, 30.
9. Robert C. Lieb, "The Use of Third-Party Logistics Services by Large American Manufacturers," *Journal of Business Logistics*, Vol. 13, No. 2 (1992), pp. 29-42.
10. Discussion with Wayne Chapman, Vice President, Roadway Logistics Services, Akron, Ohio, December 12, 1991.
11. Lieb and Millen, p. 7.

12. Ibid., p. 9.
13. See Robert Kearney, "Unlock EDI's Potential: Investigate EDI Before Investing," *Transportation and Distribution* (March, 1992), pp. 27-30.
14. James Aaron Cooke, "It's Not Easy Being Green!" *Traffic Management* (December, 1992), p. 43.
15. James Aaron Cooke, "A Quick Response Success Story," *Traffic Management* (October, 1992), p. 54.
16. For example, see Frank W. Davis, Jr. and Karl B. Manrodt, "Service Logistics: An Introduction," *International Journal of Physical Distribution and Logistics Management*, Vol. 21, No. 7 (1991), pp. 4-13.

SELECTED REFERENCES

Cooke, James Aaron. "Supply Chain Management 90s Style." *Traffic Management*, Vol. 31, No. 7 (July, 1992), pp. 33-55.

Cooke, James Aaron. "Why Sears Turned Logistics Inside Out." *Traffic Management* (May, 1992), pp. 30-3.

Coyle, John J., Edward J. Bardi, and C. John Langley, Jr. *The Management of Business Logistics*. 5th ed. (St. Paul, MN: West Publishing Company, 1992).

Fuller, Joseph B., James O'Conor, and Richard Rawlinson. "Tailored Logistics: The Next Advantage." *Harvard Business Review* (May-June, 1993), pp. 87-98.

Glaskowsky, Nicholas A., Donald R. Hudson, and Robert M. Ivie. *Business Logistics*, 3rd ed. (Chicago, IL: Harcourt Brace Jovanovich, Inc., 1992).

Johnson, James C., and Donald E. Wood. *Contemporary Logistics*. 5th ed. (New York: Macmillan Publishing Company, 1993).

Kearney, A.T. *Improving Quality and Productivity in the Logistics Process: Achieving Customer Satisfaction Breakthroughs*. (Oak Brook, IL: Council of Logistics Management, 1991).

LaLonde, Bernard J., and James M. Masters. *Bibliography on Logistics Management*, supplement (Oak Brook, IL: Council of Logistics Management, 1993).

Lieb, Robert C. "The Use of Third-Party Logistics Services by Large American Manufacturers." *Journal of Business Logistics*, Vol. 13, No. 2 (1992), pp. 29-42.

Lieb, Robert C., and Robert A. Millen. "JIT and Corporate Transportation Requirements." *Transportation Journal*, Vol. 27, No. 3 (Spring, 1988), pp. 5-10.

Lieb, Robert C., and Robert A. Millen. "The Responses of General Commodity Motor Carriers to Just-in-Time Manufacturing Programs." *Transportation Journal*, Vol. 30, No. 1 (Fall, 1990), pp. 5-11.

MacDonald, Mitchell E. "Who's Who in Third Party Logistics." *Traffic Management* (July, 1993), pp. 34-6, 38-9, 42, 44, 46.

"Shipper Super Heavyweights." *Traffic Management*, Vol. 31, No. 10 (October, 1992), pp. 32-41.

"The Language of Logistics." *Inbound Logistics*, Vol. 12, No. 1 (January, 1992), pp. 26-9.

"The State of Quality in Logistics." *Distribution*, Vol. 91, No. 8 (August, 1992), pp. 90-107.

Tyworth, John E., Joseph L. Cavinato, and C. John Langley, Jr. *Traffic Management: Planning, Operations, and Control.* (Prospect Heights, IL: Waveland Press, Inc., 1991).

Part Two

MODES OF INTERCITY CARRIAGE

Northfolk Southern Triple Crown Road-Railer Operation *Courtesy Norfolk Southern Corporation*

Chapter Three

THE RAILROAD INDUSTRY

As we approach the mid-1990s the nation's railroads are demonstrating a new vitality which, in large part, is traceable to the movement toward transportation deregulation. Operating in a more liberal regulatory environment, the railroads have sought to broaden their traffic base through aggressive marketing and service innovations. Intermodal services, including "double-stack" container operations, have enhanced their ability to compete for the carriage of manufactured goods. Nearly all of the nation's large rail systems have negotiated reduced crew size agreements which have promoted productivity gains and cost reductions. Further, the industry's structure has continued to change as a result of a number of large-scale mergers. A stronger, more streamlined industry is emerging.

As noted in Chapter 1, the industry still generates more intercity freight ton mileage than any other mode. In fact, it carries more freight now than at any time in history. Railroads generate in excess of one trillion freight ton miles each year. Rail technology's inherent capabilities coupled with its comparative energy efficiency, indicate that freight railroads will continue to be a major component of our national transportation system for many years to come.

In terms of passenger service, during the last decade Amtrak has significantly improved service levels while covering a steadily increasing portion of its operating costs through fares. Further, with increased emphasis being given to rebuilding America's infrastructure, the possibility of building new high speed rail passenger links is being more thoroughly examined. That issue received considerable attention from President Clinton during his campaign for the presidency.

This chapter examines the development and structure of the railroad industry and highlights its strength and problems. Many of these problems are examined in greater detail in later chapters.

DEVELOPMENT OF THE SYSTEM

Throughout the years, technological developments have led to major shifts in the market positions of the various forms of carriage. Typically, the newer technologies have offered speed, flexibility, and cost advantages over earlier modes; consequently, some traffic has been diverted to the newer modes. In most cases this has led to long-term adjustments in market shares as competitive reactions have surfaced in the marketplace. However, in some instances the technological change has been so great that it has overwhelmed existing competitors. That was the case during the last half of the nineteenth century following the emergence of rail technology.

Early Railroad Competition

Prior to the introduction of railroad services, economic development had been closely tied to available waterways. A variety of vessel types, including flatboats, barges, and steamboats, used the waterway system. Service was slow and expensive.[1] The canal-building era, which began in the 1820s, attempted to inject an element of flexibility into the waterway network to promote more widespread economic growth. The success of some early canal projects, such as the Erie Canal which linked the Hudson River and the Great Lakes, in stimulating economic development led to heavy state government spending for canal construction. However, overbuilding occurred, and many of the canals built during the period were financial disasters.

Highway travel at that time was quite restricted due to limited federal and state expenditures for highway development; the private sector was unable to generate adequate funds for significant highway expansion. The shortcomings of early road-building techniques and the vulnerability of many roads to adverse weather conditions also hindered travel.

The application of the steam engine to locomotives during the 1830s ushered in what was to be an extremely competitive period in transportation. Most early rail lines were local and often served in a feeder capacity to water and highway carriage. However, it soon become apparent that this new technology, with its speed and flexibility advantages, offered potential competition to the highway and waterway modes. As rail operations expanded, intermodal competition increased in intensity.

Railroad mileage expanded rapidly in the post-1830 period (See Table 3-1), and numerous end-to-end consolidations led to the emergence of the first railroad systems.[2]

Throughout that expansionary period, the bulk of the capital that financed railroad development came from the private sector. However, as the strengths of rail service become apparent, state and local governments used tax concessions,

TABLE 3-1

Railroad Mileage Operated in the United States

YEAR	*MILES OF ROAD*[a]
1830	23
1840	2,818
1850	9,021
1860	30,626
1870	52,922
1880	93,262
1890	166,703
1900	192,556
1910	240,831
1920	259,941
1930	260,440
1940	233,670
1950	223,779
1960	217,552
1970	206,265
1975	191,520
1980	164,822
1985	145,764
1990	119,758
1991	116,626
1992	113,056

[a]These figures represent the aggregate length of roadway, excluding yard tracks, sidings and parallel lines. Jointly used track is counted only once. If multiple main tracks, yard tracks and sidings are included, total railroad track totalled 196,081 in 1991.

SOURCE: Association of American Railroads, *Railroad Facts*, 1993 edition (Washington, D.C.: the Association, 1993), p. 44.

loans, security guarantees, and land grants as enticements to railroad to lay new track. Railroads also began to attract attention at the national level. In fact, during the Civil War, railroads were used as a means of securing the West to the Union. Federal assistance in the form of massive land grants was extended to a number of railroads to facilitate building of a transcontinental linkage, which was completed in 1869. Thus, a precedent was set that involved the use of railroads as an instrument of public policy.

The financial inducements not only led to tremendous expansion of the railroad network, but also provided an opportunity for financial mismanagement. A number of early railroad promoters amassed sizable fortunes by swindling railroad investors.[3] Such actions, along with growing concern for protection of the public interest against discrimination and other monopoly-related abuses, ultimately led to federal regulation of the industry. With the passage of the Act to Regulate Commerce in 1887, the Interstate Commerce Commission was created to regulate interstate rail carriage, and the pattern of extensive federal regulation of transportation was initiated.

Resurgence of Intermodal Competition

By 1900, rail carriage was the dominant mode of both intercity freight and passenger movements. There is considerable debate as to whether the diversion of traffic from water and highway carriage to the railroads was caused by the superior characteristics of rail technology or by predatory behavior in the marketplace. In any event, rail service became dominant, and from 1900 to 1920 the transportation competition that did exist was primarily intramodal in nature. At that time, federal regulation of railroads was strongly oriented toward promotion of competition among rail carriers.

The next several decades brought about changes which significantly influenced the structure and competitive position of the contemporary railroad system in the United States. The economic downturn fostered by the Depression led to widespread financial failures in the industry. The federal government, in an attempt to stabilize the transportation industries initiated regulation of several competitive modes including trucking, bus services and air carriage during the 1930s. The railroad industry handled record levels of freight and passengers during World War II and there was considerable optimism about its future as the War ended. However, government expenditure programs in the post-War period financed extensive highway, waterway and airport-airway expansion. Trucks, barges, pipelines, airplanes, buses and private automobiles subsequently emerged as viable competitors for traffic that was once tightly controlled by the railroads.

In this new competitive environment the nation's freight railroads steadily lost market share and their passenger operations proved to be a major financial burden. The industry's earnings were very depressed and many bankruptcies resulted. However, as will be discussed in detail later in this chapter, the industry's outlook has brightened substantially since the early 1970s. The passenger burden was alleviated through the creation of Amtrak, and the movement toward deregulation gave the railroads unprecedented freedom to employ new technology, market their services aggressively and use price as a competitive weapon. The industry's financial picture has brightened dramatically and rail freight service has re-emerged as a viable competitive alternative for many shippers.

INDUSTRIAL AND FINANCIAL STRUCTURE

The railroads provide service over an extensive physical network that includes approximately 113,056 miles of rail lines and 190,500 miles of track. Figure 3-1 provides a map of the contemporary railroad system. In conducting their operations, the railroads utilize more than 23,200 locomotives, approximately 1.2 million freight cars, and more than 2,000 passenger cars.[4]

Although the railroad industry might appear to be a grouping of homogeneous companies, in reality it consists of several quite different components. Predominant among these are the 12 class I freight railroads. According to the ICC class I railroads are those that generate annual operating revenues in excess of $250 million. Table 3-2 lists the Class I railroads and railroad systems in the United States in 1993.

Tremendous size differentials exist within the class I carrier group. For example, some class I carriers generate little more than the class threshold revenue minimum; conversely, five of the Class I systems, the Burlington Northern, Consolidated Rail Corporation (Conrail), CSX Transportation, the Norfolk Southern and the Southern Pacific, generate more than $3 billion in operating revenues in a typical year. There are also approximately 520 regional and local railroads. Some of those companies function in an auxiliary capacity, either originating or terminating shipments that have their line-haul movements over a class I railroad line. Others are terminal and switching railroads primarily involved in the transfer of cars from one railroad to another or in the movement of cars to and from industrial sites and railroad lines. The majority of these companies have quite limited operations, often serving lines which had been abandoned by the larger railroads. Because of their lower overhead and operating costs the smaller carriers are able to profitably serve markets which were unprofitable for the larger carriers. Many of the smaller railroads are jointly owned and operated by the line-haul railroads serving a particular area.

The dominance of the class I railroads in our national railroad system is illustrated by the fact that they account for 75 percent of total mileage operated, 89 percent of railroad employment, and 91 percent of freight revenues.[5]

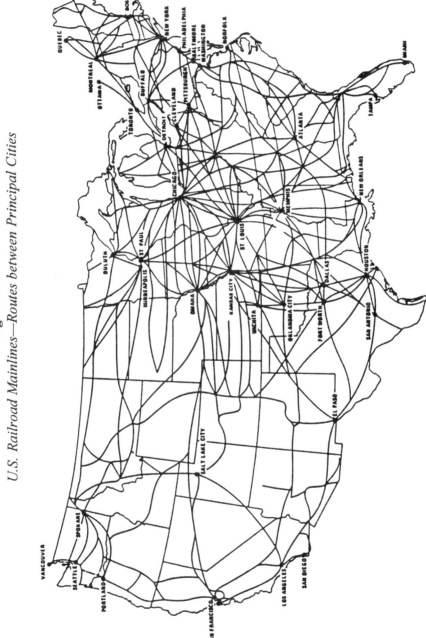

Figure 3-1

U.S. Railroad Mainlines—Routes between Principal Cities

SOURCE: U.S. Department of Transportation, Washington, D.C.

TABLE 3-2

*Class I Freight Railroad Systems
in the United States, 1993*

Atchison, Topeka and Santa Fe Railway Company
Burlington Northern Railroad Company
Chicago and North Western Transportation Company
Consolidated Rail Corporation
CSX Transportation
Grand Trunk Western Railroad Company
Illinois Central Railroad Company
Kansas City Southern Railway Company
Norfolk Southern Corporation
Soo Line Railroad Company
Southern Pacific/DRGW Companies
      Denver and Rio Grande Western Railroad Company
      Southern Pacific Transportation Company
Union Pacific Railroad Company

SOURCE: Data supplied by the Association of American Railroads, Washington, D.C., 1993.

There has been a long-term contraction in the number of railroads serving this country. Financial failure has eliminated some companies, but most have disappeared through mergers and consolidations with other railroads. As noted earlier, railroad mergers occurred with great frequency in the late 1880s, often on an end-to-end basis, as the first major railroad systems emerged. The scope of the merger movements is illustrated by the fact that over a period of years the Pennsylvania Railroad (which later became part of the Penn Central) absorbed nearly 600 independent companies. A second major wave of railroad mergers was approved by the ICC during the late 1950s and 1960s. Most of those mergers involved companies with parallel route structures; the basic motivating factor was a desire to reduce duplication of cost and service.

Another important series of rail mergers was approved by the Commission in the post-1980 period. During that period industry giants emerged such as the CSX (27,000 system miles), the Union Pacific (22,000 system miles), and the Norfolk Southern (18,000 system miles). Several of these mergers were end-to-end in nature, and the industry began to break with its earlier ICC-imposed regional form. Although interregional railroads have emerged, no transcontinental railroads exist.

In response to the deregulation movement several railroads have also moved aggressively into other modes of carriage. Before regulations were liberalized, intermodal ownership was generally prohibited. Among the most important of the intermodal combinations to emerge have been CSX-Sea Land Corporation (ocean carriage), Union Pacific-Overnite (trucking) and Norfolk Southern-North American Van Lines (trucking).

A sizable volume of railroad traffic is interregional. To service such traffic, the railroads generally must rely upon a complex pattern of through routes and joint rates as well as interchange agreements between railroads serving different regions. Even though such traffic might be handled by several railroads enroute from origin to destination, the shipper need only contact the originating carrier. Although the existence of these inter-carrier agreements facilitates the movement of interregional traffic, these movements do cause problems for the industry. The interchange process itself is time consuming and tends to slow service. Also, in most instances it is not economically feasible to unload a railroad car and reload the shipment into the car of a connecting railroad. Instead, loaded cars are interchanged. These cars must ultimately be returned to the company that owns them, and this tends to promote empty mileage and poor equipment utilization.

The railroad industry has taken several collective steps to improve this situation. The most significant of these was the formation of TTX Company. The company, which is jointly owned by 14 railroads, operates a pool of more than 80,000 specially equipped railroad flat cars which are used for transporting highway trailers and containers and for carrying new automobiles. The TTX fleet comprises most of the rolling stock used by the railroads in intermodal operations. The equipment is available for use by any railroad on a daily rental basis. The free-floating equipment moves over the lines of participating railroads and does not have to be expedited back to a particular home base. This reduces the cross-hauling of empty cars and promotes better equipment utilization.

Capital Needs

The railroad industry's net investment in road and equipment is approximately $48.6 billion.[6] Participation in the industry on a large scale necessitates heavy, fixed investment in areas such as rolling stock (equipment), terminal facilities, and the right-of-way. Only the railroads and oil pipelines own and maintain their rights-of-way. In all other forms of carriage at least part of the right-of-way expense is borne by some governmental unit. Railroads also pay substantial property taxes on their rights-of-way. Competitive forms of carriage are not similarly burdened because of public ownership of the infrastructures that they use.

In such an industry a company's ability to remain competitive through modernization and expansion is greatly dependent upon its ability to sell securities and borrow funds in the capital markets. However, a company's or an industry's access to the capital markets is dependent upon its financial performance. This has been a serious problem of the railroad industry in the post-World War II period. Contrary to widely held beliefs, the railroad industry in the aggregate is profitable. As shown in Table 3-3, railroad profitability varies by region. These variances are a function of many factors, including regional differences in economic growth rates, traffic composition, and intermodal competition. However, when the level of railroad profitability is related to the industry's investment base, it has historically yielded a rather anemic rate of return on investment. Between 1944 and 1984 the annual aggregate rate of return for the railroad industry never reached 5 percent (see Table 3-3). Since that time the industry's rate of return has increased substantially, but it is still lower than the average rate of return on investment for American industry in general which typically ranges between 9 and 14 percent. Despite the industry's improved earnings profile in recent years, there are still serious questions concerning the adequacy of those earnings. The Interstate Commerce Commission, in an ongoing attempt to determine the "revenue adequacy" of the nation's railroads, compares the industry's rate of return on investment with the industry wide cost of capital (the railroads' cost of borrowing money). In one recent annual assessment the Commission concluded that only one of the 14 Class I railroads was "revenue adequate."[7]

Regulation

The railroads are regulated as common carriers, and their interstate operations are subject to regulation by the ICC (economic matters) and the Department of Transportation (safety). Similar controls of intrastate operations exist at the state level.

Historically, the regulatory coverage of the railroad industry was extensive. Although the railroads were not restricted as to the commodities that they might carry, the following economic aspects of the industry were regulated by ICC: entry into markets, abandonment of service, initiation of new service offerings, pricing, sale of securities, and carrier mergers.

The nature of railroad regulation and its possible linkage to the industry's financial problems were extensively debated during the period that preceded the regulatory reform movement. Some critics contended that over regulation was the most serious problem faced by the industry.[8]

TABLE 3-3

Rate of Return on Investment, Class I Railroads, 1944-1992 (%)

Year	United States	Eastern District	Western District
1944	4.70	4.61	4.82
1955	4.22	4.49	3.86
1960	2.13	1.91	2.40
1965	3.69	3.50	3.87
1970	1.73	0.68	3.02
1975	1.20	Deficit	2.65
1980	4.22	2.78	5.56
1985	4.58	3.92	5.25
1986	1.30	3.81	Deficit
1987	4.75	3.33	6.29
1988	6.73	5.61	7.90
1989	6.34	6.73	5.98
1990	8.11	7.90	8.30
1991	1.30	1.21	1.39
1992	6.30	5.58	6.97

SOURCE: Association of American Railroads, *Railroad Facts*, 1993 edition (Washington, D.C.: the Association, 1993), p.18.

The most frequently criticized aspects of railroad regulation were ICC controls over abandonment of service and carrier pricing. A basic problem faced by the industry was its inability to expeditiously abandon noncompensatory freight services, particularly branch lines. Although the ICC permitted abandonment of some rail lines, it had been reluctant to permit complete curtailment of rail service to many areas. This was particularly true in areas that generated bulk traffic, such as sand, gravel, and coal, which in many cases was not subject to extensive intermodal competition. Such forced continuance of noncompensatory service was cited by many sources as a major cause of the financial collapse of the railroad system in the Northeast. As discussed later in this chapter, the government reorganization of the financially troubled carriers in that region subsequently reduced that burden.

ICC control over railroad ratemaking was also often criticized as being unresponsive to competitive dynamics.[9] The railroads long advocated more liberal ICC pricing controls. In the aftermath of the Northeast railroad crisis, Congress addressed the pricing issue in the Railroad Revitalization and Regulatory Reform

Act of 1976. Among other things, the statute gave the railroads considerably more pricing flexibility.

Two other significant changes in railroad regulation occurred during the late 1970s through administrative actions of the Interstate Commerce Commission. The commission granted railroads the authority to negotiate contract rates with shippers and deregulated railroad movements of fresh fruits and vegetables. The regulatory reform movement continued with the passage of the Staggers Rail Act of 1980, which further liberalized regulatory policies with respect to such matters as ratemaking, abandonment of service, and railroad mergers. Since that time the ICC has acted administratively to further railroad deregulation. Among the actions taken by the commission have been the exemption from regulation of all aspects of railroad intermodal services, lessening of the regulatory barriers that limited railroad movement into trucking operations, deregulation of railroad boxcar movements, and elimination of regulation of railroad movement of frozen foods.[10] The specifics of these regulatory changes are discussed in detail in Chapter 12.

COST AND SERVICE CHARACTERISTICS

The following discussion examines both the cost and service characteristics of the railroad industry. Particular attention is devoted to the competitive significance of these factors.

Railroad Costs

The total cost structure of the railroad industry is characterized by a very large fixed-cost component. It has been estimated that nearly two-thirds of the industry's costs are unrelated to volume.[11] This fixed-cost component is comprised of heavy expenditures for long-lived assets such as rolling stock, terminal facilities, rights-of-way, and yearly related outlays in interest, depreciation, and property taxes. Additionally, the industry has a large overhead burden in nonoperating salaries that is unrelated to volume.

Such an industry is often referred to as a declining-cost industry because, as output increases over some broad range, average unit costs tend to decline as fixed costs are allocated over an increasing number of units. Public utilities tend to have similar cost structures. In these industries, it is in the best interest of suppliers to attract additional volume, which results in lower average costs. These cost savings ultimately may be shared with consumers in the form of lower prices.

In contrast to the railroad industry, all other modes of intercity carriage, except oil pipelines, have total cost structures that are much less heavily weighted with fixed costs. That is, total cost is much more responsive to the volume of traffic handled. One basic reason for this structural cost difference is that in the other modes the major system cost element, the right-of-way, is not directly borne by the carriers. In some instances, user charges, including tolls and gasoline taxes, have been imposed by various governmental units. However, the aggregate amount of these charges is generally closely related to business volume. One example is provided by the trucking industry, in which fuel taxes are levied on a per-gallon-consumed basis. As a trucker's traffic volume increases, it is likely that the company's mileage and fuel tax payments will increase; hence the direct relationship between volume and cost.

Because of these differences in modal cost structures, the railroad industry possesses a theoretical pricing advantage over competitive modes. Naturally, in the long-run, all costs must be covered and a reasonable rate of return on investment must be earned. However, in the short-run, as long as the revenues generated by traffic cover the variable cost of providing the service and make some contribution to fixed cost, it makes sense for the railroad to solicit the traffic. Other forms of carriage with higher variable costs per output unit theoretically may be placed at a pricing disadvantage under these circumstances. However, except for exempt carriage, prices were historically regulated in transportation, and for many years the ICC was reluctant to allow such variable-cost pricing by the railroads due to its possible negative impact on competitive forms of carriage. The enactment of the Railroad Revitalization and Regulatory Reform Act of 1976 and the Staggers Rail Act of 1980 addressed such railroad pricing issues and provided the railroads with much greater pricing freedom. The railroads have used that pricing freedom aggressively, often lowering their prices to become more competitive. Evidence of this is provided by an Interstate Commerce Commission study which found that between 1980 and 1992 railroad freight rates dropped by almost 30 percent, when adjusted for inflation.[12]

In comparing rates, shippers would find that rail rates tend to be higher than those of water carriers and oil pipelines where competition exists among these modes (see Table 3-4). Rail rates also tend to be higher than the rates of motor carriers in short-haul markets, but often are lower than motor carrier rates for large shipments moving long distances. Due to significant speed and price differences, minimal freight competition exists between rail and air carriers. It must be remembered, however, that these are generalizations, and the relative prices of the modes will vary depending on the commodities to be shipped, the markets to be served, and the distances to be traveled.

Railroad Services

In assessing the merits of competitive forms of freight carriage, shippers are naturally concerned with service as well as price differentials. In this regard,

TABLE 3-4

Average Revenues per Ton Mile, Intercity Modes, 1960-1991 (cents)

Year	Rail[a]	Motor[b]	Barge	Oil Pipeline	Air[c]
1960	1.40	6.31	-	-	22.80
1965	1.27	6.46	0.346	0.279	20.46
1970	1.43	8.50	0.303	0.271	21.91
1975	2.04	11.60	0.518	0.368	28.22
1980	2.87	18.00	0.770	1.325	46.31
1985	3.04	22.90	0.800	1.565	48.62
1986	2.92	21.63	0.760	1.504	44.81
1987	2.73	22.48	0.733	1.453	43.47
1988	2.72	23.17	0.754	1.364	43.63
1989	2.67	23.91	0.769	1.327	48.57
1990	2.66	24.38	0.757	1.468	46.33
1991	2.59	24.86	0.778	1.398	44.45

[a]Class I freight railroads.
[b]Less-than-truckload rates of a sample of 27 general freight common carriers.
[c]Scheduled air freight service, not including Federal Express. If all scheduled and non-scheduled air freight operations, including Federal Express and UPS are included the average revenue per ton mile figure for air increases to $1.12.

SOURCE: Eno Transportation Foundation, Inc., *Transportation in America*, 11th ed., (Lansdowne, VA: the Foundation, 1993), p. 49.

service is multidimensional consisting of factors such as speed, consistency of service, reliability, and equipment availability.

Such service considerations led to the long-term erosion of the share of the freight services market held by the railroads. Historically, railroads offered carload (CL) and less-than-carload (LCL) services. LCL services tend to be rather slow when compared to less-than-truckload (LTL) services offered by motor carriers. Consequently, such traffic shifted to motor carriers and small shipments declined in importance to the railroads. Railroads also suffered from a speed disadvantage in carload services. This was particularly true in short-haul markets where the speed and flexibility of trucking was difficult to overcome. Compounding the problems of the railroads was a substantial loss and damage problem which intensified as a result of the industry's deferral of maintenance expenditures due to depressed earnings. Not surprisingly, the railroad industry's traffic base contracted, and to a great extent the industry was left to carry heavy, bulk loading, low value commodities which were not speed sensitive. Unfortunately, those same commodities could not be moved at high rates, accentuating the industry's revenue problems.

To cope with the increasingly competitive marketplace and recapture market share the railroads have invested heavily in capital improvements, upgraded the equipment fleet, and dramatically broadened their service offerings in recent years.

Intermodal Services. The most successful railroad service innovation has been the industry's expansion of intermodal services. That has involved not only traditional "piggybacking", but also double-stack container services. These services which are often offered in dedicated high-speed intermodal trains are speed competitive with motor carrier services and very competitively priced. Intermodal loadings have grown steadily, setting new volume record each year between 1980 and 1992. During the 1990s intermodal loadings have exceeded 6 million trailers and containers per year.

Piggybacking, which is the best known and most widely used of rail intermodal service offerings, consists of trailer-on-flatcar (TOFC) and container-on-flatcar (COFC) services. It involves the line-haul movement of loaded highway trailers or containers on flatcars, with the local pickup and delivery performed by truck. These services combine the best characteristics of both modes: the line-haul efficiencies of rail carriage with the pickup and delivery speed and flexibility of motor carriage. There are a variety of plans under which such services are offered, and these are detailed in Table 3-5.

An interesting technological development which has influenced the way in which some railroads provide intermodal services is the Roadrailer. It is a highway trailer which is equipped with both rubber tires for highway operation and steel wheels for direct operation on rails. This eliminates the weight of the railroad flatcar, reduces loading/unloading time, and provides maximum equipment flexibility. The Norfolk Southern Railroad, which is the strongest industry advocate of this technology, operates more than 80 Roadrailer trains each week. Some shippers, such as Ford Motor Company, find these services quite attractive. In one application, Ford uses Roadrailers to service just-in-time manufacturing operations in moving unfinished automotive parts between its plants in Detroit and St. Louis.[13] Another important intermodal development has been the introduction of double-stack container services by the railroads. In such service containers are stacked one on top of another producing less weight, and requiring fewer cars and less power to move a particular volume of freight. Double-stack services were initiated in 1984 through cooperative agreements between American President Lines (an ocean carrier) and several railroads. The

TABLE 3-5

Railroad Piggybacking Plans

Plan I   Railroad movement of trailers or containers owned by motor carriers, with shipment moving on one bill-of-lading and billing being done by motor carriers.

Plan II Door-to-door service by railroads, using their trailers or containers and making pickup and deliveries. Rates similar to those of motor carriers.

Plan II Railroad provides trailers, service, and either door-to-ramp or ramp-to-door motor service.

Plan II Ramp-to-ramp railroad service with shippers, including freight forwarders or motor carriers, providing pickup and delivery service. Modified versions of plan call for railroad pickup or delivery, but not both.

Plan III Ramp-to-ramp service with rates based on a flat charge, regardless of contents of trailers or containers which are supplied by shippers, forwarders, or motor carriers. No pickup or delivery service is performed by railroads.

Plan IV This plan is primarily designed for freight forwarders and requires them to provide either an owned or leased trailer on container-loaded flatcar. Railroads levy flat charge for loaded or empty car movements and furnish only power and rails.

Plan V   Traffic moves under joint rail-motor rates. Either mode may solicit traffic for through movement.

SOURCE: Association of American Railroads, Washington, D.C.

ocean carrier contracted with the railroads to operate double-stack trains which moved from West Coast ports served by American President ships to inland points. The shipping public has responded enthusiastically to double-stack services, which are often priced 25-30 percent lower than traditional piggyback offerings, and the number of ocean carriers and railroads offering these services has expanded steadily. While bridge and tunnel clearances have limited application of double stack technology in certain locations, such operations are now commonplace throughout the country.[14]

Increasingly, intermodal services are being offered through cooperative agreements between carriers in different modes. As noted above, double-stack operations began through ocean carrier-railroad cooperation. Similar agreements are even more common between railroads and motor carriers. For example, J.B. Hunt, the nation's largest truckload carrier, has agreements with the Santa Fe, Burlington Northern, Southern Pacific, and Florida East Coast Railroads to jointly develop intermodal opportunities. Under one of those agreements, the Santa Fe hauls nearly 2,000 trailers per week for Hunt.[15] Another large trucker, Schneider National, has similar agreements with the Southern Pacific and Burlington Northern Railroads. Schneider has estimated that its use of double-stack rail services saves the company approximately $400 per container compared with over the road highway movements of the same traffic between Chicago and Los Angeles.[16]

Cooperative agreements between railroads serving different parts of the country to provide high quality, long-distance intermodal services have also become common. In one such instance Conrail and the Santa Fe provide premium coast-to-coast piggyback services in 76 hours. The services, known as the California Connection westbound and the Manhattan Chief eastbound, are heavily used by United Parcel Service, the U.S. Postal Service, and Yellow Freight (a large LTL trucker).[17]

Another rail service innovation which should be mentioned is the "unit train". It is essentially a rent-a-train concept, and it typically involves the contractual movement of a bulk commodity, such as coal, in trainload quantities. It has often been applied in the movement of coal to public utility power generation plants. The cars, which are generally owned by the shipper, are only loaded in one direction, and return empty to the commodity source. However, the guaranteed volume and expedited services make the concept attractive to railroads and large-volume shippers alike.

Such service innovations, coupled with dramatic improvements in both the railroad industry's tracking and tracing capability and its loss and damage performance have increased the industry's ability to be competitive for the movement of a broader range of commodities. The industry has employed such diverse technology as satellite tracking and electronic date interchange connections with large customers to provide timely information to shippers concerning rail movements. At the same time improvements in roadbed and equipment allowed the industry to reduce its loss and damage claims from 1.97 percent of industry revenues in 1970 to 0.40 percent in 1991.[18] As a result of such improvements, the railroads have been able to regain a considerable amount of high-valued manufactured commodities (at attractive higher rates) which had been lost to motor carrier competition.

The Role of Middlemen. Two forms of transportation intermediaries or middlemen play important roles in marketing and purchasing intermodal services offered by the railroads. These are shippers agents and freight forwarders.

Shippers agents are classic transportation middlemen who buy intermodal capacity from the railroads on a wholesale, multiple-carload basis, then retail the services to individual shippers. Because of the sizeable quantity discounts offered to the agents by the railroads, agents are able to offer lower prices to shippers than the shippers would be able to obtain in dealing directly with the railroads. The range of services offered by agents has expanded broadly during the past several years and now often includes pickup and delivery, tracking, tracing and information services. The largest intermodal agent is the Hub Group which annually handles in excess of $600 million in intermodal business.[19]

Freight forwarders have also been active buyers of railroad intermodal services. In contrast to shippers agents who typically deal in at least carload size shipments, freight forwarders are primarily involved in gathering small shipments that subsequently move in consolidated form over intercity routes. At the forwarder's local terminal the shipments are sorted according to destination cities and consolidated into carload (or truckload) quantities. The forwarders then arrange for an intercity carrier to move the consolidated shipments to the various destination cities. Upon arrival at the destination city, the shipments are disaggregated in a break-bulk operation and delivered to customers.

The forwarder is perceived as a carrier by the shipper and as a shipper by carriers. Forwarders negotiate contract rates with the railroads and truckers and make their money on the spread between the rates which they charge shippers for the service and the lower rates they have negotiated with the line-haul carriers.

Commodities Carried. While expansion of intermodal services has allowed the railroads to increase the volume of manufactured goods which they handle, they are still heavily involved in long-distance, large-volume movements of low-valued, high-density commodities. Products of forests, mines, and agriculture, all exhibiting low-value, high-density characteristics, are the major products transported by the railroads. Railroads are still the principal mode of carriage for many bulk materials and agricultural products. They handle over 70 percent of coal ton miles and 60 percent of grain ton miles. (Coal comprises nearly 27 percent of railroad carloadings). They are also the primary mode for manufactured products such as pulp and paper products (84 percent), automotive products (73 percent), foodstuffs (56 percent), chemicals (52 percent), and primary metals (54 percent).[20]

The long-distance nature of railroad freight service is illustrated by the fact that the average length of railroads hauls in 1991 was 751 miles.[21] Reflecting the large-shipment concentration of railroad traffic, the average carload moved by railroads in 1991 exceeded 66 tons.[22]

THE NORTHEAST RAILROAD CRISIS

One of the most significant transportation developments of this century was the financial collapse of the Northeast railroad system in the early 1970s. Its negative significance, including deteriorating railroad services and carrier bankruptcies, has been well documented in the media. However, the collapse also had positive implications, because it focused national attention on the economic significance of the railroads and led to an examination of the many problems that threatened future railroad viability.

The problems faced by the Northeast railroads were multifaceted.[23] Intermodal competition in the region was intense. As previously noted, government spending programs, especially the construction of high-speed, high capacity highways, greatly contributed to that competitive intensity. Additionally, many traffic flow patterns in the region were relatively short-haul (less than 300 miles), and motor carriage, due to its speed and flexibility, was a quite formidable competitor for many types of traffic moving such distances.

The railroads of the region also suffered because of shifts in industrial location patterns. Much heavy manufacturing has shifted to the South and West, reducing the high-volume traffic available in the region. New traffic emanating from the region has tended to be high in value and low in volume, and such traffic is not well suited to railroad movement. In many instances these competitive and locational factors led to decreased traffic density, particularly in branch-line operations. This promoted numerous railroad abandonment applications to the ICC; but the commission, as in the case of passenger discontinuance applications, was reluctant to permit broad-scale service cutbacks. Complicating these problems were rather questionable management practices, including diversion of capital into nonrailroading ventures, and low labor productivity among the regions railroads compared to class I railroads in general.[24] Finally, the burden of passenger service losses in the pre-Amtrak period also drained much needed capital from the Northeast railroads.

Bankruptcies

This combination of problems led to continued cash flow and refinancing difficulties for the railroads of the region and ultimately resulted in the bankruptcy of seven major carriers by 1973. Those railroads declaring bankruptcy were the Ann Arbor, the Boston and Maine, the Central of New Jersey, the Erie Lackawanna, the Lehigh Valley, the Penn Central, and the Reading. Collectively, these carriers served 19 states and the District of Columbia, while generating nearly 18 percent of the industry's revenues and employing nearly 20 percent of the industry's workforce. Because of the public dependence upon continued rail services in the region, these lines were not liquidated; rather, each entered court-supervised reorganization proceedings in hopes of becoming viable.

However, by early 1973 it was apparent that the individual reorganizations were not working. Services continued to deteriorate, cash flow and deferred maintenance problems persisted, and deficits grew. As a result,

Congress considered a number of courses of action, including nationalization, that might be used to rehabilitate rail services in the Northeast.

Regional Rail Reorganization Act

After considering a variety of restructuring plans, which had been suggested by such parties as the Department of Transportation, the ICC, several congressmen, and a number of railroad executives, in late 1973 Congress enacted the Regional Rail Reorganization Act.[25] The bill was signed into law by President Ford in January 1974.

The legislation created two new organizations that were to bring about an unprecedented collective reorganization of the region's bankrupt railroads. One was a government agency, the United States Railway Association (USRA), which functioned as the planning and financing agency in bringing about the restructuring. The second organization was the Consolidated Rail Corporation (Conrail), which was to operate the restructured system as a private, for-profit organization.

To facilitate the reorganization, Congress provided nearly $2.1 billion in federally guaranteed loans, direct loans, and direct grants. Included in this total was $180 million to subsidize unprofitable lines that might otherwise be abandoned. Also included was $250 million in job protection funds for workers who would be displaced.

Working in conjunction with the Rail Services Planning Office of the ICC and the Department of Transportation, the USRA was charged with development of a final system plan, which would be subject to congressional approval. The task faced by USRA was monumental. There was no precedent for a reorganization of this scale. The number of lines and facilities to be evaluated in the development of the final system plan, which was to preserve essential rail services while equitably reimbursing previous security holders, was mind boggling. At the same time, political pressures were immense, particularly from elected officials whose districts were faced with a decrease or loss of rail services.

Essentially, the planning process was a classic confrontation between public and private interests. For years the railroads of the Northeast and many other regulated carriers have been used as instruments of public policy. Governmental desire to promote competition and service continuity has often led to carriers being forced to continue noncompensatory services. In the long-run, such action may run counter to the public interest by draining needed capital from private companies. Although resolution of this conflict is difficult and multidimensional, it is also essential.

After nearly two and a half years of planning, Conrail initiated operations on April 1, 1976. At that time, the company employed nearly 87,000 workers and serviced 17,000 route miles in 16 states. It also operated trains over approximately 900 route miles of light-density lines under a subsidy program established by the Reorganization Act. Those light-density lines that were not conveyed to Conrail were subsidized by federal and state funds in the amount of the difference between revenues and operating costs. Additionally, Conrail operated commuter passenger services under contracts with state and local transportation authorities.

Much of the initial federal appropriation for Conrail was used for upgrading track and equipment. Despite these expenditures, Conrail's financial performance during its first five years of operation was disappointing. During its first nine months of operation in 1976, the company incurred a $205.5 million loss, followed by a $366.6 million loss in 1977, and a $385.3 million loss in 1978. Also, the $250 million in federal funds to finance the employee protection program, which had been projected to last until 2016, was depleted by 1978. That necessitated annual supplemental congressional funding to continue those benefits. The operating loss was trimmed to $178.2 million in 1979. However, losses continued into 1980, with the carrier registering a deficit of $243.7 million. Throughout the 1976-1980 period, Conrail, which originated, terminated, or handled nearly 22 percent of the nation's rail traffic, was plagued by a variety of problems. These included poor equipment utilization, old facilities, and an excessively large workforce.

The federal financial commitment to Conrail was expanded to $3.3 billion during 1980. By early 1981, serious questions had been raised as to whether Conrail would ever achieve financial viability. However, several steps were taken during that year that were to prove quite important in promoting improvements in Conrail's financial performance. In January, L. Stanley Crane, former chairman of the Southern Railway, was appointed chairman and chief executive officer of Conrail. Crane accelerated the company's ongoing cost-cutting efforts and sought ways to eliminate noncompensatory operations. That summer, Congress passed the Northeast Rail Service Act of 1981.[26] The legislation provided for the eventual return of Conrail to the private sector, and required the USRA to determine by June 1983 if the carrier was profitable and also to evaluate its prospects for long-term viability. If the USRA found the company to be profitable by that time and determined that its prospects were good, steps would be taken to dispose of the system as a whole. If it was determined that the system was not profitable, the Secretary of Transportation was to take action to dispose of the system on a piecemeal basis. The act also required Conrail to transfer all of its commuter operations to state and local government units by January 1983. Additionally, it substantially reduced the duration of the employee protection period that had been accorded Conrail's employees, and provided funds for lump-sum severance payments that might be used by the carrier to reduce its workforce through early retirements.

Conrail registered an operating profit of $39.2 million, during 1981 and followed that with another profit of $174.2 million in 1982. By June 1983 USRA had determined that the carrier was profitable and the Department of Transportation had begun to solicit offers to purchase the system. The system had been pared to 15,000 miles and the number of employees had been reduced to 42,000. During 1983 Conrail realized an operating profit of $313 million.

The DOT began accepting bids for the system in early 1984 and closed the bidding period on June 18, 1984. By that time the agency had received 14 bids. Among the bidders were several railroads (including CSX and Norfolk Southern), a group of railroad labor unions, and several private investment groups. Throughout this process Conrail's management argued against merging with another railroad, and contended that the railroad should be privatized as an independent company. The offers received by the DOT were quite complex and involved various combinations of cash payments and waivers of Conrail's tax credits and tax loss carry-forwards. After concluding its evaluation of the offers, the DOT supported sale of Conrail to the Norfolk Southern. However, congressional leaders, clearly influenced by the arguments of Conrail's management, opted to spin the company off as a stand-alone entity. Under the provisions of The Conrail Privatization Act of 1986 a public sale of 85 percent of Conrail's common stock was initiated by the government in 1987. The remaining 15 percent was held by Conrail employees. The government received approximately $1.6 billion as a result of the sale.[27]

In the years which have followed the sale, Conrail has continued to make progress. By 1993 Conrail's workforce had been reduced to 25,000, approximately one-quarter of what it had been when it began service in 1976. During 1992 the company negotiated an agreement with the United Transportation Union to reduce the number of crew members from three to two on most of its trains.[28] The company continues to be among the most profitable and productive railroads in the country which reflects a strong management performance in a region which has been less than robust in economic terms during the past decade.

AMTRAK

To this point this chapter has primarily focused on the railroad industry's freight-carrying capability. However, railroad passenger services are also important from a public policy standpoint. As government spending programs have promoted the expansion of our highway and airway systems, intercity rail passenger service has been affected negatively. The railroads carried 77 percent of all for-hire intercity passengers in the United States in 1929, but their share of that traffic declined to 7.2 percent by 1970.[29] If that passenger volume is expressed as a percentage of all intercity travel, including automobile trips which dominated such movements, railroads accounted for less than 1 percent of passenger volume.[30]

The reasons for the precipitous decline in rail passenger service were numerous. They included the expansion of the other modes of intercity carriage, our growing national affluence, and our society's every-increasing commitment to the automobile. As the shift in passenger preference accelerated following World War II, many railroads incurred sizable deficits in passenger operations. At the same time, railroad management was reluctant to commit scarce capital to declining passenger operations, and consequently service deteriorated. The ICC responded to these developments by permitting the railroads to discontinue nearly one-third of intercity passenger trains between 1958 and 1970. Although these actions partially alleviated the problem, they did not prevent deficits. In fact, between 1963 and 1970 the aggregate passenger service deficit of the railroads exceeded $400 million annually.

In response to this problem and undoubtedly prompted by the June 1970 bankruptcy of the Penn Central, which had annually incurred approximately one-third of the aggregate national passenger loss, Congress enacted the Rail Passenger Service Act in October 1970.[31] This legislation created a quasi-public company, the National Railroad Passenger Corporation (Amtrak), to manage the national intercity rail passenger service network. Amtrak was charged with the development of a modern and efficient passenger network that would ultimately operate on a profitable basis.

Amtrak initiated service in May 1971 over a reduced passenger network, which had been jointly determined by the Department of Transportation, Congress, and Amtrak's board of incorporators. Figure 3-2 illustrates the scope of the Amtrak network. Carriers that had previously served the routes included in the initial Amtrak network were given the option of becoming affiliated with Amtrak or continuing the services independently. If the carriers chose not to become a party to the Amtrak agreement, they were not to be permitted to drop any of those services for a period of at least five years. Three railroads, the Denver & Rio Grande Western, the Rock Island, and the Southern Railway, chose not to become affiliated with Amtrak and continued to operate passenger service independently.

The carriers that opted to become affiliated with Amtrak were assessed entry fees based on their prior passenger service losses. Such payments totaled $197 million; these funds, coupled with congressional appropriations, provided the initial funding of the new passenger system.

Initially burdened by a congressionally-imposed network which made little economic sense, an outdated equipment fleet, scarce capital and a traveling public which expected immediate improvements, Amtrak still succeeded in quickly reversing a long-term decline in intercity rail passenger ridership. During

Figure 3-2

Amtrak's National Rail Passenger System

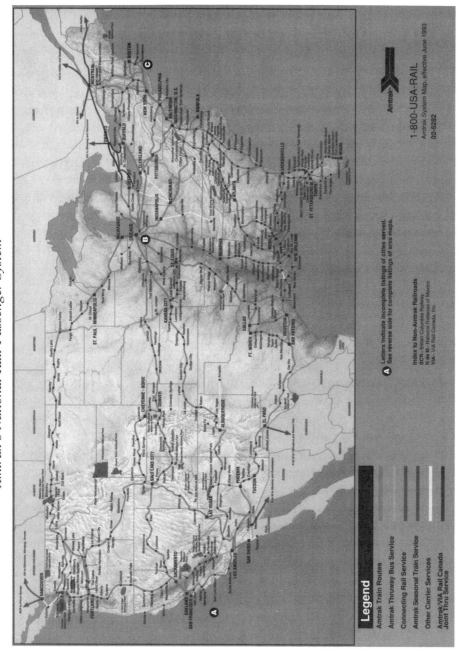

SOURCE: *National Railroad Passenger Corporation (Amtrak), Washington, D.C*

its first decade of operation Amtrak experienced a 96 percent increase in passengers carried and generated a 125 percent increase in revenue passenger miles.[32]

However, Amtrak's operating deficit continued to climb (see Table 3-6). The deficits, which necessitated congressional subsidies to cover both operating losses and capital needs, had become increasingly visible in the late 1970s.

In the early 1980s Amtrak's ridership trends reversed. The effects of both the national economic slowdown and the aggressive pricing tactics of many of the new airlines and bus companies which had entered the marketplace through deregulation began to be felt. By that time, the Department of Transportation had become a vocal critic of Amtrak. Among the Amtrak-related matters criticized by the department were the inclusion of many long-distance trains in the system, Amtrak's policy of maintaining relatively low fares, and the congressional extension of nearly $900 million in loan guarantees to Amtrak. Those guarantees eventually were transformed into grants by Congress given Amtrak's inability to repay the related obligations. During 1979 the department called for a 43 percent cutback of Amtrak's 27,700-mile route system.[33] At the same time, the federal Office of Management and Budget, faced with an Amtrak request for nearly a billion dollars for the following fiscal year, advocated sizable service reductions. Congress responded by directing Amtrak to drop six routes in the fall of 1979.

The Reagan administration, which began in 1980, opposed continued funding for Amtrak. The President called for elimination of the system in several budget messages to Congress. While there was sufficient support for Amtrak among congressional leaders to offset the pressures to shut down the system, those individuals intensified their calls for greater Amtrak efficiency and less reliance upon federal subsidies.

Congress mandated that Amtrak cover a steadily increasing portion of its operating costs through fare increases, and over the past decade the company has responded aggressively. As shown in Table 3-7 Amtrak's revenue to expense ratio had improved to 79 percent by 1992 (it was slightly greater than 50 percent in 1983).

Amtrak's ridership, as measured in terms of passenger miles, grew significantly between 1983 and 1992, reaching nearly 6.1 billion intercity passenger miles in 1992. In addition, the company has increasingly pursued commuter rail contracts with state and regional commuter authorities. Its success in obtaining such contracts is demonstrated by the fact that in 1992 Amtrak carried 20.3 million passengers in commuter services versus 21.3 million passengers in intercity operations.[34]

With continued congressional funding Amtrak has dramatically upgraded its equipment fleet and roadbed and as a result on-time performance has been steadily enhanced. There is a strong demand for first-class and sleeper service in many markets, and the company continues to develop new fare programs targeted

TABLE 3-6

Selected Amtrak Operating Statistics, 1971-1992

Year	Rev. Passengers Carried (Millions)	Commuter Passengers Carried (Millions)	Rev. Passenger Miles[b] (Billions)	Operating Deficit (Millions)
1971[a]	10.6		2.0	$ 55
1972	16.6		3.0	148
1973	17.0		3.8	159
1974	18.3		4.3	273
1975	17.4		3.9	352
1976	18.2		4.1	441
1977	19.0		4.2	552
1978	19.2		4.2	582
1979	21.5		4.9	595
1980	20.8		4.5	599
1981	19.4		4.4	760
1982	18.2		4.0	707
1983	18.9		4.2	797
1984	19.9	.5	4.6	763
1985	20.8	.6	4.8	774
1986	20.3	.7	5.0	702
1987	20.4	10.2	5.2	699
1988	21.5	15.4	5.7	650
1989	21.4	17.4	5.9	665
1990	22.2	18.0	6.1	703
1991	22.0	18.1	6.3	722
1992	21.3	20.3	6.1	712

[a]Reflects operations for 7-month period, May 1-December 31, 1971.
[b]Passenger miles generated in contract commuter operations are not included.

SOURCE: National Railroad Passenger Corporation, *Annual Reports*, 1971-1992 (Washington, D.C.: the Corporation, 1971-1992).

at off-season travel, families and international travelers. In one of its more innovative marketing efforts Amtrak has initiated an air-rail program with United

Table 3-7

Amtrak Revenue/Expense Ratios and On-time Performance, 1986-1992

Year	Revenue/Expense Ratio	Systemwide On-Time Performance
1986	.62	74%
1987	.65	74%
1988	.69	71%
1989	.72	75%
1990	.72	76%
1991	.79	77%
1992	.79	77%

[a]Beginning in 1991 the Federal Railroad Administration (FRA) began paying excess Railroad Retirement and Unemployment Insurance Taxes on behalf of Amtrak to the Internal Revenue Service. This change resulted in a .06 improvement in Amtrak's revenue/expense ratio for the year. The FRA will continue to make these payments in subsequent years.

SOURCE: National Railroad Passenger Corporation, *Annual Reports*, 1986-1992 (Washington, D.C.: the Corporation, 1986-1992).

Airlines which is based on travel by Amtrak in one direction and by air in the opposite direction. The joint fares offered compare favorably with round-trip excursion air fares.[35]

Congress continues to provide both operating subsidies and capital grants to Amtrak. During the early 1990s those payments averaged nearly $1 billion per year. The most ambitious of the rail passenger programs approved by Congress in recent years was the Northeast Corridor Improvement Project. The project, which focuses on Amtrak's strongest market, will substantially reduce operating times between New York and Boston while supporting 24 daily roundtrips between those cities by 1997.

By 1993 Amtrak's passenger system had been substantially reconfigured and consisted of a 25,000 mile route network which included 500 stations. The system was served by 24,000 employees and by nearly 2,000 owned and leased passenger cars. In view of the route network served by the company (which is highly influenced by political considerations) and the competitive marketplace in which it operates, Amtrak will never be profitable. The company does hope to eliminate the need for federal operating subsidies by the year 2000.[36] Regardless, it must be recognized that the company provides a safe, energy efficient mode of travel to an increasing number of passengers while taking pressure off highways and airports in many of our nation's most congested travel markets.

It has been suggested that Amtrak be privatized, but in view of economic realities, this is very unlikely to happen. Amtrak will continue to operate at the discretion of Congress, and its support base in that forum continues to be solid.

Auto-Train

One of the major railroad passenger service innovations of the 1970s was the initiation of service by Auto-Train. The private company was granted authority by the ICC to operate trains carrying passengers and their automobiles between Lorton, Virginia, and Sanford, Florida. Similar service was also operated between Louisville, Kentucky, and Sanford, Florida. Locomotives and operating crews were provided on a contractual basis by the railroads that owned the rights-of-way over which Auto-Train traveled. Substantial ridership was attracted, but the company was plagued by numerous financial problems, which ultimately led to its declaration of bankruptcy in 1980. In 1983, Amtrak paid the estate of Auto-Train $200,000 for the name of the company, its operating manuals, and a list of former passengers. Amtrak initiated its Auto-Train operations in October 1983 and continues to provide the services between Lorton, Virginia and Sanford, Florida.

HIGH-SPEED RAIL SERVICE

In recent years there has been a resurgence of interest in high-speed passenger trains in the United States. Such trains are typically defined as those which can operate at average speeds of at least 125 miles per hour (mph). In the U.S. only Amtrak's Metroliner, which operates between Washington and New York, reaches that speed, and then only for short distances. While the federal government showed considerable interest in various high-speed rail options in the early 1970s, Congress severely reduced development funds on related projects in the mid-1970s, effectively abandoning those efforts.

Other countries, such as France and Japan, were also involved in the development of high-speed rail technology, and their efforts yielded "conventional" high-speed rail networks which are electrically powered. In France, the highly publicized TGV system has a top operating speed of 186 mph and the "bullet trains" of Japan reach top speeds of 163 mph. It has been estimated that top speeds of 200 mph will be possible on both systems by the late 1990s.[37]

Based on the success of TGV operations in both attracting ridership and easing highway and airport congestion the 12-nation European Community has agreed to expand the current 1,800 miles of high-speed rail lines in Europe to 18,000 miles by the year 2000. The cost of building the system has been estimated at $76 billion plus billions to be spent on equipment for the system.[38]

The impressive operating performance of the French and Japanese high-speed rail systems has rekindled interest in such systems in the United States. By 1993 thirteen states were studying the possibility of constructing such systems. But, supporters of high-speed rail applications in the U.S. are faced with rather formidable obstacles. These include a reluctance in the financial community to commit capital to such projects, the opposition of many state regulatory bodies, and hostile members of the general public who oppose the initiation of high-speed operations in their geographical areas.

The capital costs of high-speed rail passenger service projects are quite limiting. A recent Transportation Research Board study estimated that the cost of acquiring land and building high-speed rail links in the U.S. to be at least $10 million to $20 million per mile.[39] While the nationalized railroads of countries like Japan and France have ready access to the required governmental funds to support such ventures, until recently the federal government has been hesitant to provide the necessary capital to promote development in the United States. However, during the Bush administration the Department of Transportation devoted considerable attention to high-speed rail issues and began to explore the concept of magnetically levitated trains (maglev) which use powerful electromagnetic fields to levitate vehicles a few inches above a fixed guideway at speeds approaching 300 mph. Prototypes of maglev systems have already been built in Germany and Japan and the U.S. is about to enter the field. The Intermodal Surface Transportation Act of 1991 provided $725 million over six years for development and production of the nation's first maglev prototype.

While maglev systems may sound like a dream come true for high-speed rail advocates, there are several significant problems associated with the technology. Construction of maglev systems is likely to be far more costly than conventional high-speed rail links. Energy consumption also appears to be a problem. It has been estimated that the Japanese maglev would consume 40 times the electricity used by the nation's bullet trains.[40] Further, the noise levels generated by maglev prototypes will have to be dramatically lessened if such technology is to be accepted by environmentalists.

During his campaign for the presidency President Clinton advocated construction of an extensive high-speed rail network for the United States. However, he neither addressed the choice between conventional high-speed rail technology and maglev nor did he identify potential funding sources for such systems. Any attempt on his behalf to deliver such services on a large scale to the traveling public will face sizeable obstacles.

SUMMARY

Despite competitive inroads by other modes of carriage, the railroad industry still remains the dominant form of intercity freight movement as measured in terms of intercity ton mileage. As a result of mergers and carrier failures the industry has undergone a substantial transformation in recent years. The regulatory reform movement has allowed the industry to eliminate unnecessary services and concentrate on its core business. The service offerings of freight railroads have become more diverse and they have finally been allowed to use price as a competitive weapon. As the industry's profitability has increased carriers have been able to upgrade their physical plant and equipment fleets thereby fostering service improvements.

In terms of passenger service, Amtrak has substantially improved its service while setting new ridership records. However, it still generates substantial operating losses and relies upon federal subsidies to cover those losses and its capital needs. At the federal level increasing attention is being devoted to the concept of high-speed rail passenger service. However, any attempt to introduce such services on a broad scale, either using conventional rail or maglev technology, faces substantial obstacles not the least of which is the enormous capital costs of such projects.

DISCUSSION QUESTIONS

1. Discuss briefly the cost structure of the railroad industry.
2. Explain the reasons for the necessity of traffic interchange in the railroad industry and outline the problems which such interchange causes.
3. Outline the structural changes which have occurred in the railroad industry during the past two decades.
4. What were the pressures which led to the creation of Amtrak? In your opinion, what role should the company play in the future intercity transportation network?
5. What role, if any, should high-speed rail passenger service play in the United States? What factors might limit that role?

NOTES

1. D. Philip Locklin, *Economics of Transportation*, 7th ed. (Homewood, IL: Richard D. Irwin, Inc., 1972), p. 95.

2.   U.S. Congress, Senate, Committee on Interstate and Foreign Commerce, Special Study Group on Transportation Policies in the United States, *National Transportation Policy* (Doyle Report), 87th Cong., 1st Sess., 1960 (Washington, D.C.: U.S. Government Printing Office, 1961), p. 232.

3.   Dudley F. Pegrum, *Transportation: Economics and Public Policy*, 3rd ed. (Homewood, IL: Richard D. Irwin, Inc., 1973), pp. 55-6.

4.   Eno Transportation Foundation, Inc., *Transportation in America*, 10th ed. (Lansdowne, VA: the Foundation, 1992), p. 63.

5.   Association of American Railroads, *Railroad Facts*, 1992 ed. (Washington, D.C.: the Association, 1992), p. 5.

6.   Ibid., p. 42.

7.   "ICC Finds Just One Railroad Revenue Adequate," *Traffic Management* (October, 1991), p. 18.

8.   See Association of American Railroads, "AAR Proposals for Deregulating the Railroad Industry" (Washington, D.C.: the Association, 1979), 20 pp. (Mimeographed).

9.   U.S. Department of Transportation, Office of the Secretary, *Rail Service in the Midwest and Northeast Region* (Washington, D.C.: U.S. Government Printing Office, 1974), p. 10.

10.   "ICC Stays Boxcar Deregulation Decision," *Transport Topics* (October 24, 1983), p. 6.

11.   Roy J. Sampson and Martin T. Farris, *Domestic Transportation: Practice, Theory and Policy*, 4th ed. (Boston, MA: Houghton Mifflin Company, 1979), p. 59.

12.   Association of American Railroads, "ICC Reports Additional Rail Rate Reductions," *On Track* (June 29, 1992), p. 4.

13.   Association of American Railroads, "RoadRailers Prove Answer to Ford's Transport Needs," On Track (November 1-15, 1987), p. 1.

14.   "Stack Trains Now Reaching Across U.S.," *Traffic Management* (January, 1989), p. 17.

15.   "The Great Train Turnaround," *Business Week* (November 2, 1992), p. 56.

16.   "Intermodal Transportation: Key to a "Win-Win" Freight Transportation System," *Defense Transportation Journal* (August, 1992), p. 9.

17.   Association of American Railroads, "Conrail, Santa Fe Offer Premium Piggyback Train," *On Track* (September 15-30, 1987), p. 4.

18.   Association of American Railroads, *Railroad Facts*, 1992 cd. (Washington, D.C.: the Association, 1992), p. 61.

19.   Rip Watson, "Hub Plan May Usher in New Intermodal Era," *Journal of Commerce*, New York, February 2, 1993, pp. 1A and 3B.

20. Data supplied by the Association of American Railroads, Washington, D.C.

21. *Railroad Facts*, p. 36.

22. Ibid., p. 37.

23. U.S. Railway Association, *Preliminary System Plan* (Washington, D.C.: the Association, 1975), I, p. 3.

24. Railroad labor relations have been quite controversial throughout the years, and labor agreements have a decided impact on worker productivity and carrier costs. These issues are discussed in depth in Chapter 14.

25. *Regional Rail Reorganization Act*, Public Law 93-236 (1973).

26. *Northeast Rail Service Act*, Public Law 97-35 (1981).

27. Association of American Railroads, "Conrail Sale Garners $1.6 Billion for US," *On Track* (April 1-15, 1987), p. 1.

28. Association of American Railroads, "UTU Ratifies Crew Reduction Agreement with Conrail," *On Track* (February 19, 1992), p. 1.

29. National Railroad Passenger Corporation, "Amtrak News," Washington, D.C., 1972, p. 1.

30. *Transportation in America*, p. 48.

31. *Rail Passenger Service Act*, Public Law 91-518 (1970).

32. National Railroad Passenger Corporation, *Annual Reports*, 1971-1981 (Washington, D.C.: the Corporation, 1971-1981).

33. "U.S. Eases Stance on Cutting Back Amtrak System," *Wall Street Journal*, New York, June 21, 1979, p. 5.

34. National Railroad Passenger Corporation, *Annual Report, 1991* (Washington, D.C.: the Corporation, 1991), p. i.

35. Ibid., p. 6.

36. U.S. Department of Transportation, *Moving America-New Direction, New Opportunities: A Statement of National Transportation Policy-Strategies for Action* (Washington, D.C.: the Department, 1990), p. 64.

37. "High Speed Rail," *Journal of Commerce*, New York, November 19, 1991, p. 8A.

38. Ferdinand Protzman, "To Track Unity in Europe, Watch Its Fast Trains," *New York Times*, October 25, 1992, p. 5.

39. "High Speed Rail," p. 8A.

40. "Will Magnetic Levitation Ever Get Off the Ground?" *Business Week* (December 30, 1991), p. 44.

SELECTED REFERENCES

Armstrong, John H. *The Railroad: What It Is, What It Does.* 3rd ed. Omaha, NEB: Simmons-Boardman Books, Inc., 1991.

Association of American Railroads. *An Integrated Transportation Policy for an Era of Rising Expectations.* Washington, D.C.: the Association, 1989.

"Big Rail is Finally Rounding the Bend." *Business Week* (November 11, 1991), pp. 128-29.

Elliott, Kathleen M. "Is This Any Way to Run a Railroad?" *The Babson Staff Letter*, September 18, 1992, pp. 1-4.

Fogel, Robert W. *Railroads and American Economic Growth.* Baltimore, MD. Johns Hopkins Press, 1964.

Gellman, Aaron J. "Barriers to Innovation in the Railroad Industry." *Transportation Journal*, Vol. 25, No. 4 (Summer, 1986), pp. 4-11.

Hilton, George W. *The Northeast Railroad Problem.* Washington, D.C.: American Enterprise Institute for Public Policy Research, 1975.

Higginson, James K. and James H. Bookbinder, "Implications of Just-in-Time Production on Rail Freight Systems." *Transportation Journal*, Vol. 29, No. 3 (Spring, 1990), pp. 29-35.

Lee, Tenpao, Philip C. Baumael, and Patricia Harris. "Market Structure, Conduct and Performance of the Class I Railroad Industry, 1971-1984." *Transportation Journal*, Vol. 26, No. 4 (Summer, 1987), pp. 53-65.

Nice, David C. "Financial Performance of the Amtrak System." *Public Administration Review*, Vol. 51 (March-April, 1991), pp. 138-44.

Roberts, Robert. "New Directions for Amtrak." *Railway Age* (June, 1991), pp. 59-60, 62-3, 66.

Rockey, Craig F. "The Formation of Regional Railroads in the United States." *Transportation Journal*, Vol. 27, No. 2 (Winter, 1987), pp. 5-13.

Orenstein, Jeffrey. *United States Railroad Policy: Uncle Sam at the Throttle.* Chicago, IL: Nelson-Hall, Inc., 1990.

"The Great Train Turnaround." *Business Week* (November 2, 1992), pp. 56-7.

U.S. Department of Transportation. *Moving America-New Directions, New Opportunities: A Statement of National Transportation Policy-Strategies for Action.* Washington, D.C.: the Department, 1990.

U.S. General Accounting Office. *Railroad Regulation: Economic and Financial Impacts of the Staggers Rail Act of 1980.* Washington, D.C.: U.S. General Accounting Office, 1990.

U.S. General Accounting Office. Report to the Committee on Commerce, Science and Transportation, U.S. Senate. *Railroad Competitiveness: Federal Laws and Policies Affect Railroad Competitiveness.* Washington, D.C.: U.S. General Accounting Office, 1991.

Wilner, Frank N., Association of American Railroads, Information and Public Affairs Office. *Railroads and Productivity: A Matter of Survival.* Washington, D.C.: the Association, 1991.

Santa Fe Con-Quest Double Stack Train *Courtesy Consolidated Freightways*

Roadway Express Twin Trailer *Courtesy of Roadway Express*

United Parcel Service "Feeder" Operation Transporting Packages Between Hubs *Courtesy of United Parcel Service*

CHAPTER FOUR

THE HIGHWAY SYSTEM

This chapter focuses on another major component of the national transportation network, highway carriage. Primary attention is given to the intercity for-hire freight movement by truck, but passenger carriage by bus and automobile is also discussed.

The movement toward federal deregulation of the trucking industry has dramatically changed not only the structure of the industry, but the way in which it operates. Regulatory reform has had similar effects in the intercity bus industry.

Those concerned with the deterioration of our nation's infrastructure often focus on our nation's highway system which has suffered from the deferral of nearly a trillion dollars in maintenance. In response to that problem, gasoline taxes have been increased at both the federal and state level. President Clinton's call for rebuilding our nation's infrastructure indicates that further fuel tax increases are likely.

Government pressures continue to be directed at automobile manufacturers to emphasize energy efficiency and safety in vehicle design. Consumers increasingly reflect similar desires in their purchase of automobiles. At the same time, reduction of automobile, truck and bus pollution has become an important national priority.

The primary purpose of this chapter is to explore the industry structure of intercity highway carriage and to focus attention on the contemporary strengths and problems of this system. Urban or metropolitan highway transportation issues are examined in depth in Chapters 18 and 19.

DEVELOPMENT OF THE SYSTEM

Little highway development occurred in this country prior to 1800, and that which did take place was in the form of turnpike or toll roads financed by private capital. Many toll roads were financial successes, but it was apparent that private capital was inadequate to meet the highway needs of the country's expanding economy.

Initial Government Funding

Responding to this need, in 1797 Congress authorized construction of a National Pike to connect major population centers. Yearly federal highway appropriations followed that action, and the highway system expanded to approximately 27,000 miles by 1830.[1] However, during the 1830s, a dispute over states' rights and the desirability of federal involvement in the internal affairs of the states led to curtailment of federal highway spending. Further development of the highway system was viewed as a state function, but most states lacked the financial capability to promote such development. Consequently, highway expansion decelerated and received relatively little attention until the latter part of the century.

The lobbying efforts of farmers, railroads, and bicyclists led several states to create highway departments and to increase state funding of highway programs in the 1890s, but the real impetus for renewed highway expansion was the invention of the internal combustion gasoline engine. As automobile ownership increased during the early 1900s, growing attention was devoted to highway expansion. Rekindled state interest in highway programs was illustrated by the creation of state highway aid laws in 45 states by 1915.[2] However, state funding of highway projects was still rather limited.

Expansion of Federal Funding

Federal involvement in highway construction was renewed in the Federal-Aid Road Act of 1916, which established a program of federal-state cooperation in highway construction that continues to the present. The statute established a program of formula grants under which states were allocated federal highway funds on the basis of several variables, including state population and area. To qualify for these grants, the states were required to establish state highway departments to cooperate with the federal government.[3]

Highway expansion continued following World War I. The growth was financed by a combination of federal, state, and local government outlays. Gasoline taxes were levied in many states and soon became a major source of state highway funds. Underlying these levies was a basic philosophy that relies upon users to pay for publicly provided facilities. Such "user charges" still generate much of federal and state funding for highway programs.

As the highway system both expanded and improved in quality, the number of people attracted to for-hire trucking and bus operations steadily increased. Intermodal competition grew in intensity during the 1920s, and the competitive impact of the highway modes began to be felt by the railroads. The

ICC, concerned not only with the diversion of traffic from the railroads but also with questionable competitive practices in trucking, called for federal regulation of trucking as early as 1925.[4] By that time, a number of states had already enacted regulations governing intrastate motor carriage.

Competitive conditions between truckers and railroads intensified even further with the onset of the Depression. Highway building programs were expanded to stimulate the economy, and the number of people engaged in for-hire highway carriage increased dramatically. Ultimately, these conditions led to passage of the Motor Carrier Act of 1935, which established ICC control over many aspects of interstate highway carriage. The scope and coverage of these regulatory controls are discussed later in this chapter.

National priorities dictated suspension of federal-aid highway projects during World War II. As a result, highway expansion slowed considerably during the conflict. Even in the years immediately following the war, material and personnel shortages continued to severely restrict highway programs. It was not until the early 1950s that the pace of highway development accelerated appreciably.

Post-World War II Highway Expansion

The most significant highway development since World War II has been the building of the Interstate Highway System, which is illustrated in Figure 4-1. This high-speed, limited-access highway network, which was designed to link most major cities and state capitals was originally approved by Congress in 1944, but financing was not finalized until 1956. The Interstate extends approximately 43,000 miles. Ninety percent of the cost of constructing the Interstate has been financed by the federal government. The federal share has been funded through the Highway Trust Fund, which was created for that purpose in 1956. The fund accumulates revenues from a federal gasoline tax and other federal highway excise taxes. Expenditures for the construction of the Interstate exceeded $100 billion, making it the largest peacetime public works program in our country's history. The high-quality roads of the Interstate have not only reduced highway travel times, but have also lowered vehicle operating costs. While the Interstate comprises only one percent of the nation's total roadway miles, it carries about 20 percent of highway travel in this country.

The federal role in highway expansion has not been limited to the Interstate Highway System. The Intermodal Surface Transportation Efficiency Act of 1991 established a 155,000 mile National Highway System (which includes the Interstate) that also qualifies for federal assistance. Roads included in the National Highway System carry 75 percent of the nation's truck traffic.

Figure 4-1
The Dwight D. Eisenhower System of Interstate
and Defense Highways

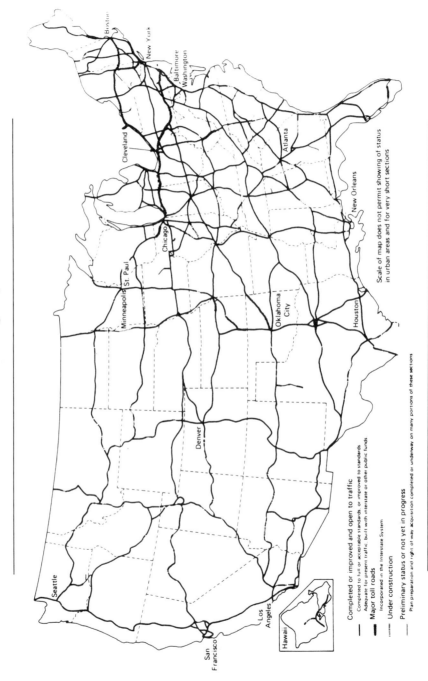

Completed or improved and open to traffic
    Completed to full or acceptable standards, or improved to standards.
    Adequate for present traffic built with interstate or other public funds.
Major toll roads
    Incorporated in the Interstate System
Under construction
Preliminary status or not yet in progress
    Plan preparation and right of way acquisition completed or underway on many portions of these sections

Scale of map does not permit showing of status
in urban areas and for very short sections

SOURCE: U.S. Department of Transportation, Federal Highway
Administration, Washington, D.C.

The 1991 legislation established a six-year $151 billion spending program. Of that amount $119.5 was to be spent on highway improvements and $31.5 was to be used for mass transit projects. The law also granted the states unprecedented flexibility in determining how the federal funds were to be used at the state level.[5]

While the Intermodal Surface Transportation Efficiency Act did not increase federal gasoline taxes, it extended through 1999 2.5 cents of an incremental 5 cent per gallon gasoline tax which had been enacted one year earlier. That fuel tax increase had originally been scheduled to expire in 1995. Federal gasoline taxes were increased by 4.3 cents per gallon in 1993. The increase was approved by Congress in response to President Clinton's fiscal year 1994 budget proposals. By 1993 federal gasoline taxes, per gallon were 18.63 cents per gallon of gasoline and 24.3 cents per gallon of diesel fuel.

The role of state and local government in financing highway expansion and improvement should not be underestimated. In fact, such outlays far outweigh federal highway expenditures. The relative highway funding role of these governmental units is illustrated by the fact that while federal highway outlays were estimated to be $16.3 billion in 1992, state and local highway spending exceeded $62.8 billion.[6] The highway modes now play major roles in intercity markets. Trucks move approximately one-fourth of intercity freight ton mileage, and buses play a major role in intercity passenger movement. The speed and convenience of the automobile have led to its emergence as the dominant form of intercity passenger carriage, accounting for nearly 81 percent of intercity passenger mileage.[7]

Development of the contemporary highway network has yielded enormous benefits to our nation. Because of the transportation cost savings that the network has generated, it has tended to lower the prices of many goods while increasing their availability. It has also given our population unparalleled mobility. However, the highway system also has had tremendous costs. From a purely economic standpoint, nearly one trillion dollars has been spent for highway purposes by various governmental units since World War II.[8] Social costs have also been substantial. Air pollution has become a national concern, and nearly 40,000 people lose their lives on our highway each year, while millions are injured. Our great reliance upon highway modes, particularly the automobile has accelerated the depletion of precious energy resources. Consequently, a major challenge in the years to come will be a reassessment of national transportation priorities and a determination of appropriate highway spending levels, given society's other goals.

INDUSTRIAL AND FINANCIAL STRUCTURE

The structure of the trucking industry which is illustrated in Figure 4-2, is rather complex. It involves both for-hire and private carriage. Included in for-hire carriage are both regulated motor carriers and carriers that are exempt from the economic controls of regulatory agencies. The nature and significance of these exemptions are discussed later in this chapter. It has been estimated that nearly two-thirds of intercity truck ton mileage is carried by private and exempt carriers, with the balance being moved by regulated carriers.[9] Total trucking industry revenues for 1991 were estimated to be $278 billion[10]

The composition of truck traffic is quite different from that carried by the railroads. As discussed in Chapter 3, the majority of rail tonnage consists of products of mines, forests, and agriculture. Less than one-third of rail traffic is comprised of manufactured products. In contrast, more than 85 percent of the tonnage originated by class I motor carriers of freight consists of manufactured products.[11] The degree of motor carrier control over high-valued commodity movements is illustrated by the American Trucking Associations' estimate that truckers deliver more than 70 percent of all radios, televisions, phonograph records, clothing, and office and accounting machines.[12] Additionally, truckers now deliver the largest percentage of such mineral products as sand, gravel, and crushed stone. Truckers also deliver the majority of livestock and fresh fruit and vegetables to major markets.

ICC Regulated Carriers

In the post World War II period the number of interstate motor carriers subject to ICC regulation declined rather steadily from 20,872 in 1945 to 15,100 in 1974. Mergers were the major reason for the contraction. Due to rather restrictive federal entry regulations, mergers often provided the most effective means for a trucking company to broaden its market coverage.

The movement toward reduced federal regulation of trucking, which began in the mid-1970s, substantially liberalized entry requirements and as a result the long-term contraction in the number of carriers has been dramatically reversed. By 1993 nearly 45,000 trucking companies were subject to ICC regulation.[13] Their aggregate annual operating revenues exceed $78 billion.[14]

The ICC classifies regulated motor carriers on the basis of annual gross operating revenues. Class I carriers are those which generate annual operating revenues of more than $5 million. Motor carriers generating between $1 and 5 million in annual operating revenues are considered class II carriers, and those with annual operating revenues of less than $1 million are categorized as class III carriers. As

FIGURE 4-2

Legal Structure of the Motor Carrier Industry

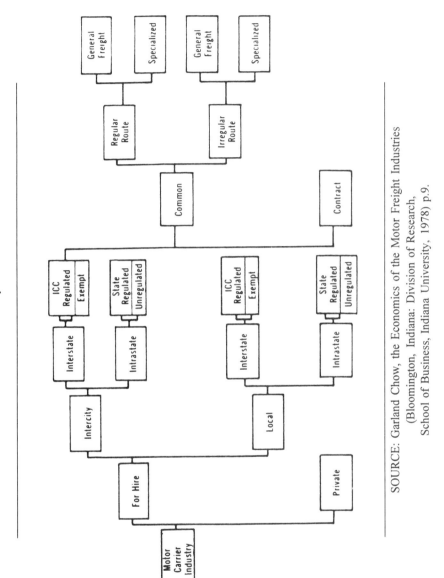

SOURCE: Garland Chow, the Economics of the Motor Freight Industries (Bloomington, Indiana: Division of Research, School of Business, Indiana University, 1978) p.9.

the classifications would indicate, there are substantial size differentials in the regulated portion of the trucking industry. While nearly 95 percent of the trucking companies regulated by the Commission are class III carriers, in 1992 there were 863 class I carriers, the largest being United Parcel Service which had operating revenue in excess of $15 billion.[15] The ICC also categorizes motor carriers according to the types of commodities that they are permitted to carry. The agency maintains 17 different commodity classifications for truckers. The largest carrier grouping consists of general freight carriers who are permitted to haul a wide variety of packaged goods that are referred to as general commodities.

Separate ICC authority is needed to handle traffic covered by the 16 special commodity categories. Those categories cover such freight as household goods, heavy machinery, petroleum products, motor vehicles, building materials and hazardous materials. It is not unusual for a carrier that is primarily engaged in the carriage of general commodities to establish one or more subsidiaries to handle special commodities.

General Commodity Carriage. The general commodity sector of ICC regulated trucking was dramatically affected by the regulatory reform movement. Entry policies were liberalized and thousands of new carriers entered the marketplace. At the same time, many existing carriers broadened their geographical coverage. In examining this sector of the industry it is useful to distinguish between truckload (TL) and less-than-truckload (LTL) operations. Individual carriers tend to specialize in one or the other of those operations. For statistical purposes, the ICC defines truckload shipments as those weighing in excess of 10,000 pounds.

In truckload operations the shipment moves directly from the shipper to the consignee with no terminal handling or consolidation activity. It has been estimated that nearly 40,000 ICC regulated carriers specialize in TL movement of general commodities, and that most of them are quite small.[16] Nearly all of the new companies which have entered the industry as the ICC has liberalized its entry policies have entered this sector of the industry. These companies have typically been low cost, non-union operations and they have proven to be formidable competitors for such traffic. The three largest carriers in this sector of the industry in 1991 were Schneider National with revenues of $760 million, J.B. Hunt Transport ($732 million) and Werner Enterprises ($323 million). The 10 largest TL carriers control about 10 percent of the TL market. Some believe their share will increase to 25 percent by the end of the 1990s.[17] The average length of haul in the TL sector of the industry was 228 miles in 1991.[18]

In contrast, other general commodity carriers focus their efforts in the less-than-truckload (LTL) shipment business. Much of the traffic handled by these carriers consists of small shipments. The average shipment handled by these carriers weighs 1,000-1,200 pounds. The carriers provide pickup service on small shipments in the originating city. Shipments then move through one or more consolidation and/or breakbulk terminals enroute to their final destination. Delivery service is then provided at the destination city. Due to the flow pattern of these shipments, each shipment is handled at least several times, and labor costs are quite high, as is the susceptibility of the shipment to loss and damage. The average LTL shipment moved 589 miles in 1991.[19]

Prior to the movement toward deregulation, carriers that were primarily LTL-oriented tended to view TL freight as backhaul traffic. It was not uncommon for such carriers to generate three-fourth of their revenues from LTL freight with the balance coming from TL shipments.

However, that backhaul traffic was also very attractive to many of the new carriers who entered the industry as regulations liberalized, and they aggressively used price competition to take that traffic from the LTL carriers. As a result, the large LTL carriers have become even more specialized in handling small shipments with truckload traffic often comprising no more than 5-10 percent of their revenue base. For example, during 1992 TL traffic accounted for only 9 percent of Yellow Freight Systems revenues, 10 percent of Roadway's revenues, and 9 percent of Consolidated Freightways revenues.[20]

While there has been massive new entry into the TL sector of the industry, there has been a growing concentration of business in LTL operations. It has been estimated that only 150 carriers participate in this industry sector, and as a result of failures and mergers, 13 of the largest 20 LTL carriers in 1979 had disappeared by the early 1990s.[21] The "Big Three" companies, Consolidated Freightways, Roadway Express, and Yellow Freight Systems dominate the market by offering extensive LTL services on the regional and national levels. Their combined revenues comprise approximately one-third of the aggregate LTL market. [22]

Some ICC regulated motor carriers of general commodities specialize in parcel delivery service and limit the size of the shipments which they handle. Foremost among these is United Parcel Service (UPS) which is the nation's largest motor carrier. The company offers parcel delivery services to every address in the contiguous 48 states for packages weighing up to 70 pounds each. The maximum package size is 130 inches in length and girth combined and the maximum package length is 108 inches.

UPS is a privately held company with approximately 244,000 employees, many of those working on a part-time basis. The company generated $15 billion in parcel revenues in 1992 while delivering more than 2.94 billion parcels and documents.[23] It has expanded aggressively into air cargo services and has become a major international carrier which services 180 countries and territories worldwide. By combining its ground and air capabilities in the domestic marketplace the company is able to offer a variety of service options to shippers.

The United States Postal Service (USPS) has traditionally competed with UPS in the parcel delivery market. The USPS also limits shipment size to 70 pounds, and will handle packages up to 106 inches in length and girth combined with a maximum length of 72 inches. The service quality offered by the Postal Service has improved significantly in recent years, and as a result its overnight and second day delivery services have become far more attractive to shippers. While the USPS has emphasized cost reductions in recent years it still registers operating losses in excess of $2 billion per year.[24]

Another major competitor in the parcel delivery market is Roadway Package System (RPS). The company was established in 1985 as a non-union subsidiary of Roadway Express. It relies heavily upon owner-operators as drivers. RPS has expanded its route network steadily and in the early 1990s its traffic volume was expanding at 20-25 percent annually.[25]

Further competition is provided by many smaller companies providing parcel delivery services over much more limited route networks. For certain classes of parcel service there is also considerable competition between truckers and the air express services offered by such companies as Federal Express. The specific nature of air cargo services is discussed extensively in Chapter 6.

Exempt Carriage and Owner-Operators

The interstate movement of unprocessed agricultural goods is exempt from regulation of the Interstate Commerce Commission. Therefore, truckers may carry such traffic without obtaining the approval of the Commission. While some agricultural goods are carried as backhauls by regulated carriers, the majority is hauled by carriers often referred to as owner-operators. These carriers do not have ICC operating authority to provide regulated services. It has been estimated that there are approximately 100,000 owner-operators, most of whom operate one truck.[26]

Some owner-operators are also involved in the movement of regulated commodities under subcontract with regulated carriers. In operating on a subcontract basis, the owner-operator receives a percentage of the total revenues paid to the regulated carrier (under whose operating authority the owner-operator is working) by the shipper. By using owner-operators a regulated carrier is effectively able to expand and contract its equipment fleet and workforce according to current business volume. As a result of regulatory changes, owner-operators are also permitted to work on a subcontract basis with companies which have private trucking fleets. Although the scale of individual operation is relatively small, it has been estimated that owner-operators collectively carry between 25 and 40 percent of intercity trucking tonnage.[27]

Private Trucking

There are nearly 50,000 private trucking fleets in the United States.[28] While transportation is not the primary business of the companies which establish private fleets, those fleets handle a considerable volume of local and intercity truck tonnage.[29] One study concluded that about one-third of all manufacturers, 75 percent of producers of construction materials, 65 percent of lumber and wood producers, and 55 percent of food processors operate private fleets.[30]

Private trucking fleets range in scope from one to several hundred vehicles. Companies establish private trucking operations for a variety of reasons including specialized service requirements, the desire for greater shipment control and lack of satisfaction with the rates charged by for-hire carriers. The majority of private trucking fleets operate on a local basis; however, many conduct interstate operations.

Historically, private truck fleets operating on an interstate basis experienced empty backhaul problems. For example, a company would move its products from a manufacturing facility to a regional distribution center in another state. Typically, the company had nothing to move from the distribution center to the manufacturing facility and the truck returned empty. Tight federal regulation of interstate trucking generally precluded private trucking operations from providing for-hire services for another company on the backhaul. However, the regulatory reform movement has changed that situation, and hundreds of private trucking operators have acquired backhaul operating authority from the ICC.[31]

The Role of Middlemen

Two forms of transportation middlemen serve the trucking industry. They are brokers and freight forwarders.

Brokers act as classic transportation middlemen in arranging transportation services for shippers and soliciting and booking freight for carriers. While brokers were originally limited to playing those roles in the movement of exempt commodities, they now play a very significant role in the movement of regulated commodities.

To become a broker, one has to be licensed by the ICC. Prior to the movement toward deregulation, there were relatively few brokers (less than 100 in 1980). However, since that time the number of brokers has grown to more than 7,000 and they now handle more than $5 billion per year in trucking services.[32] While most brokers are relatively small, some are quite large and serve thousands of customers.

Brokers can use the services of common, contract, exempt and private trucking operations in linking shippers and carriers. For their services they are paid a commission which averages 7-10 percent of the freight bill. The broker bills the shipper, deducts the commission, then gives the balance to the carrier.

The services offered by brokers are of value to many parties. Many small shippers, with limited expertise in transportation, not only rely upon brokers to identify carriers and route shipments, but also to handle administrative issues for them including such matters as rate negotiation, billing and tracing. Many small to medium size truckers use brokers to find backhauls, particularly in markets in which they have no direct sales representation. Similarly, companies operating private trucking fleets use brokers to identify potential backhaul traffic. Finally, owner-operators serving exempt markets generally use brokers to market their services.

As noted in Chapter 3, freight forwarders also tender some of their consolidated freight to truckers for line-haul movements. However, the importance of freight forwarders in intercity freight markets has declined precipitously as regulatory controls in transportation have lessened. The traffic base which they once controlled has eroded due to such factors as the aggressive marketing of air cargo services and the deep discounts offered to large shippers of LTL freight by truckers.

REGULATION

The Motor Carrier Act of 1935 established extensive ICC control over a variety of the economic and safety aspects of the interstate motor carriage. Despite the changes fostered by the regulatory reform movement, the Commission still controls many of the economic aspects of interstate trucking. Control over safety matters was transferred to the Department of Transportation when it was established in 1967.

Under the provisions of the act, all motor carriers serving interstate routes on a for-hire basis are classified as common, contract, or exempt carriers. Common carriers hold themselves out to the general public, which they have authority to serve. Their operating rights may be for regular route service (over designated highways on a regular basis) or irregular route service between designated points or areas on a nonscheduled basis. Contract carriers operate under continuing contracts with one or more shippers. As noted earlier, exempt carriers are those engaged in certain commodity movements or types of operation that are considered to be outside the economic jurisdiction of the ICC. Included are trucks used exclusively for transportation of unprocessed agricultural commodities or newspapers, and vehicles used incidental to air carriage.

Among those aspects of regulated motor carrier operations historically controlled by the ICC have been entry into common and contract carriage, prescription of commodities to be carried, specification of routes to be traveled and points to be served, pricing, mergers, and the sale of securities. The development and evolution of these regulatory controls are discussed in Chapters 10-12.

Interstate Commerce Commission regulation of interstate trucking was widely criticized throughout the years. Entry and pricing controls were often challenged as being overly restrictive and inflexible. Similarly, route restrictions were attacked as not only generating excessive cost and time delays, but also as causing unnecessary fuel consumption. In response to both these criticisms and a growing ICC commitment to regulatory reform, the commission substantially liberalized trucking regulations in the late 1970s. These administrative actions, in turn, prompted congressional reassessment of the propriety of the statutes that governed the economic aspects of interstate trucking. This reassessment ultimately resulted in passage of the Motor Carrier Act of 1980, which made substantial regulatory changes. Since that time the ICC, through administrative actions, has reduced the extent of trucking regulation. However, many aspects of the industry are still tightly regulated. In recognition of this fact, in 1992 the Commission joined the Department of Transportation in calling upon Congress to totally deregulate the economic aspects of interstate trucking.[33] These issues are discussed extensively in subsequent chapters.

State Regulation

Regulation of intrastate motor carriage rests with state authorities. Of the 50 states only seven have significantly deregulated intrastate trucking. Those states are Alaska, Arizona, Delaware, Florida, Maine, New Jersey and Wisconsin.[34] Although there are considerable differences in the economic regulation of motor carriage in the other 43 states, state controls are often quite similar to the pattern of federal controls that existed prior to the regulatory reform movement. In the area of motor carrier safety, state governments regulate such matters as licensing, speed, and vehicle weights and lengths.

Intrastate trucking regulation been the topic of considerable public policy debate in recent years. Carrier groups, shippers and the Interstate Commerce Commission have all called for reduction or elimination of economic regulation of trucking at the state level.[35] Critics of those regulations have estimated that their elimination would save the shipping public $6-8 million per year.[36] Through administrative actions the ICC has effectively broadened the definition of interstate trucking, thereby reducing the scope of state controls. This matter is examined more extensively in Chapter 12.

CAPITAL NEEDS

The average net investment per firm of class I intercity motor carriers of freight is slightly more than $9.2 million.[37] In contrast, the average net investment of class I railroads (those generating annual operating revenues in excess of $250 million) exceeds $1 billion.[38] Reflection on these figures indicates that there are considerable scale differences between the two modes; consequently, motor carriers tend to have rather different capital requirements than those of railroads, as discussed in Chapter 3.

The most important factor that leads to these differences in average investment is the fact that highways, the major cost element of the total motor carrier system, are financed by various government units, whereas railroads own and maintain their own rights-of-way. Motor carriers contribute to the financing of highways through a variety of user payments, but they are not individually burdened with investment in highway facilities.

Because there are many comparatively small companies and their related capital requirements are limited, much trucking industry financing is accomplished without reliance on capital markets. Capital for smaller companies is frequently provided by a few individuals, and in many instances a large part of the capital invested represents reinvested earnings of the business. However, as noted earlier, concentration is increasing in the industry, and the emergence of large companies, such as Roadway Express, Consolidated Freightways, and Yellow Freight System, has led to a growing industry participation in capital markets through the sale of securities and borrowing from major financial institutions.

It should be noted that there are substantial differences in the magnitude of capital needs of carriers in different sectors of the trucking industry. This is particularly true with respect to terminal and real estate needs. At one end of the scale is the owner-operator who tends to specialize in truckload movements that are solicited either directly or through arrangements with a broker or larger carrier. Under such circumstances, the owner-operator has little need for elaborate terminal facilities because his operation consists primarily of truckload, line-haul movements between the location of the shipper and the consignee. Further along the terminal/real estate need continuum is the carrier of specialized commodities. Again, their terminal/real estate needs tend to be somewhat limited due to the specialization in truckload movements that tends to occur in this sector of trucking. However, on average these firms tend to be considerably larger than the individual owner-operators and consequently are likely to support somewhat larger administrative and operational facilities. At the other end of the terminal/real estate needs scale is the carrier of general commodities which primarily handles LTL traffic. Effective solicitation and handling of such traffic requires large-scale investments in consolidation and break-bulk facilities—hence their financing needs tend to be considerably greater than motor carriers operating in other sectors of the industry.

The equipment needs of carriers also vary by sector of the industry, with the needs of the large-scale, LTL carrier typically being the greatest. While the larger carriers generally have a variety of equity and debt options available for financing equipment, the smaller carriers tend to be heavily dependent upon the equipment manufacturer who offers credit arrangements either directly or through "captive" finance companies. Carriers regulated by the ICC also rely heavily upon owner-operators as a source of equipment. As discussed earlier in this chapter, under certain circumstances, the owner-operator effectively rents his vehicle to a regulated carrier. This reliance upon owner-operators is heaviest in movements of household goods and in truckload shipments of other specialized commodities.

Rental of owner-operator equipment allows many regulated carriers, particularly those in the special commodity categories, to limit their capital commitment to the industry. Continuation of such arrangements is dependent upon the financial viability of owner-operators. However, in recent years owner-operators have been confronted with several serious problems including skyrocketing insurance costs, rising equipment costs, lagging revenues, and extreme vulnerability during periods of economic slowdown. At the same time, the ICC's liberalized entry policies have led many former owner-operators to obtain operating authority from the Commission. If the number of owner-operators declined significantly that development could lead to a substantial increase in the financial needs of regulated truckers in the future. However, the limited capital requirements associated with becoming an owner-operator makes that scenario unlikely.

Although regulated intercity motor carriers transport only two-thirds as much traffic volume as the railroads, the aggregate operating revenues of the motor carriers exceed those of rail carriers. In 1991 regulated motor carriers generated $78.3 billion in operating revenues, compared to $29.5 billion for the railroads.[39] To a great degree, this reflects a difference in the composition of the traffic carried by the two modes. Much of the traffic moved by the railroads consists of heavy bulk commodities that move at low rates, whereas the truckers dominate the carriage of manufactured goods that have higher absolute rates.

As discussed in Chapter 3, a major factor in a company's or industry's ability to obtain financing in the capital markets is its rate of return on investment. Table 4-1 contains a summary of return on investment data for class I intercity motor carriers of freight. In comparison, the aggregate rate of return on investment for U.S. industry has ranged between 9 and 14 percent during the same period. This fact, coupled with the long-term growth of industry traffic and profitability, has tended to provide the industry with needed capital access. It must be remembered, however, that it is difficult to generalize about the financial

TABLE 4-1

Rate of Return on Net Investment,
Class I Intercity Motor Carriers of Property
1960-1991

Year	Rate of Return (%)
1960	11.53
1965	22.56
1970	13.90
1975	18.59
1980	19.32
1985	19.42
1986	22.38
1987	12.06
1988	15.61
1989	13.31
1990	15.19
1991	13.49

SOURCE: U.S. Interstate Commerce Commission, *1992 Annual Report* (Washington, D.C.: U.S. Government Printing Office, 1993), p.131, and additional information supplied by the American Trucking Associations.

condition of approximately 45,000 thousand ICC regulated trucking companies. This is particularly true in view of the fact that the largest group of regulated truckers, Class III carriers, are not required to report financial data to the Commission. Naturally, differences in earnings, volume, and growth prospects of individual companies can lead to major differences in ease of capital access.

The failure rate among regulated truckers has increased substantially as federal regulation of the industry has diminished. While 382 ICC regulated truckers declared bankruptcy in 1980, the number increased to 1,589 in 1990.[40] While it might be argued that there were substantially more ICC regulated in 1990 and that more failures should be expected, the failure rate among those companies was nearly twice that of American industry in general.[41]

COST AND SERVICE CHARACTERISTICS

The cost and service characteristics of the motor carrier industry are examined in the following discussion. Particular attention is devoted to the competitive significance of these factors.

Motor Carrier Costs

As noted earlier, the cost structure of the motor carrier industry is substantially different from that of rail carriage in that it is much more heavily weighed with variable costs. It has been estimated that only 10 percent of a motor carrier's cost structure is fixed in nature. Therefore, the total cost structure of the industry is quite responsive to the volume of traffic handled. Because of the current nature of the majority of motor carrier costs, these carriers are rather restricted in terms of the limits within which they can reduce rates below fully allocated costs to meet competition.

Major Cost Elements. Several of the major cost elements of the industry deserve mention. Fifty to sixty percent of the operating costs of regulated common and contract carriers using unionized employees consists of wages and fringe benefits.[42] The labor costs of non-union companies comprise a substantially smaller component of total costs. Nevertheless, in any motor carrier operation management must devote considerable attention to controlling labor costs and improving worker productivity. Related labor-management issues are discussed in depth in Chapter 14.

Another major element of cost in the industry is highway user payments. For their use of the nation's highway system in 1991, truck owners (private and for-hire) paid more than $18 billion in federal and state highway use taxes.[43] Approximately two-thirds of this total was paid to state governments. There are several different forms of highway use tax. At the state level, the major highway user charges consist of motor fuel taxes and truck and trailer registration fees. The major categories of federal highway use payments are motor fuel taxes and excise taxes on new trucks, trailers, tires, and tubes. For a given vehicle class, user fees vary substantially from state to state. Sizable variations also exist in the user charges levied on various vehicle classes.

There has been a long-standing controversy concerning the adequacy of the highway user payments made by for-hire motor carriers. The carriers contend that they are assessed a disproportionate share of highway cost responsibility; critics suggest that they underpay. Numerous cost allocation methods might be used in judging the cost responsibilities of various vehicle classes so as to establish equitable user charges. Each method is quite complex, and the basic assumptions concerning the costs and benefits realized by users and nonusers are debatable. A comparison of these techniques and the results that they generate would be interesting, but such a task is obviously beyond the scope of this book. However, highway cost allocation studies conducted by the Department of Transportation have led the department to consistently contend that the users of light trucks tend to be overcharged in user payments, while those owning buses operating in intercity service and owners of diesel-powered combination trucks tend to be undercharged.[44] These conclusions have been challenged routinely by the American Trucking Associations.

One additional cost element of significance in motor carriage is the expenditure for fuel. The significance of fuel expenses varies substantially in different sectors of the industry. They comprise approximately 15 percent of regulated TL carrier expenses, but only 5 percent of the operating costs of more labor-intensive LTL operators.[45] Major increases in fuel costs have necessitated numerous general freight rate increases in motor carriage in recent years. These fuel cost increases are passed along to shippers through rate increases, but if continued they threaten to impair the competitive position of motor carriage, which has a proportionately higher fuel consumption rate than rail carriage.

Operating Ratio. One measure of the revenue needs and financial condition of a motor carrier is its operating ratio. This ratio expresses a percentage relationship between the operating expenses and operating revenues of the company. The greater the spread between operating expenses and revenues, the larger the amount of residual revenue that is available to cover nonoperating expenses such as interest payments and income taxes. Any remaining revenues are profits.

Much attention is devoted to prevailing operating ratios in the trucking industry; these figures are often used as a criterion for proving the need for rate increases before the ICC. The ratio of nonoperating expenses to total expenses is quite low in motor carriage compared with the magnitude of nonoperating expenses incurred by railroads. As a result, it is possible for a motor carrier to operate profitably with an operating ratio in the low nineties. There is general agreement among motor carriers that a company's stability and service are impaired when its operating ratio rises above 95 percent.

Although the operating ratio provides some indication of the operating condition of a company, it must be remembered that it does not consider how efficiently resources are being used. Nor does it differentiate between the carrier whose costs are high due to inefficiency and one whose operating ratio is high because of circumstances beyond its control, despite the carrier's efficient use of the resources.

Motor Carrier Rates and Price Competition. The average revenue per intercity ton mile realized by class I intercity motor carriers was 10 cents for TL service and nearly 25 cents for LTL service in 1991.[46] The TL rate was nearly four times the average revenue per ton mile earned by railroads that year. The LTL rate was more than eight times the rail rate. At first glance, it would appear that there is little price competition between these two modes, and in fact there is little direct competition between those modes in the movement of small shipments. However, such average figures reveal little about the actual degree of competition in a given market situation. Generalizations can be drawn about the relative rates of regulated motor carriers and railroads in several different settings. As a result of differences in both terminal and line-haul expense characteristics, truck rates are generally lower than rail rates on small shipments and on short-hauls. But, in intermediate to long-distance moves of large quantities of high-valued commodities there tends to be considerable parity in the rates of railroads and regulated motor carriers. In contrast, in long-haul volume movements of bulk commodities, motor carriers are typically unable to quote rail-competitive rates. Nevertheless, it must be remembered that rate differences are only one decision variable considered by shippers in making modal selections, and that a variety of service quality issues are at least as important to most shippers.

The intensity of intramodal competition has increased substantially as ICC motor carrier entry standards have liberalized. This is particularly true with respect to TL services due to the dramatic increase in the number of carriers providing such services. In some TL markets private trucking competes aggressively with the regulated carriers. In the market for LTL service, while the number of major carriers has declined, there is still intense competition on both a price and service basis in this market.

To a lesser extent, there is also competition between regulated motor carriers operating over long distances and air freight movements. The expansion of second and third day air options by companies such as Federal Express and UPS has created new competition for traffic which was once viewed as tied to the trucking industry. In response to the long-term challenge of air cargo, a number of motor carriers, such as Consolidated Freightways, have established either air freight forwarding subsidiaries or direct air cargo operations to share in the possible growth of such service.

There is also strong competition between owner-operators engaged in exempt commodity movements and railroads. These truckers tend to compete more on a price basis with the railroads, while their regulated counterparts tend to place more emphasis on service competition. In exempt commodity movements by truck, prices fluctuate substantially, often on a daily basis. The pricing decisions of owner-operators often have been attacked as being irrational. Some credibility was given to this charge by a national survey of owner-operators in which nearly 30 percent of the respondents admitted that they did not know their operating cost per mile.[47] Regardless of this fact, owner-operators remain a major competitive force in the industry, and shippers appear to be generally satisfied with their prices and service.

Motor Carrier Services

As discussed earlier in this chapter, for-hire motor carriers offer a variety of services to the shipping public including truckload, less-than-truckload and parcel delivery services. Within the industry such services can be offered directly by a carrier to destinations within its route network or on an interline basis with other motor carriers. Interline agreements between truckers effectively allow a company to broaden its service area.

In an effort to further diversify their service offerings many truckers have moved aggressively into intermodal services. As noted in Chapter 3, companies such as Schneider and J.B. Hunt have established alliances with railroads to jointly promote intermodal services. They, and many other motor carriers, now commonly substitute rail intermodal services for what previously would have been a line-haul trucking movement. UPS has also established an extensive air cargo network to supplement its ground capabilities.

Realizing that shippers are increasingly interested in total logistics management and not just transportation, some trucking companies have formed third party logistics enterprises to offer a full range of logistics services. Among the companies that have expanded in that direction are UPS, Yellow Freight System and Roadway Express.

The broad adoption of Just-in-Time manufacturing approaches by American manufacturers has also pressured carriers to modify their service offerings. One recent study found that approximately 80 percent of the 500 largest general commodity motor carriers had modified the nature of their services to meet the needs of JIT accounts.[48] Many motor carriers have also made sizeable investments in information technology to provide improved information services to customers. The importance of improved information flows between carriers and shippers has been demonstrated by some large shippers requiring Electronic Data Interchange (EDI) capabilities of carriers as a prerequisite for giving a carrier any business.

Some of America's largest motor carriers have further diversified into international operations. While many carriers have begun to develop alliances with carriers in Mexico and Canada to take advantage of liberalized North American trade policies, others have taken a more global approach. Roadway Express has launched a program linking the 58,000 U.S. communities it serves with 10 Asian countries, Australia and New Zealand. The international freight is consolidated into containers at the ports of Los Angeles and Long Beach. Five overseas agents are responsible for customs clearance and local delivery from the foreign ports into which the containers are delivered. Yellow Freight System has also initiated international services on a trans-Atlantic basis. The service, called YMF Direct, is offered in conjunction with the Royal Frans Maas Group, a Dutch logistics enterprise. Similarly, ABF Freight System offers worldwide intermodal service to 67 ports through an agreement with Voltainer International of the Netherlands.[49] Other American truckers, most notably UPS, have established extensive land-based operations in other countries.

Other Service Considerations. Due to the nature of their operations and the extensive coverage of the national highway system, motor carriers tend to have a decided speed advantage over other forms of intercity carriage, excluding air freight. This is particularly true in short-distance markets, but the development of the Interstate System has also enabled truckers to become speed-competitive with railroads in many long-haul markets. Speed of service is a major variable to be considered by shippers of high-valued goods, which lead to very high inventory carrying costs. The sooner such goods are delivered, the sooner the customer payment cycle is likely to begin.

Another important aspect of motor carrier service to be considered by shippers is the packaging requirements for shipments. Generally, these are less stringent in motor carriage than they are in rail service. Improvements in truck tires and suspension systems have led to quite smooth riding characteristics. These factors have contributed to a long-term decline in motor carrier loss and damage claims expressed as a percentage of revenues. For LTL carriers only 1.2 percent of total LTL revenues were absorbed by loss and damage claims in 1991.[50] Naturally, this is important to shippers in meeting customer service standards. The reduction of the claim rate as a percentage of motor carrier revenue should not mislead one to believe that loss and damage claims are of little importance in trucking. Consequently, a high-priority item in the industry is continued improvement of cargo security systems.

A major strength of the motor carrier industry is the extensive coverage of the highway network. Because of this, the great majority of industrial shippers have door-to-door trucking services available to them. In contrast, many industrial sites are off-line from rail facilities. Additionally, shippers often find a greater number of motor carriers than rail carriers in a given market, resulting in a greater choice of carriers in trucking than in rail carriage.

Although motor carriers do have advantages over rail service in both flexibility and accessibility, they are at a distinct capacity disadvantage to railroads. Given existing regulation of truck weights and the nature of contemporary truck design, motor carriers can seldom carry more than 30,000 to

50,000 pound payloads. In contrast, the carrying capacity of modern railroad freight cars often exceeds 200,000 pounds.

TRUCK SIZE AND WEIGHT ISSUES

The trucking industry has attempted to strengthen its competitive position through a variety of innovations. Of major importance has been the development of twin and triple trailers, pulled by a single power unit, which provide substantially greater productivity per vehicle combination. The use of lighter and stronger materials in vehicle construction has also significantly improved fuel efficiency. These factors have tended to offset some of the capacity disadvantage suffered by truckers in competing with railroads.

During the early 1990s the trucking industry mounted a strong campaign for federal approval of the use of longer combination vehicles (LCV). At that time, 20 states allowed their use, with the largest of those tandem trucks consisting of a tractor with three 28 foot trailers. While the trucking lobby argued that allowing LCV operations in the other 30 states would significantly reduce motor carrier costs and lower prices to shippers, the railroad countered with claims that unrestricted LCV operations could cost railroads 45-50 percent of their profits.[51] The federal General Accounting Office also opposed expansion of LCV operations due to safety concerns related to the sway characteristics of the longer combination vehicles. The issue was subsequently addressed by Congress in the Intermodal Surface Transportation Efficiency Act of 1991 which limited LCV use to those states which already allowed them. The legislation also provided for a two year study of the issue. The trucking industry has vowed to continue their efforts to promote LCV operations at both the federal and state levels.

PASSENGER CARRIAGE

Passenger travel on the national highway system occurs in both private automobiles and buses. As noted earlier, automobiles dominate intercity passenger travel, accounting for more than 81 percent of intercity passenger mileage. The relative roles of these two forms of passenger carriage are examined in the following discussion.

Intercity Bus Operations

Many of the companies presently engaged in intercity bus operations began in short-route automobile passenger service. Others began as a form of substitute service for expensive railroad passenger operations in low-density areas. The extent of railroad involvement in early bus operations is illustrated by the fact that, during the early 1930s, railroads had a financial interest in companies operating 50 percent of Greyhound's route mileage.[52]

The intercity bus industry now serves approximately 5,700 communities (down from nearly 12,000 in the early 1980s), of which only about 1,000 are served by other for-hire intercity modes.[53] Buses account for approximately 6 percent of commercial intercity passenger mileage (but only 1.2 percent of total intercity passenger mileage).[54] While they carry nearly three-fourths as many intercity passengers as the airlines (339 million versus 436 million in 1992), the intercity passenger mileage which they register is only 6 percent of that of the airlines. This is due to due to the substantial difference in the average passenger trip length between the two modes (143 miles for bus passengers versus 806 miles for airline passengers).[55]

Bus passengers tend to be drawn from lower-income and nonprofessional occupational categories. The relatively young and old, students, military personnel, and retirees are heavy users. Moreover, a high proportion of trips taken are nonbusiness oriented and are for relatively short distances. The Regulatory Reform Act of 1982 liberalized entry into the interstate bus industry and there are now more than 2,000 companies engaged in such service. While most of those companies are quite small, the industry is dominated by Greyhound Lines, Inc., which generates nearly 75 percent of the industry's interstate revenues. Greyhound developed from a holding company established in 1926, and grew, to a great extent, by absorbing bus lines and acquiring authorities for bus services from railroad subsidiaries.

The bus company, Greyhound Lines, was sold to an investment group by its parent company, Greyhound Corp., in March, 1987 for $350 million. The sale followed several years of labor turmoil within the company as the company sought concessions from its workers to improve its competitive position.[56] Later that year the bus company acquired its large, financially strapped competitor, Trailways, Inc., and became the country's only nationwide interstate bus company. Greyhound has extensive interline arrangements with other bus operators, making it possible for passengers to purchase through tickets to most destinations.

Following the acquisition of Trailways, Greyhound dropped services to many marginal markets and substituted vans for full-size bus operations over other light routes. Despite those changes, the company has continued to experience financial difficulties which were intensified by a three month strike in 1990. In June 1990 Greyhound filed for bankruptcy protection. In the subsequent reorganization the company eliminated many unprofitable routes and schedules, reduced its long-term debt, and instituted computerized fleet allocation, reservation, and yield management systems.[57] It also streamlined its management structure. Greyhound emerged from the reorganization in October, 1991. While focusing on improving service and controlling costs the company realized a $10.9 million net income the following year. The company generated $581 million in passenger revenues in 1992.[58]

Regulation. Bus operators engaged in interstate service are subject to economic regulation by the ICC and safety regulation by the DOT, as well as state regulation of intrastate operations. Among those aspects of industry operations regulated by the ICC are entry, rates, and mergers. Carriers are also classified by the commission according to revenues; in early 1991 there were 21 class I intercity motor carriers of passengers (at least $5 million in average annual gross operating revenues).

Federal and state regulation of the bus industry also received close scrutiny during the late 1970s. In the early 1980s several states enacted bus deregulation statutes and the ICC took steps to liberalize its regulation of interstate bus operations. Congressional action, in the form of the Bus Regulatory Reform Act, followed in 1982.[59] The provisions of that statute, which made extensive changes in federal policies governing such matters as entry, abandonment of service, and ratemaking are discussed in Chapter 12.

Cost and Service Characteristics. Because most of the highway system's cost structure is financed by the governmental units that provide the highways, the majority of bus costs are variable in nature, with nearly 60 percent of operating expenses being comprised of labor costs.[60] User taxes paid by class I carriers to federal, state, and local government units have annually exceeded $50 million in recent years.[61] However, it should be noted that bus operators are exempt from federal excise taxes on motor fuels.

The ICC gives considerable attention to the operating ratios of regulated bus companies. It has been suggested by the ICC that an operating ratio of 85 percent or less would be appropriate for the industry. However, the industry's operating ratio has been considerably above that level in recent years.

In excess of 70 percent of class I bus operating revenues are generated by regular route intercity service. The balance of the revenues is generated by package express, charter, and tour services.[62]

In short-distance markets, buses are generally speed-competitive with other modes of intercity passenger carriage. In longer haul markets, buses tend to register slower speeds than both rail and air service. However, highway improvements have reduced the magnitude of this disadvantage. Traditionally intercity bus operations have been quite competitive with other for-hire modes on a price basis, and that has helped define their market niche. However, as price competition has intensified between airlines the gap between air and bus prices has narrrowed considerably. For example, in 1991, the average revenue per passenger mile of the bus industry was 11.3 cents, compared with 12.1 cents for airline coach service (21.5 for first class, and 12.8 cents for Amtrak.)[63]

Financial Status. As a group, class I intercity bus operators have experienced financial difficulty since the mid-1970s. As shown in Table 4-2 net income has been relatively stagnant and return on equity has declined significantly. Operating costs have increased more rapidly than operating revenues. The revenue softness has been precipitated by a downward trend in the number of passengers carried in regular route intercity service.

Private Automobiles

The American love affair with the automobile is a well-documented phenomenon. Automobile registrations were nearly 143 million in 1991, up from 127 million in 1980. Two or three automobile families are no longer rare. Access to the private automobile provides a degree of convenience and flexibility that cannot be matched by for-hire passenger carriage.

Although we generally think of the automobile in terms of local movement within a given metropolitan area, it has become the dominant mode of intercity passenger carriage. The tremendous expansion and upgrading of intercity highway facilities following World War II, coupled with design improvements in the automobile, have strengthened the role of the automobile by making long-distance driving safer, faster, and less tiring.

As the prices of new automobiles and gasoline have increased, the cost of owning and operating automobiles has naturally risen. The DOT recently estimated that the cost of owning and operating an intermediate-size automobile was approximately 33.4 cents per passenger mile, assuming slightly more than one passenger per trip.[64] In contrast, as noted earlier in this chapter, the average fare per passenger mile charged by for-hire carriers ranges between 11 and 13 cents. Based on these figures, the automobile would appear to be a rather high-cost mode of intercity passenger carriage. However, it should be realized that the addition of a second, third, or fourth passenger to the automobile for the trip reduces the cost per passenger mile dramatically. Consequently, for many intercity family trips, the automobile is quite price-competitive with for-hire carriage. Its speed, flexibility, and convenience also offer value to the traveler.

Critics often have argued that individuals irrationally select the automobile for such trips because they are not aware of the total capital and operating costs on a per-mile basis. Although it may be true that the individual is not aware of all costs, it is questionable whether or not total costs are relevant to such mode-selection decisions. A more relevant consideration is the marginal cost of operation, because the individual has already committed himself to the ownership of the vehicle for multiple trip purposes (e.g., to drive to work or to the shopping center). If the individual were to compare the marginal cost of intercity trips by

TABLE 4-2

Selected Financial and Operating Statistics
Class I Intercity Motor Carrier of Passengers
1975-1991

Year	No. of Carriers	Rev.Pass. Carried	Rev.Pass. Miles (Millions)	Net Income (Millions)	Return on Equity (Billions)
1975	85	351	25.4	55.8	12.2
1980	46a	370	27.4	88.5	14.5
1981	46	375	27.1	54.7	9.5
1982	46	370	26.9	29.3	4.8
1983	49	365	25.6	27.2	3.1
1984	47	352	24.6	NA	NA
1985	43	348	23.8	52.6	9.7
1986	29b	336	23.7	36.3	7.5
1987	32	333	23.0	-21.6	Negative
1988	21c	334	23.1	-.2	Negative
1989	21	343	24.0	7.1	6.0
1990	21	322	23.0	-180.3	Negative
1991	21	317	23.5	NA	NA

[a]The reduced number of Class I carriers reflects ICC reclassification of class I carriers in 1976.
[b]The reduced number of Class I carriers reflects mergers of subsidiaries of Trailways Lines, Inc. into parent company.
[c]The reduced number of Class I carriers reflects ICC reclassification of Class I carriers. The limits were raised from $3 million in annual operating revenues to $5 million.

SOURCE: U.S. Interstate Commerce Commission, *1992 Annual Report* (Washington, D.C.: U.S. Government Printing Office, 1993), p. 132 and previous editions; also, Eno Transportation Foundation, Inc., *Transportation in America*, 10th ed., December supplement (Lansdowne, VA: the Foundation, 1992), p.8.

automobile with the tickets of for-hire carriers, the automobile would often represent a quite rational choice.

The role of the automobile as a form of intercity passenger carriage may well change over time due to rising petroleum prices and energy shortages.

Increasing gasoline prices are naturally a deterrent to automobile usage, and consumers have increasingly opted to purchase more energy efficient automobiles. Clearly, that has been somewhat a function of availability as automobile producers responded to government mandates to build more energy efficient vehicles. Reflecting this change in the national automobile fleet, petroleum consumption by automobiles actually declined slightly from 1.747 billion barrels in 1980 to 1.684 billion barrels in 1991.[65]

Future intensification of our national energy problems might promote some mode switching behavior. However, a major shift in travel patterns would cause severe capacity problems in the other modes of intercity carriage. Therefore, any national attempt to de-emphasize the automobile as a form of intercity passenger carriage would have to be coupled with related adjustment of the passenger-carrying capabilities of the for-hire modes, or a substantial reduction in intercity travel.

SUMMARY

Our nation's highway system has played a steadily increasing role in meeting our national transportation needs. As government highway spending programs have accelerated, the highway network has both expanded and improved in quality. The trucking industry has undergone a major restructuring as a result of the regulatory reform movement and now offers a much broader array of price and service options to the shipping public.

In intercity passenger carriage, the automobile has become the dominant form of transportation. Automobiles annually account for approximately 81 percent of interrcity passenger mileage. The intercity bus industry, while continuing to play a major role in the provision of a low-cost travel alternative to passengers, has been hurt by intense price competition from the airlines and continues to struggle financially.

Obviously, the highway modes will continue to play major roles in our national transportation system; however, several factors, including environmental and energy concerns and the enormous capital requirements to rehabilitate the existing highway system, may combine to limit their future growth. Government policy decisions concerning each of these matters will have a decided impact on the relative roles to be played in the future by the highway modes.

The regulatory reform movement has profoundly affected the structure and performance of both the intercity trucking and bus industries. The collective response of these carriers to the rapidly changing competitive environment will be one of the most significant transportation developments of the 1990s.

DISCUSSION QUESTIONS

1.   What are user charges? How are they applied in motor carriage and what is their function?
2.   Distinguish between common, contract, and exempt motor carriage; explain the significance of each in the transportation marketplace.
3.   Discuss the importance of owner-operators in intercity trucking operations.
4.   Compare the cost structure of the motor carrier industry with that of the railroad industry.
5.   Distinguish between the truckload and less-than-truckload segments of the intercity trucking industry.
6.   What are longer-combination-vehicles and what is their significance?
7.   Why would a company choose to establish a private trucking fleet?
8.   As the marketplace has become more competitive, how have motor carriers attempted to differentiate themselves?

NOTES

1.   Charles A. Taff, *Commercial Motor Transportation*, 4th ed. (Homewood, ILL., Richard D. Irwin, Inc., 1969), p. 12.
2.   Roy J. Sampson and Martin T. Farris, Domestic Transportation, 4th ed. (Homewood, ILL.: Richard D. Irwin, Inc., 1969), p. 12.
3.   Taff, p. 16.
4.   *Motor Bus and Truck Operations*, 140 ICC 685 (1928); also, Coordinator of Motor Transportation, 182 ICC 263 (1932).
5.   See Mitchell E. MacDonald, "Congress Passes Highway Bill With A $151 Billion Price Tag," *Traffic Management* (January, 1992), pp.
6.   Eno Transportation Foundation, Inc., *Transportation in America*, 11th ed. (Lansdowne, VA: the Foundation, 1993), p. 73.
7.   Ibid., p. 47.
8.   Ibid., p. 73.
9.   D. Daryl Wyckoff and David H. Maister, *The Owner-Operator: Independent Trucker* (Lexington, MA: D.C. Heath and Company, 1975), p. 2.
10.   Eno Transportation Foundation, Inc., p. 40.
11.   American Trucking Associations, *American Trucking Trends*, 1979-1980 (Washington, D.C.: the Associations, 1981), p. 18.
12.   Ibid., p. 55.
13.   Lawrence J. Kaufman, "ICC Chairman Favors Trucking Deregulation," *Journal of Commerce*, New York, August 14, 1992, p. 2B.

14. Eno Transportation Foundation, p. 53.
15. Standard and Poor's Corporation, Standard and Poor's Industry Surveys, "Trucking Industry Structure," Vol. 2 (October 22, 1992) p. R50; also, "UPS: Up From the Stone Age," *Business Week* (June 15, 1992), p. 132.
16. Standard and Poor's Corporation, p. R46.
17. Ibid., p. R48.
18. Eno Transportation Foundation, p. 71.
19. Ibid.
20. Standard and Poor's Corporation, *Standard and Poor's Industry Surveys,* "Railroads and Trucking," Section 3 (June 17, 1993), p. R8.
21. James Aaron Cooke, "The Shakeout Intensifies," *Traffic Management* (May, 1990), p. 39.
22. Standard and Poor's Corporation, p. R50.
23. Mark B. Solomon, "Schedule Changes Could Help Ease UPS Pact's Bite," *Journal of Commerce,* New York, (September 29, 1993), p. 1A.
24. "Management Update," *Traffic Management* (September, 1991), p. 2.
25. Data supplied by Roadway Packaging System.
26. Wyckoff and Maister, p. 1.
27. Ibid.
28. Standard and Poor's Corporation, pp. R46-7.
29. Ibid.
30. Ibid., p.R47.
31. Ibid.
32. U.S. Interstate Commerce Commission, *1991 Annual Report* (Washington, D.C.: the U.S. Government Printing Office, 1992, p. 47; also, Mitchell E. MacDonald, "Forwarder vs. Broker," *Traffic Management* (June, 1992), pp. 61-3.
33. Kaufman, p. 2B.
34. "Management Update," *Traffic Management* (May, 1987), p. 1.
35. Mitchell E. MacDonald, "ICC, States Move Toward Head-On Collision Over Trucking Regulation," *Traffic Management* (July, 1992), p. 15.
36. Ibid.
37. U.S., Interstate Commerce Commission, *1989 Annual Report* (Washington, D.C.: U.S. Government Printing Office, 1990), p. 134.
38. Association of American Railroads, *Railroad Facts*, 1992 ed. (Washington, D.C.: the Association, 1992), p. 9.
39. Eno Transportation Foundation, p. 17.
40. Mitchell E. MacDonald, "It's Still Survival of the Fittest," *Traffic Management* (June, 1991), p. 31.
41. "Management Update," *Traffic Management* (May, 1991),p. 1.
42. Standard and Poor's Corporation, (October, 1992), p. R56.

43.   Standard and Poor's Corporation, (October, 1992), p. R58.
44.   For an example of the Department's views concerning this matter, see U.S. Department of Transportation, *Transportation Trends and Choices to the Year 2000* (Washington, D.C.: U.S. Government Printing Office, 1977), pp. 176-77; also, George F. Hoffer, "Estimating the Impact of Changes in Recent Cost Allocation Methodology and Highway User Fees on the Allocated Cost and Revenue Responsibility of Motor Carriers," *Transportation Journal*, Vol. 33, No. 1 (Fall, 1983), pp. 31-7.
45.   Standard and Poor's Corporation, p. R58.
46.   Eno Transportation Foundation, p.49.
47.   D. Daryl Wyckoff, "Which Truckers Compete with Us?" *Modern Railroads* Vol. 29, No. 11 (November, 1974), p. 66.
48.   Robert C. Lieb and Robert A. Millen, "The Responses of General Commodity Motor Carriers to Just-in-Time Manufacturing Programs," *Transportation Journal* (Fall, 1990), Vol. 30, No. 1, pp. 5-11.
49.   Chris Barnett, "Trucks Across the Water," *International Business* (September, 1992), p. 31.
50.   "Management Update," *Traffic Management* (September, 1992), p. 2.
51.   See Mitchell E. MacDonald, "A Year of Hope for Shippers," *Traffic Management* (January, 1991), p. 29.
52.   Taff, p. 429.
53.   Department of Transportation, *Trends and Choices*, p. 151.
54.   Eno Transportation Foundation, p. 70.
55.   Ibid., p. 30.
56.   "Leave the Driving to Fred Currey," *Business Week* (August 24, 1987), pp. 62-3.
57.   Greyhound Lines, Inc., *1991 Annual Report* (Dallas, TX: the company, 1992), pp. 2-3.
58.   Greyhound Lines, Inc., *The 1992 Greyhound Annual* (Dallas, TX: the company, 1993), pp. 15-6.
59.   Bus Regulatory Reform Act, Public Law 97-261 (1982).
60.   Data supplied by the American Bus Association.
61.   Ibid.
62.   Ibid.
63.   Eno Transportation Foundation, p. 15.
64.   U.S. Department of Transportation, Reasearch and Special Programs Administration, *National Transportation Statistics* (Washington, D.C.: U.S. Government Printing Office, 1992), pp. 91/92.
65.   Eno Transportation Foundation, p. 56.

SELECTED REFERENCES

Andel, Tom. "Parcel Shippers Are Put to the Test." *Transportation and Distribution* (April, 1992), pp. 34-6.

Brown, Terrence A. "Property Brokers: A Pilot Study of Carriers' Perspectives." *Transportation Journal*, Vol. 30, No. 2 (Winter, 1990), p. 32-9.

Brown, Terrence A. "Size and Operating Characteristics of Property Brokers." *Transportation Journal*, Vol. 29, No. 4 (Summer, 1990), pp. 52-7.

Brown, Terrence A. *Transportation Brokers: History, Regulation and Operations.* Alexandria, VA: Transportation Brokers Conference of America, 1993.

Corsi, Thomas M. and Curtis M. Grimm. "Changes in Owner-Operator Use, 1977-1985: Implications for Management Strategy." *Transportation Journal*, Vol. 26, No. 3 (Spring, 1987), pp. 4-16.

Corsi, Thomas M. and Joseph R. Stowers. "Effects of a Deregulated Environment on Motor Carriers: A Systematic, Multi-Segment Analysis." *Transportation Journal*, Vol. 30, No. 3 (Spring, 1991), pp. 4-28.

Crum, Michael R. and Benjamin J. Allen. "The Changing Nature of the Motor Carrier-Shipper Relationship: Implications for the Trucking Industry." *Transportation Journal*, Vol. 32, No. 2 (Winter, 1991), pp. 41-54.

Felton, John Richard and Dale G. Anderson, eds. *Regulation and Deregulation of the Motor Carrier Industry.* Ames, IA: Iowa State University Press, 1989.

Kling, Robert W. "Deregulation and Structural Change in the LTL Motor Freight Industry." *Transportation Journal*, Vol. 29, No. 3 (Spring, 1990), pp. 47-53.

Lieb, Robert C. and Robert A. Millen, "The Responses of General Commodity Motor Carries to Just-in-Time Manufacturing Programs." *Transportation Journal*, Vol. 30, No. 1 (Fall, 1990), pp. 5-11.

MacDonald, Mitchell E. "It's Still Survival of the Fittest." *Traffic Management* (June, 1991), pp. 30-3, 35.

MacDonald, Mitchell E. "The Big Guys Move in on the Regionals." *Traffic Management* (May, 1992), pp. 42-5.

McMullen, Starr B. "The Impact of Regulatory Reform on U.S. Motor Carrier Costs." *Journal of Transport Economics and Policy* (September, 1987). pp. 307-19.

Min, Hokey and Martha Cooper. "A Comparative Review of Analytical Studies of Freight Consolidation and Backhauling." *Logistics and Transportation Review*, Vol. 26, No. 2 (June, 1990), pp. 149-69.

Morash, Edward A. and George D. Wagenheim. "State Regulation of Motor Carriers in a Deregulated Transportation Environment." *Transportation Journal*, Vol. 30, No. 3 (Spring, 1991), pp. 39-56.

Richardson, Helen L. "Are Bigger Trucks Coming?" *Transportation and Distribution* (July, 1991), pp. 24-6.

Southern, R. Neil and James P. Rakowski. "An Analysis of the Changing Nature of the Deregulated Trucking Industry." *Business Perspectives* (Spring, 1991), pp. 4-6.

U.S. General Accounting Office. *Surface Transportation: Availability of Intercity Bus Service Continues to Decline*. Washington, D.C.: General Accounting Office, 1992.

Winston, Clifford, Thomas M. Corsi, Curtis M. Grimm and Carol A. Evans. *The Economic Effects of Surface Freight Deregulation*. Washington, D.C.: the Brookings Institution, 1990.

Wyckoff, D. Daryl and David Maister. *The Motor Carrier Industry*. Lexington, MA: Lexington Books, 1978.

Wyckoff, D. Daryl and David Maister. *The Owner-Operator: Independent Trucker*. Lexington, MA: Lexington Books, 1975.

Consolidated Freightways Twin Trailer Operation *Courtesy of Consolidated Freightways*

Towboat and Barge Operations *Courtesy of American Waterway Operators Association*

CHAPTER FIVE

THE OIL PIPELINE AND WATER CARRIAGE INDUSTRIES

Attention now shifts to two major modes of intercity freight transportation, oil pipelines and domestic water carriage, which are little understood by the general public. The recent financial problems of many for-hire carriers and the regulatory changes in the airline, motor and rail carrier industries have given those modes high public profiles, but the oil pipeline networks and water carriage continue to function in relative obscurity.

It may be surprising to the reader to learn that the oil pipeline network of the United States extends nearly 214,000 miles and that each year it carries approximately 20 percent of intercity freight ton mileage. It is also likely that the reader is unaware that the U.S. water way system is the most extensive in the world. It consists of nearly 26,000 miles of navigable waterways, and commodity movements over the system account for approximately 16 percent of annual intercity ton mileage.

This chapter focuses on the nature of these two industries and examines their relative roles in our national transportation system. The international water carriage component of the U.S. transportation system is discussed in Chapter 7.

OIL PIPELINE INDUSTRY

In the following pages, the development, industrial and financial structure, and cost and service characteristics of the oil pipeline system are examined. The discussion is limited to companies primarily involved in the for-hire pipeline movement of petroleum products.

Development of the System

The oil pipeline industry began in 1865 in the oil fields of western Pennsylvania. A number of entrepreneurs financed short, two-inch diameter pipelines to feed oil to barge and rail facilities located several miles away. The pipelines offered lower rates than horse-drawn wagons and soon attracted a substantial share of short-haul crude oil traffic. As had been the case in the early years of railroading, the profitability of the first pipeline companies attracted many new entrants into the business, and cutthroat competition and bankruptcies became commonplace.[1]

The high risk associated with investment in pipeline facilities and the threat of bankruptcy led to a growing reluctance on the behalf of many financiers to invest in pipeline operations. As a result, the industry came to be dominated by the oil companies and their subsidiaries, which needed uninterrupted transportation service. Many smaller independent companies were later consolidated into such organizations as the National Transit Pipeline Company, which was controlled by Standard Oil.

Emergence of Trunk Lines. Until the late 1870s the oil pipelines were primarily limited to short-haul gathering activities that connected with other modes for line-haul carriage. However, as pipeline technology progressed, it became possible to move crude oil over longer distances by pipeline. This led to the construction of several six-inch diameter trunk lines, which carried crude oil more than 100 miles.[2] When these ventures proved successful, the major oil companies took the next logical step and connected their large refineries directly to the oil fields by pipeline. Consequently, much of the longer haul crude oil traffic was diverted from rail and barge movements. Thus, the pipeline emerged as a viable competitor for this traffic in intercity markets.

The growth of the oil pipeline network continued to parallel that of the oil industry, and the system expanded steadily into the twentieth century. Throughout that period of growth, pressures increased to make interstate oil pipelines common carriers. Supporters of that proposal believed that such action would provide small independent oil producers and refiners with nondiscriminatory access to this mode. Congressional acceptance of the concept was signified by the passage of the Hepburn Act of 1906, which gave the Interstate Commerce Commission (ICC) economic jurisdiction over for-hire interstate oil pipeline carriage. This regulatory authority was transferred to the Department of Energy's Federal Energy Regulatory Commission (FERC) in 1977. The scope of federal regulation of oil pipelines is discussed later in this chapter; the pressures that led to this regulation are examined in detail in Chapter 10.

Emergence of Product Lines. Prior to 1930, pipeline carriage of oil had been limited to the movement of crude oil because of pipeline leakage problems, which made the movement of refined products such as gasoline impractical.[3] However, welding techniques improved and product lines became a reality. Because of that development, oil pipelines began attracting an increasing percentage of such product movements from other modes.

Federally Funded Oil Pipelines. During World War II, two major oil pipeline projects were financed and operated by the federal government. These pipelines were built to provide the capacity to handle overland oil movements from Texas to the Northeast. Prior to the war, much of the traffic moved in coastwise tankers, but the activity of enemy submarines off our coasts made such shipments quite dangerous. One federally funded pipeline project, the Big Inch, carried crude oil from Longview, Texas, to the New York-Philadelphia refining area. The system, which extended 1,340 miles and cost $78 million, operated from 1943-1945. The other project, the Little Inch, extended 1,475 miles and cost $67.3 million.[4] This line basically ran parallel to the Big Inch and moved products from the Texas Gulf Coast refineries to the New York area during 1944 and 1945. The Little Inch was somewhat revolutionary in that its 20-inch diameter made it the first large-diameter products line; it provided an impetus toward larger diameter pipelines following the war. Both federally financed pipeline projects were sold to private interests following the war and were later converted to natural gas lines.[5]

Growth of Large Diameter Pipelines. Before World War II, the majority of oil pipelines had diameters of less than ten inches. However, as pipeline technology progressed, the desirability of larger diameter pipelines became apparent. Because of the technical characteristics of pipelining, the larger the diameter of the pipe, the lower the per-unit cost of transportation, assuming good utilization. In recent years there has been a decided trend toward the use of large-diameter pipeline.

While 90 percent of the crude oil gathering lines in the United States are six inches in diameter or less, the crude oil trunk lines that receive oil from those lines and other modes of carriage range from 8 to 56 inches in diameter.[6]

As the volume of oil consumption has risen in this country, making large-diameter pipelines feasible, oil companies have often jointly financed pipeline projects over common routes. Such joint financing under "undivided interest" agreements has lowered financing costs by reducing duplicate investment and has promoted cost efficiencies due to better pipeline utilization. Under joint financing agreements, pipeline capacity and profits are typically prorated on the basis of each participating company's investment in the project.

Alaskan Pipeline. Probably the most significant development in the oil pipeline industry in the post-World War II period was the construction of the Trans Alaska Pipeline System. In 1968 one of the richest oil and gas areas in the world was discovered on the North Slope of Alaska. To bring this oil to the lower 48 states, a consortium of seven oil producers and pipeline companies formed the Alyeska Pipeline Service Company to design, construct, and maintain the pipeline. After successfully defending the pipeline project in a series of court challenges related to environmental concerns and the property rights of native Alaskans,

Alyeska spent more than three years building the pipeline system. The completed system, which commenced operations in mid-1977, stretches nearly 800 miles from Prudhoe Bay on the Arctic Ocean to Valdez on Alaska's southern coast. At Valdez the oil is loaded aboard tankers for shipment to West Coast refineries.

The Alyeska system, which utilized 48-inch pipe, cost more than $9.3 billion and was the largest construction project ever undertaken by private industry.

Contemporary Oil Pipeline System. Oil pipeline mileage exceeds 214,000 miles, with nearly 60 percent of the mileage dedicated to the movement of crude oil and the balance consisting of product pipelines for the movement of various refined products. Figures 5-1 and 5-2, respectively, illustrate the major interstate crude oil and products pipeline networks of the United States.

As noted earlier in this chapter, oil pipelines annually carry approximately 20 percent of intercity freight ton mileage. The volume of traffic handled by pipelines might seem somewhat surprising, but it reflects the tremendous consumption rate of petroleum products in this country for both consumer and industrial purposes. Each year pipelines account for approximately 58 percent of all domestic petroleum freight ton mileage. The participation of other modes in such traffic is as follows: water carriage (33 percent); motor carriage (6 percent), and rail carriage (3 percent).[7]

Industrial and Financial Structure

Approximately 135 pipeline companies are federally regulated as common carriers. The capital investment in these companies exceeds $21 billion. Forty percent of those carriers are undivided-interest or joint-venture companies. Sixteen percent are wholly owned by a single oil company, and the remaining companies are independents.[8] The independents are primarily involved in the movement of refined products.

There is a substantial degree of concentration in the industry, with 20 integrated oil companies controlling two-thirds of pipeline mileage. The regulated carriers generate nearly 85 percent of the industry's ton mileage and the balance is handled by private operations.

One interesting development in this area has been the establishment of pipeline subsidiaries by several railroads, including the Southern Pacific, the Santa Fe and the Burlington Northern. These railroad-controlled pipelines have not only provided the railroads with a means of recapturing some traffic that had been lost to the pipelines, but have also diverted some oil traffic that previously moved in the railroads' less efficient tank cars.

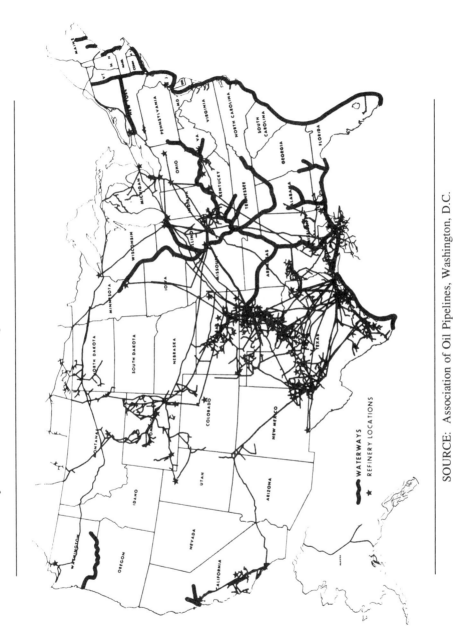

Figure 5-1

Major Interstate Crude Oil Pipelines in the United States

SOURCE: Association of Oil Pipelines, Washington, D.C.

Figure 5-2

Major Interstate Products Pipelines in the United States

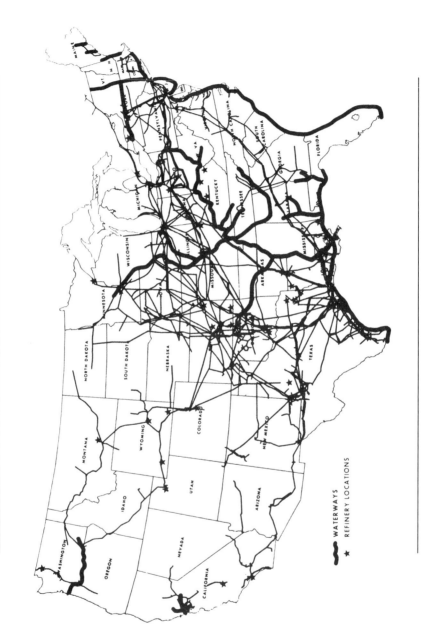

SOURCE: Association of Oil Pipelines, Washington, D.C.

Regulation. Federal regulation of interstate oil pipeline operations was established by the Hepburn Act of 1906, which created a pattern of regulation similar to that which had previously been applied to the railroads.[9] The ICC was vested with control over oil pipeline rates of common carriers, and personal discrimination was forbidden. Reporting requirements were also established. However, entry into the industry was not controlled by the ICC, nor were line extensions. Theoretically, this provided open entry into the industry. Realistically, the substantial capital costs and the difficulties inherent in acquiring the necessary rights-of-way constituted quite formidable nonregulatory entry barriers. There were several other areas in which pipeline regulation was not as comprehensive as railroad regulation. The ICC was not given control over pipeline abandonments, sale of securities, or consolidations. However, pipelines were subjected to the antipooling provisions of the Interstate Commerce Act.

In 1977, when Congress established the federal Department of Energy, the ICC's powers over oil pipeline ratemaking and valuations were transferred to the department's Federal Energy Regulatory Commission. The remaining economic regulations of oil pipelines were shifted to other components of the department. The safety aspects of interstate oil pipeline operations are administered by the Department of Transportation, and the industry has an admirable safety record.

As the other modes of interstate transportation have been at least partially deregulated there has been pressure to apply a similar regulatory approach to the oil pipeline industry. During the Reagan administration the DOT called for less regulation of oil pipelines, but Congress did not respond. Similarly, during the Bush presidency the department called for complete deregulation of the economic aspects of oil pipelines, but no congressional action followed.[10]

More than half the states have adopted some form of regulation pertaining to oil pipelines. Generally, these states require common carrier status of companies operating on an intrastate basis. Some states impose common carrier status as a prerequisite to exercise the right of eminent domain to acquire property for pipeline rights-of-way.

Capital Needs. Oil pipeline operations are capital intensive in nature, and it has been estimated that between 80 and 90 percent of the total investment in the industry consists of pipelines and rights-of-way.[11] Earnings of the industry have been quite stable, averaging 7 to 8 percent on net investment on an annual basis. In pipeline rate cases the ICC historically tended to allow an 8 percent rate of return for crude oil lines and a 10 percent return for product line operations.[12] One reason for different treatment of crude and product lines was the higher risk associated with handling the more valuable refined products. The maximum earnings of shipper-owners (parent oil companies that ship by pipeline) were limited to 7 percent by the ICC and a Justice Department consent decree signed by a number of pipeline companies in 1940.[13] The consent decree was accepted by the companies following a Justice Department investigation of alleged rebating practices involving the major oil producers. The average annual earnings of oil pipeline companies have not changed significantly under FERC regulation.

Cost and Service Characteristics

The cost and service characteristics of the oil pipeline industry are examined in the following discussion. Particular attention is devoted to the competitive implications of these factors.

Oil Pipeline Costs. The aggregate cost structure of the oil pipeline industry is characterized by a large fixed-cost component. Because of the substantial fixed investment in pipeline and rights-of-way, the industry resembles the railroad industry in that, as volume increases, average costs per unit of output tend to decline steadily over a broad range of output. Also, as noted earlier, as the diameter of a pipeline increases, given steady high-volume utilization, costs per unit of output tend to decline. Because of these two factors, there is a strong incentive for the industry to use large-diameter pipelines when possible and to operate at high levels of traffic volume.

The industry is highly automated, having approximately 19,000 employees. The use of more efficient pumping equipment and large-diameter pipe, increases in long-haul movements, and improvements in detecting pipeline failure have all contributed to major increases in industry productivity. Similarly, the development of more durable pipe that is highly resistant to corrosion has substantially reduced industry maintenance costs.

The cost structure of the industry is such that it gives oil pipelines a substantial cost advantage over competing modes (except water carriage) on large-volume movements of petroleum products. Reflecting their lower costs, pipelines tend to have lower rates on high-volume petroleum shipments than either rail or motor carriage. For example, the typical long-haul pipeline rate is slightly more than one-half the railroad rate for similar movements.[14] The rates of water carriers tend to be lower than those of pipelines. However, large-diameter pipelines (in excess of 30 inches) appear to be cost-competitive with water carriage. Nevertheless, pipelines are often used in a feeder capacity in connection with water carrier operations.

Oil Pipeline Service. To the shipper of either crude or refined petroleum, the pipeline system offers a continuous, uninterrupted mode of carriage that is unaffected by weather conditions. The average length of a crude oil shipment by pipeline is approximately 824 miles, while products move an average of 378 miles.[15] Many movements requested by petroleum shippers involve origins and destinations on the lines of different pipeline companies. In some cases the movement from the producing field to the refinery involves the lines of five or six different companies. To facilitate these movements, pipeline companies have established a complex system of through tariff rates. Because of the existence of interline agreements, the refiner or purchaser of petroleum has a broad choice of suppliers; conversely, the owners of crude oil or refined products are given a wider market for their products.

Pipeline companies specify a minimum tender size (the minimum quantity of petroleum acceptable for shipment); this typically ranges between 10,000 and 100,000 barrels. Federal regulation of these tender-size guidelines has effectively scaled the requirements down so as to prevent discrimination against smaller shippers.

Crude oil and refined petroleum products move through pipelines at speeds ranging from three to eight miles per hour. The speed of movement varies according to such factors as line size, line pressure, and the density and viscosity of the liquid being transported. At typical rates of speed, it takes between 14 and 22 days to move liquids between Houston and New York City.[16]

COAL SLURRY PIPELINES

The efficiencies of pipeline movements have led to consideration of the movement of other commodities through pipelines. In fact, there are more than 100 slurry pipelines in the United States, which use water as a propellant to move coal, gilsonite, limestone, sulfur, and metal concentrates.[17] To date, most such lines are relatively short and quite limited in their application. However, the possibility of further expansion of coal slurry pipelining became quite controversial during the past two decades. Private interests have proposed the construction of several long-distance slurry lines for the movement of low-sulfur western coal to consumption points. These lines would move a 50/50 mixture of finely ground coal and water.

The coal slurry interests, which include the Coal Slurry Technology Association, some utilities, coal companies, investment groups, and construction unions, continue to seek a congressional grant of federal eminent domain to construct these lines. However, many environmental and agricultural groups oppose construction of these lines because of the pipelines' water consumption in already arid regions. Further, the railroad industry, which fears loss of coal traffic to slurry pipelines, strongly opposes their construction.[18] In some instances, railroad efforts to stop slurry construction appear to have been overzealous. In 1989 a federal district court awarded $45 million in damages to Energy Transportation Systems in a case in which they alleged a railroad conspiracy to stop its construction of a 1,400 mile slurry line between Wyoming and Texas.[19]

In comparing the relative advantages of rail versus slurry pipeline movement of coal, the congressional Office of Technology Assessment has concluded that slurry lines tend to have a cost advantage over rail under certain circumstances. These were: very high traffic volume, long-distance movements, closely spaced mines, secure markets, sufficient water supplies, and the existence of inefficient or circuitous rail service.[20]

This controversy clearly illustrates the intermodal linkages involved in congressional decision-making in transportation. A congressional decision in favor of the slurry interests would represent a serious setback in the railroads' attempt to sustain financial viability.

Some attention also has been devoted to the future potential of pipelines as movers of hollow capsules filled with such commodities as wheat and chemicals. However, given the present capital requirements of the industry and innovations in other modes of carriage such as railroads offering attractive contract rates, it does not appear likely that such pipeline services will be commercially feasible in the foreseeable future.

DOMESTIC WATER CARRIAGE

There are several distinct forms of domestic water carriage: (1) movements over the inland waterway, which consists of the river and canal system of the country; (2) movements on the Great Lakes; and (3) domestic deep-sea transportation, which includes coastal shipping between ports of the Pacific coast and between ports on the coastline of the Gulf of Mexico and the Atlantic seaboard, and intercoastal shipping between ports on the Pacific coast and the ports of the Gulf of Mexico and the Atlantic coast. The following discussion examines the significance of domestic water carriage and explores the nature of the industry. American carrier participation in international ocean transportation is examined in Chapter 7.

Development of the System

The waterway system has played an important role in development of the United States. This was particularly true in the pre-railroad period. Overland travel was generally slow and expensive and often dangerous. Initially, coastal water carriage by ship served as the major link between the colonies, which were clustered along the coastline.

As settlement proceeded inland, natural lakes and rivers provided access to new lands. In subsequent years the waterways served as channels of commerce for various forms of rafts and boats, which moved excess farm production to colonial markets.

Although the natural waterway system was extensive, geographical and navigational limitations led to public efforts to improve and expand the system. The rivers of the United States historically have been owned and controlled by the federal government in the name of the people, and federal funding has promoted the bulk of waterway development. As early as 1789, federal monies were appropriated for harbor improvements; in the years that followed, numerous federal river and harbor projects were initiated.[21]

Canals. State participation in the promotion of waterway development during the formative years of our nation primarily involved canal building. The era of canal building, which witnessed the construction of more than 4,400 miles of artificial waterways linking various bodies of water, really began with completion of the Erie Canal in 1825. The canal, which was built by the state of New York at a cost of nearly $7 million, stretched 364 miles and linked Buffalo on Lake Erie with Albany on the Hudson River.[22] It provided low-cost transportation between the East and the West. Consequently, it diverted much of the traffic eastward that had previously moved from the West down the Mississippi River to New Orleans. The canal was a great success, and not only was an important factor in promoting development of the West, but also led to the emergence of New York City as an important commercial center on the Atlantic coast.

The financial success of the Erie Canal and widespread desire for low-cost transportation led to construction of canals in many other states. Some of those projects were financially viable, but many were economic failures that placed heavy financial burdens on the sponsoring states. By 1880 the superiority of rail carriage and the inability of most canal projects to generate adequate toll revenues had led to the abandonment of more than half of all canal mileage.[23] The present domestic waterway system contains fewer than 700 miles of canals.

Steam Technology. While canal building was increasing the scope and coverage of the waterway system, the introduction of steam technology to water transportation was revolutionizing the mode of carriage. The relative increase in speed introduced by the steamboat and its ability to undertake upstream journeys led to a position of transportation dominance prior to the Civil War. Steamboat traffic, particularly on the Mississippi and Ohio rivers, grew steadily into the 1850s, when the competition of railroads began to have an impact. Railroads had outgrown their roles as feeders to water facilities and were now actively competitive with water operations over longer routes. Within the decade following the Civil War, steamboats had practically disappeared, and railroads had clearly emerged as the leading mode of both passenger and freight movement.

Resurgence of Water Carriage. The near-monopoly power of the railroads in many markets at the turn of the century was a matter of considerable public concern. In response to this situation, the federal government took both regulatory and financial action. From 1900 to 1920, Congress substantially tightened railroad regulations, thereby strengthening the relative competitive position of water carriers. At the same time, federal outlays for waterway development, which were made yearly following the Civil War, increased substantially. Although many of these outlays were considered primarily conservation measures, their secondary effect was the improvement of the waterways for commercial purposes. One measure of the extent of federal commitment to waterway development is the fact that more than $213 million was appropriated for such projects between 1900 and 1940.[24] The resurgence of water carriage was slow but steady, and by the 1930s approximately 15 percent of intercity freight was moving over the U.S. waterway system. Barge operations had made sizable inroads on bulk and liquid commodity movements that had previously been carried by rail, and the railroads advocated federal regulation of water carriage to ease the competitive intensity. Congress responded to these conditions with the passage of the Transportation Act of 1940, which, among other things, established ICC control over certain aspects of domestic water carriage. These regulatory controls are discussed later in this chapter.

Public financing of waterway development and improvement has continued (see Table 5-1). It should be noted that expenditures for multiple-purpose waterway projects are not included in the table. Most new construction is carried out by the Army Corps of Engineers, with congressional funding involving both user fees and general tax revenues.

Contemporary Network. The combination of a vast natural waterways system and sizable public outlays has yielded a domestic waterway network that is the most extensive in the world. Excluding seacoasts and Great Lakes routes, the network consists of nearly 26,000 miles of commercially navigable waterways. Annually the system accounts for approximately 16 percent of intercity ton mileage.[25] The nature of carriers operating over this system and their cost and service characteristics are discussed in the following sections.

Industrial Structure

Domestic water transportation consists of several major industrial components: companies conducting barge services on the river and canal portion of the inland waterway system, companies conducting steamship and ferry operations on the Great Lakes and companies providing ocean-going vessel service in coastal and intercoastal transportation.

Inland Waterway Operations. Barge operations, which consist primarily of multiple-barge tows pushed by a power unit, comprise the most significant segment of domestic water carriage; they account for approximately 13 percent of intercity freight ton mileage.[26] More than 1,800 companies provide services on

TABLE 5-1

Public Expenditures for Waterway Development (in millions)

YEAR	FEDERAL	STATE AND LOCAL	TOTAL
1950	$ 189	$ 136	$ 325
1955	119	154	273
1960	287	237	524
1965	391	276	667
1970	376	444	820
1975	526	742	1,268
1980	1,156	1,168	2,324
1985	1,189	1,495	2,684
1986	1,075	1,725	2,800
1987	1,043	1,744	2,787
1988	1,134	1,842	2,976
1989	1,134	1,923	3,057
1990	1,303	1,968	3,271
1991	1,540	2,000	3,540
1992	1,498	2,018	3,516

SOURCE: Eno Transportation Foundation, Inc., *Transportation in America*, 11th ed. (Lansdowne, VA: the Foundation, 1993), p. 73.

a for-hire basis. Of these, 360 are regulated as common or contract carriers by the ICC.[27] The remaining companies operate as exempt carriers and engage in the unregulated movement of bulk and liquid commodities. Additionally, more than 400 companies, such as public utilities, oil companies, and food processors, conduct private barge operations. The Interstate Commerce Act permits both private and regulated water carriers to act as exempt carriers on back-haul movements.

In total, about 36,500 towboats, tugs, and barges are involved in operations over the river and canal network.[28] There are several large companies engaged in for-hire barge operations, but the typical operator is a relatively small businessman in transportation terms. Because of the scale of the typical barge operation and the limited regulatory entry controls in this form of carriage, it is often assumed that entry into such operations is relatively easy. However, the cost of a modern towboat is several million dollars, so capital entry barriers are rather significant.

Great Lakes and Deep Sea Operations. The second major component of domestic water carriage operations consists of movements on the Great Lakes. An additional 3 percent of intercity freight ton mileage moves on the Great Lakes by freighter or ferry services.[29] About 70 commercial harbors exist on the lakes, and the traffic flow consists primarily of ore and grain movements. Opening of the St. Lawrence Seaway has provided lake ports with access to service by all but the largest ocean-going vessels and has stimulated the growth of import-export traffic. The seaway, which was completed in 1959, stretches 160 miles from Lake Ontario to Montreal, providing deep-sea access to traffic from lake ports. It is capable of servicing both deep water ocean vessels and shallow-draft vessels. The project was financed jointly by the United States ($131 million) and Canada ($340 million).

The third component of the domestic water system is coastal (along either the Pacific coast or the Atlantic coast, or between Atlantic and Gulf Coast ports) and intercoastal (connecting East and West Coast Ports through the Panama Canal or around South America). Historically, the federal government has restricted such services to vessels that are built, owned, and operated by U.S. citizens. Such stipulations, both here and abroad, are generally referred to as "cabotage" laws. The related guidelines that cover the U.S. situation are contained in the Jones Act, also known as the Merchant Marine Act, which was passed in 1920.

A considerable volume of coastal traffic moves by barge, with the remainder moving by regular cargo ship. Prior to World War II, 19 companies offered package and volume service on intercoastal movements.[30] These services were interrupted by the war, and the business never recovered. Contributing to its decline was increasing rate and service competition from railroads, oil pipelines, and motor carriers. Traffic volume moving over the intercoastal routes has dwindled, and the number of companies serving the routes has similarly contracted.

Regulation. Responsibility for the economic regulation of domestic water carriage was given to the ICC by the Transportation Act of 1940. A regulatory pattern was adopted that was quite similar to that applied to the railroads. Major provisions of the act stipulate regulation of the following aspects of the industry: entry into common and contract carriage, common carrier ratemaking (contract carriers must publish minimum rates only), and carrier mergers.

However, a significant difference exists between the regulation of railroads and water carriage in that all water carriers of bulk commodities are exempt from regulation, provided that not more than three commodities are carried in the same vessel or tow. Liquid cargo movements are similarly exempt from regulation. The combined effect of these exemptions and the existence of private carriage is that only 3 percent of domestic water carriage traffic is subject to ICC regulation.[31] The balance is moved by exempt carriers (71 percent) and private carriers (26 percent).[32]

For nearly two decades the ICC has called upon Congress to eliminate the limited economic regulation of domestic water carriage which does exist. Similarly, the Department of Transportation has urged complete deregulation of interstate barge operations.[33] However, Congress has not yet responded to those requests.

The U.S. Coast Guard, now a component of the federal Department of Transportation, enforces federal maritime safety regulations and is charged with provisions of navigational aids. It is also responsible for enforcing the antipollution laws that apply to the waterway system.

Capital Needs. According to the ICC, the financial condition of regulated water carriers appears to be generally sound. However, the earnings pattern of these carriers has been subject to considerable year-to-year fluctuations.

One factor that has contributed to the industry's financial strength is the recent inflow of capital to the industry from nontransportation companies. Some of the largest barge operations have been acquired by conglomerate (multi-industry) companies, and the capital backing of the conglomerates has led to equipment modernization and related operating cost reductions. This movement of conglomerate companies into for-hire transportation is the subject of considerable controversy; it is discussed at length in Chapter 15.

The major cost element of the domestic water carriage industry, the right-of-way, is provided, maintained and operated primarily at public expense. Government spending for these purposes has averaged slightly more than $3.5 billion annually in recent years. Unquestionably, these outlays strengthen the competitive position of water carriers by opening new markets and reducing operating costs. Competitive modes long contended that such public outlays, if not recovered through user charges, gave water carriage an artificial price advantage in intermodal competition. Water carriers counter by claiming that waterway expenditures generally have multiple purposes, such as promotion of national defense, flood control, or improved irrigation, and that commercial water carriage is an indirect beneficiary.

This debate continued for many years, and throughout that period the only instance in which waterway user charges were levied in domestic water carriage was on movements through the St. Lawrence Seaway. Then, in 1978 Congress established a waterway fuel tax program to recover a portion of federal waterway expenditures.[34] The program, which began in 1980, levied a 4 cents per gallon tax on the diesel fuel used by water carriers. The tax increased annually until it reached 10 cents per gallon by 1985. The federal user fee program expanded further with passage of the Inland Water Resources Act of 1986. The statute provided for steadily escalating fuel taxes on inland waterway users. It froze fuel taxes at 10 cents per gallon until the end of 1989 then provided annual step increases up to a maximum fuel tax of 20 cents per gallon in 1995. The legislation also stipulated a 50-50 shared funding structure for waterway capital improvements with half of the money coming from the Inland Waterways Trust Fund (which accumulates the user fees) and the other half coming from general tax revenues.[35] While this expansion of federal fuel taxes on inland waterway users puts federal funding of related projects on a more equitable footing, waterway interests contend that funds accumulated (and the matching funds from general tax revenues) will not be sufficient to reconstruct and expand the nation's lock and dam network.

Cost and Service Characteristics

The following discussion examines the cost and service characteristics of domestic water carriage. Particular attention is devoted to the competitive significance of these factors.

Water Carrier Costs and Rates. Extensive governmental participation in construction, operation, and maintenance of domestic waterways significantly lowers the cost structure of firms that perform water transport services. Because the right-of-way is provided at limited carrier expense, the major capital outlays of carriers are related to vessel ownership and terminal facilities.

The cost structure of inland and coastal water carriers is lightly weighted with fixed costs, the majority of costs being variable in nature. In that respect, their cost structure resembles that of trucking rather than that of railroads or oil pipelines. The unit costs of water carriers in moving freight tend to be considerably lower than those of competitive modes, with the possible exception of pipelines in certain instances. Several factors combine to make water carriage such a low-cost mode: the public provision of the right-of-way, extremely low operating costs, and the favorable impact on unit costs of handling large-volume shipments, which further reduces the already low overhead expenses per unit.

In contrast, the capital investment of water carriers involved in Great Lakes and intercoastal shipping tends to be much larger than that of the typical barge operator because of the relative costs of the vessels employed-freighters and tankers versus barges. That sector of the industry consequently has a cost structure that exhibits, as do the cost structures of the railroad and pipeline industries, a significant difference between fully distributed and variable costs.

Line-haul costs in inland and coastal water carriage tend to be quite low, not only because the industry is very energy efficient, but also because the introduction of more powerful towboats has increased possible tow lengths and reduced labor requirements. Terminal costs and the costs of loading and unloading tend to be proportionately higher.

A lack of information concerning exempt and private water carriage makes it impossible to comment on their operating ratios. However, the ICC reports that regulated water carriers operating on the inland and coastal waterways, taken collectively, have had average operating ratios between 85 and 93 percent in recent years.[36] The fact that these carriers could report high operating ratios and yet register average rates of return on investment between 8 and 21 percent during the same period attests to the low nonoperating cost structure of this sector of the industry. During the same period, regulated coastal and intercoastal carriers reported average operating ratios between 89 and 100 percent.[37]

It is difficult to generalize about the rate structure of the domestic water carrier industry because of the diversity of water carrier services and the existence of major exemptions. However, it was estimated that the average revenue per ton mile realized by barge operators in 1991 was .778 cents.[38] This is approximately one-fourth the average revenue per ton mile earned by railroads during the same year; but comparison of these figures is of limited value, because it fails to reflect the impact of rail-water competition over a given route. Where such competition has existed between regulated carriers, water carriers have traditionally attempted to establish prices that were about 20 percent below rail rates.[39] Under these circumstances, shippers must weigh this price difference against several other factors, including the relative speeds and route distances of the two modes. Where competition exists between exempt water carriers and railroads, the ICC has tended to allow the railroads to meet the prices of the exempt carriers.

To a great extent, the nature of rail-water competition has changed significantly in recent years. The railroads have aggressively pursued contract rate negotiations with many major bulk commodity shippers. This development has increased the intensity of price competition between the two modes.

In some markets, competition has also developed between water carriage and oil pipelines on petroleum traffic. Improvements in the pumping technology and the use of wide-diameter pipe have allowed the pipelines to quote rates that are quite competitive with water carriage over long-distance movements.

There is also a certain degree of competition between water carriers engaged in common and contract carriage. Where such competition exists, the rates of common carriers tend to be higher than the rates of contract carriage. Some joint rail-water ratemaking also exists. Such agreements, which effectively extend the markets that might be served by individual carriers, are subject to ICC approval.

Water Carrier Service. Domestic water carriage primarily serves industries that generate, process, or consume bulk-loading commodities. These commodities do not tend to be time sensitive, and their shippers trade off the relative slowness of water carriage for its low price. A limited number of commodity categories account for the majority of water traffic. Coal, scrap metals, sand, stone, iron, steel, and petroleum constitute the bulk of the industry's traffic base.[40] As indicated by the average length-of-haul figures registered by water carriers operating over the various segments of the U.S. waterway system, water carriers are generally engaged in long-distance movements. During one recent year these figures were river and canal movements, 449 miles; Great Lakes operations, 540 miles; and coastwise, 1,585 miles.[41]

Typically, water traffic moves in large quantities, taking advantage of a major strength of the mode, its ability to handle large-volume shipments. In barge operations, waterway improvements and introduction of towboats with up to 9,000 horsepower have combined to yield astounding capacity. Dry-cargo barges have capacities ranging from 800 to 3,000 tons; tank barges have capacities ranging from 1,000 to 3,800 tons. Given these barge capacities and towboat capabilities, tow loads of 50,000 tons are not uncommon. In contrast, 20 years ago a tow of 10,000 tons was considered huge. These capacity figures are more meaningful when it is realized that some barges are capable of carrying as much bulk traffic as 40 railroad cars, and that tows consisting of 40 to 50 barges are possible.

In coastal and intercoastal service there have been several recent changes in service offerings. Much of this traffic now moves in unitized loads relying upon loaded container or trailer movements on container-ships. This has not only reduced loading and unloading times, but has also lowered longshoring costs and reduced loss and damage. Probably the most dramatic innovation in water carriage in recent years is the development of barge-carrying, ocean-going ships. This system, LASH (lighter aboard ship), has provided shippers located on practically any segment of the inland waterway system with access to seaports and inland water destinations throughout the world. Barges having capacities ranging from 250 to 750 tons are moved along the inland waterways to a deep-water port. There they are loaded upon ocean-going vessels for ocean movement. Upon arrival at the destination port, the barges are unloaded from the mother ship and moved by towboat to their final destination. Although the concept has some application in domestic movements, its primary purpose will be to serve international markets.

Shipper Assessment of Water Carriage. In considering the possible use of water carriage, the shipper is confronted by the fact that the capacity strength and low rate structure of the mode are offset to varying degrees by certain disadvantages inherent in the mode. For example, even under ideal conditions water operations generally operate between 8 and 15 miles per hour. Contributing to this relative slowness is waterway congestion at some key locks during certain seasonal peaks. Also, some segments of the waterway system are impassable during winter months. Additionally, many water routes are quite circuitous, which effectively increases origin-destination times.

Because of the geographical limitations of the waterway system, services are not readily available at all locations, and the cost and time involved in the transfer from rail or truck to water carrier are often prohibitive. However, frequent shippers and receivers of bulk-loading commodities often locate facilities on waterways to assure access to water service. Finally, in employing the services of water carriers, shippers will find that the carrier's liability is more limited than that of carriers of other modes; the shipper must often take a marine insurance policy to assure total coverage.

Despite these disadvantages, domestic water carriage has maintained a relatively stable share of intercity freight ton mileage in recent years, and it continues to serve as a major component of our national transportation network.

SUMMARY

Oil pipelines play a dominant role in domestic petroleum movements. The steady earnings of the industry and its affiliation with the major oil companies have allowed the industry to continuously modernize and automate, thereby keeping costs relatively low. In the long-run, the industry may well expand into movements of other commodities on a broad scale. At the present, however, such movements are limited. Therefore, the industry's main contribution to the economy in the immediate future will likely be the provision of continuous, low-cost petroleum carriage.

Domestic water carriage has benefitted from significant technological changes and a capital infusion from conglomerate companies. The industry's cost structure, which benefits from major public spending for waterways, is generally lower than that of competitive modes. Although the mode suffers some competitive disadvantage due to such factors as the limitations of the waterway network, climatic conditions, and relative slowness, technological improvements and federal construction projects have combined to alleviate some of these problems. Consequently, both the regulated and exempt sectors of the industry will continue to play a major role in the intercity movement of bulk and liquid commodities.

DISCUSSION QUESTIONS

1. Explain the concept of undivided interest as it applies to the oil pipeline industry.
2. In several instances, Congress has granted certain exemptions from economic regulation. What are these exemptions, and what is their significance in the transportation marketplace?

3.   Discuss the ability of barge operators to be competitive with other modes of freight movement on the basis of both price and service characteristics.

4.   What are coal slurry pipelines and if they are constructed on a broad scale what competitive impact would they have?

5.   Compare the cost structures of carriers in the inland waterways and oil pipeline segments of the transportation industries.

NOTES

1.   J.L. Burke, "Oil Pipelines' Place in the Transportation Industry," *ICC Practitioners' Journal*, Vol. 31, No. 7 (April, 1964), p. 782.

2.   Ibid., p. 783.

3.   Fred S. Steingraber, "Pipeline Transportation of Petroleum and Its Products," in *Transportation: Principles and Perspectives* by Stanley J. Hille and Richard F. Poist (Danville, ILL: Interstate Printers and Publishers, 1984), p. 147.

4.   D. Philip Locklin, *Economics of Transportation*, 7th ed. (Homewood, ILL: Richard D. Irwin, Inc., 1972), p. 608.

5.   Ibid.

6.   Association of Oil Pipelines, *Oil Pipelines in the United States: Progress and Outlook* (Washington, D.C.: the Association,1983), pp. 2-3.

7.   Eno Transportation Foundation, Inc., *Transportation in America*, 11th ed. (Lansdowne, VA: the Foundation, 1993), p. 59.

8.   Association of Oil Pipelines, p. 7.

9.   Burke, p. 787.

10.   U.S. Department of Transportation, Moving America - New Directions, New Opportunities: A Statement of National Transportation Policy (Washington, D.C.: the Department, 1990), p.69

11.   Burke, p. 801.

12.   Charles F. Phillips, *The Economics of Regulation*, rev. ed. (Homewood, ILL: Richard D. Irwin, Inc., 1969), p. 276.

13.   John Guandolo, *Transportation Law* (Dubuque, IA: William C. Brown Company, 1965), p. 215.

14.   Eno Transportation Foundation, p. 49.

15.   Ibid., p. 31.

16.   Association of Oil Pipelines, p. 15.

17.   "Pipeline Transportation Technology," *Handling and Shipping*, Vol. 10, No. 1 (January, 1969), p. 66.

18.   See Association of American Railroads, "House Panel Sets Slurry Markup,"*On Track* (April 1-15, 1989), pp. 1,4.

19.   Dennis Melamed, "Slurry Advocates Fail to Overcome Opposition," *Journal of Commerce*, June 18, 1992, p. 6c.

20.   See U.S.Congress, Office of Technology Assessment, *A Technology Assessment of Coal Slurry Pipelines* (Springfield, VA: National Technical Information Service, 1978).

21.   Roy J. Sampson and Martin T. Farris, *Domestic Transportation: Practice, Theory, and Policy*, 4th ed. (Boston, MA: Houghton Mifflin Company, 1979), p. 23.

22.   Locklin, p.97.

23.   Ibid., p. 102.

24.   Charles W. Howe, *Inland Waterway Transportation: Studies in Private and Public Management and Investment Decisions* (Baltimore, MD: Johns Hopkins Press, 1969), p. 9.

25.   Eno Transportation Foundation, p. 44.

26.   Ibid.

27.   U.S. Interstate Commerce Commission, *1992 Annual Report* (Washington, D.C.: U.S. Government Printing Office, 1993), p. 127.

28.   Eno Transportation Foundation, p. 63.

29.   Ibid., p. 44.

30.   Paul T. McElhiney, *Transportation for Marketing and Business Students* (Totowa, NJ: Littlefield, Adams, and Company, 1975), p. 105.

31.   U.S. Army Corps of Engineers, *Waterborne Commerce in the United States* (Washington, D.C.: the Corps, 1988).

32.   Ibid.

33.   U.S. Department of Transportation, p. 69.

34.   Public Law 95-502 (1978).

35.   Dave Higdon, "Waterway Operators Fear Fuel Tax Boost Will Not Be Enough to Fund Improvements," *Journal of Commerce*, December 7, 1989, p. 5B.

36.   Data supplied by the U.S. Interstate Commerce Commission.

37.   Ibid.

38.   Eno Transportation Foundation, p. 49.

39.   U.S. Interstate Commerce Commission, *92nd Annual Report* (Washington, D.C.: U.S. Government Printing Office, 1978), p. 145.

40.   Mitchell E. MacDonald, "Don't Overlook Barges," *Traffic Management* (February, 1992), p. 58.

41.   Eno Transportation Foundation, p. 71.

SELECTED REFERENCES

Burke, J.L. "Oil Pipelines' Place in the Transportation Industry." *ICC Practitioners' Journal*, Vol. 31, No. 7 (April, 1964), pp. 780-802.

Campbell, Thomas C. "Eminent Domain: Its Origin, Meaning and Relevance to Coal Slurry Pipelines." *Transportation Journal*, Vol. 17, No. 1 (Fall, 1977), pp. 5-21.

Chancellor, Andrea. "Will Coal Slurry Pipelines Survive?" *Modern Railroads* (August, 1988), pp. 37-40.

Coyle, John J., Edward J. Bardi, and Joseph L. Cavinato. *Transportation*, 3rd ed. St. Paul, MN: West Publishing Company, 1990. Chapter 7. "Domestic Water Carriers," pp. 141-60. Chapter 8. "Pipelines," pp. 161-76.

Dupin, Chris. "Inland Towing Moves Into Current of Recovery." *Journal of Commerce*, December 7, 1989, pp. 5B, 7B.

Johnson, A.M. *Petroleum Pipelines and Public Policy, 1906-1959*. Cambridge, MA: Harvard University Press, 1967.

National Waterways Foundation. *U.S. Waterways Productivity: A Private and Public Partnership*. Huntsville, AL: The Strode Publishers, 1983.

MacDonald, Mitchell E. "Don't Overlook Barges!" *Traffic Management* (February, 1992), pp. 57, 58, 60 and 62.

Wood, Donald F. and James C. Johnson. Contemporary Transportation, 4th ed. New York: Macmillan Publishing Company, 1993.
Chapter 7. "Pipelines," pp. 143-72.
Chapter 8. "Domestic Water Carriers," pp. 173-201.

U.S. Department of Transportation. *Transportation Trends and Choices to the Year 2000*. Washington, D.C.: U.S. Government Printing Office, 1977. Chapter IX. "Marine," pp. 253-88. Chapter X. "Pipelines," pp. 289-302.

United Airlines 747 Courtesy United Airlines

Crowley Maritime successfully completes the largest civilian maritime sealift in history with transportation of 187,000 tons of cargo to Prudhoe Bay, Alaska. *Courtesy of Crowley Maritime*

CHAPTER SIX

THE U.S. AIRLINE INDUSTRY

Among the modes of intercity transportation, the airline industry has clearly been the most visible. The technology employed, the speed of service and the advertising appeals used have combined to attract and hold the public interest.

During the past two decades the industry has undergone an unprecedented transformation as carriers have responded to the freedoms granted by airline deregulation. The industry has emerged as the dominant form of for-hire intercity passenger movement in the United States, accounting for approximately 84 percent of for-hire passenger mileage. Air cargo service has also increased in significance as those buying the service seek to use speed to create competitive advantage. Large American passenger carriers such as American, Delta and United (the "Big Three") have become major factors in international aviation as they have expanded their route networks. Similarly, cargo carriers such as United Parcel Service (UPS), Federal Express and DHL have become global players.

While some carriers have prospered in this environment, others have failed and been liquidated. The financial problems experienced by many airlines in the early 1990s have raised serious questions about the industry's long-term viability.

This chapter explores the industry structure of the U.S. airline industry and focuses on its contemporary strengths and problems. The international aspects of the industry are examined in detail in Chapter 7.

DEVELOPMENT OF THE SYSTEM

Since the inception of manned aircraft flight in this country in 1903, the development of commercial aviation has had a strong connection with government and military endeavors. Although experimentation continued following the successful efforts of the Wright brothers, it took World War I to trigger large-scale development and production of aircraft. During the war years, much of the productive capacity of the automobile industry was redirected into production of more than 17,000 aircraft under federal contracts. The number of pilots trained by the military during this period exceeded 10,000.[1]

United States involvement in the war clearly demonstrated the future military significance of aircraft and thereby established a pattern of joint military-industry development efforts that continues to the present.

Following the war, surplus planes were sold to private parties (including many ex-military pilots), and small-scale commercial operations surfaced. In 1918 the federal government initiated experimentation with airmail service. By 1924 the government provided continuous day and night transcontinental airmail service.[2] The feasibility of such service having been demonstrated, the Kelly Act of 1925 permitted the Post Office Department to award airmail contracts to private companies. The significance of this legislation in promoting the growth of commercial aviation cannot be overstated. By the mid-1930's, airmail contracts (which included a major subsidy element) comprised the bulk of the aviation industry's operating revenues.[3] Further, the Kelly Act and several later statutes also stimulated expansion of passenger services by requiring companies that were awarded airmail contracts to provide passenger facilities as well.

Throughout this early period in aviation history, the federal government assumed responsibility for developing and operating the national airway system. This responsibility continues to the present time, whereas the bulk of the responsibility for construction and operation of airport facilities rests with municipalities and public authorities.

Commercial aviation continued to expand during the 1930's, but at a slow pace. Passenger carriage was still in its infancy, and aircraft development efforts were limited. During that period many carriers experienced financial difficulties and air safety deteriorated. These factors contributed to passage of the Civil Aeronautics Act of 1938, which created the Civil Aeronautics Board (CAB) and established an extensive pattern of federal regulation of commercial air carriage to be administered by the board.

With the onset of World War II, increased government spending led to accelerated efforts in aircraft design and rapid expansion of the national aircraft fleet. During the conflict the number of people exposed to air travel grew dramatically, setting the stage for expansion of commercial airline capacity and demand in the post-World War II period.

The years following the war witnessed rapid expansion of commercial aviation. The route mileage served by the "trunk" airlines, which linked major population centers, grew steadily. The base of the industry was further broadened by establishment of a group of "local service" lines to provide links between smaller communities and major cities. In doing so, they functioned in a feeder role relative to the trunk lines. Another group of passenger carriers known as "air taxi" operators emerged to serve low-density points that did not have sufficient traffic to support a local service airline. "Charter" airlines began to provide non-scheduled passenger and cargo services. "All cargo" carriers and the middlemen which served them, air freight forwarders, completed the industry picture.

Passenger and cargo volume continued to grow into the early 1970s and the scope of the national passenger and cargo network grew with it. The mid 1970s witnessed a major movement toward airline deregulation. Through a combination of administrative actions at the CAB and statutory changes the industry was effectively deregulated. These regulatory changes affected both passenger and cargo operations. The CAB was abolished in 1985. The specifics of the regulatory changes are discussed later in this chapter.

During the late 1970s the industry experienced considerable financial problems. Unfortunately, at the same time liberalized entry policies allowed many new carriers to enter the industry the economy experienced its worst recession since the Depression. Industry profits plummeted and many carriers failed, including a number of the new entrants. The industry recovered during the 1980s, and each year between 1981 and 1990 set new records in terms of revenue passengers served and revenue passenger miles generated. Cargo volume nearly doubled during that period.[4]

The 1990s have not been as kind to the industry. Recessionary pressures and the Gulf War, which not only reduced passenger travel but also raised fuel prices dramatically, combined to produce the three worst years in commercial aviation history between 1990-1992. Many airlines declared bankruptcy, and some, including Eastern Air Lines, Pan American and Midway, were liquidated. The long-term impact of those problems are discussed later in this chapter.

The growth of commercial aviation during the past two decades is shown in Table 6-1. In servicing more than 1.3 million passengers each day, the airlines account for more than 84 percent of for-hire passenger mileage in the United States and handle nearly 80 percent of all first-class intercity mail.[5] Air cargo volume has also continued to grow. As these carriers have continued to expand internationally, the portion of their passenger revenues generated in international operations has surpassed 22 percent.[6]

The U.S. airport-airway system has expanded tremendously, and the airway system now extends more than 390,000 statute miles.[7] Nearly 211,000 aircraft utilize the system. There are more than 17,300 airports in the United States.[8] Of those approximately 16,700 are small facilities used almost exclusively for general aviation. About 600 airports are regularly served by scheduled airlines. During 1992, the nation's airlines offered more than 19,000 daily flights in servicing these facilities.[9]

A significant proportion of the expansion of the airport-airway system has been financed by the federal government. Prior to 1970 little of the related federal expenditure was recovered through user charges. The Airport-Airway Development Act of 1970 established a user charge program that was later

TABLE 6-1

Passenger and Cargo Statistics, U.S. Scheduled Airlines,
1961-1992

Year	Rev.Passengers Enplaned (000)	Rev.Passenger Miles (000,000)	Cargo Ton Miles (000)
1961	63,012	39,831	1,093,343
1965	102,920	68,677	2,303,131
1970	169,922	131,710	4,984,197
1975	205,062	162,810	5,892,605
1980	296,749	254,180	7,188,610
1985	344,683	305,116	8,185,366
1986	418,946	366,546	9,071,136
1987	447,678	404,472	10,014,494
1988	454,614	423,302	11,469,193
1989	453,692	432,714	12,186,497
1990	465,557	457,915	12,603,656
1991	452,301	447,954	12,129,963
1992	473,305	478,081	13,053,681

SOURCE: Air Transport Association, *Air Transport, 1993* (Washington, D.C.: the Association, 1993) p.2; also earlier editions.

expanded in the Airport and Airway Improvement Act of 1982. The fees established in the 1982 legislation were subsequently raised in 1990 and include a ten percent airline ticket tax and a seven percent air cargo tax as well as a per gallon fuel tax which applies to general aviation.[10] These and related user fees recover all of the costs associated with airport improvement grants and the modernization of the Federal Aviation Administration (FAA) capital plan. They also recover a portion of the costs incurred by the FAA in operating and maintaining the airway system.

INDUSTRIAL AND FINANCIAL STRUCTURE

The nation's airlines employ more than 540,000 workers and utilize nearly 4,300 aircraft in providing passenger and freight services.[11] Approximately 90 percent of the industry's operating revenues, which were nearly $78 billion in 1992, are generated by passenger services.[12] An additional 5-6 percent of operating revenues originate in freight and express services. The balance represents revenue sources such as airmail contracts and government subsidies.

DOT Classification of Airlines

Prior to the movement toward airline deregulation the CAB classified the nation's airlines on an industry segment basis. Air carriers were classified as trunk lines, local service lines, air taxi operators, charter airlines, air cargo carriers, and air freight forwarders.

The federal government no longer classifies air carriers on that basis. The Department of Transportation now classifies air carriers on an annual revenue basis. The classifications are: Majors (annual revenues of over $1 billion), Nationals (annual revenues of $100 million to $1 billion), and Regionals (annual revenues of less than $100 million). The major and national carriers are listed in Table 6-2.

Major Airlines. There are ten major airlines, including one cargo carrier, Federal Express. The number of majors declined by two between 1990 and 1992 as Eastern Air Lines and Pan American Airlines were liquidated. By mid-1993 two of the remaining majors, Continental and TWA, had declared bankruptcy but continued to operate while in reorganization. The majors are generally viewed as the backbone of the commercial aviation industry and they not only provide the bulk of services between large American cities, but also most U.S. based international airline services. They carry nearly 86 percent of the industry's domestic passenger traffic.[13]

National Airlines. The 14 nationals serve route systems which are much more limited than those of the majors and primarily link small population centers with the larger airports served by the majors. As a result of acquisitions by majors and failures (the most significant being Midway Airlines) the number of nationals has continued to decline and by 1993 they only generated approximately four percent of the industry's passenger traffic.[14] Alaska Airlines is the largest and most successful of the remaining nationals.

Regional Airlines. The regional carriers, generally operating aircraft with fewer than sixty seats, not only link smaller communities to larger airports, but also provide scheduled service between small and medium size communities. The number of such carriers, sometimes referred to as "commuters", peaked at 246 in 1981, but has subsequently been reduced to 144 by acquisitions and failures. The top 50 regional carriers account for more than 97 percent of the revenues generated by this industry grouping.[15]

In recent years, regionals have experienced a growth rate in traffic which has surpassed that of the larger carriers. The more successful regional carriers have generally formed alliances with the majors and nationals which have been

TABLE 6-2
Major and National Airlines, 1993

Majors (Annual Revenues over $1 billion)	*Nationals* Annual Revenues of ($100 million-$1 billion)
America West Airlines	Air Wisconsin
American Airlines	Alaska Airlines
Continental Airlines	Aloha Airlines
Delta Airlines	AmericanTrans Air
Federal Express	Emery
Northwest Airlines	Evergreen
Southwest Airlines	Hawaiian
Trans World Airlines	Horizon Air
United Airlines	Markair
USAir	Midwest Express
	Southern Air
	Tower
	United Parcel Service
	USAir Shuttle
	West Air
	World

SOURCE: Air Transport Association, *Air Transport, 1993* (Washington, D.C.: the Association, 1993), p. 19.

mutually beneficial. The larger carriers get the feed from the smaller communities and through the practice of "code sharing" the smaller carriers are listed under the code of the larger carriers on computer reservation systems. In some cases the regionals also benefit from use of the larger carrier's gates and joint advertising outlays.[16]

Air Taxi Operators. The services offered by the major, national and regional airlines are also supplemented by those provided by several thousand air taxi operators. These companies, which operate very small aircraft, play an important role in providing commercial air transportation linkages into remote communities.

Regulation and Promotion

The Civil Aeronautics Act of 1938 established the regulatory structure of air transportation. The statute sought to stabilize conditions in the still-infant industry. During the period immediately preceding passage of the act, the industry was in a rather chaotic state. Operating problems were widespread, accidents were increasing at an alarming rate, and several major carriers were faced with the prospect of bankruptcy.

The act created the CAB to function in both a regulatory and a promotional capacity with respect to commercial air carriage. The board was given independent status and was required to report to Congress, as was the Interstate Commerce Commission. It was granted authority over such matters as fares and rates, routes served, operating rights, mergers, and subsidy payments. It also was charged with promoting development of international air transportation. In that capacity, the CAB, subject to presidential approval, granted foreign operating certificates to U.S. Carriers and U.S. operating permits to foreign carriers.

For many years the CAB was the subject of criticism concerning its economic regulation of air carriage. This criticism, which intensified in the mid-1970s, charged that the board had discouraged price competition between carriers, thereby fostering expensive service competition, which increased customer costs. It was further contended that the board was overly concerned with protection of the regulated carriers and gave inadequate attention to consumer interests.

During the final stages of the Ford administration the CAB, responding to these pressures, agreed that regulatory reform appeared to be desirable. The movement toward reform accelerated with the appointment of Alfred Kahn as chairman of the CAB in 1977. Under Kahn the board aggressively pursued administrative deregulation, which liberalized both fare and entry policies. During that same period, Senators Edward Kennedy and Howard Cannon led the congressional movement toward airline deregulation. These efforts initially led to legislation in 1977 that brought about the deregulation of air cargo operations and later led to passage of the Airline Deregulation Act of 1978.[17] The latter statute provided for a dramatic reduction of the economic regulation of commercial passenger service. Specifically, it not only provided for elimination of CAB route and fare controls by 1983, but also for the abolition of the agency by 1985. When the agency was abolished, the remaining economic regulatory responsibilities in aviation were shifted to the DOT, and primarily assumed by the office of the Assistant Secretary for Policy and International Affairs. In 1989 the Department's antitrust powers in aviation were transferred to the Department of Justice. These regulatory changes and their effects on commercial aviation in the United States are discussed extensively in Chapter 12.

The Federal Aviation Administration (FAA), which is a component of the Department of Transportation, is charged with development and enforcement of safety regulations in air transportation. It also develops and operates the airways and administers the federal airport program. Another federal agency, the independent National Transportation Safety Board, is responsible for investigation of fatal airline crashes. The board plays a similar role with respect to the other modes of transportation.

State Regulation

The federal government, through the FAA, has the power to regulate all interstate or intrastate flying to the extent that it may be necessary to protect interstate, overseas, or foreign air commerce. This greatly limits the authority of the states in the field of air safety.

However, with respect to economic regulation, the powers of CAB were limited to jurisdiction over interstate, overseas, and foreign commerce as well as the carriage of mail. This left the field of intrastate commerce by air to the jurisdiction of the states. Consequently, individual states can certify carriers for intrastate air service and can similarly regulate the fares charged in these operations. Given this ability, 28 states have chosen to regulate at least some economic aspects of intrastate air carriage.

Capital Needs

As noted earlier, various governmental units have played major roles in financing the growth and development of the U.S. airport-airways system. The federal government, relying extensively upon user-charges, has played the predominant role in this regard. The magnitude of the federal commitment in this area is illustrated by the fact that the federal budget for Fiscal Year 1994 included $8.85 billion for Federal Aviation Administration.[18] Public authorities and local governments generally own and operate the airports. In many instances, the fees charged for landing aircraft, office and operational space, and maintenance and administrative quarters do not repay the operating costs of the airport. Even when the fees repay operating costs, they commonly do not cover capital costs. Consequently, the airline industry has historically benefitted from the partial financing of the major cost element of the industry, the airport-airways system, by various governmental units.

During the 1990s the airlines have often been critical of the FAA for what they perceive to be the agency's relative slowness in upgrading and effectively staffing the nation's air traffic control system. The 18,000 controllers who staff the system are FAA employees. The carriers contend that delays caused by system inefficiencies cost the industry more than $2 billion per year in wasted fuel and added crew costs.[19] If the value of time lost by passengers is included, the figure grows to $5 billion annually.[20] While the airlines have called for an overhaul of the agency's structure and priorities, they have also lobbied to have the industry's user-charges reduced. In this era of budget deficits, those positions appear rather inconsistent.

There have also been periodic calls for privatization of the air traffic control system. Advocates suggest that the federal government should contract with private companies to operate at least part of the system. Limited forms of such privatization have emerged in Britain, New Zealand and Switzerland.[21]

Airline Finances and Capital Requirements. Prior to World War II, the capital requirements of most commercial airlines were modest, and many airlines were closely controlled by individuals or small groups that had little dependence on outside sources of capital. However, as the scale of the industry increased, and jets and wide-bodied aircraft were introduced, capital requirements increased tremendously. As a result, it has been necessary for many carriers to rely heavily upon borrowing and the sale of securities (primarily bonds) to generate the necessary investment capital. This has led to sizable debt-servicing obligations for many airlines.

Reliance upon external sources of financing focuses the attention of the investment community on the performance and potential of those companies seeking financing. One commonly used measure of the financial strength of a company is its rate of return on investment. In 1979, the CAB set 12.0 percent as a "fair and equitable" target annual rate of return on investment for the scheduled airline industry.[22] However, as shown in Table 6-3, the industry has never achieved that target rate of return.

While the industry as a whole was consistently profitable during the 1980s, the 1990s have witnessed severe financial problems for the airlines. Recessionary pressures, heavy debt loads, rising costs, traffic declines precipitated by the Gulf War and intense price competition have combined to send the industry into a financial spiral. Financially, 1990-1992 was the worst three year period in the history of commercial aviation in the United States. Industry losses for the period were $4 billion in 1990, $1.9 billion in 1991 and $4 billion in 1992.[23] The losses of that three year period exceeded the cumulative earnings of the industry since 1945.[24] By mid-1993 Continental Airlines and Trans World Airlines were struggling through reorganizations following bankruptcy declarations, and several other majors appeared to have serious financial problems. Even the "Big Three" were not insulated from the problems. The losses reported by those carriers for 1992 were as follows: American Airlines ($935

TABLE 6-3

Rate of Return on Investment,
U.S. Scheduled Airlines, 1950-1992

Year	Rate of Return (%)
1950	11.2
1955	11.8
1960	2.8
1965	11.2
1970	1.5
1975	2.5
1980	5.3
1985	9.6
1986	4.9
1987	7.2
1988	10.8
1989	6.3
1990	(6.0)
1991	(0.5)
1992	(6.4)

SOURCE: Air Transport Association, *Air Transport, 1993* (Washington, D.C.: the Association, 1993), p.2; also earlier editions.

million), Delta Air Lines ($565 million), and United Airlines ($957 million). USAir, struggling to avoid bankruptcy, lost an astonishing $1.23 billion.[25] These losses prompted the airlines to make numerous changes in their operating and capital plans. Those changes are discussed below.

COST AND SERVICE CHARACTERISTICS

Although modern aircraft represent multi million dollar investments, fixed costs such as interest, depreciation, and amortization comprise a relatively small percentage of the industry's cost structure. It has been estimated that nearly 80 percent of the industry's cost structure is variable in nature. Contributing to this situation is the provision of airways and airports by various governmental units. While charges are levied on the users of these system elements, these payments, such as landing fees, are variable with operations.

Major Cost Elements

Among the major costs incurred by the airlines are labor, fuel, equipment and user-charge outlays.

Labor Costs. The cost of labor is the largest airline cost element, on average accounting for approximately 35 percent of airline operating costs.[26] There is some variation in wage rates within the industry; nevertheless, controlling labor costs and stimulating labor productivity continue to be major areas of management concern in all airlines.

The wave of new entrant airlines, including companies like New York Air and People Express, which entered the industry in the late 1970s used their non-union, low labor costs status as a means of establishing an immediate market presence. That labor cost differential provided an important cost advantage to the newer companies, and they aggressively challenged the more established companies with deep discount fares in the early 1980s. The labor cost advantage of the newer market entrants prompted an unprecedented wave of concession bargaining in the industry between 1982-1984.[27]

In the years which followed, for a variety of reasons discussed later in this book, many of the new entrants failed and as the earnings of the more established carriers rebounded, the unions sought to reassert themselves in bargaining with the airlines. As a result, airline employee compensation resumed its growth pattern and by 1993 average employee compensation was approximately $52,200.[28]

In response to their financial difficulties many of the larger airlines, including American, Delta, United and Northwest resorted to large-scale employee layoffs during 1992-1993.[29] The specifics of those efforts are discussed in Chapter 14.

Fuel Costs. Fuel expenditures comprise the second largest operating cost in the industry. On an annual basis they account for 15-20 percent of operating costs. The price of airline fuel has increased dramatically over the past two decades. Jet fuel cost about 12 cents per gallon in 1973, but by 1993 exceeded 60 cents per gallon.[30] Over that period jet fuel prices exhibited substantial volatility, reaching $1.40 per gallon during the Gulf War. The industry attributed most of its record $4 billion loss in 1990 to the doubling of fuel costs which occurred during the fourth quarter of that year.[31]

In analyzing the significance of fuel costs, the Air Transport Association has estimated that each one-cent increase in fuel costs means approximately $150 million in additional costs to the industry.[32]

Jet aircraft are major consumers of fuel. For example, on average the Boeing 747-100 consumes 3,464 gallons of fuel per flight hour.[33] The smaller Airbus 332-100/200 consumes 751 gallons per hour.[34] Continued concern with effective management of fuel costs led many airlines to order new, more fuel-efficient aircraft. However, the additional debt required to finance the new equipment has increased carrier vulnerability to short-term cyclical fluctuations in business volume.

Equipment Costs. While equipment costs in the airline industry comprise a relatively low percentage of the industry's cost structure, they and the debt-servicing obligations that they entail are by no means trivial. The price of new planes has continued to escalate. This is illustrated by the projected price of $120 million for Boeing's new 777 which will be introduced in 1995.[35]

U.S. airlines had nearly 4,300 jets in their collective fleet in 1993 and the FAA has projected that the total will grow to more than 5,700 by 2004.[36] On average, the airlines' current fleet is the oldest in U.S. history. Clearly, however, to finance a new generation of planes, the carriers will have to return to profitability. Because of the magnitude of their recent losses several of the nation's largest airlines including United and Northwest have canceled or renegotiated delivery dates with Boeing and other aircraft manufacturers. A record number of used aircraft have also been available in the 1990s leading some carriers to reconsider previous orders for new planes. If that option is pursued aggressively by the carriers this would cause serious financial problems not only for equipment manufacturers, but also for companies specializing in leasing new planes.[37]

Fares and Price Competition. Collective pricing behavior has played a far more limited role in domestic air carriage than it has in surface transportation. In fact, air carriers traditionally had to obtain CAB permission before they could engage in collective discussion on matters such as fares. While the board relied upon the initiative of individual carriers in the establishment of fares (subject to board approval), prior to the deregulation movement it did not foster extensive price competition within the industry. Competition tended to have a service orientation, with emphasis placed on frequency of service, type of aircraft flown, and a variety of accessorial services.

However, price competition in the industry increased significantly with the movement toward deregulation. In 1977-1978 the CAB administratively gave the carriers more pricing freedom than they previously had experienced. This action was reinforced by the provisions of the Airline Deregulation Act of 1978, which initially permitted airlines to lower fares by as much as 50 percent or raise fares by up to 5 percent without CAB interference. The statute's provisions ultimately ended airline fare regulation by the federal government on January 1, 1983.

Since that time, price has become an important competitive variable in the industry. Initially, the primary price-cutting thrust came from the new entrant airlines which could not match the more established carriers in terms of service, but could attract passengers through lower fares.

Even though many of the new entrants subsequently failed, intense price competition has continued over many routes, thereby depressing passenger yield (revenue per passenger mile). Table 6-4 provides airline yields between 1975-1992 and compares those yields with those of other forms of intercity passenger carriage.

In absolute terms, the domestic airline yield increased only slightly, from 11.5 cents to 12.9 cents, between 1980 and 1992. However, when adjusted for inflation, the real yield in 1992 was only two-thirds what it had been in 1976.[38]

Yield management has become an important industry issue in the 1990s, and the presidents of several of the largest airlines have argued that a continuation of this yield pattern will bankrupt the industry.[39] They have blamed the "Chapter 11 carriers", those in bankruptcy reorganizations, for the industry's continued deep discounting practices. It has been asserted that those carriers, and others on the brink of bankruptcy, have been so desperate for cash flow that they have instituted non-compensatory prices to continue operations in the short-term.[40] In response to these and other concerns about the industry's future, President Clinton signed a bill in early 1993 establishing the National Commission to Ensure a

TABLE 6-4

Average Revenue Per Revenue Passenger Mile,
Intercity Carriers (in cents per mile), 1975-1992

Year	Scheduled Airlines[a]	Amtrak[b]	Class I Buses
1975	7.7	5.7	4.9
1980	11.5	8.2	7.3
1985	12.2	10.5	9.9
1986	11.1	10.6	10.5
1987	11.4	10.6	10.1
1988	12.3	11.5	10.7
1989	13.1	12.6	11.2
1990	13.4	12.9	11.6
1991	13.2	12.8	12.0
1992	12.9	NA	NA

[a]Includes domestic first-class and coach services.
[b]Includes first-class and coach services.
SOURCE: Eno Transportation Foundation, Inc., *Transportation in America*, 11th ed. (Lansdowne, VA: the Foundation, 1993), p. 50.

Strong, Competitive Airline Industry. The 26 member commission was directed to investigate the problems of the industry and make recommendations to congress to assure the industry's future viability.[41] The final report of the Commission, which was issued in August, 1993, is discussed in later chapters.

User Charges. As previously noted, user charges in the aviation industry have increased significantly. The bulk of existing user fees are borne directly by the traveling public in the form of excise taxes on passenger tickets and freight waybills. Although the airlines do not bear these costs directly, the taxes increase airline ticket prices and cargo rates, and in the opinion of some industry executives, divert passengers and cargo to competitive modes. The Air Transport Association of America, the industry's main trade association, agrees with that assertion and has called upon Congress to roll back federal aviation user fees to pre-1990 levels.

Airports also levy fees on airlines to support runways, taxiways, apron areas, terminal buildings, parking facilities, and airport access roads. These fees have increased substantially over the past decade; landing fees have also grown significantly.

Airline Service

The basic differentiating factor of air transportation is its speed. Aircraft speed far surpass that of competitive modes of surface carriage and tends to give air carriage a decided advantage, particularly in long-distance markets.

However, several factors tend to offset some of the line-haul speed advantage of air carriage. One factor is the airport access-egress problem. The traveler must get to and from the airport. Air transportation experiences a "peaking" of demand that coincides roughly with the peaking of travel in urban transportation during the morning and evening rush hours. If the airport is located near center city, it leads to a mix of urban and air travelers at peak hours. Consequently, this adds considerable time to air travel on a door-to-door basis. The individual making the line-haul journey by automobile does not have to contend with this problem. Nor do rail and bus travelers who board at suburban terminals. Conversely, some airports, such as those in Houston and New Orleans, are located considerable distances from center city. As planes have become larger and more space has been needed to accommodate the aircraft, the trend toward outlying airports has accelerated. Suburbanization had already consumed large masses of property; consequently, some new air facilities have had to locate many miles from the center city. Once again, many travelers find that this adds considerable time to their total trip.

Another factor that offsets some of the line-haul speed advantage of air travel is airport congestion. Many domestic airports are operating at flight levels that approach maximum capacity. Community resistance and environmental concerns have made it increasingly difficult to expand airport capacity. As a result, congestion has become a fact of life at many major commercial air facilities. This also tends to be a problem during adverse weather conditions. Frequent air travelers usually have experienced "stacking" over some airport, caused either by traffic peaks or poor visibility. In all fairness, it should be noted that even though air carriage is somewhat more vulnerable to weather conditions than are competitive modes, it has compiled an excellent reliability record.

Because of the combination of factors that offset some of the line-haul speed advantage of air carriage, airlines are more susceptible to competition from auto, bus, and rail operations in short-distance markets than they are in long-distance operations. The airline speed differential is so great in serving long-distance markets that it easily offsets the cumulative effects of the previously mentioned factors, even when stop-offs at intermediate cities are included. The extent of airline participation in long-distance travel markets is indicated by the average length of passenger haul for the scheduled airline, which has increased steadily from 736 miles in 1980 to 806 in 1991.[42]

One important operational change in the airline industry which has significantly affected its service pattern has been the post-1980 movement of large carriers to reconfigure their operations on a "hub and spoke" basis. Under this system, flights originating in smaller cities (spokes) are channeled into a large (hub) airport where connecting flights link passengers with their final destinations. Operating in this manner, airlines are able to significantly increase the number of cities which they service without providing direct service between each city pair. This promotes much better equipment utilization. Table 6-5 lists the principal hub cities used by the major airlines.

In an effort to broaden their geographical coverage, thereby broadening their customer base, many airlines have not only entered new markets, but also acquired carriers or developed marketing alliances with other airlines. These matters are discussed extensively in subsequent chapters.

Load Factors. Given the multimillion dollar investment represented by the modern jet liner, airlines are naturally concerned with equipment utilization. One measure of utilization is the revenue passenger load factor. This figure expresses the relationship between available seat miles and revenue passenger miles realized. The load factor realized by the industry in a given year is a function of many factors, including prevailing economic conditions, carrier pricing strategy, composition of the equipment fleet, and the extent of market competition.

Table 6-6 contains the load factor figures for U.S. scheduled airlines between 1975 and 1992. Industry load factors fluctuated between 53.7 and 63.6 percent during that period.

TABLE 6-5
Principal Hubs of the Major Airlines, 1992

Carrier	Hubs
American Airlines	Dallas/Fort Worth, Chicago, San Juan, Nashville, Raleigh/Durham, San Jose
America West	Phoenix, Las Vegas
Continental Airlines	Houston, Denver, Newark
Delta Airlines	Atlanta, Dallas/Fort Worth, Salt Lake City, Los Angeles, Cincinnati
Northwest Airlines	Minneapolis/St. Paul, Detroit, Memphis
TWA	St. Louis, New York
United	Chicago, Denver, Washington, D.C., San Francisco
USAir	Pittsburgh, Philadelphia, Charlotte, Baltimore

SOURCE: Standard and Poor's Corporation, "Major Airlines," *Industry Surveys*, Vol 160, No. 26,Sec. 1 (June 25, 1992), p. A-35.

DOMESTIC AIR CARGO

The domestic air cargo market was estimated at $15.4 billion in 1992 and projected to grow to $27 billion by 1995.[43] In generating that revenue, air carriers handled approximately 740 million shipments. The projected 1995 volume is 1.6 billion shipments.[44] Average shipment size continues to fall as much of industrial output becomes lighter and more valuable. In 1986 average shipment size was 18 pounds; by 1995 it is expected to be 10.8 pounds.[45]

Air cargo moves in a variety of service classes. These include overnight, second day and deferred air. The traffic carried is generally categorized as letters/envelopes, packages (generally viewed as any shipment under 70 pounds), and "air freight" (generally viewed as any shipment over 70 pounds). During 1992 air freight generated approximately 68 percent of domestic air cargo revenues, packages 26 percent, and letters/envelopes 6 percent.[46] Among the major product

TABLE 6-6
Revenue Passenger Load Factor
U.S. Scheduled Airlines, 1975-1992

Year	Load Factor (%)
1975	53.7
1980	59.0
1985	61.4
1986	60.3
1987	62.3
1988	62.5
1989	63.2
1990	62.4
1991	62.6
1992	63.6

SOURCE: Air Transport Association, *Air Transport, 1993* (Washington, D.C.: the Association, 1992), p. 2; also earlier editions.

categories moving as air cargo are computer components, electronics, fashion goods and cut flowers.

Shippers, considering the use of air cargo, have a variety of carrier options to consider. Carriers providing air cargo service may be grouped into "integrated air cargo companies", "scheduled combination carriers", charter operators and air freight forwarders. That group is supplemented by the air services of the U.S. Postal Service (USPS). There is considerable concentration in the business with the five largest air cargo carriers and the USPS handling nearly 92 percent of domestic air cargo shipments.[47]

Integrated Air Cargo Companies

Integrated air cargo companies have integrated air service and related ground support systems and handle air cargo from origin to destination. The companies which dominate the air cargo industry, including Federal Express, United Parcel Service, DHL, Airborne Express, Burlington Air Express and Emery Worldwide are illustrations of such companies. These companies own extensive aircraft and trucking support fleets and blanket the domestic air cargo marketplace. While there has traditionally been some degree of specialization within this group, based on the size of shipments handled, the lines of distinction are becoming less clear. Federal Express, which entered the industry in 1973 with 8 small planes, to a great extent defined the overnight letter and package business. By concentrating on 70 pound and under business and giving excellent service, the company has grown at an incredible pace. During its 1993 fiscal year the company generated $5.82 billion in domestic air cargo sales.[48] As shown in Table 6-7 that represented 43.3 percent of the domestic air cargo market. While the company became known as a parcel carrier, it has taken important steps to diversify its service offerings. In 1989 the company acquired Flying Tigers which was the dominant carrier in the heavy freight segment of the business. The nearly $900 million acquisition was also motivated by Federal's desire to acquire Tigers' extensive international route network. In 1989 Federal also raised its shipment size limit to 150 pounds. Federal's most significant competitor in the domestic air cargo market is UPS which entered the air market late, in 1982. Since that time its air volume has grown rapidly and the company now handles more than one-quarter of domestic air cargo volume.

TABLE 6-7
Market Share of Domestic Air Cargo Revenues
Selected Carriers, 1992

Carrier	*Market Share*
Federal Express	43.3%
United Parcel Service	25.2
Airborne	14.3
United States Postal Service	7.6

SOURCE: "Just the Facts," *Air Commerce*, New York, May 24, 1993, p.9A.

Two other competitors, Emery Worldwide and Burlington Air Express, are best known for the handling of heavy air cargo shipments. Emery was acquired by Consolidated Freightways (one of the three largest general commodity truckers in the U.S.) in 1989 and merged with Consolidated's much smaller CF Air Freight operation. Two years earlier, Emery had acquired one its major competitors, the financially troubled Purolator Courier.

Scheduled Combination Carriers

The nation's scheduled passenger airlines, which are often referred to as "combination carriers" in the context of air cargo operations also provide air cargo services. On average, air cargo generates about 5 percent of the revenues of the scheduled airlines in the U.S.[49]

Most of the cargo which they handle moves in the bellies of passenger planes. Among the combination carriers only Northwest continues to operate cargo freighters. Most of the freight moved by these carriers consists of second day and deferred air cargo. With the exception of American Airlines, none of the other combination carriers maintains a dedicated air cargo sales and marketing organization. Therefore, they rely almost exclusively on the services of air freight forwarders to generate their air cargo volume.

Air Freight Forwarding

As is the case with their surface carriage counterparts, air freight forwarders are transportation middlemen which link carriers that provide intercity services with shippers. In the case of "pure" air freight forwarding, shipments destined for air movements are picked up at shipper location, consolidated into air containers, and delivered to combination carriers or integrated air cargo companies for movement by air. Upon arrival at the destination airport the containers are generally delivered to the forwarder's local terminal for breakbulk operations and local delivery. Most of the traffic handled by the forwarders has historically consisted of second day and deferred air freight. Forwarder profits come from the difference between the volume rates which they receive from the air carriers and the rates the forwarders charge individual customers.

Prior to the movement toward air deregulation, air freight forwarders were generally precluded from operating their own aircraft unless they were unable to obtain sufficient "lift capacity" from the direct air carriers. Under those infrequent circumstances they were able to lease and operate aircraft. Few forwarders had the financial capability to pursue such an option. Most of the several hundred air forwarders operating at that time were very small and thinly capitalized. Several large air freight forwarders had emerged prior to deregulation. They included Emery Air Freight, Burlington Air Express (which was established as subsidiary of the Burlington Northern Railroad), and Purolator Courier.

In 1979 the Civil Aeronautics Board voted to deregulate air freight forwarding. That decision was closely related to the air cargo deregulation effort which had begun in 1977. As a result of those actions, the economic aspects of air forwarding, including entry and ratemaking, are no longer subject to federal regulation.

As the industry moved into the deregulation era several of the largest air forwarders, including the three mentioned above, decided to buy their own aircraft and become "integrated air forwarders." Those companies were then able to provide door-to-door, single carrier service to air cargo customers. Subsequently, those companies were able to offer complete, integrated services in some markets and act as "pure" forwarders in other markets relying upon other carriers to provide the air portion of the service. By acquiring aircraft the larger air forwarders changed the financial nature of their companies and took on substantial debt loads. The related debt servicing obligations, coupled with fluctuations in business volume, would later cause serious financial problems for several of those companies.[50]

The air freight forwarder industry in the U.S. consists of approximately 1,500 companies. Only 25 of those are of any significant size and the several remaining large, integrated forwarders dominate this industry sector.[51] It is interesting to note that two of those large companies, Emery Worldwide and Burlington Air Express, operate as integrated forwarders domestically, but use scheduled combination carriers for their international cargo movements.

Charter Operators

Charter operators provide another option for shippers originating large air cargo shipments. Under such circumstances the shipper may charter all or part of the aircraft. One industry which has relied heavily upon air charter services has been computer manufacturers who have used such service to move completed systems to customers.

United States Postal Service

The USPS has become an important participant in the overnight and second day delivery market of letters/envelopes. Its overnight express mail service handled 55 million pieces in 1992 while its second day priority mail accounted for 551 million pieces.[52]

Air Cargo Rates and Competition

For many years it appeared that the shipping public viewed air cargo as emergency service. However, during the past two decades many shippers have come to realize that in certain instances air cargo movements can become an integral part of a company's distribution system. Air cargo service is expensive and that expense must be weighed against potential improvements in such areas as customer service levels and inventory requirements.

The relative expense of air cargo service is illustrated by the fact that the average revenue per ton mile of air cargo carriers in 1991 was 44.45 cents versus 24.82 cents for trucking and 2.67 cents for rail.[53] The difference is even more dramatic if the small package traffic handled by Federal Express and UPS is included in the air cargo figures. When those operations are included, the industry's revenue per ton mile jumps to $1.12.[54]

Price competition within the domestic air cargo industry, and between that industry and LTL trucking, has intensified during the 1990s. To a great extent this has been precipitated by significant price cuts and aggressive marketing efforts by the two industry leaders, Federal Express and UPS. Air cargo yields have fallen and industry participants have increasingly emphasized value-added services such as inventory management and improved tracking and tracing systems as a means of differentiating their services. At the same time, the larger carriers have expanded their international networks dramatically. This issue is addressed extensively in the next chapter.

GENERAL AVIATION

This chapter has devoted primary attention to commercial air carriage in the United States. However, the significance of "general aviation" should not be overlooked. The term general aviation is applied to a heterogeneous group of aircraft types and uses. It includes instruction and personal flying, and a variety of commercial operations, such as crop dusting, surveying, and business travel in corporate planes. The nearly 215,000 aircraft utilized in general aviation represent more than 92 percent of the civil aviation fleet and annually account for nearly 75 percent of aircraft operations at airports with Federal Aviation Administration control towers.[55] Among the various classes of general aviation, business use is predominant with respect to hours and miles flown. This reflects the growth of corporate fleets and the flexibility of general aviation in serving communities with airports that do not receive regularly scheduled service by commercial carriers.

The sheer number of aircraft in general aviation causes problems in terms of compatibility with other users of the aviation system, particularly at higher altitudes and within terminal airspace. The management of airspace and the physical constraints of the domestic aviation system pose sizable challenges to the federal government in the years ahead.

SUMMARY

The airline industry has emerged as the dominant form of for-hire intercity passenger carriage in the United States, accounting for nearly 84 percent of such traffic. The speed of air transportation allows it to dominate long-distance, for-hire passenger carriage, particularly with respect to business travelers. Although the airlines still account for less than one percent of intercity freight ton mileage, air cargo continues to grow in size and importance.

The airport-airway network of the United States is the most extensive domestic system in the world. However, the network faces significant physical capacity problems in the years ahead.

The commercial airline industry has undergone a major transformation as a result of the movement toward airline deregulation. During the past several years the industry has recorded enormous operating losses and many large carriers have failed financially. The airlines face an increasingly competitive marketplace and their actions during the next several years will be very important in determining the future form and viability of the U.S. airline industry.

During the past decade many U.S. airlines have expanded the scope of their international operations and the international aviation industry has reconfigured itself on a global basis. The nature of those expansion efforts and their significance are examined in the next chapter.

DISCUSSION QUESTION

1. How has the nature of competition changed in the airline industry since 1978?
2. What factors combined to depress airline earnings in the early 1990s?
3. What is the role of air freight forwarders in the air cargo market?
4. Discuss the relative significance of labor and fuel costs in the domestic airline industry.
5. What are the major factors which will influence the future of air transportation in the United States?

NOTES

1. U.S. Department of Commerce, Bureau of Air Commerce, Aeronautics Bulletin No. 1, *Civil Aeronautics in the United States* (1937), as cited by D. Philip Locklin, *Economics of Transportation*, 7th ed. (Homewood, ILL: Richard D. Irwin, Inc., 1972), p. 770.
2. Roy J. Sampson and Martin T. Farris, *Domestic Transportation: Practice, Theory, and Policy*, 4th ed. (Boston: Houghton Mifflin Company, 1979), p. 33.
3. For an excellent discussion of the early airline subsidy programs, see John H. Frederick, *Commercial Air Transportation*, 4th ed. (Homewood, ILL: Richard D. Irwin, Inc., 1955), pp. 79-86.
4. Air Transport Association, *Air Transport 1993* (Washington, D.C.: the Association, 1993), p. 3, and earlier editions.
5. Eno Transportation Foundation, Inc., *Transportation in America*, 11th ed., December supplement (Lansdowne, VA: the Foundation, 1993), p. 47.

6. Air Transport Association, p. 2.
7. Eno Transportation Foundation, p. 64.
8. U.S. Department of Transportation, *Moving America-New Directions, New Opportunities: A Statement of National Transportation Policy* (Washington, D.C: the Department, 1990), p. 66.
9. Air Transport Association, p. 1.
10. Air Transport Association, *Air Transport, 1992* (Washington, D.C.: the Association, 1992), p. 2.
11. Air Transport Association, *Air Transport, 1993*, p. 10.
12. Ibid., p. 2.
13. Standard and Poor's, "Air Transport Outlook," *Industry Surveys*, Vol. 160, No. 26, Sec. 1 (June 25, 1992), p. A35.
14. Ibid., p. A39.
15. Ibid., p. A40.
16. Ibid.
17. Public Law 95-163 (1977).
18. U.S. Executive Office of the President. *Budget of the United States Government, Fiscal Year 1994*. Washington, D.C.: U.S. Government Printing Office, 1993, p. 846.
19. "Privatizing the FAA," *Journal of Commerce*, New York, February 26, 1992, p. 8A.
20. Ibid.
21. Ibid.
22. Air Transport Association, *Air Transport, 1993*, p.3, and earlier editions.
23. Air Transport Association, *1993 State of the U.S. Airline Industry* (Washington, D.C.: the Association, 1993), p. 3.
24. Ibid.
25. John Boyd, "Aviation Red Ink Swells as Delta, UAL Report Big Losses," *Journal of Commerce*, New York, January 29, 1993, p. 3B.
26. Standard and Poor's, p. A43.
27. Robert C. Lieb and James Molloy, "The Major Airlines: Labor Relations in Transition," *Transportation Journal*, Vol. 26, No. 3 (Spring, 1987), pp. 17-29.
28. Air Transport Association, *Air Transport, 1993*, p. 11.
29. James Ott, "Airlines Fight Labor for Survival," *Aviation Week & Space Technology* (April 5, 1993), pp. 20-1.
30. Air Transport Association, *1993 State of the U.S. Airline Industry*, p. 7.
31. Air Transport Association, *Air Transport, 1991* (Washington, D.C.: the Association, 1991), p. 2.
32. Air Transport Association, *1993 State of the U.S. Airline Industry*, p. 7.
33. Air Transport Association, *Air Transport, 1993*, p. 13.

34.   Ibid.
35.   "Boeing Knocks Down the Wall Between the Dreamers and the Doers," *Business Week* (October 28, 1991), p. 121.
36.   Air Transport Association, *Air Transport, 1993*, p. 10.
37.   "All the Trouble Isn't in the Sky," *Business Week* (March 11, 1991), pp. 84.
38.   Steven A. Morrison and Clifford Winston, "Cleared for Takeoff: The Evolution of the Deregulated Airline Industry," *The Annual Review of Travel*, 1992 ed. (New York: American Express, 1992), p. 79.
39.   See "The Airlines Are Killing Each Other Again," *Business Week* (June 8, 1992, p. 32; also, "Airline Woes," *Journal of Commerce*, New York, February 25, 1993, p. 6A.
40.   "Airline Woes," p. 6A.
41.   Stephanie Nall, "New Panel May Recommend Partial Airline Re-Regulation," *Journal of Commerce*, New York, May 5, 1993, p. 3B.
42.   Eno Transportation Foundation, p. 70.
43.   See "Just the Facts," *Air Commerce*, New York, May 24, 1993, p. 9A; also, James Aaron Cooke, "How the Integrated Carriers Changed an Industry," *Traffic Management* (August, 1991), p. 37.
44.   Michael S. Lelyveld, "US Air Cargo Growth Expected to Double over Next Decade," *Journal of Commerce*, New York, September 17, 1992, p. 3B.
45.   "How the Integrated Carriers Changed an Industry," p. 42.
46.   "Just the Facts," p. 9A.
47.   Estimate supplied by the Colography Group, Marietta, Georgia.
48.   "Fedex: Europe Nearly Killed the Messenger," *Business Week* (May 25, 1992), p. 126.
49.   Perry A. Trunick, "Domestic Air Offers Shippers Options," *Transportation and Distribution* (December, 1991), p. 32.
50.   See Mark B. Solomon, "Emery Rises Up from the Ashes," *Air Commerce*, New York, February 22, 1993, p. 4.
51.   Trunick, p. 32.
52.   John Davies, "Express Mail Volume Expected to Decline," *Journal of Commerce*, New York, September 21, 1992, p. 1A.
53.   *Transportation in America*, 10th ed, December supplement, p. 9.
54.   Ibid.
55.   Data supplied by the Federal Aviation Administration.

SELECTED REFERENCES

Air Transport Association. *Air Transport, 1993*. Washington, D.C.: the Association, 1993.

Air Transport Association. *1993 State of the U.S. Airline Industry.* Washington, D.C.: the Association, 1993.

Caves, Richard E. *Air Transport and Its Regulators.* Cambridge, Ma: Harvard University Press, 1962.

Chow, Garland, Richard D. Gritta, and Ronald Hockstein. "Airline Financing Policies in a Deregulated Environment." *Transportation Journal*, Vol 27, No. 3 (Spring, 1988), pp. 37-48.

Douglas, George W., and James C. Miller, *Economic Regulation of Domestic Air Transport: Theory and Policy.* Washington, D.C.: Brookings Institution, 1974.

"Eastern: The Wings of Greed." *Business Week*, November 11, 1991, pp. 34-6.

Gesell, Laurence E. *Airline Re-Regulation.* Chandler, AZ: Coast Aire Publications, 1990.

Meyer, John R., and Clinton V. Oster, Jr. *Deregulation and the New Airline Entrepreneurs.* Cambridge, MA: the MIT Press, 1984.

Morrison, Steven A., Clifford Winston, Elizabeth E. Bailey, and Alfred E. Kahn. "Enhancing the Performance of the Deregulated Air Transport System: Comments and Discussion." *Brookings Papers on Economic Activity.* Washington, D.C.: the Brookings Institution, 1988.

Morrison, Steven A., and Clifford Winston. *The Economic Effects of Airline Deregulation.* Washington, D.C.: the Brookings Institution, 1986.

National Commission To Ensure A Strong Competitive Airline Industry. *A Report to the President and Congress.* Washington, D.C.: U.S. Government Printing Office, 1993.

Oum, Tae Hoom, Allison J. Taylor and Anming Zhang. "Strategic Airline Policy in the Globalizing Airline Networks." *Transportation Journal*, Vol. 32, No. 3 (Spring, 1993), pp. 14-30.

Rackowski, James P., and David Bejou. "Birth, Marriage, Life and Death: A Life-Cycle Approach for Examining the Deregulated U.S. Airline Industry." *Transportation Journal*, Vol. 32, No. 1 (Fall, 1992), pp. 15-29.

Standard and Poor's. "Aerospace and Air Transport." *Industry Surveys*, Vol. 160, No. 26, Sec. 1, June 25, 1992, pp. A33-43.

U.S. Department of Transportation, Office of the Secretary. *Secretary's Task Force on Competition in the U.S. Domestic Airline Industry: Industry and Route Structure.* Washington, D.C.: the Department, 1990, Vols. I and II.

U.S. Department of Transportation, Office of the Secretary. *Secretary's Task Force on Competition in the U.S. Domestic Airline Industry: Pricing.* Washington, D.C.: the Department, 1990, Vols. I and II.

U.S. Department of Transportation, Office of the Secretary. *Secretary's Task Force on Competition in the U.S. Domestic Airline Industry: Regional Airline Competition.* Washington, D.C.: the Department, 1990.

U.S. General Accounting Office. *Airline Competition: Effects of Airline Market Concentration and Barriers to Entry on Airfares*. Washington, D.C. General Accounting Office, 1991.

U.S. General Accounting Office. *Airline Competition: Fares and Concentration at Small-City Airports*. Washington, D.C.: General Accounting Office, 1991.

U.S. General Accounting Office. *Airline Competition: Weak Financial Structure Threatens Competition*. Washington, D.C.: General Accounting Office, 1991.

Air Containers are unloaded from UPS DC-8 at Boston Logan Airport *Courtesy United Parcel Service*

Container Facility, Moran Terminal, Boston, Massachusetts. *Courtesy of Massachusetts Port Authority*

CHAPTER SEVEN

U.S. PARTICIPATION IN THE INTERNATIONAL MARITIME AND AVIATION INDUSTRIES

Although this book is primarily concerned with the domestic transportation system, it is appropriate that attention also be devoted to America's international transportation linkages. The markets served by many American companies have become increasingly international in nature, as has the mix of products sold in the United States. American manufacturers also rely extensively upon foreign sources for materials to be used in the production process. The aggressive free trade policies articulated early in the Clinton administration seem likely to support even further internationalization of American business.

The annual value of U.S. foreign trade (exports plus imports) exceeds $900 billion and is larger than that of any other country.[1] It is the equivalent of 20 percent of Gross National Product.[2]

For the country to remain competitive in the world marketplace its transportation system must be able to support the large-scale movement of materials and products to and from the United States. America's international ocean and air transportation industries have undergone significant changes in recent years. The merchant marine fleet has dwindled in size while the last several federal administrations have attempted to address the industry's problems. The U.S. airline industry, plagued with financial problems at home, has become increasingly global in scope. Similarly, large railroads and truckers, through alliances with ocean and air carriers, are now defining themselves in international terms.

This chapter examines not only the nature of the U.S. carrier involvement in the international maritime and aviation industries, but also the related programs and policies of the federal government.

INTERNATIONAL MARITIME OPERATIONS

As world trade volume has continued to expand, reaching nearly $5 trillion annually, and national economies have become more interdependent, the role of ocean transportation has become more important.[3] Nearly 90 percent of long-distance international trade volume is moved in ships. The merchant ships of many nations compete, to varying degrees, in various segments of the maritime industry. A significant number of factors, including governmental maritime policies, trade route traffic volume, and industry capacity affect the nature of that competition.

The world's merchant marine fleet consists of nearly 24,000 ships comprising 652,025,000 deadweight tons (deadweight tonnage is a measure of the weight of a ship without cargo).[4] The composition of the world fleet, by vessel type, is shown in Table 7-1.

TABLE 7-1

Composition of the World Merchant Fleet, 1992

Type of Ship	Number of Ships
Freighters	12,581
Combinations	347
Bulk Carriers	5,446
Tankers	5,361
Total	23,735

SOURCE: U.S. Department of Transportation, Maritime Administration, *Merchant Fleets of the World* (Washington, D.C.: the Department, 1992), p. 9.

Freighters are involved in the movement of non-bulk general cargo. There are a variety of types of freighters. The most important of those are intermodal ships. One form of intermodal ship, the "containership", handles most of the general cargo moving along the world's major trade routes. These ships are equipped with permanent container cells to accommodate 20 and 40 foot steel ocean containers. Other intermodal ship types include Roll-On/Roll-Off (RO/RO) ships designed to carry wheeled containers or trailers, and barge carriers which are ocean-going vessels which move loaded barges between ports. The freighter category also includes a number of older breakbulk vessels which handle non-containerized freight. In aggregate, freighters account for the largest portion of world trade when measured according to the value of goods transported.

Bulk ships are designed to carry dry bulk cargo such as ore, coal, or grain. Tankers move such commodities as crude petroleum, petroleum products and chemicals. Companies operating dry bulk ships and tankers move the largest portion of world trade when measured according to the tonnage handled. This traffic moves in shipload quantities under contracts that range in length from a single voyage to long-term charters lasting several years.

Vessels operating in world trades may either be registered in their owner's country or in another nation. Since the 1960s an increasing number of countries, including Panama, Liberia and the Bahamas, have developed fleets of "flags of convenience" which do not require owner citizenship in those countries. In most instances those nations offer tax advantages and less stringent vessel inspection standards. As a result, flags of convenience vessels have become increasingly important in maritime markets. As shown in Table 7-2 Panama now has the largest maritime fleet in the world (the U.S. ranks 16th). Many American owned ships are registered under flags of convenience.

The following discussion examines not only the structure and operations of the U.S. merchant marine fleet, but also reviews the maritime policies and programs of the federal government.

Industry Structure

The relative significance of the privately-owned U.S. merchant marine fleet has declined substantially during the past several decades. In 1951 the fleet consisted of 1,300 ships; by 1992 the number had declined to 397.[5] The 1992 fleet consisted of 168 freighters, 201 tankers, 25 bulk vessels, and three combination passenger/cargo carriers.[6] The U.S. fleet carries only 4.8 percent of the country's ocean borne commerce, as measured in terms of tonnage handled.[7]

As outlined above, U.S. flag maritime operations include carriers serving the general cargo, dry bulk and tanker segments of the industry. In addition, the activities of these carriers are facilitated by the support services offered by a variety of specialized middlemen. Each of these distinct components of the U.S. maritime industry provides important services to the importing and exporting public.

General Cargo Operations. The most important component of the freighter segment of the industry is "liner" service. Liners move general cargo, usually in containerships, from port to port at fixed rates according to a regular schedule.

The liner segment of the U.S. flag international maritime industry is composed of seven ship-operating companies, down from 18 in 1970. As shown

TABLE 7-2

Principal Merchant Fleets of the World, by Number of Ships, 1992

Country	Number of Ships	Rank
Panama	3,040	1
Liberia	1,550	2
China	1,359	3
Cyprus	1,210	4
Japan	944	5
Greece	914	6
Norway	770	7
Bahamas	756	8
British Dep. Terr.	712	9
Malta	640	10
Philippines	536	11
Italy	493	12
Germany	492	13
Singapore	478	14
South Korea	445	15
U.S. (Privately Owned)	394	16
All Others[a]	9,210	
Total	23,943	

[a]Includes ships owned by the United States government.

SOURCE: U.S. Department of Transportation, Federal Maritime Administration *Merchant Fleets of the World* (Washington, D.C.: the Department, 1992), p. 10.

in Table 7-3, these companies vary considerably in size. Two of those companies, Sea-Land Service Inc. (41 containerships), and American President Lines Ltd.(27 containerships), control approximately 84 percent of the capacity of the U.S. containership fleet.[8]

The market share of oceanborne foreign trade tonnage handled by the American liner fleet declined from 30.7 percent in 1975 to 18.6 percent in 1990, but in terms of absolute tonnage handled its traffic has grown steadily in recent years.[9] In terms of value of liner traffic handled by U.S. carriers, their market share declined from 31.2 percent in 1970 to 21.5 percent in 1990 (see Table 7-4).

TABLE 7-3

Containership Fleets of U.S. Flag Liner Companies, 1993

Company	Number of U.S. Flag Containerships
Sea-Land	41
American President	27
Lykes Brothers	14
Matson Navigation	6
Crowley	3
Farrell Lines	2
Central Gulf/Waterman	1
Total	94

SOURCE: Data supplied by U.S. Department of Transportation, Maritime Administration, Washington, D.C, 1993.

The commodities handled by the U.S. liner fleet vary in the export and import markets. The leading export commodities are pulp and wastepaper, paper and paper products, wood and cork and plastics. The most significant import traffic consists of iron and steel, fruits and vegetables, and road vehicles and parts.[10]

The U.S. flag liner fleet is among the most modern in the world. While its operating costs are quite high relative to its competition, it has attempted to remain competitive through maintenance of high quality service, aggressive marketing, and the provision of door-to-door intermodal services through alliances with railroads and trucking companies. As discussed in earlier chapters, landbridge and related service offerings provide land-sea combination service under through-rates, and have become increasingly important as a competitive factor. The volume of intermodal traffic moving via such plans has grown dramatically. In one interesting international development, Sea-Land has initiated a joint venture program within the former Soviet Union to provide landbridge services between the Far East and Eastern Europe.[11]

Over many international trade routes liner operators have established a variety of agreements to restrict competition and/or limit overcapacity. One such form of cooperative agreement is the liner "conference" system, which is prevalent in most developed trade routes. The conferences are granted immunity from U.S. antitrust laws. There are several hundred liner conferences throughout the world. Some are very narrowly defined, covering specific ports in one

TABLE 7-4

U.S. Oceanborne Liner Trade and Market Share of U.S. Flag Carriers

Tonnage (Millions)	1980	1985	1986	1987	1988	1989	1990
Total Tons	59.3	66.7	71.8	79.4	83.3	91.6	85.4
US Flag Tons	16.2	14.0	14.3	11.9	14.0	17.5	15.9
US Flag Percentage	27.3	21.0	19.9	14.9	16.9	19.1	18.6

Value ($Billions)	1980	1985	1986	1987	1988	1989	1990
Total Value	136.9	181.2	199.9	221.9	253.4	279.7	286.3
US Flag Value	39.2	43.4	46.5	41.7	53.1	65.0	61.6
US Flag Percentage	28.7	24.0	23.3	18.8	21.0	23.3	21.5

SOURCE: U.S. Department of Transportation, Maritime Administration, *1991 Annual Report* (Washington, D.C.: the Department, 1992), p. 17 and earlier editions.

direction. Others cover multiple ports and broad geographic regions. During the past several years a number of "superconferences" have emerged through conference mergers. In the Pacific-Far East trade, 19 conferences have consolidated into three.[12] Similarly, 11 liner companies have formed the Trans-Atlantic Agreement (TAA) which covers the U.S. East Coast-North Europe trade. Members of that conference control nearly 84 percent of the liner traffic that moves over those routes. The balance is handled by independents, including the world's largest liner operator, Evergreen Line of Taiwan.[13]

U.S. flag carriers are active participants in liner conferences. While most conferences are "closed" (not open to new membership), according to U.S. maritime regulations, all conferences serving U.S. ports must be "open" to all new members who are willing to abide by terms of the conference agreement. These terms, which essentially provide for collective ratemaking, must be filed with the U.S. Federal Maritime Commission (FMC), and the terms are made public.

Shippers planning to use liner services typically have a variety of options. They can use the services of conference members at normal conference rates, use independents (which often offer rates which are 10-15 percent lower), or they can sign "service contracts" with the conferences or independents. Such contracts, which have been permitted since passage of the Shipping Act of 1984, provide discounted rates in return for time-volume guarantees from shippers. To date, all ocean conferences serving U.S. ports have prohibited their members from individually entering service contracts with shippers. That is, the service contract is written between the conference and shippers. Independents often write service contracts with shippers.[14] In the first seven years following passage of the 1984 legislation nearly 32,000 service contracts were filed with the FMC.[15]

U.S. flag liner operators also participate in other types of collective agreements involving specific trade routes. One increasingly important area of cooperation involves capacity restriction agreements. The market for liner services has often been plagued with overcapacity, which in turn has depressed rates. To address this issue carriers are now permitted to collectively restrict capacity over particular routes through a variety of agreements which include joint sailing schedules, equipment interchange and "vessel-sharing" programs through which two or more companies jointly operate a single ship.[16] Another common form of cooperation is the "revenue pool". Under the terms of such pooling agreements (which are subject to FMC approval), each pool member receives a specified percentage of the total freight revenues earned by all pool members, and agrees to a minimum number of sailings along that trade route.

Liner conferences have been subjected to considerable criticisms concerning their collective ratemaking and capacity restriction activities. Critics contend that collective pricing agreements protect inefficient carriers and stifle innovation, while supporters argue that the reduction in competition is more than offset by the stability in rates and carrier finance fostered by the conferences.

The cost structure of U.S. flag liner operations tends to be heavily weighted with fixed costs. This is particularly true with respect to the companies whose fleets consist primarily of container ships. It has been estimated that nearly 75 percent of the costs incurred by such operations do not vary with traffic volume.[17]

Generally speaking, U.S. flag liner companies incur higher capital and operating costs than their foreign-flag competitors. Their ship acquisition costs are higher because they historically purchased vessels built in U.S. shipyards, and their crew costs are typically two to six times greater than those of their foreign-flag competitors.[18] The crew cost differential is caused by their use of U.S. crews rather than foreign crews, and U.S. regulations which dictate higher "manning" requirements for U.S. flag operators. These cost-related matters are discussed later in this chapter.

The financial performance of U.S. flag liner companies engaged in foreign trade has been rather erratic in recent years. While the industry has been marginally profitable in recent years, its return on equity has been substantially lower than that of American industry in general. That financial performance, coupled with the large-scale capital needs of liner operators to modernize their fleets, has raised serious questions concerning the future capital access of such operators. This has prompted those companies to call upon Congress to provide financial assistance to the industry.

Tanker and Dry Bulk Operations. U.S. flag carriers also participate in the movement of liquid and dry bulk commodities in international markets. The liquid traffic, which moves in tankers, consists almost exclusively of crude petroleum and petroleum products. The major dry bulk commodities moved are grain, forest products, coal and iron ore.

In terms of total tonnage carried, the U.S. tanker and dry bulk trades greatly exceed U.S. liner volume (by nearly 10 to 1).[19] However, U.S. flag carriers handle only a small percentage of that traffic. American operators historically have had trouble competing with foreign-flag carriers due to their relatively high vessel acquisition and operating costs. Their most significant cost disadvantage involves crew costs. On the average, the crew costs of U.S. flag tanker and dry bulk carriers are approximately three times as great as those of their foreign-flag competitors. Further, crew costs are a much higher percentage of total costs in tanker and dry bulk operations than in the liner trades.

International tanker and dry bulk markets are very price competitive. Overcapacity has been a chronic problem, and collective pricing agreements do not exist in those markets.

The U.S. tanker fleet consists of approximately 200 ships, down nearly one-third since the early 1980s. It carries less than three percent of the petroleum moving to and from the country.[20] However, vessels controlled by U.S. companies but registered under flags of convenience carry most of the balance of that traffic. The flags of convenience carriers are able to operate at lower costs through use of foreign-built vessels and foreign crews. The competitive pressures in international trade routes have been so intense that a number of U.S. flag tankers have withdrawn from international operations and are now providing domestic services.

The U.S. flag dry bulk fleet in foreign trade service consists of 25 ships, many of which are more than 20 years old.[21] They face formidable foreign-flag competition, which generally uses newer, more efficient vessels and lower cost foreign crews. Among their competitors are the U.S. controlled, foreign-flag operators that carry a large portion of American coal and grain exports. Many industry observers believe that the U.S. flag dry bulk operations are only able to survive through carriage of "cargo preference" traffic that the federal government effectively reserves for them. Cargo preference policies are discussed later in this chapter.

Specialized Middlemen. There are a variety of middleman who also play important roles in international waterborne commerce. Foremost among these are ocean freight forwarders, non-vessel operating common carriers (NVOCCs), and customs brokers.

Ocean freight forwarders are licensed by the Federal Maritime Commission. More than 3,200 forwarders act as agents for shippers in dealing with ocean carriers. Most are quite small and localized in nature, many serving only one international port. Due to the nature of their operations, there are quite modest capital requirements to enter the industry, and turnover has historically been substantial. Nevertheless, some large forwarders, such as Fritz Companies, have emerged and their operations are international in scope. Many of the smaller forwarders effectively broaden their service areas through agency agreements with other forwarders.

The relationship between ocean freight forwarders, ocean carriers and shippers is quite interesting. Generally, shippers do not deal directly with ocean carriers. Rather, ocean forwarders function in a classic middleman capacity linking shippers and the carriers. Shippers typically contact the forwarders to discuss their transportation requirements. Although they generally do not take possession of the cargo, forwarders can provide a wealth of information concerning such matters as ocean carrier schedules, rates and documentation requirements. Having decided which service best suits the needs of the specific shipper, the forwarder books the shipment with the carrier.

In addition to booking space for shippers with ocean carriers, ocean freight forwarders may also:

1. obtain the necessary equipment, such as ocean containers, for shippers
2. arrange for pick up and delivery of containers in both the port of origin and the destination port
3. arrange for customs clearance at the destination port
4. handle the related shipment documentation and review it prior to shipment
5. provide shippers with the import regulations of the destination country
6. arrange for shipment insurance
7. and, identify warehousemen and distribution channels in the destination market.

Not all shippers want the full range of these services; however, many do. The forwarding fees charged vary according to the services required. In addition, the forwarders also receive a commission from the ocean carriers, usually a minimum of 1.25 percent of the ocean freight charges paid by the shipper.[22]

Under federal law, NVOCCs are considered to be common carriers which do not operate ocean vessels. As such they are subject to FMC regulations. The approximately 1,500 NVOCCs are primarily freight consolidators whose business essentially consists of consolidation less-than-container freight into container shipments which are subsequently tended to ocean carriers. They often negotiate discounted service contract rates with the ocean carriers and make most of their money on the spread between the full container rates they obtain from the carriers and the less-than-container rates which they charge shippers. As common carriers the NVOCCs assume full responsibility for shippers' cargoes and issue their own bills of lading. They must file their rates with the FMC (ocean freight forwarders are not required to do so).

The services of customs brokers may also be of value to those importing goods into the United States. These intermediaries facilitate the movement of goods through customs while attempting to assure that the goods bear the lowest legal import duties. They are licensed by the U.S. Treasury Department.

There has been a recent consolidation of companies which act as intermediaries in ocean transportation. Many mergers have occurred, and as a result it is not uncommon to find a single company offering "one stop shopping" as an ocean forwarder, an NVOCC and a customs broker.

"Shippers' associations" also act as intermediaries in international ocean transportation. The Shipping Act of 1984 made formation of such associations possible, and many have been subsequently formed. They are voluntary, non-profit organizations formed by shippers to take advantage of their collective purchasing power in dealing with ocean carriers. To a great extent shipper associations perform many of the same functions for its members which would have been performed for them individually by ocean freight forwarders and NVOCCs. Cost savings are shared by association members.

Federal Regulatory and Promotional Activities

Federal involvement in U.S. maritime affairs dates back to the 18th Century, when Congress developed a system of tariffs to protect U.S. shipbuilding and ship-operating companies. Since that time, federal maritime policy has evolved into a complex pattern of regulatory and promotional activities. Proponents of this governmental involvement have traditionally argued that it is justified not only in economic terms, but also with respect to national military preparedness.

Regulation. Federal economic regulation of the maritime industry is administered by the Federal Maritime Commission (FMC). The regulatory powers of the agency originated in the Shipping Act of 1916 and subsequent revisions of that statute. The most important of those revisions were contained in the Shipping

Act of 1984. That legislation not only redefined the agency's regulatory powers, but also authorized the use of service contracts and the establishment of shippers' associations.[23]

While the FMC has no control over entry of new carriers or carrier mergers, it has considerable power with respect to carrier ratemaking and conference agreements. The agency has the authority to grant antitrust immunity to conferences and can approve, cancel, and modify conference agreements. Prior FMC approval is needed for any form of anticompetitive agreement such as collective ratemaking or pooling.

Ocean carriers and conferences are required to file their rates on all commodities (except those moving in dry bulk and tanker operations) with the Commission. Under the 1984 Act the Commission monitors and enforces tariff rates and service contracts and prosecutes any violation of the Act's tariff provisions including charging other than filed rates or illegal rebating. If foreign flag carriers violate FMC guidelines, the agency is empowered to deny the offending country's national flag lines access to U.S. ports. Further, if the agency believes that foreign governments are discriminating against U.S. flag carriers the agency can take action against ocean carriers flagged in those countries. In response to such threats, in 1992 the South Korean government changed its rail and trucking policies which clearly discriminated against U.S. carriers which were attempting to offer door-to-door service between the U.S. and South Korea.[24]

The regulatory responsibilities of the FMC also include the licensing and regulation of ocean freight forwarders and NVOCCs.

Federal maritime safety regulations are administered by the U.S. Coast Guard, which is an operating unit of the Department of Transportation. The Coast Guard enforces regulations governing navigation, vessel inspection, port safety and security, marine environmental protection, and resource conservation. It also sets ship construction and safety standards, and maintains a fleet of rescue vessels, aircraft, and communications facilities to aid vessel operators.

Promotion. Throughout the years the federal government has played a major promotional role with respect to the development of the U.S. maritime industry. In addition to a variety of tax incentives, the promotional programs have included construction differential subsidies (CDS), operating differential subsidies (ODS), ship financing guarantees, cargo preference laws, and "cabotage" requirements. Development and administration of these promotional programs are the responsibilities of the federal Maritime Administration (MARAD) which in 1982 ceased to operate as an independent agency and became a component of the Department of Transportation.

The Merchant Marine Act of 1936 authorized construction and operating differential subsidies to U.S. maritime operators to help offset the vessel acquisition and operating cost disadvantages faced by U.S. flag operators. As

TABLE 7-5

U.S. Maritime Subsidy Outlays, 1936-1991

Fiscal Year	CDS	Reconstruction CDS [a]	CDS	ODS	Total ODS & CDS
1936–1955	$ 248,320,942	$ 3,286,888	$ 251,607,830	$ 341,109,987	$ 592,717,817
1956–1960	129,806,005	34,881,409	164,687,414	644,115,146	808,802,560
1961	100,145,654	1,215,432	101,361,086	150,142,575	251,503,661
1962	134,552,647	4,160,591	138,713,238	181,918,756	320,631,994
1963	89,235,895	4,181,314	93,417,209	220,676,685	314,093,894
1964	76,608,323	1,665,087	78,273,410	203,036,844	281,310,254
1965	86,096,872	38,138	86,135,010	213,334,409	299,469,419
1966	69,446,510	2,571,566	72,018,076	186,628,357	258,646,433
1967	80,155,452	932,114	81,087,566	175,631,860	256,719,426
1968	95,989,586	96,707	96,086,293	200,129,670	296,215,963
1969	93,952,849	57,329	94,010,178	194,702,569	288,712,747
1970	73,528,904	21,723,343	95,252,247	205,731,711	300,983,958
1971	107,637,353	27,450,968	135,088,321	268,021,097	403,109,418
1972	111,950,403	29,748,076	141,698,479	235,666,830	377,365,310
1973	168,183,937	17,384,604	185,568,541	226,710,926	412,279,467
1974	185,060,501	13,844,951	198,905,452	257,919,080	456,824,532
1975	237,895,092	1,900,571	239,795,663	243,152,340	482,948,003
1976 [b]	233,826,424	9,886,024	243,712,448	386,433,994	630,146,442
1977	203,479,571	15,052,072	218,531,643	343,875,521	562,407,164
1978	148,690,842	7,318,705	156,009,547	303,193,575	459,203,122
1979	198,518,437	2,258,492	200,776,929	300,521,683	501,298,612
1980	262,727,122	2,352,744	265,079,865	341,368,236	606,448,102
1981	196,446,214	11,666,978	208,113,192	334,853,670	542,966,862
1982	140,774,519	43,710,698	184,485,217	400,689,713	585,174,930
1983	76,991,138	7,519,881	84,511,019	368,194,331	452,705,350
1984	13,694,523	–0–	13,694,523	384,259,674	397,954,197
1985	4,692,013	–0–	4,692,013	351,730,642	356,422,655
1986	–416,673	–0–	–416,673	287,760,640	287,343,867
1987	420,700	–0–	420,700	227,426,103	227,846,803
1988	1,236,379	–0–	1,236,679	230,188,400	231,425,079
1989	–0–	–0–	–0–	212,294,812	212,294,812
1990	–0–	–0–	–0–	230,971,797	230,971,797
1991	–0–	–0–	–0–	217,574,038	217,574,038
Total	$3,569,648,434	$264,904,682	$3,834,553,116	$9,069,965,572	$12,904,518.688

a Includes $131.5 million CDS adjustments covering the World War II period, $105.8 million equivalent to CDS allowances which were made in connection with the Mariner Ship Construction Program, and $10.8 million for CDS in fiscal years 1954 to 1955.

b Includes totals for FY 1976 and the Transition Quarter ending September 30, 1976.

SOURCE: U.S. Department of Transportation, Maritime Administration, *1991 Annual Report* (Washington, D.C.: the Department, 1992), p. 81.

shown in Table 7-5, since that time nearly $13 billion in construction and operating subsidies has been granted under those programs.

The problems that originally led Congress to provide financial assistance to U.S. operators still exist, and in some instances they have intensified. Because of their high cost structure and the relative efficiency of their foreign competitors, U.S. shipyards are not competitive in the world market. To partially offset the related cost disadvantage, MARAD was empowered to provide construction subsidies of up to 50 percent of the cost of U.S. built vessels that were purchased by U.S. operators. However, because of the magnitude of the existing cost differential between U.S. shipyards and shipyards in countries such as Korea and Japan, construction subsidy levels still failed to equalize the competitive situation. In reality, construction differential subsidies were indirect subsidies to U.S. shipyards and without them those shipbuilding facilities and their employees would have been quite vulnerable to foreign competition. A combination of the CDS payments and cargo preference and cabotage policies (see later discussion) created an artificial market for U.S.built vessels. Despite the existence of these programs, U.S. shipyards continued to experience financial problems into the early 1980s.

The Reagan Administration, which had been quite critical of the CDS program in terms of its cost effectiveness, cut off CDS funding in fiscal year 1982. The DOT subsequently announced that it intended to phase out the program and that no future CDS funding would be made available. Despite continuing pressures from shipbuilding interests the Bush administration did not reinstate CDS funding. During the early days of his administration President Clinton showed little sign of reversing that policy.

Consequently, U.S. shipyards now seldom build merchant ships. In fact, only one new commercial ship was under contract with a U.S. shipyard in 1993.[25] However, those shipyards are still among world leaders in building military vessels. While the CDS program has been eliminated, the U.S. Navy has continued to give large-scale ship construction contracts to the shipyards. Without a major shift in federal policy, it appears quite likely that U.S. shipbuilding capacity will continue to decline and that U.S. vessel operators will acquire most of their vessels from foreign shipyards. The military preparedness implications of this reduction in U.S. shipyard capacity are unclear and continue to be debated in Congress.

The Merchant Marine Act of 1936 also established an operating differential subsidy program. As noted earlier in this chapter, U.S. vessel operating costs have been much higher than those of foreign competitors, primarily due to differences in crew costs. Under the provisions of the ODS program, MARAD has provided up to 20 percent of ship operating costs to U.S.

flag companies operating in competition with lower cost foreign vessels over what MARAD has deemed to be essential trade routes.

ODS payments have been quite important to U.S.-flag carriers in the liner trades. During 1991 58 liners and 34 bulk ships qualified for such payments. That year Lykes (25 ships) and American President Lines (23 ships) were the major beneficiaries of the program.[26] In recent years, ODS payments have comprised approximately 6 to 7 percent of the revenues of these firms. As shown in Table 7-5, ODS payments were more than $217 million in 1991.

Cargo preference programs and cabotage requirements also effectively reserve some waterborne traffic for U.S. flag operators. The federal government grants preference to U.S. flag operators in the movement of government traffic in international markets. The traffic involved consists primarily of Agency for International Development and Export-Import Bank cargoes and military traffic. The movement of preference traffic has been particularly important on major U.S. liner routes, because historically, commercial traffic along these routes has been predominantly inbound in nature. Thus the preference traffic provides U.S. flag liner operators with more balanced traffic flows and facilitates better equipment utilization. On an annual basis, cargo preference traffic generates 16 to 17 percent of U.S. flag liner operating revenues.[27] U.S. flag vessel operators also benefit from cabotage requirements. Under the provisions of the Jones Act (1920), all vessels operating in domestic trade, including coastwise, intercoastal, noncontiguous (shipping routes serving Alaska and non-continental U.S. states and territories), and on inland routes must have been constructed in the U.S. They must also be registered in the U.S. and manned by U.S. crews. Restriction of such "coasting" traffic to vessels registered in the country involved is a common maritime policy throughout the world. It has been periodically suggested that the U.S. built requirement be eliminated, and that foreign-built, U.S. registered vessels be permitted to enter the domestic trades. While this would substantially lower the acquisition cost of such vessels, Congress has not chosen to waive this requirement.

The federal government also provides a variety of tax incentives and loan guarantee programs to support U.S. flag ocean carriers.

Important Policy Issues

U.S. maritime policy is obviously complex and subject to ongoing federal analysis. In attempting to formulate rationale public policy, Congress, the FMC and MARAD must weigh the interests of many parties including the shipping public, the military, ocean carriers, shipbuilders, and seafaring and shipyard labor organizations.

The continuing financial problems of the ocean carrier and shipbuilding industries in the U.S. continue to attract considerable attention at the federal level. During each presidential campaign the candidates promise a thorough reassessment of related policies, but progress has been slow.

U.S. shipbuilding interests continue to lobby for reinstitution of the CDS program and sanctions against what they believe to be heavily subsidized foreign shipyards. They contend that those subsidies, and the absence of similar supports in the U.S., make it impossible for them to compete effectively in world markets. U.S. flag ocean carriers maintain that extensive federal regulations, which govern their operations in such diverse areas as manning requirements and ship repairs, artificially inflate their costs and limit their competitiveness.

During the Bush administration the President appointed several study groups and task forces to evaluate the regulatory structure, tax policies and shipbuilding laws which affect our maritime industries.[28] Similarly, at the urging of the White House, the FMC conducted its own analysis of maritime regulations.[29] While those efforts led to suggestions for change, Congress failed to act. Early in the Clinton administration maritime interests met with Secretary Pena to discuss the need for change, but by mid-1993 no congressional action had been taken. In frustration, the two largest U.S. flag liner companies, Sea Land and American President Lines, announced their intention to begin the process of reflagging a large percentage of their fleets outside the United States.[30]

INTERNATIONAL AVIATION

While international air operations began prior to World War I, the international aviation system as it exists today was shaped primarily in the post-World War II period. Many airlines (most of them government owned) had instituted international service prior to the war, but much of the industry's capacity was destroyed during the conflict.

Toward the end of the war, representatives of 54 nations met in Chicago to establish a framework to facilitate the exchange of international aviation traffic between nations. At the conference there was considerable diversity of opinion among representatives concerning the most appropriate format for international aviation agreements. The polar positions were represented by the United States, which sought equality of opportunity for carriers in an essentially unregulated environment, and the United Kingdom, which advocated strict regulation of entry, fares, flight frequencies, and market share. The position of the United Kingdom was undoubtedly influenced by the relative strength of American carriers at that time, since their European counterparts had been devastated by the war.

While these differences, and many others, could not be resolved at the Chicago conference, the participants created the International Civil Aviation

Organization (ICAO), which later became a component of the United Nations. The ICAO has subsequently played an important role in standardizing the technical aspects of international civil aviation. The organization's primary mission has been the promotion of safety in international air transportation, while encouraging the development of airports, airways, and air navigation facilities. Due to the complexity of international law, ICAO recommends safety rules and standards, but their actual implementation is left to the individual nations participating in ICAO agreements.

Bilateral Agreements and the Role of IATA

In an attempt to resolve their differences, the United States and the United Kingdom met again in Bermuda in early 1946. This meeting established the pattern for international aviation agreements which, to a great extent, continues today. In a compromise agreement, the United Kingdom agreed to relax its posture concerning strict capacity limitation, and the United States agreed to accept fares set by carrier agreement through the International Air Transport Association (IATA), subject to government approval.[31] The two countries exchanged traffic rights between specific city pairs, and carriers were selected. The carriers were then permitted to provide service between those city pairs.

The "bilateral" negotiating format established in the Bermuda Agreement became the model for many subsequent agreements between nations. That format was later modified by the United States and the United Kingdom in the "Bermuda 2" agreement which is discussed later in this chapter.

As a result of the Chicago and 1946 Bermuda meetings, "five freedoms of the air" were recognized by the United States and the United Kingdom. They were to provide the "freedom" to:

1.   fly across territory of a foreign nation without landing
2.   land for purposes other than traffic
3.   set down in a foreign country traffic coming from the country of the airline's nationality
4.   pick up in a foreign country traffic destined for the country of the airline's nationality
5.   carry traffic from a point of origin in one foreign country to a point of destination in another foreign country.

While these freedoms were subsequently recognized by many other nations in their aviation agreements, their specific application or non-application in aviation agreements between any two countries was, and is, a function of the negotiations carried out between those nations. A "sixth freedom" was later added to the list. It gives a carrier the freedom to pick up traffic in one country, move it through the country of the airline's nationality, then fly it to a third country.

The Bermuda agreement on pricing legitimized the concept of collective ratemaking in international aviation. IATA was originally established in 1919 by a group of European airlines to facilitate cooperation between carriers and to provide a forum for discussion and agreement on rates. It became worldwide in scope in 1944 when it absorbed a rival organization, the Conference of International Air Transport Operators. By 1946, the organization had achieved sufficient stature in the international aviation community that both the United States and the United Kingdom were willing to entrust basic international airline ratemaking responsibility to the organization.

Status of International Commercial Aviation

International commercial aviation has expanded dramatically since the Bermuda agreement was signed. The number of air carriers providing international service has grown steadily, and some of the larger carries such as American Airlines, United Airlines, Delta Air Lines, Air France, British Airways, Lufthansa German Airlines and Japan Airlines have embarked on globalization strategies.[32] Many airlines have developed alliances with carriers in other countries to effectively broaden their global market coverage.

More than 200 airlines provide regularly scheduled international services. They include both passenger and cargo carriers. The services of the scheduled carriers are supplemented by those offered by many non-scheduled (charter) operators. The charter operators generally offer lower fares and fewer amenities than their scheduled counterparts, and they have become formidable competitors over many international routes. Thousands of international air freight forwarders also support the cargo operations of scheduled and non-scheduled carriers.

IATA has become the dominant industry trade association consisting of 210 airlines that offer scheduled international airline services. Membership in IATA is voluntary, and some scheduled airlines have chosen not to become members of the organization. However, IATA members generate nearly 97 percent of the world's total scheduled airline traffic.[33]

For the purpose of collective pricing, IATA operates through three conferences that correspond to different areas of the world. All member carriers in a particular conference area may participate in fare discussions, and each carrier, regardless of size, has one vote in the ratemaking process. The resulting fare schedules are then subject to the approval of each member carrier's government. The organization also has joint conferences to deal with matters that affect more than one conference, and a composite conference that deals with matters on a worldwide basis. Each conference is supported by committees, subcommittees, and working groups and meets once each year to discuss and agree upon fare policies for both passenger and freight movements. It often has been quite difficult for IATA to reconcile member differences concerning fare policies, and in some instances a new agreement has been reached just prior to the expiration of an existing one. As previously noted, some international airlines are not members of IATA, and those carriers sometimes offer fares that differ substantially from those of IATA members.

While IATA's existence has contributed to stability in the fare structure of scheduled operators, it often has been criticized as being an ineffective pricing cartel. This matter is discussed later in this chapter.

TABLE 7-6

Financial Results, IATA International Scheduled Services,
1987-1991, in Billions of Dollars

	1987	1988	1989	1990	1991
Operating Revenues	53.8	60.9	70.7	91.0	91.7
Operating Expenses	51.3	57.5	68.1	90.5	92.3
Result before Interest	2.5	3.4	2.6	0.5	-0.6
Net Interest Payable	1.6	1.8	2.3	3.2	3.4
Result after Interest	0.9	1.6	0.3	-2.7	-4.0

SOURCE: International Air Transport Association, Market and Economic Analysis Division, Montreal, Canada.

As shown in Table 7-6, the aggregate financial performance of IATA members in international operations has been quite poor in recent years. During the three year period, 1990-1992, IATA members registered aggregate losses of approximately $8.7 billion in providing international scheduled services.[34] Those losses, which have threatened the financial viability of many international carriers, have been caused by a variety of factors. These include world wide recessionary pressure, the precipitous decline in international traffic related to the Gulf War, heavy debt loads, and rising fuel costs.

These continuing losses have troubled both private and government-owned airlines operating in international markets. Many of the world's international airlines are government-owned and exist for a variety of reasons including national prestige, military preparedness, and balance-of-payments considerations. While they have not typically been subjected to the same rigorous profit/loss scrutiny that their private-sector counterparts experience, the size of their recent losses has led some national governments to aggressively pursue the option of "privatization."

Despite the softening of demand for international passenger and cargo services which occurred during the early 1990s, industry officials are quite optimistic about future traffic volume. IATA has forecasted an annual growth in international passenger traffic of 7.4 percent between 1992 and 1996. If realized, the number of passengers carried in scheduled international service would reach 376 million by 1996.[35] International air cargo volume was projected to grow by 6.9 percent per year during the same period, reaching 13.1 million tons by 1996.[36]

The U.S. Role in International Aviation

U.S. carrier participation in international aviation includes the operations of scheduled and non-scheduled (charter) airlines, air cargo carriers, and air freight forwarders. These carriers participate in a market that has grown substantially during the past several decades. In many segments of this market they face considerable foreign carrier competition.

The American carrier share of the U.S. international passenger market, as measured in terms of both inbound and outbound passenger trips, has averaged 50 percent in recent years.[37] Approximately 90 percent of all passenger traffic moving between the U.S. and foreign countries moves via scheduled service. In scheduled operations, nearly 80 percent of U.S. carrier revenues are generated by passenger traffic, and the balance originates in freight and mail.[38]

U.S. based charter airlines cater to the more price-sensitive segments of the international travel markets, and their fares and cargo rates are generally much lower than those of scheduled airlines flying the same routes. In certain markets, particularly Transatlantic routes, charters provide important competition for the scheduled airlines.

A number of large, U.S. based airlines have become major factors in international passenger travel. These carriers, including such companies as American Airlines, Continental Airlines, Delta Air Lines, Northwest Airlines, United Airlines and USAir, are among the largest airlines in the world and have each increasingly "globalized" their route networks in recent years. They have done so in several ways. First, they have applied to the Department of Transportation (DOT) and been granted additional international route awards. Second, as shown in Table 7-7, some have purchased international routes from other airlines. Such purchases are subject to DOT approval. Third, some airlines have established alliances with foreign carriers to effectively broaden their markets. The marketing and operational alliances established between USAir and British Airways in 1993 and those which exist between Northwest Airlines and KLM Royal Dutch Airlines provide illustrations of such linkages. In some instances,

TABLE 7-7

Selected International Route Sales Between Major U.S. Airlines,
1986-1992

Buyer	Seller	Route	Price ($Millions)
American	Eastern	Latin American System	$471
	TWA	3 US-London Routes	445
Delta	Pan Am	European Routes	526
	Pan Am	New York-Mexico City	25
Northwest	America West	Honolulu-Nagoya, Japan	15
	Hawaiian	Pacific Routes	9
USAir	TWA	2 US-London Routes	50
United	Pan Am	Pacific Routes	716
	Pan Am	US-London	400
	Pan Am	Latin American System, Los Angeles-Mexico City	148

SOURCE: U.S. General Accounting Office, *Airline Competition: Impact of Changing Foreign Investment and Control Limits on U.S. Airlines* (Washington, D.C.: General Accounting Office, 1992), p. 40.

such alliances have involved investment by foreign carriers in U.S. airlines. Federal law limits such investment to 25 percent of the voting stock of the U.S. carrier.[39] This issue has become quite controversial, particularly in view of the failure of such companies as Eastern Airlines and Trans World Airlines and the continuing financial problems of several other U.S. carriers flying international routes (see subsequent discussion later in this chapter).

Despite the financial problems of some of the U.S. carriers flying international routes, companies such as American Airlines, Delta Air Lines and United Airlines are among the strongest in the world. Their extensive route structures and reputations for high quality service cause concerns in many other countries about their potential domination of international passenger transportation. Such concerns have led not only to exploration of possible mergers between the nationalized airlines of other countries, but also to calls for limiting their impact through more restrictive bilateral agreements with the United States.

U.S. participation in the movement of international air cargo has also expanded significantly during the past several years. The passenger airlines, who historically carried the bulk of U.S. international air cargo in the bellies of passenger planes, have now been joined by such air cargo specialists as DHL Worldwide Express, Emery Worldwide, Federal Express (which paid $880 million for Tiger International in 1989 to obtain its international route network) and United Parcel Service in providing frequent, dependable air cargo service on a worldwide basis. Collectively those carriers provide cargo linkages between the U.S. and thousands of foreign destinations. The majority of traffic handled by those carriers consists of perishable foodstuffs, fashion goods, cut flowers, computers, electronics, and documents.

Some of the larger U.S. based air cargo companies have not only attempted to establish effective ground handling and distribution systems in foreign countries, but also sought to offer other services within those countries. In some cases their service offerings have also expanded to include services between foreign countries. This managerial process has been complex, very expensive, and often constrained by foreign governments. In most instances, those factors have combined to produce sizeable losses for the carriers. During 1992, Federal Express, after losing several hundred million dollars in its European operations, dramatically scaled-back its involvement in Europe.[40] United Parcel Service, which expects to generate one-third of its revenues from international operations by 2000, has also registered sizeable international losses, but expects many of those operations to begin to generate profits by the mid-1990s.[41]

The international cargo operations of both the passenger and cargo carriers are supported by a network of several thousand air freight forwarders. Those forwarders generally provide a range of services similar to those outlined in the earlier discussion of ocean freight forwarding. Their services are particularly important to the U.S. based passenger airlines in generating international air cargo volume because most of those carriers do not maintain sales and marketing organizations to sell those services.

Federal Regulation. The federal government plays an active role in international aviation. That role involves negotiation of aviation agreements with other countries, awarding of international routes to U.S. carriers, controlling foreign investment in U.S. carriers, price regulation, and safety regulation.

Bilateral Agreements. Aviation agreements between the United States and other countries are primarily based on the bilateral agreements negotiated by the two countries. The U.S. currently has more than 70 aviation bilaterals in effect.[42] In addition to specifying the "freedoms" to be granted, a bilateral may also specify such issues as the number of carriers permitted to fly the routes involved, airports to be served, frequency of service offered by those carriers, and the capacity to be offered.

The U.S. strategy for a particular bilateral negotiation is typically developed by the Department of Transportation and the State Department in consultation with U.S. airlines, airports, labor representatives and industry groups. The negotiating team is led by the State Department and generally includes DOT officials and representatives of carrier, airport and labor interests. The U.S. representatives meet with their foreign counterparts and the details of the bilateral are negotiated.

The nature of bilateral aviation agreements between the U.S. and other nations has changed considerably since the 1946 Bermuda agreement was signed. Under the terms of that agreement and subsequent bilaterals involving the U.S., the capacity of U.S. carriers on related routes typically was not limited; that is, carriers were relatively free to add flights if they believed that demand conditions warranted such action. That freedom prompted a major confrontation between the United States and the United Kingdom during 1976-1977. In June, 1976 the British announced their intention to terminate the Bermuda 1 agreement effective June 1, 1977. While there were many reasons for this action, the primary complaint of the British was that U.S. carriers were offering excessive capacity on United States-United Kingdom routes, and that this produced a commercial imbalance. At the time U.S. carriers were generating three times the revenues of British carriers serving those routes.[43] The British sought to tighten regulation of capacity over those routes, which clashed with the prevailing pro-competitive U.S. regulatory philosophy. After long and tense negotiations, Bermuda 2 was signed on July 23, 1977.

While neither American nor British carriers were completely satisfied with the terms of the "Bermuda 2" agreement, it represented a significant compromise. Some new carriers from both countries were permitted to enter the markets, but they had to submit schedules to their governments for prescreening. If problems arose, a mechanism was provided whereby the governments would contact each other and work out their differences.

In the years which have followed the signing of the Bermuda 2 agreement the United States has pushed aggressively for "open skies" bilaterals which would open international markets to more American carriers while increasing service levels and carrier capacity along those routes. While some countries agree with this concept, most notably the Netherlands which signed such an agreement with the U.S. in 1992, many other countries are strongly opposed to it.[44]The United Kingdom, France, Germany, Spain, Italy and Japan have all called for new bilateral aviation agreements with the United States which would be more restrictive than those currently in place.[45] Clearly those positions have been taken because of fear of the potential market impact of the "Big Three" U.S. carriers in an unrestricted international aviation marketplace. Along many international routes American carriers already have established dominant market positions (for example, 65 percent of the passengers in the United States-France market by 1992). France felt so strongly about this issue that it renounced its 46 year old bilateral agreement with the U.S. in 1992, triggering a new wave of negotiations. Germany and Japan threatened similar action. While the U.S. cannot unilaterally force an "open skies" philosophy on the international aviation community, it is clear that it will continue to aggressively negotiate on behalf of the concept.

International Route Awards. The procedures by which a U.S. company is permitted to institute international air passenger or cargo service have been summarized as follows by the U.S. General Accounting Office: International route awards are currently awarded to U.S. airlines through an administrative process overseen by DOT's Office of International Aviation. International routes on which entry is limited (i.e., the number of U.S. airlines that can offer service or the number of flights that can be operated are limited) are awarded for a period of 5 years. When a new route becomes available or an existing route is up for renewal, airlines submit applications to DOT detailing their service proposals. In selecting which U.S. airline will receive authority, DOT considers, among other factors, which proposal will generate the most competition among the airlines in the market.[46]

Subject to DOT review, U.S. airlines are free to sell their routes to another U.S. airline. DOT considers the effect of the transfer on competition between U.S. airlines and between U.S. airlines and foreign airlines, and the impact on the trade position of the United States in the international transportation market.

Foreign Investment in U.S. Airlines. During the past several years a number of factors have combined to highlight the issue of foreign investment in U.S. airlines. The most important of these have been the continuing financial difficulties of some U.S. carriers and the desire of foreign carriers to obtain greater access to U.S. markets. Under federal law, at least 75 percent of the voting stock of a U.S. airline must be held by U.S. citizens. To attract additional investment in such airlines, in 1991 Secretary of Transportation, Sam Skinner, announced that the DOT would subsequently interpret the law so as to allow a foreign investor to hold as much as 49 percent of an airline's total equity, as long as the investment did not exceed the 25 percent voting stock guideline.

This issue became active during 1992 when British Airways proposed a $750 million investment in financially-troubled USAir in return for 44 percent of the company's voting stock. The investment was strongly opposed by American, Delta and United who argued that the investment should only be permitted if the United Kingdom signed an "open skies" agreement with the U.S.[47] Further, the DOT, while welcoming the potential financial assistance to USAir, could not accept the proposal in view of the 25 percent statutory restriction. After several months of negotiations involving the carriers and the DOT British Airways invested $300 million in USAir in return for 19.9 percent of the company's voting stock. It also took an option to invest $450 million more over the next five years if U.S. regulations changed.[48]

British Airways is not the only foreign carrier interested in investment linkages to U.S. airlines. By late 1992 KLM Royal Dutch Airlines owned 20 percent of Northwest Airlines, Singapore Airlines owned 5 percent of Delta Airlines, SAS had an 18 percent interest in Continental Airlines and Ansett (Australian) owned 20 percent of America West Airlines.[49] By mid-1993 the Department of Transportation was still involved in analysis of the desirability of changing the foreign investment guideline. Congressional action would be necessary to make the change.

Regulation of Pricing. Prior to its elimination in 1985, the CAB regulated international airline pricing over routes linking the United States to other countries. Since 1985 the Department of Transportation has played that role.

International air passenger fares and cargo rates must be filed with the DOT. Those prices may be filed collectively by the carriers through IATA conferences, or individually. All carriers participating in IATA, including U.S. flag airlines, are guaranteed the right to "independent action." Increasingly, those carriers are filing individual prices with the DOT which are lower than official IATA prices. Very few of the proposed prices are challenged by the DOT as the agency seeks to promote the "open skies" pricing philosophy which was discussed earlier.[50]

The specific international aviation prices which are filed with the Department may be subject to three different approval processes, depending upon the nature of the bilateral agreement which has been signed by the U.S. and the foreign country involved. The first of these is the "double approval" standard which means that the DOT and its foreign counterpart must both approve the price before it can take effect. A second standard is "double disapproval" which means that both countries must oppose the price to stop its implementation. If one of the countries approves the proposal, it can take effect. The third standard is "country of origin" which vests final approval with the country from which the flight originates. If that country approves the proposed price, it takes effect; if it opposes the price, it does not. That standard is incorporated into the U.S. bilateral with Germany and has been used by the German government to stop U.S. carriers from lowering prices on routes between the two countries.[51]

Supersonic Transport

The idea of flying at supersonic speeds has intrigued people for many years. In the late 1960s, projects to develop supersonic aircraft for long-distance passenger service were initiated in the United States and the Soviet Union. A similar venture was jointly undertaken by the British and French governments.

The U.S. project relied heavily upon congressional funding. As development progressed in the United States, a variety of questions arose concerning the environmental impact of the supersonic transport (SST). Although the speed advantages of the aircraft were obvious, serious questions were raised about the SST's noise levels and its possible contribution to atmospheric pollution. Others questioned the absolute cost of the project versus the rather limited market applicability of the aircraft. After extensive debate on the merits and costs of the SST, in mid-1971 Congress voted to terminate the U.S. SST project, leaving future development efforts to the Russian and British-French interests.

SST service has since become a reality in international markets, with the British-French Concorde initiating service between Paris and South American cities in early 1976. The Russian TU-144 SST also instituted limited commercial operations. As these services were initiated, pressures grew for the United States to permit the Concorde to service some U.S. cities with transatlantic flights. Once again, this prompted extensive congressional debate. It was decided that the Department of Transportation would make the final determination in this matter. In February 1976, Secretary of Transportation William Coleman announced that the Concorde would be permitted to land at Kennedy International Airport and Dulles International Airport on an experimental basis. Concorde operations into Dulles commenced in May 1976 and service to Kennedy followed.

The DOT decision to permit the Concorde to land in the United States was strongly influenced by political considerations. The British and French governments had invested heavily in the SST development project, and potential markets for SST service were quite limited without landing rights in North America. The decision to allow SST landings in the United States also gave indications that the United States might consider re-entry into supersonic development efforts, the DOT decision having legitimized the concept.

The Concorde has continued to operate and British Airways and Air France contend that their SST services generate an operating profit. The speed of the plane is illustrated by the fact that it provides three and one-half hour service between New York and London, versus six hour service via regular commercial service. However, the two governments, having invested $2.5 billion in the project, stopped producing the plane in 1979 because of lack of market acceptance.

That experience did not mark the end of interest in the concept of commercial supersonic aircraft. To the contrary, the supersonic issue was revived in the U.S. in 1985 when the National Aeronautics and Space Administration awarded contracts to Boeing and McDonnell Douglas to investigate whether a second generation SST could be developed which was not only environmentally more acceptable, but also more efficient to operate. Among the environmental requirements for such a plane are no significant effect on the ozone layer, no community noise created during takeoffs and landings, and no perceptible sonic booms. Economically, it would have to carry more than the 100 passenger payload of the first generation plane.[52]

Small scale SST research continues in the United States. In view of the pace of technological change in the industry, and the continued growth of international passenger travel, a second generation SST commercial aircraft seems quite likely to emerge early in the 21st century.

SUMMARY

The United States is the world's largest trading nation. As such it is very dependent upon high quality transportation linkages to assure the efficient flow of goods to and from the country. The U.S. flag merchant marine fleet, despite continuing financial and competitive problems, continues to play an important role in that regard. While U.S. flag liners have been more successful than their bulk counterparts in attracting maritime traffic, both groups of carriers have been troubled by cost disadvantages in their competition with foreign vessels. These disadvantages are at least partially caused by heavy U.S. regulation of the industry. While the federal government has traditionally offered operating subsidies and other forms of financial assistance to U.S. flag operators to help offset those cost disadvantages, the future of those programs is in doubt. Without decisive congressional action, it appears that the U.S. flag maritime industry will continue to decline.

U.S. air carriers have participated extensively in the globalization of the airline industry. Despite the failure of some large carriers, American carriers are still among the most efficient in the world. The national governments of other country's clearly fear their impact in international markets and have generally resisted U.S. efforts to promote open-skies aviation agreements.

U.S. based companies such as United Parcel Service, Federal Express, and DHL Worldwide have become major participants in international cargo markets. They have not only established linkages between the U.S. and other countries, but have also built extensive ground systems abroad.

DISCUSSION QUESTIONS

1.   Discuss the factors which have led to the decline of the U.S. flag merchant marine since World War II.

2. What was the rationale for the federal Construction Differential Subsidy (CDS) program?
3. Identify and discuss the maritime policies of the Reagan administration.
4. Discuss the role of IATA in the pricing of international airline service.
5. What are bilaterals and why are they important in international aviation?
6. What are the implications of an "open skies" policy in international aviation?

NOTES

1. Vern Terpstra and Ravi Sarathy, *International Marketing*, 5th ed. (Chicago: the Dryden Press, 1991), p. 23.
2. Ibid.
3. Data provided by the International Monetary Fund, Washington, D.C.
4. U.S. Department of Transportation, Maritime Administration, *Merchant Fleets of the World* (Washington, D.C.: the Department, 1992), p. 6.
5. U.S. Department of Transportation, Maritime Administration, *Vessel Inventory Report* (Washington, D.C.: the Department, 1991), p. v.
6. Ibid.
7. U.S. Department of Transportation, Maritime Administration, *1991 Annual Report* (Washington, D.C.: the Department, 1992), p. 10.
8. Transportation Research Board, Special Report 236, *Intermodal Container Transportation: Impediments and Opportunities* (Washington, D.C.: National Research Council, 1992), p. 30.
9. U.S. Department of Transportation, Maritime Administration, *United States Oceanborne Foreign Trade Routes* (Washington, D.C.: the Department, 1992), p. 5.
10. Ibid.
11. Mark Magnier, "Sea-Land Chief: Cost Control to Remain a Priority of Carriers," *Journal of Commerce*, New York, October 11, 1991, p. 5B.
12. Julian Weiss, "Batten Down the Hatches," *Inbound Logistics* (August, 1992), p. 25.
13. Allen S. Roberts, "Race is on to Lure N. Europe Ship Pacts," *Journal of Commerce*, New York, November 4, 1992, p. 1A.
14. *Report to the President and the Congress of the Advisory Commission on Conferences in Ocean Shipping*, p. ix.
15. "Trends in Service Contracting," *American Shipper* (February, 1992), p. 40.
16. Advisory Commission on Conferences in Ocean Shipping, *Report to the President and the Congress of the Advisory Commission on Conferences*

in Ocean Shipping (Washington, D.C.: U.S. Government Printing Office, 1992), p. iii.

17. For a discussion of ship operating costs, see Roy Nersesian, *Ships and Shipping* (Tulsa, OK: Pennwell Publishing, 1981), Chapter 9.

18. U.S. Congress, Office of Technology Assessment, *An Assessment of Maritime Trade and Technology* (Washington, D.C.: U.S. Government Printing Office, 1983), p. 66.

19. Ibid., p. 73.

20. *United States Oceanborne Foreign Trade Routes*, p. 14.

21. *Vessel Inventory Report*, p. v.

22. *Report to the President and the Congress of the Advisory Commission on Conferences in Ocean Shipping*, p. 22.

23. U.S. Congress, *The Merchant Marine Act, 1936-The Shipping Act of 1984 and Related Acts*, as amended through the 101st Congress, 1st Session, January, 1990 (Washington, D.C.: U.S. Government Printing Office, 1991.

24. "Shipyard Subsidies," *Journal of Commerce*, New York, November 10, 1992, p. 8A.

25. Information supplied by the U.S. Department of Transporation, Maritime Administration, Washington, D.C.

26. U.S. Department of Transportation, Maritime Administration, *1991 Annual Report*, pp. 20-1.

27. Office of Technology Assessment, p. 68.

28. William DiBenedetto and Tim Shorrock, "Industry Lauds Creation of Bush Policy Group," *Journal of Commerce*, New York, April 17, 1992, p. 1B.

29. William DiBenedetto, "FMC Panel Lists Possible Deregulation Moves," *Journal of Commerce*, April 1, 1992, p. 1B.

30. Peter M. Tirschwell and Allen R. Wastler, "Sea-Land, APL Move to Reflag Containerships," *Journal of Commerce*, New York, June 30, 1993, p. 1A.

31. For an extensive discussion of Bermuda 1, see Nawal K. Taneja, *U.S. International Aviation Policy* (Lexington, MA: Lexington Books, 1980), pp. 11-14.

32. See "Snapshots of the World's Major International Airlines," *The Wall Street Journal*, New York, January 14, 1992, p. A8.

33. International Air Transport Association, *Annual Report*, 1992 (Montreal, Canada, 1992), p.38

34. See Leo Ryan, "Airlines Now Face Losses for 1993, IATA Head Says," *Journal of Commerce*, New York, October 3, 1992, p. 2B; also, "Global

Airlines Could Lose $2 Billion in '92, IATA Says," *Journal of Commerce*, New York, July 9, 1992, p. 3B.

35. John Zarocostas, "Growth in World Air Freight Traffic Expected to Average 6.9% in 1992-96," *Journal of Commerce*, New York, October 25, 1992, p. 3B.

36. Ibid.

37. Data supplied by the U.S. Department of Transportation, Washington, D.C.

38. Data supplied by the Air Transport Association, Washington, D.C.

39. See U.S. General Accounting Office, *Airline Competition: Impact of Changing Foreign Investment and Control Limits on U.S. Airlines* (Washington, D.C.: General Accounting Office, 1992), p. 2.

40. Bruce Barnard, "Federal Express' European Retreat May Boost Rates," *Journal of Commerce*, New York, March 18, 1992, pp. 1A and 10A.

41. "UPS Aims to Turn Profit in Europe by '94," *Journal of Commerce*, May 7, 1992, p. 3B.

42. U.S. General Accounting Office, *Airline Competition: Impact of Changing Foreign Investment and Control Limits on U.S. Airlines* (Washington, D.C.: General Accounting Office, 1992), p. 42.

43. Taneja, pp. 21-5.

44. Mark Solomon, "US-Dutch Open-Skies Agreement Raises European Aviation Stakes," *Journal of Commerce*, New York, September 10, 1992, p. 2B.

45. Keith M. Rockwell, "US is Prepared to Let Bonn, Paris Air Pacts Lapse," *Journal of Commerce*, New York, August 6, 1992, pp. 1A-2A.

46. U.S. General Accounting Office, *Airline Competition: Impact of Changing Foreign Investment and Control Limits on U.S. Airlines*, p. 18.

47. Mark Solomon, "Executives Seek Open Skies in Return for BA-USAir Deal," *Journal of Commerce*, New York, October 2, 1992, p. 3B.

48. Bernie Kohn, "Big 3 Carriers Again Join to Fight USAir-BA Pact," *Journal of Commerce*, New York, January 28, 1993, p. 2B.

49. "Major Alliances between U.S. and Foreign Air Carriers," *Time* (October 5, 1992), p. 22.

50. Conversation with David O'Connor, International Air Transport Association, Washington, D.C., July 12, 1993.

51. Ibid.

52. Alfred Borcover, "Plenty of Ifs Stand between Boeing and an SST of Its Own," *The Honolulu Advertiser*, Honolulu, Hawaii, September 9, 1991, pp. A11 and A13.

SELECTED REFERENCES

Advisory Commission on Conferences in Ocean Shipping. *Report to the President and the Congress of the Advisory Commission on Conferences in Ocean Shipping*. Washington, D.C.: U.S. Government Printing Office, 1992.

Collison, Frederick M. "Liner Shipping and the U.S. International Trades." *Journal of Transportation Management*, Vol. 1, No. 1 (1990), pp. 1-29.

"Dogfight! United and American Battle for Global Supremacy." Business Week (January 21, 1991), pp. 56-60 and 62.

Estis, Toby B. "How to Choose an Ocean Carrier." *Traffic Management* (October, 1987), pp. 66, 69-72.

Gooley, Toby B. "You Can Negotiate International Freight Rates." *Traffic Management* (September, 1991), pp. 51-4.

Lieb, Robert C. "Logistics as a Strategic Variable in Post-1992 Europe." *Transportation Journal*, Vol 30, No. 4 (Summer, 1991), pp. 56-62.

Murphy, Paul R., James M. Daley and Douglas R. Dalenberg. "Selecting Links and Nodes in International Transportation: An Intermediary's Perspective." *Transportation Journal*, Vol. 31, No. 2 (Winter, 1991), pp. 33-40.

U.S. Department of Transportation, Maritime Administration. *Inventory of American Intermodal Equipment, 1991*. Washington, D.C.: the Department, 1991.

U.S. Department of Transportation, Maritime Administration. *Merchant Fleets of the World*. Washington, D.C.: the Department, 1992.

U.S. Department of Transportation, Maritime Administration. *United States Oceanborne Foreign Trade Routes*. Washington, D.C.: the Department, 1992.

U.S. Department of Transportation, Maritime Administration. *Vessel Inventory Report*. Washington, D.C.: the Department, 1991.

U.S. Department of Transportation, Maritime Administration. *1991 Annual Report*. Washington, D.C.: the Department, 1992.

U.S. General Accounting Office. *Airline Competition: Impact of Changing Foreign Investment and Control Limits on U.S. Airlines*. Washington, D.C.: General Accounting Office, 1992.

U.S. General Accounting Office. *Airline Competition: Weak Financial Structure Threatens Competition*. Washington, D.C.: General Accounting Office, 1992.

Cargo being loaded through the nose door of a Lufthansa Boeing 747F Jumbo Freighter *Courtesy of Lufthansa German Airlines*

American President Lines Containership, President Truman *Courtesy American President Lines, LTD.*

Part Three

COST, DEMAND AND RATEMAKING

CHAPTER EIGHT

COST AND DEMAND IN INTERCITY TRANSPORTATION

Ratemaking activities of carriers are quite important in determining both a carrier's long-term survival and its relative role in the transportation marketplace. In the aggregate, rates must be high enough to allow the carriers to generate a reasonable rate of return on invested capital to assure the long-term continuance of carrier services. However, the rate structure must also be low enough to foster the movement of traffic.

In approaching the critical and complex pricing process, the carrier must necessarily consider not only the costs of providing the services, but also the demand characteristics of the various markets and customers that it serves.

This chapter examines the nature of cost and demand in intercity transportation and prepares the reader for a detailed discussion of the pricing process, which follows in Chapter 9.

TRANSPORTATION COSTS

Comprehension of the ratemaking process in transportation requires an understanding of several basic cost concepts and cost relationships. These matters are examined in the following discussion.

Fixed and Variable Costs

As is the case in any industry, an intercity carrier's cost structure consists of fixed and variable cost components. Fixed costs are those not related to output in a direct fashion. They remain independent of output regardless of output changes. Such costs include depreciation on buildings, equipment, and rights-of-way caused by time or weather rather than usage; interest on bonds; executive salaries; property taxes; and long-term leases. Fixed costs must be calculated for a particular time period, because in the long-run all costs are variable.

In contrast to fixed costs, certain costs fluctuate directly with a company's rate of output during a particular time period. These costs are known as variable costs and include outlays for materials, operating supplies, and direct labor. In a transportation context, variable costs might include outlays for fuel, crew salaries (although part of this might be considered to be fixed in nature), tolls, and depreciation related to usage, such as deterioration of engines on power units. In the short-run, variable costs constitute the controllable portion of the cost of production; they can be decreased by reducing output or increased by increasing output. When the rate of output is increased, total variable cost increases. Conversely, when the rate of output declines, total variable costs decrease.

As long as the scale or size of the company is constant, fixed costs will remain the same for the period. However, during the period, average fixed cost per unit will decline as output increases.

As discussed in Chapters 3 through 7, there are significant differences in the relative proportions of fixed and variable costs experienced in the different modes of transportation. At one end of the spectrum, railroad and pipeline companies incur proportionately higher fixed costs, and consequently realize declining average total costs over broader ranges of output as fixed cost per unit declines. Truckers, water carriers, and forwarders, with proportionately higher variable costs, experience declining per-unit costs over substantially smaller ranges of output.

Cost Traceability

Although some costs are related to the rate of output and others are independent of it, certain costs are attributable to specific units of output while others are not. In the transportation industries, services are often performed under conditions of "common" cost. That is, some productive unit generates several distinct services, and a portion of the costs of this process cannot be directly traced to individual output units. For example, passenger trains and freight trains may share the same rights-of-way under common cost conditions. Similarly, passengers, cargo, and mail may be carried in a single plane. In these two illustrations, and many similar situations in transportation, some costs are common to several services and can only be allocated to particular services on an arbitrary basis. Similar allocation problems also arise with respect to "joint" costs, which are found when two or more services are necessarily produced together in fixed proportions. One of these services may be said to be the byproduct of the other. The most common illustration of joint cost behavior is provided by the back-haul situation. Return capacity is a byproduct of the loaded trip to the original destination. The bulk of the return trip costs will be generated whether or not any return traffic is obtained. However, if such return traffic is solicited, this will necessitate apportioning of joint expenses between the primary and back-haul movements. Once again, the allocation will be arbitrary.

Economies of Utilization

Having defined broad cost categories, let us now consider the impact of utilization on the per-unit cost of transportation output. Throughout the years there has been some controversy concerning definition of the most appropriate unit for defining transportation output.[1] However, for the purposes of this illustration, output will be expressed in terms of ton miles (one ton of freight carried one mile) and passenger miles (one passenger carried one mile).

While the scale of an enterprise remains constant, average unit costs tend to decline as output volume increases over a specific output range. Because of the sizable fixed investment incurred in several modes of carriage, it is quite advantageous for a carrier to use its facilities to full physical capacity, since fixed costs must be met regardless of the traffic volume handled. Therefore, carriers of freight seek heavier and more frequent loads coupled with rapid equipment turnaround, and passenger carriers seek to intensively utilize facilities by attempting to generate higher load factors.

However, there are limitations to utilization economies. Pushing equipment and employees beyond their effective limits can lead to increasing equipment failure and operating problems. At this point, per-unit cost rises and the carrier is better off reducing volume. The carrier may also consider scale expansion if the traffic currently being handled appears to offer stable potential in the future.

Economies of Scale

As implied in the preceding discussion, average unit costs in transportation may also be influenced by the scale or size of the carrier. In certain industries the scale of operation is an important determinant of production costs; larger firms tend to realize lower per-unit output costs compared to smaller firms.

A brief discussion of the principle of returns to scale should clarify the concept of "economies of scale". The principle of returns to scale involves three stages of company activity. In the first stage, which is referred to as increasing returns to scale, output increases more than proportionately to the increase in all factor inputs. As a result, long-run average cost per unit of output declines. The forces that lead to increased productivity in response to increased scale may be referred to as economies of scale. The second phase, constant returns to scale, occurs when output expands in direct proportion to the increase in the factors of production. Average unit cost is constant within this range. Studies of returns to scale indicate that a long phase of constant returns to scale is typical.[2] The final stage, decreasing returns to scale, occurs when output increases less than proportionately to the increase in input factors. The forces that lead to this rise in long-run average cost per unit of output might be referred to as "diseconomies of scale." Public utilities tend to experience such economies of scale. The incidence of scale economies in the gas and electric industries has influenced regulatory policy toward promotion of regional monopolies in hopes of realizing lower average unit production costs, and hence lower prices to consumers.[3]

In the long-run a company might seek to lower average unit costs by expanding the scale of existing operations so as to realize economies of scale.

Causes of Economies of Scale. Several factors may lead to realization of economies of scale. First, as the scale of an operation is increased, the possibility of division and specialization of labor also increases. By performing fewer diverse tasks, workers may become more adept in completing a narrower range of jobs and consequently become more productive. Also, the time sacrificed as a worker transfers from one job to another may be eliminated. Such opportunities of specialization are not limited to production workers. In fact, potential specialization in management may be far more important. The ability of management to concentrate in specific functional areas, such as personnel, logistics, finance, and marketing, may also lead to increased productivity. Machine specialization may also be of significance in lowering long-run unit costs as company scale expands.[4]

Closely related to machine specialization is the element of "factor indivisibility." Input units may not be completely divisible. Certain types of capital goods will not perform their functions properly if they are built on too small a scale, since weight is important in their operation.[5] Division of size may lead to lower levels of productivity. Therefore, larger machines (purchased as firm scale expands) may be cheaper to obtain per unit of output capacity than similar machines of a smaller scale. Indivisibilities may also exist in a variety of managerial areas, such as advertising, research work, and financing. Advertising on a small scale tends to be relatively less effective than large-scale advertising, and research activities cannot be carried on effectively on a small scale. In the financial area, the cost of floating a bond issue is, to a large extent, independent of the size of the issue. Thus this method of financing is expensive to a firm until it has expanded beyond a certain size.[6]

Any of these factors may be of significance in realizing increasing returns to scale. However, such improvements cannot indefinitely continue to lower long-run average cost. Once the company has attained a size that is sufficient to realize all scale economies, there may be a wide range of company sizes for which returns to scale are constant. Expansion beyond this range of company size may lead to diseconomies of scale.

Causes of Diseconomies of Scale. If expansion continues, firm size may eventually increase to a point at which operations become somewhat unmanageable. The increased size of the labor force causes supervision and coordination of problems that management may be unable to cope with. Similarly, employees may be overworked at such output levels. Top management finds it increasingly difficult to coordinate the efforts of various operating units of the firm. Overexpansion may similarly cause the company's communications network to fail. As a result of these factors, productivity is likely to decrease, and average unit costs will rise, thereby incurring diseconomies of scale.

Instances of Economies of Scale. There is considerable difference of opinion in economic circles concerning both the importance and the incidence of economies of scale. Nevertheless, there are indications that such economies do exist in certain industries, such as automobile manufacturing, natural gas distribution, telephone and telegraph services in long-distance markets, and the generation, transmission, and distribution of electric power.[7] More importantly, from the standpoint of this book, the existence of economies of scale appears to vary considerably across the modes of carriage.

Several studies have indicated that there are economies of scale in the railroad industry. In addition to the economies that might arise through equipment and managerial specialization and through use of large-size vehicles, there are also indications that railroads are subject to the types of indivisibilities discussed earlier in this chapter.[8]

The movement of petroleum products through pipelines seems to be subject to considerable economies of scale. This is particularly true with regard to pipeline diameter. As discussed in Chapter 5, studies have indicated that the unit cost of crude oil pipeline transportation declines rapidly with increases in throughput and diameter of the pipeline.[9]

A considerable number of studies have addressed the issue of scale economies in motor carriage. Interest in the topic increased in response to both the movement toward deregulation and related concerns about potential market dominance by large carriers. However, the findings of these studies have varied substantially and therefore have provided limited guidance for public policy formulation. While several studies have concluded that there are no significant economies of scale in motor carriage, one work suggested that economies of scale do exist in the less-than-truckload segment of general commodity trucking.[10] Unfortunately, variations in the approach, methodology, and coverage of these studies has made it difficult to reconcile the conflicting conclusions.

Studies of air transportation have concluded that once moderate size has been attained by individual airlines, there do not appear to be any significant economies of scale. Prior to achievement of moderate size, economies appear to stem from a decline in operating costs per available seat mile, or ton mile, as the size of the plane increases.[11]

Relevance of Scale Studies. Studies of economies of scale in transportation are far from being definitive. Typically, the studies have been quite limited in coverage. Also, there is considerable debate concerning how scale economies should be measured. Therefore, caution must be used in attempting to employ the findings of such studies as the basis for transportation policy formulation with respect to such issues as entry and merger guidelines.

Other Major Cost-Influencing Factors

Many factors influence the costs of providing various transportation services. Understanding of these factors is important because of the role they play in the pricing process. As a prelude to the detailed pricing discussion contained in Chapter 9, attention now shifts to several other major factors that influence the costs incurred by carriers in offering specific services. These factors may be separated into commodity and route characteristics.

Commodity Characteristics. Some characteristics of a particular commodity that influence the costs of moving the commodity are loading characteristics, susceptibility to loss and damage, volume and regularity of movement, and the nature of the equipment required to move it.

The loading characteristics of products vary widely. For example, some bulk and liquid products, like grain, sand, and petroleum products, are loaded through automated processes with little labor input. Other commodities, such as manufactured items, are typically loaded through more labor-intensive processes. If items are packaged in standardized units, it may be possible to load and unload them using equipment such as wooden pallets that hold multiple units. In contrast, other items that are odd-shaped must be handled individually, possibly by hand. The more labor intensive the handling process, the more time consuming and costly the process is, and the greater the likelihood of damage to the shipment.

Another important loading characteristic of a particular commodity is its use of the cubic capacity of the vehicle. If the product is light but bulky, it will tend to use up the cubic capacity of the vehicle without approaching the vehicle's weight-carrying potential. Under such circumstances, it is quite common for the carrier's rate to reflect this by assessing higher charges per unit of weight to light-loading commodities.

One final loading consideration in terms of cost generation is who actually does the loading and unloading of the vehicle. This varies from mode to mode and by commodity grouping. In rail carriage, loading and unloading are typically handled by shippers and consignees. Consequently, this cost factor is more meaningful to shippers and consignees than it is to the rail carrier, because the costs are not borne directly by the carrier. The loading and unloading pattern is rather different in motor carriage. Drivers frequently assist in the loading and unloading process, thereby generating carrier costs that are not necessarily reflected in rates.

An additional factor influencing unit cost in the provision of transportation service is the commodity's susceptibility to loss and damage, which varies quite widely across commodity groupings. Certain products, such as glassware and computers are quite fragile and require special carrier treatment. In contrast, movement of many bulk commodities, such as sand and gravel, do not require special handling efforts and consequently generate lower costs. Other products, like agricultural goods, are perishable. This may necessitate use of special refrigerated trailers or rail cars, and this generates additional costs.

Certain products are quite vulnerable to pilferage, particularly items that are small and valuable, such as pocket calculators and cameras. Because of the high incidence of pilferage in certain product categories and due to the resulting high cost of claims, at various times certain carriers have unofficially attempted to embargo carriage of such items. However, a carrier cannot legally do that, and such action can be stopped by the regulatory agencies.

Some pilferage occurs in carrier terminal areas; this has led to a variety of cargo security measures, ranging from placement of security guards on carrier docks to installation of surveillance cameras.

Pilferage in transportation is not limited to small-scale theft. Hijacking is still a problem in the trucking industry, particularly involving truckloads of such commodities as cigarettes, razor blades, or pharmaceuticals. Hijacking is so serious a problem in certain cities that some truckers number the tops of trailers so that stolen trailers might be spotted by police helicopters. Such extraordinary security efforts naturally generate additional costs in serving certain commodity groupings that are highly susceptible to theft.

Loss and damage considerations provided a major stimulus in the movement toward containerization of both domestic and international traffic. Placement of items in sealed containers not only facilitates ease of handling, but also provides additional cargo security.

The costs generated by loss and damage are not limited to the amount of loss and damage claims; they also include the costs of claim investigation and payment processing.

Nature of Equipment Required. As discussed earlier in this chapter, some cargo can be handled by general-purpose equipment such as straight trailers, but other types of cargo necessitate carrier purchase and operation of more costly specialized equipment. Due to the nature of the commodities carried, some transportation vehicles may have to be specially cushioned, refrigerated, or equipped to handle liquid commodities. Naturally, these equipment modifications add to the costs incurred by the carrier.

Traffic Volume and Regularity. The volume in which a commodity moves also influences the per-unit cost of providing the service. Any unit of transportation output is burdened with some arbitrary overhead allocation. As shipment size increases, these fixed costs are spread over greater traffic volume, and average costs per unit of output tend to taper off. This phenomenon is reflected in the rate structure, which generally assesses lower transportation charges per unit of traffic handled as shipment size increases.

Also, as shipment size increases, the likelihood of application of labor-saving devices such as palletization also increases. Potentially, this can lower handling costs per unit. This situation tends to lead to considerable differences in the costs of handling truckload versus less-than truckload (LTL) freight. The smaller average shipment size of LTL traffic tends to generate considerably more manual handling, and hence higher costs.

The regularity with which specific traffic types are handled also influences the cost of the movement. Frequent movement, particularly of commodities that necessitate use of specialized equipment, facilitates improvements in scheduling and equipment utilization.

Route Characteristics. The characteristics of the route over which traffic moves also influence the costs of providing the service. Foremost among these cost-influencing factors are route distance, operating conditions, and traffic density.

The distance over which traffic moves between origin and destination naturally influences the carrier's costs. Total cost rises as distance increases, but the cost per mile tends to decline. Certain rather fixed costs, such as those associated with moving the transportation vehicle through terminal facilities, are spread over longer distances. The following example illustrates this concept. Assume that it costs $200 to move a loaded rail car through a railyard and terminal facility. If the car moves 100 miles to its destination, the "recovery rate" on these terminal costs is $.02 cents per mile. In contrast, if the shipment moves 1,000 miles, the recovery rate becomes 20 cents per mile. This spreading out of terminal expenses is reflected in the rate structure, which tends to assess tapering rates as shipment distance increases. That is, total transportation charges do not tend to increase proportionately with shipment distance.

The distance a shipment travels between origin and destination may vary considerably across the modes due to the circuitry of the routes traveled by certain carriers. For example, quite often water carriers' distance between two cities is considerably greater than that of their railroad competitors due to the limitations of the natural waterway system.

Costs are also influenced by the operating conditions that prevail over specific routes. The route's topography is important in that regard. Negotiation of grades and curves generates higher costs than operation over rather flat routes. In the railroad industry, grade crossings force reduction in speed, which tends to raise operating costs. Consequently, it is generally more expensive to operate in heavily populated areas. In the trucking industry the nature of the highway system to be traveled is important. Stop-and-go operation over unlimited-access highways not only tends to be more time consuming, but also more costly in terms of fuel consumption than operation over interstate highways.

A final route characteristic that has a major influence on carrier costs per unit of traffic handled is the traffic density of the route. Traffic density may be defined as the amount of traffic that a carrier handles per mile over a given route. Earlier in this chapter the impact of increasing shipment size on average cost was discussed. The same basic principle applies to a given route as volume or density increases over the route. The fixed-cost burden of each unit of traffic moving over the route lessens as density increases.

Often traffic density over a particular route is lower in one direction than the other. As a result (ignoring topographical considerations), costs per unit of traffic carried tend to be higher in the lighter traffic direction. In response to this situation, carriers often establish lower incentive rates in the lighter density direction to stimulate additional traffic.

TRANSPORTATION DEMAND

Whereas cost considerations tend to establish a lower limit in transportation pricing decisions, demand considerations set the effective pricing ceiling. Understanding the demand characteristics of potential customers is important to carriers, because these characteristics, in the aggregate, determine the quantity of carrier services that will be consumed at a particular price at a given time.

Transportation demand analysis and forecasting are not nearly as refined as carriers and government officials would like them to be. Nevertheless, the pricing decisions of carriers are at least partially based on an evaluation of customer demand schedules. Carriers are constantly faced with such questions as how responsive will passenger demand be if air coach fares between Boston and Miami are lowered from $125 to $99, or how will demand react to a 5 percent increase in the rate charged for moving wheat from Minneapolis to Chicago? As discussed later in this chapter, the ultimate answer to questions like these is based on the elasticity of demand for those services.

The demand for transportation services is derived in nature. That is, the level of transportation demand is dependent upon societal demands for other goods and services. This is particularly true with respect to freight services. People do not purchase ton miles solely for the sake of consuming them. Ton miles of transportation service are purchased because they add value or place utility to the commodity that is to be moved. For example, raw materials and finished products generally must be moved from their point of production to potential markets to realize an increase in value. Hence transportation services create additional value by providing place utility.

Similarly, in a passenger context, people do not generally purchase passenger miles because they enjoy consuming them. Rather, there is some specific trip purpose, such as increasing individual place utility for either personal or business reasons through travel.

Because of the derived demand nature of transportation, particularly in the area of freight movements, carriers must be sensitive to conditions that prevail in the markets for final products to accurately forecast their demand picture and to plan marketing strategies.

Determinants of Demand

The demand for transportation services, at any level of aggregation, is a function of many factors, including economic, social, and political considerations. Let us first examine transportation demand at the macro level by looking at national freight and passenger demand in totality. This is often referred to as aggregate demand. The level of aggregate demand for transportation services in a country is closely related to the general level of economic activity in the country. Because of this close relationship, railroad and truck loadings have long been viewed as indexes of national business activity.

During periods of rising business activity, aggregate demand for freight services tends to increase as the volume of raw materials and finished goods consumed in the economy rises. As disposable personal income rises, people tend to spend more on transportation, particularly on pleasure travel.[12]

As business activity slows, the situation is reversed with respect to freight volume, and personal expenditures for pleasure travel tend to be reduced. Even the business portion of passenger demand is affected by economic slowdowns. During such periods, many firms reduce employee travel and rely upon other, less expensive forms of communications.

The proportion of Gross National Product (GNP) devoted to freight movements tends to remain stable or decline as an economy matures. Movement from an extractive, raw material orientation generally witnesses a growth in service-oriented industries. The service share of GNP increases, but services require less movement of goods than mining or manufacturing. As a result, the freight transportation proportion of GNP declines. Somewhat offsetting this trend, however, in terms of aggregate transportation demand, is the fact that the demand for passenger movement tends to increase as the economy matures and discretionary income rises.

In the United States transportation outlays as a percentage of GNP has declined significantly in recent years. While those outlays comprised 19.8 percent of GNP in 1980 they declined to 16.8 percent in 1991.[13] That decline reflected not only the country's evolution to a service based economy, but also the increased price competition fostered by deregulation.

Modal Demand. The aggregate transportation demand of an economy is divided among the several modes and between for-hire and private carriage. The relative national market share of each form of carriage (modal split) is a function of many factors. In the freight sector, the most important mode-determining factors are the composition of the traffic moved, availability of alternative modes, service characteristics, prices of alternative modes, the geographical dispersion of economic activity, and the regulatory environment.

As industrialization expands in a country, transportation alternatives tend to increase, and growing emphasis is placed on faster, more expensive modes for movement of manufactured goods. In many instances this has reduced the market share of railroads and water carriers, which had dominated bulk commodity movements in the earlier stages of economic growth. This pattern has been visible in the United States over the past 40 years, with the long-term shift of high-valued commodities from rail to motor and air carriage. Technological and regulatory changes, coupled with aggressive marketing behavior, may contribute to shifts in the aggregate freight modal split. While such shifts tend to be rather gradual, some occur rapidly due to changes in significant competitive variables. For example, the pricing freedom accorded the railroads in intermodal and agricultural traffic deregulation led to substantial railroad traffic gains in a matter of months.

The aggregate modal split of passenger carriage is also influenced by a variety of factors. Predominant among these factors are the availability of alternatives, comparative prices, and numerous service considerations, including speed, convenience, comfort, dependability, and safety. In intercity markets, the U.S. public has clearly demonstrated a preference for the automobile; nearly 81 percent of intercity passenger miles are registered in automobiles.[14] It is clear that the convenience of the private automobile outweighs other choice variables for most intercity travels. The modal choice of passengers is explored further in subsequent chapter which examine urban travel.

Specific Demand. At the micro level, the shipper generally weighs a number of variables in making carrier selection decisions. Assuming that the shipper does not engage in private carriage, he must choose among the modes then select a particular carrier within the mode chosen. The shipper ordinarily weighs a variety of price-service considerations in assessing possible tradeoffs. The decision is often guided by company policies that call for certain levels of customer service. Under those circumstances the individual attempts to realize those levels of service while minimizing transportation outlays. In negotiations with carriers, the shipper often attempts to play one carrier, or mode, off against the other. Depending on the volume of freight that he controls, the shipper may influence carrier price levels and service offerings.

In soliciting traffic, the carrier is faced with many potential customers, each being unique in its needs. Consequently, to be effective the carrier must develop some understanding of these needs while realizing his own capabilities. The carrier naturally would like to carry nothing but high-density, high-rated traffic that has limited susceptibility to loss and damage. Unfortunately for the carrier, the transportation marketplace in which it operates does not generally conform with this ideal. Consequently, the carrier will attempt to cultivate the more desirable traffic while tolerating other accounts.

The factors that affect the demand for specific passenger services vary somewhat between business and nonbusiness travelers. The business traveler, often traveling on an expense account, tends to be somewhat less concerned with the price differences of his alternatives and somewhat more concerned with the value of his time. Consequently, the business traveler is likely to be influenced in his carrier selection by such factors as service frequency, speed of service, his past experience with the companies serving the market, and the total package of amenities offered by the competitors. To a certain extent, long-distance business travel is somewhat captive to the airline industry; as a result, the traveler's choice tends to be limited to selection of one of several airlines serving the cities he is moving between. In shorter distance markets, rail and bus alternatives become available, as does the automobile, and the carrier selection process becomes more complex.

The nonbusiness traveler is likely to be somewhat more concerned with the comparative costs of modal alternatives than his business counterpart, because direct costs will come from the nonbusiness traveler's personal budget. Nevertheless, even though considerable evidence has been compiled which suggests that for-hire modes are less expensive than the private automobile for many intercity trips, the automobile continues to dominate such private travel because of other attributes such as convenience.

Elasticity of Demand

The supplier of any transportation service is naturally concerned with the responsiveness of customer demand to price changes, which is usually referred to as the "price elasticity of demand." If total revenues vary inversely with price changes, demand is said to be elastic. In contrast, if revenues vary directly with price changes, demand is said to be inelastic. An illustration should serve to clarify this concept. If an airline lowered its one-way coach fare between Boston and Miami from $125 to $99, and total market revenues rose (due to an increase in market demand), demand would be considered to be elastic. Conversely, if revenues fell following the price reduction, demand would be considered to be inelastic. In that case, even though passenger demand may have risen, its growth was not sufficient to offset the $26 per passenger revenue reduction related to the price cut.

Naturally, management of carrier operations would be simplified considerably if a data base existed that documented demand elasticity by market and class of service, but such a data base is lacking in most instances. Even when price experimentation has occurred, a number of intervening variables, such as changes in economic conditions, has tended to cloud the results. Consequently, much of transportation pricing represents sophisticated guesswork, and the results are not always favorable. For example, the intense price competition among airlines in the early 1990s depressed the industry's yield per passenger in heavily traveled markets and contributed to record losses by many carriers.[15] Fortunately, not all carrier price reduction efforts have resulted in such performance. Following ICC deregulation of railroad intermodal traffic, the railroads effectively employed selective price reductions as a means of promoting the growth of such traffic.[16]

The aggregate demand for transportation services tends to be rather price inelastic in the short-run. However, over longer periods, aggregate demand has demonstrated a responsiveness to changing price levels. As might be expected, modal demand tends to be more price elastic than aggregate demand. At the specific carrier-shipper level, the relative elasticity or inelasticity of demand for particular services is determined to a great extent by what competitors charge for their services and the availability of such services. Further, it might reasonably be expected that services for which there are adequate substitutes will show higher elasticities than services for which there is little or no competition. Also of importance is the ability of the purchaser of transportation service to pass along price increases to other members of the production-consumption channel. If the rate increase does not have to be absorbed by the party paying the transportation bill, demand for the specific service is not likely to be impaired. However, the ability to pass such increases along the channel is a function of the demand situation faced by the commodity in final markets.

Value of Service

As implied in the preceding discussion, different commodities and passenger groups exhibit different demand elasticities. That is, various customer groups tend to react differently to price modifications. These differences are reflected in the concept of "value of service" in transportation. The value of a specific transportation service might be said to be the upper limit of the freight or passenger charge. Essentially, this is the highest price that can be assessed for that particular service without diverting the traffic to another carrier or stopping its movement altogether.

Carrier and regulatory agency assessment of value of service plays a major role in transportation pricing. Although cost certainly plays a role in price setting in transportation, the most important reason for differences in prevailing rates on low and high-value commodities is the greater ability of the valuable articles to stand higher rates. These differences in ability to pay are consequently reflected in the transportation pricing structure, which, as discussed in Chapter 9, discriminates among various classes of passenger service and among commodity types according to value.

This philosophy of pricing leads to charging what the traffic will bear: carriers will strive to charge the rate on each commodity or significant traffic movement that, when the volume of traffic is considered, will make the largest total contribution to fixed expenses.

SUMMARY

The cost characteristics of the several modes of intercity carriage differ significantly. These differences involve not only fixed/variable cost proportions, but also include differences in the incidence of economies of scale. Numerous factors influence the costs incurred by a company in providing transportation services. Among the most important cost-influencing factors in freight movements are the loading characteristics of the commodity being shipped, the equipment used, the volume in which it moves, and the route over which it travels. In passenger movements, costs are highly influenced by the density of passenger volume, the equipment employed, and regulatory guidelines.

Basically, the demand for transportation services is derived in nature. The level of aggregate transportation demand tends to be closely related to the level of economic activity in a particular country. Modal demand is a function of many factors, including the range of available alternatives and price-service relationships. The demand for service at the specific shipper-carrier level is similarly influenced by a multitude of considerations.

The demand for transportation services may be discussed in terms of elasticity or responsiveness to price changes. Different commodities and passenger groups exhibit varying demand elasticities. This has led to a heavy reliance upon value-of-service considerations in transportation pricing.

The blending of such cost and demand considerations in the transportation pricing process is discussed in Chapter 9.

DISCUSSION QUESTIONS

1. How do the proportions of fixed and variable costs vary among the transportation modes?
2. Explain the concept of economies of utilization.
3. What are scale economies and what are their significance from a regulatory standpoint?
4. Explain the importance of the concept of value-of-service pricing to carriers in determining the rates to be charged for various transportation services.

NOTES

1. For a summary of this controversy, see Hugh S. Norton, *Modern Transportation Economics*, 2nd ed. (Columbus, OH: Charles E. Merrill Publishing Company, 1971), pp. 99-101.
2. John F. Due and Robert W. Clower, *Intermediate Economic Analysis*, 5th ed. (Homewood, ILL: Richard D. Irwin, Inc., 1966), p. 111.
3. Charles F. Phillips, *The Economics of Regulation*, rev. ed. (Homewood, ILL: Richard D. Irwin, Inc., 1969), pp. 22-3.
4. Joe S. Bain, *Industrial Organization*, 2nd ed. (New York: John Wiley and Sons, Inc., 1968), p. 166.
5. Due and Clower, p. 108.
6. Ibid., p. 109.
7. John B. Lansing, *Transportation and Economic Policy* (New York: Free Press, 1966), p. 16. For a discussion of the lack of agreement concerning the existence of scale economies, see Richard D. Low, *Modern Economic Organization* (Homewood, ILL: Richard D. Irwin, Inc., 1970), pp. 147-80.
8. Due and Clower, p. 108.
9. Leslie Cookenboo, Jr., "Costs of Operating Crude Oil Pipe Lines, *Rice Institute Bulletin* (April, 1954), as cited by Charles F. Phillips, *The Economics of Regulation*, p. 23.

10.   For an excellent discussion of economies of scale in trucking, see Garland Chow, "The Status of Economies of Scale in Regulated Trucking: A Review of the Evidence and Future Directions," in *Proceedings of the Nineteenth Annual Meeting of the Transportation Research Forum* (Oxford, IN: Richard B. Cross Company, 1978), pp. 365-73.

11.   Richard E. Caves, *Air Transport and Its Regulators* (Cambridge, MA: Harvard University Press, 1962), pp. 57-61.

12.   Martin T. Farris and Forest E. Harding, *Passenger Transportation* (Englewood Cliffs, NJ: Prentice-Hall, Inc., 1976), pp. 22-3.

13.   Eno Transportation Foundation, Inc., *Transportation in America*, 11th ed., (Lansdowne, VA: the Foundation, 1993), p. 6.

14.   Ibid., p. 47.

15.   See John Boyd, "Aviation Red Ink Swells as Delta, UAL Report Big Losses," *The Journal of Commerce* New York, January 29, 1993, p. 3b; also, "The Airline Mess," *Business Week* (July 6, 1992), pp. 50-5.

16.   Norman Thorpe, "Piggyback Rail Traffic Catching On," *Wall Street Journal* New York, December 27, 1983, p. 15.

SELECTED REFERENCES

Coyle, John J., Edward J. Bardi, and Joseph L. Cavinato. Transportation. 3rd ed. St. Paul, MN: West Publishing Company, 1990. Chapter 13. "Cost and Pricing in Transportation,"pp. 251-75.

Chow, Garland. "The Status of Economies of Scale in Regulated Trucking: A Review of the Evidence and Future Directions." *Proceedings of the Nineteenth Annual Meeting of the Transportation Research Forum*. Oxford, IN: Richard B. Cross Company, 1978, pp. 365-78.

Corsi, Thomas M. and Joseph R. Stowers. "Effects of a Deregulated Environment on Motor Carriage: A Systematic Multi-Segment Analysis." *Transportation Journal*, Vol. 30, No. 3 (Spring, 1991), pp. 4-28.

Elliott, Russell S. "Motor Carrier Cost Analysis." *Journal of the Transportation Research Forum* (1987), pp. 194-99.

Friedlaender, Ann F. "Hedonic Costs and Economies of Scale in the Regulated Trucking Industry." *Proceedings of a Workshop on Motor Carrier Economic Regulation*. Washington, D.C.: National Academy of Sciences, 1978, pp. 141-62.

Grimm, Curtis M., Thomas M. Corsi, and Judith L. Jarrell, "U.S. Motor Carrier Cost Structure Under Deregulation.' *The Logistics and Transportation Review*, Vol. 25, No. 3 (Spring, 1989), pp. 23-50.

Harmatuck, Donald J. "Motor Carrier Cost Function Comparisons." *Transportation Journal*, Vol. 31, No. 4 (Summer, 1992), pp. 31-46.

Healy, Kent T. *Effects of Scale in the Railroad Industry*. New Haven, CT: Committee on Transportation, Yale University, 1961.

Keeler, Theodore E. "Railroad Costs, Returns to Scale, and Excess Capacity." *Review of Economics and Statistics*, Vol. 56 (May, 1974), pp. 201-8.

Lawrence, Michael E. "Economies of Scale in the General Freight Motor Carrier Industry: Additional Evidence." *Proceedings of the Seventeenth Annual Meeting of the Transportation Research Forum* (1976), pp. 169-76.

Meyer, John R., Merton J. Peck, John Stenason, and Charles Zwick. *Economies of Competition in the Transportation Industries*. Cambridge, MA: Harvard University Press, 1964. Chapter 7. "Transportation Rates and Demand Characteristics of the Transportation Market," pp. 168-202.

Rackowski, James. P. "Marketing Economies and the Results of Trucking Deregulation in the Less-than-Truckload Sector." *Transportation Journal*, Vol. 27, No. 3 (Spring, 1988), pp. 11-22.

Rinehart, Lloyd M. and Shaoming Zou. "Modeling Customer Behavior in Negotiations for Motor Carrier Contracts." *Transportation Journal*, Vol. 31, No. 3 (Spring, 1992), pp. 39-45.

Sugrue, Paul K., Manfred H. Ledford, and Nicholas A. Glaskowsky, Jr. "Operating Economies of Scale in the U.S. Long-Haul Common Carrier, Motor Freight Industry." *Transportation Journal*, Vol. 22, No. 2 (Fall, 1982), pp. 27-41.

Wang Chang, Judy S. and Ann F. Friedlaender. "Truck Technology and Efficient Market Structure." *Review of Economics and Statistics*, Vol. 67 (1988), pp. 250-8.

Wilson, George W. "Notes on the Elasticity of Demand for Freight Transportation." *Transportation Journal*, Vol. 17, No. 3 (Spring, 1978), pp. 5-15.

Wood, Donald F., and James C. Johnson. *Contemporary Transportation*. 4th ed., New York: Macmillan Publishing Company, 1993. Chapter 11. "Transportation Pricing, Rates, and Negotiations, pp. 263-89.

CHAPTER NINE

CARRIER RATEMAKING

The pricing of transportation services takes place in two quite different environments. As discussed in earlier chapters, in the markets for transportation services which are not subject to federal economic regulation, rates are freely determined through interaction of carriers and shippers. In contrast, carriers that are subject to economic regulation must price their services in a rather constrained environment in which regulation significantly influences pricing decisions.

This chapter examines those pricing processes and gives attention not only to carrier ratemaking issues, but also to the interaction which takes place between carriers, shippers, rate bureaus and regulatory agencies.

RATEMAKING IN NON-REGULATED TRANSPORTATION MARKETS

While trucking movements of agricultural commodities and water carrier handling of bulk and liquid commodities have never been subject to federal economic regulation, the deregulation movement has dramatically expanded the portion of interstate transportation which is exempt from those regulations.

In surface transportation regulatory changes have led to several significant exemptions being extended to rail traffic since 1978. Railroad movements of fresh fruits and vegetables (1978), piggyback traffic (1981), boxcars and frozen food (1984), and various lumber, plywood and treated wood products (1991) are no longer subject to ICC regulation.

In air transportation the rates charged by air carriers providing cargo service and the rates of air freight forwarders were deregulated between 1977-1979. Similarly, passage of the Airline Deregulation Act of 1978 began a gradual process by which federal control of domestic airline passenger fares was completely eliminated by 1985.

In these exempt markets, carriers are able to vary rates with market conditions, and there is no advance notice requirement related to rate changes. Consequently, carrier prices may vary from day to day.

RATEMAKING IN REGULATED TRANSPORTATION MARKETS

Despite the deregulation movement, there are still many sectors of interstate surface transportation in which prices are regulated by the ICC. In pricing movements of regulated commodities, carriers generally file individual rates with the Interstate Commerce Commission. The rates filed may cover either common carriage service under which a carrier offers its service to all customers on a non-discriminatory basis, or contract carriage under which services are offered only to those customers with whom the carrier has negotiated a specific contract.

Under certain circumstances, carriers may engage in collective pricing activities through rate bureaus. The collective rates are then filed with the ICC. While such collective pricing behavior has become far less significant in transportation in recent years it still exists, and is quite controversial.

The Nature of Government Involvement

The federal government has been involved in the ratemaking activities of interstate carriers since passage of the Interstate Commerce Act in 1887. That involvement emerged not only to protect the shipping public from potential carrier abuses, but also to protect carriers from destructive competition. While there have been variations across the modes, federal regulation of transportation prices generally has entailed specification of filing requirements, rate publication guidelines, and control over the maximum, minimum and actual rates which a carrier could charge. The rates filed with the regulatory agencies have typically been subject to suspension and review by the agencies if complaints were filed about those rates and the agency believed there was substance to the complaint. The specifics of this process are discussed in detail later in this chapter.

Federal regulation of transportation rates has often been criticized. Obviously, government involvement in carrier ratemaking generates filing and publication costs for carriers as well as the costs which might be incurred in defending rate proposals which have been suspended by the regulatory agency. Ultimately those costs must be borne by the shipping public. Critics argue that these costs are unnecessary and would be minimized in a non-regulated transportation marketplace. It is further argued that federal regulations stifle ratemaking innovation and reduce carrier responsiveness to short-term market conditions.

Single Carrier Ratemaking

In the regulated sectors of the transportation industries, most rates are filed individually by carriers with the ICC. As noted above, they can cover either common or contract carriage. The rate filings can be very specific, such as a railroad rate for moving coal between two points, or they can take the form of a general rate increase.

A general rate increase proposal filed by a carrier typically seeks to raise rates on all commodities handled by that carrier. In certain circumstances, due to competitive conditions, some commodities may be excluded from the increase. Usually, general rate increases are expressed in percentage terms; for example, in October 1992 Roadway Express announced it would raise its rates an average of 4.64 percent. Soon after that announcement, Roadway's major competitors in LTL trucking, Yellow Freight System, CF Motor Freight, ABF Freight System, and Carolina Freight Carriers Corporation, all announced general rate increase filings in the range of 4.6 percent.[1]

A carrier petition for a general rate increase may be prompted by rising costs, depressed carrier earnings, or a combination of the two.

Collective Ratemaking

For many years collective ratemaking played an important role in railroad, trucking, and water carrier pricing.[2] While such behavior is generally illegal, carrier rate bureaus have been granted antitrust exemptions. The bureaus are nonprofit, carrier-maintained organizations that are legally permitted to initiate joint carrier pricing action. Such collective pricing in transportation is often referred to as the "conference method" of ratemaking. It must be stressed, however, that, although these organizations have been permitted to initiate rate changes, such pricing modifications typically are subject to possible regulatory agency review.

Bureau Structure and Functions. Rate bureaus are generally organized on a regional basis, and interregional rates are established between each territory. The membership of a particular bureau is limited to carriers within a single mode. Because the operating rights of a particular carrier may encompass a broad geographical region, the carrier may be a member of more than one bureau.

Membership in a particular bureau is typically open to all carriers (in that mode) that serve the bureau's region. Rate bureau operations are primarily supported by member contributions, which are usually assessed as a percentage of each member's gross operating revenues. Additional bureau income is often generated through sale of bureau publications to carriers and shippers.

Following several bureau mergers, there are seven major rate bureaus in the trucking industry and two railroad rate bureaus.[3] Additionally, there are several domestic water carrier bureaus.

In addition to providing a mechanism for collective ratemaking, rate bureaus perform several other functions. Among these are the dissemination of information concerning matters such as regulatory changes, provision of a forum to discuss problems of mutual concern, and publication of rates in "tariffs," which are the equivalent of transportation price lists.

Bureau Procedures. The antitrust exemption granted to rate bureaus has provided a means by which carrier representatives have been able to meet, discuss proposed rate changes, vote on those changes, and, if the changes are approved, file them with the Interstate Commerce Commission. At that stage, if a bureau member does not agree with the bureau's decision it may choose to "flag out" and not participate in the official rate.

In all such bureau proceedings, individual carriers maintain the right of "independent action" which allows them to file their own rates, which differ from the rates of the bureau, with the ICC.

It should be noted that in the trucking industry rate bureaus are permitted to submit collective general rate increase proposals to the ICC on behalf of their members. Since 1984 railroad bureaus have not been permitted to do so.

Regulatory Reform and Rate Bureaus. The collective pricing activities of carrier rate bureaus have always been the subject of considerable controversy. Supporters have traditionally argued that such collective action is necessary to promote stability in prices and carrier earnings. Critics have countered by charging that rate bureaus stifle competition and protect inefficient carriers to the detriment of the shipping public.[4]

One of the most vocal attackers of the conference method of ratemaking has been the federal Department of Transportation. Beginning in 1971, the DOT periodically submitted legislative proposals to Congress that sought to limit the scope of bureau influence. DOT criticisms of collective pricing in transportation brought considerable attention to the issue, and steps have been taken to reduce bureau power.

Several actions have been taken to limit the power of motor carrier bureaus. In 1975, the ICC issued an order that prohibited motor carrier bureaus from opposing independent filings by member carriers that were published in bureau tariffs.[5] Further, the Motor Carrier Act of 1980 stipulated that only those carriers with authority to participate in the proposed service were permitted to vote on specific rate proposals. This guideline applied to both single and joint line rates. Beginning in 1984 discussion and voting on single line rates was prohibited. The legislation also established the Motor Carrier Ratemaking Study Commission to re-examine the collective pricing issue. In its final report the commission recommended abolition of the antitrust exemption for collective ratemaking in the trucking industry.[6] Congress did not heed that recommendation.

The ICC has continued to criticize rate bureaus, and in 1990-1991 conducted an investigation to determine if bureaus should be eliminated. However, at the conclusion of that investigation the ICC announced that it saw no reason for curtailing bureau activity.[7]

The activities of railroad rate bureaus have also been limited by the regulatory reform movement. The Railroad Revitalization and Regulatory Reform Act of 1976 specified that railroad bureaus were no longer permitted to allow agreement or voting on single line rates, and that only carriers that could practicably participate in the movement could vote on joint line rates.[8] As previously noted, collective pricing activity in the rail industry was constrained further by the Staggers Rail Act of 1980 which provided for elimination of general rate increases through rail bureaus by January 1, 1984.

Collective ratemaking has become steadily less significant in the transportation marketplace. Administrative and statutory changes have dramatically reduced the permissible scope of such agreements, and many carriers have voluntarily severed their ties with rate bureaus. For example, during 1991 five of the nation's largest LTL truckers, Yellow Freight System, CF Motor Freight, Carolina Freight Corporation, ABF Freight System, and Overnite Transportation, withdrew from most motor carrier rate bureaus. Yellow and CF each estimated that membership in bureaus was costing them approximately $1 million per year, while Overnite said it would save $300,000 annually by withdrawing.[9] Further eroding the importance of the bureaus have been the individual pricing policies of the thousands of new entrants in the trucking industry who have chosen not to join the bureaus.

These developments raise serious questions concerning the long-term survival of rate bureaus in transportation. If they survive their role may well be limited to serving as publishing agents for carrier tariffs.

RATEMAKING AND THE INTERSTATE COMMERCE COMMISSION

Rate change proposals of individual carriers or rate bureaus must be filed with the ICC prior to their effective date. During 1992 there were nearly 1.4 million common carrier tariff filings with the ICC. Included in that total were slightly more than one million motor carrier tariff filings, 116,000 railroad filings, 57,000 international ocean/land intermodal freight agreements, 56,000 water carrier filings, and 3,500 bus passenger submissions.[10] In addition, 38,000 new railroad contracts were submitted to the agency.[11] It should be noted that motor carrier contracts are no longer required to be filed with the commission.

In the trucking industry, rate decrease proposals must be filed at least one day prior to their implementation while rate increase proposals must be filed at least seven days before their effective date. Proposed rail decreases must also be filed one day in advance, but increase proposals must be filed 20 days in advance.

Any interested party, including the ICC itself, may protest a rate change that has been filed with the commission. However, far less than one percent of the rate changes filed with the ICC are suspended for commission investigation, and there has been a steady decline in rate complaints in recent years.[12]

Rate Change Protests

Normally, if a rate filed with the ICC is protested, the commission will suspend the rate proposal to allow itself sufficient time to study the proposal. The burden of proof in such proceedings rests with the party filing the complaint. Prior to the deregulation movement, the burden rested with the carrier proposing the rate change.

In judging the merits of a specific rate proposal that has been protested, the ICC must consider many factors. Naturally, the cost and demand data presented will be evaluated. Additionally, the ICC must ultimately decide if the proposed rates are "reasonable," and it must determine that they are not "unduly discriminatory." In terms of reasonableness, the rates must at the same time be low enough to facilitate traffic movement, yet high enough to generate adequate carrier revenues. It must also be established that the rates are not unduly discriminatory against particular persons, firms, or places. The meanings of both reasonable and unduly discriminatory are somewhat vague and, consequently, are subject to considerable ICC interpretation. In evaluating these factors, the ICC must also be sensitive to the potential impact of the rate change on shippers and carriers.

Once a rate change has been approved by the commission, it may be implemented by the carrier. However, the orders of the agency may, in certain cases, be appealed in the federal courts. For example, a party to a case might believe that the agency had misinterpreted the law or ignored important facts in making its decision. There are precedents for court reversal of ICC decisions in such cases.

THE RATE QUOTATION PROCESS

One seemingly simple but rather complex and important process in transportation is the quotation of rates to shippers. The complexity becomes obvious when one considers not only the millions of different commodities that are shipped, but also the multitude of origins and destinations between which these commodities might move. Further complicating this situation are the many routes that might be used in moving traffic between any specific origin-destination combination. The following discussion examines a variety of types of rates which are applied in the transportation industries.

Commodity and Contract Rates

Most regulated railroad, trucking and domestic water carrier traffic moves under "commodity" or "contract" rates. Commodity rates, which are often viewed as discount rates, are often established for a commodity which moves in large quantities on a rather regular basis, or if the traffic is needed by the carrier due to unused capacity or empty backhauls. Such rates generally state the commodity involved, the origins-destinations involved, and the minimum volume required to qualify for the rate.

As illustrated in Figure 9-1, commodity rates are quoted directly in a commodity tariff rather than through the medium of a freight classification. Commodity tariffs often make extensive use of grouping points of origin and destination. Many important commodities, such as coal, ore, cement, brick, grain, and livestock, generally move at commodity rates.

Companies offering "contract" carrier services do not hold themselves out to provide service to the general shipping public, but rather establish individual contracts with one or more shippers. Rates are agreed upon through negotiation between shippers and the contract carrier. Consequently, the collective pricing activities of rate bureaus do not apply to the contract carriage ratemaking process.

While the establishment of contract services had traditionally been permitted in both motor and water carriage, it was not until November 1978 that the ICC voted to allow railroads to offer such services to the shipping public. This marked a significant reversal of commission policy. Previously, the agency had contended that railroad contract ratemaking would be potentially anti-competitive. However, in its 1978 ruling the ICC concluded that adequate safeguards existed to protect the public interest. The Staggers Rail Act of 1980 authorized contract ratemaking by the railroads and required that such rates be filed with the Interstate Commerce Commission.[13] As noted in Chapter 3, the railroads have aggressively utilized their contract ratemaking authority in negotiating rates with large-volume shippers. It has been estimated that more than half of all railroad traffic now moves under contract rates.[14] The extent of railroad use of contract carriage is illustrated by the fact that the railroads filed more than 38,000 new contracts with the ICC during 1992.[15] More than 190,000 rail contracts were filed between 1985-1992.[16] In September 1992 the commission exempted railroads from contract filing requirements with the exception of

FIGURE 9-1

Sample Page from Trunk line Rail Commodity Tariff 3003D

Rates are in cents per 100 pounds, unless otherwise specified (See Item 190 and 195)

ITEM NO.	COMMODITIES & STCC (In carloads, unless otherwise stated)	APPLICATION	RATES	ROUTE (See page 45)
760	Liquors, Malt, Ale, Beer, Beer Tonic, Cereal Beverage, Porter or Stout as described in Item 56850.1 series, TL-CTR Freight Tariff E-2009-I, ICC C-1008. (20-821-10)			

FROM MERRIMACK, NH

To		A	B	To		A	B
Alexandria.	.VA	133	118	Fairmont.	.WV	153	138
Allentown	.PA	118	116	Farmington.	.VA	142	133
Altoona	.PA	140	124	Frederick.	.MD	133	118
Asbury Park . . .	.NJ	108	102	Front Royal	.VA	140	124
Atlantic City . . .	.NJ	121	107	Frostburg.	.MD	142	133
Baltimore	.MD	126	116	Georgetown Jct. . . .	.MD	133	118
Berlin.	.MD	133	118	Glyndon	.MD	126	116
Bluefield	.WV	179	158	Greenwich.	.VA	142	133
Bradford.	.PA	133	118	Hagerstown.	.MD	133	118
Bristol	.VA	179	158	Hampton.	.VA	142	133
Cape Charles. . . .	.VA	140	124	Harrisburg.	.PA	126	116
Carlisle.	.PA	126	116	Hazelton.	.PA	121	107
Chambersburg. . . .	.PA	133	118	Hinton.	.WV	174	151
Charleston.	.WV	174	151	Homer City.	.PA	142	133
Clarksburg.	.WV	153	138	Honesdale	.PA	118	105
Curwensville. . .	.PA	140	124	Huntington.	.WV	179	158
Easton.	.MD	126	116	Johnstown	.PA	142	133
Easton.	.PA	118	105	Kennett Square. . . .	.PA	119	106
Elkins.	.WV	158	140	Kingwood.	.WV	153	138
Elkton.	.MD	121	107	Lancaster	.PA	121	107
Erie.	.PA	138	122				

A - Minimum weight 60,000 pounds.

B - Minimum weight 80,000 pounds; not subject to rule 24 of UFC or Exceptions thereto nor to stopping-in-transit to complete loading or to partially unload.

Rates named in this Item are subject to the provisions of Item 245 and are not subject to the provisions of Items 80 and 85.

(0-B19-1)

765	Liquors, Malt, Ale, Beer, Beer Tonic, Cereal Beverage, Porter or Stout as described in Item 56850.1 series, TL-CTR Freight Tariff E-2009-I, ICC C-1008. (20-821-10)			

FROM MERRIMACK, NH

To		A	B	To		A	B
Lebanon.	.PA	121	107	Ridgway.	.PA	138	122
Lewiston	.PA	133	118	Roanoke.	.VA	167	151
Lynchburg.	.VA	153	138	Romney	.WV	142	133
Marlboro	.MD	127	118	Salisbury.	.MD	126	116
Martinsburg. . . .	.WV	127	118	Shamokin	.PA	121	107
Milford.	.DE	127	118	State College. . . .	.PA	133	118
Montandon.	.PA	127	118	Staunton	.VA	151	135
Morgantown.	.WV	127	118	Tamaqua.	.PA	121	107
Newark.	.NJ	105	88	Trenton.	.NJ	108	102
New Brunswick. . .	.NJ	108	102	Uniontown.	.PA	151	135
New Castle. . . .	.DE	118	105	Vineland	.NJ	119	106
Norfolk.	.VA	142	135	Washington	.DC	133	118
Norristown	.PA	118	105	Waterloo.	.VA	133	118
Petersburg. . . .	.VA	151	153	Waverly	.NJ	105	88
Philadelphia . . .	.PA	118	105	Welch.	.WV	180	159
Portsmouth. . . .	.VA	151	153	West Pittston. . . .	.PA	119	106
Pulaski.	.VA	174	151	Wildwood.	.NJ	121	107
Quantico	.VA	138	122	Williamson.	.WV	183	163
Reading.	.PA	119	106	Williamsport	.PA	126	116
Richmond	.VA	142	133	York.	.PA	126	116

A - Minimum weight 60,000 pounds.

B - Minimum weight 80,000 pounds; not subject to rule 24 of UFC or Exceptions thereto nor to stopping-in-transit to complete loading or to partially unload.

Rates in this Item are subject to the provisions of Item 245 and are not subject to the provisions of Items 80 and 85.

(0-B19-1)

SOURCE: Boston and Maine Railroad Corporation. Used by permission

contracts involving agricultural commodities.[17] That decision substantially reduced the contract filing burden of the railroads. It should be noted that very few rail contracts have been challenged at the ICC, and none have been suspended.[18]

Motor carriers are also extensively involved in contract carriage. The ICC has estimated that two-thirds of the nearly 50,000 motor carriers regulated by the agency engage in at least some contract carriage.[19] Truckers offering contract services are not required to file those contracts with the commission.

Rate Classification Systems

An alternative way for a carrier to quote a rate to a customer is through a rate classification. Rather than quoting an individual rate on each commodity moving between every possible origin-destination combination over every possible route, carriers have long attempted to simplify rate quotation through freight classification systems. These systems group commodities into a limited number of classes according to their transportation characteristics and then prescribe rates on the various classes. Rates quoted through such a process are called "class" rates. For many years classification systems were viewed as the foundation of the rate quotation process in transportation. However, due to the extensive contemporary use of commodity and contract rates, class rates are only applied to a very small percentage of the traffic which moves in interstate commerce. While classification systems can be used to determine a class rate for any commodity moving between any two points in the United States, there may also be a commodity rate which covers the movement. Invariably, the commodity rate is lower, and the shipper is entitled to the lowest rate available.

Understanding Classification Systems. A basic understanding of freight classification systems is useful to employees of carriers and shippers alike. To the carrier the classification system is still an important component of the rate quotation process. Knowledge of the system may be useful in developing prices for new commodity movements. Understanding of classification systems and their role in carrier pricing also enhances the ability of carrier employees to communicate with each other on important issues.

As viewed by the shipper, classification systems are still significant. Many commodities move in small quantities and therefore carriers do not offer commodity rates on such moves. Hence the traffic may move at class rates. Further, understanding of these systems may be useful in attempts to gain lower classifications for existing products and in getting new commodities classified. Communications with carrier representatives are also improved if both parties have a common frame of reference.

Although a shipper can request rate quotes from carriers, it is impractical to do so in some instances. This is particularly true if the company is conducting research such as market analysis that involves estimation of delivered prices (including freight charges) into many areas. Similarly, forecasts of expected transportation costs in markets presently served are simplified if shipper employees have a working knowledge of such classification systems. Finally, as discussed in Chapter 2, the shipper may want to audit a carrier's freight bills, and some of those may involve class rates. Due to the complexity of the pricing process, mistakes are common. For example, one source has estimated that mistakes are made on 5 to 6 percent of the freight bills sent to shippers by the motor carrier industry.[20] Freight bill auditing may be conducted internally if employees are familiar with carrier pricing systems. If not, freight bill audits would have to be conducted by outside auditors.

Development of the Rail Classification System. Development of freight classification systems predated the railroads. To simplify their pricing systems, early barge and wagon operators established limited numbers of freight classes and grouped commodities into these classes for rate quotation purposes.[21] For similar reasons, the railroads soon developed far more elaborate classification systems. However, as many railroads adopted individual classifications, different classification systems abounded. This caused problems in quoting rates on traffic that moved over the lines of more than one railroad.

Classification differences were quite cumbersome, and, following its creation in 1887, the ICC prodded the railroads to streamline the classification system.[22] Regional classification systems emerged before 1900, but it was not until 1956 that the Uniform Freight Classification system, which had been developed by the railroads, was extended to the entire country. Adoption of that system meant that the same commodity moving by rail anywhere in the United States would be placed in the same class.[23]

The rail industry maintains the Uniform Classification Committee, which handles classification of new commodities and applications for reclassification of commodities. In many instances, the committee holds hearings and takes testimony from carriers and shippers on such classification matters.

The Uniform Freight Classification contains 31 classes, 8 above class 100 and 22 below. Class 100 serves as the base class; other classes are stated as percentages of class 100. The highest is class 400; the lowest is class 13. Although these class numbers have no inherent meaning in terms of specific transportation charges, the higher the class number, the higher the related rate. This matter is explained in greater detail later in this chapter.

Classification Systems of Other Modes. The motor carrier industry has also developed several freight classification systems. Most motor carriers adopted the National Motor Freight Classification (NMFC) following passage of the Motor Carrier Act of 1935. The act required motor carriers to file rates with the ICC, and, rather than undertaking development of a completely new classification system, the motor carriers simply followed the rail classification. Consequently, most entries in the original National Motor Freight Classification had descriptions that were identical to those in the rail classification.[24] In fact, many entries are still identical due to rail-motor competition. The NMFC contains 18 different numerical classes, or ratings, ranging from a low of class 50 to a high of class 500.[25]

In 1952 the National Motor Freight Classification was modified to provide a single set of national ratings. A National Classification Board is maintained by the industry, and it functions in a parallel capacity to that of the Uniform Classification Committee of the railroads.

The other modes of intercity carriage have not developed similar national classification systems. Domestic water carriers often use the rail or motor classification systems.

Factors Considered in Rating Freight. Many factors are likely to be considered in establishing a classification "rating" for a particular commodity. These include:

1. Shipping weight per cubic foot
2. Liability for damage
3. Liability for damage to other commodities with which is transported
4. Perishability
5. Liability for spontaneous combustion or explosion
6. Susceptibility to theft
7. Value per pound in comparison with other articles
8. Ease or difficulty in loading or unloading
9. Stowability
10. Excessive weight
11. Excessive length
12. Care or attention necessary in loading and transporting
13. Trade conditions
14. Value of service
15. Competition with other commodities transported
16. Quantity offered as a single consignment.[26]

As might be expected, the importance assigned to each of these considerations is likely to vary from item to item.

Many commodities, particularly new commodities for which a rating has not yet been established, are classified by comparison with other commodities possessing similar transportation characteristics. This is often referred to as "classification by analogy." In fact, pending establishment of a specific rating for his traffic, a shipper may use such an analogy to determine the applicable rate on his shipments. That action, however, may be appealed by carriers.

Shippers may use similar logic in protesting to a classification committee that the rating on an existing commodity is too high (and hence related rates are too high). Carriers may also use such comparisons in attempting to get the ratings of specific commodities raised, thereby leading to higher rates on the traffic.

It must be remembered that determination of the rating of a specific commodity is just the first step in determining the applicable rate. The following discussion illustrates the class rate-determination process from beginning to end.

Use of a Classification System. As illustrated in Figure 9-2, which is a page from the National Motor Freight Classification of the trucking industry, items are listed alphabetically in classifications, and item descriptions are quite detailed. Consequently, the first step involved in using a freight classification is determination of the proper item description for the product being shipped. Once this definition is established and the item is located in the classification, the user must next determine the applicable item rating. Figure 9-2 also shows that motor carrier classifications typically specify less-than-truckload (LTL) and truckload (TL) ratings for a particular item.

It should be noted that there tend to be considerable absolute differences in the LTL and TL ratings. Remember, these are not rates, but the larger the rating, the higher the related rate. Also notice that the classification specifies a truckload minimum; this establishes the minimum shipment size that qualifies for the lower TL rating.

As discussed later in this chapter, in some instances shippers will send a lower quantity than the minimum TL shipment size "as the truckload minimum" to qualify for the lower TL rating.

Shipping Illustration. The following example will illustrate the use of a motor carrier classification system to determine a class rate for a shipment. Assume that you are shipping 10,000 pounds of self-developing photographic film from Needham, Massachusetts to Hempstead, New York. As shown in Figure 9-2, this is item number 39655. This quantity is less than the necessary volume to qualify for the truckload rating (24,000 pounds). Consequently, the relevant LTL rating for the shipment is 100.

At this point, you have only established the "rating" of the commodity being shipped. To obtain the related rate, you must now refer to a class tariff, a separate publication that is the equivalent of a transportation price list. This is no simple task because there are literally thousands of tariffs, some issued by bureaus and some by individual carries. Fortunately, due to the limited number of commodities shipped and destinations involved, most shippers generally use only a few tariffs on a regular basis. Consequently, the tariff-search process tends to be streamlined with more frequent use. However, shipments to new points tend

FIGURE 9-2

Sample Page for National Motor Freight Classification 100T

NATIONAL MOTOR FREIGHT CLASSIFICATION 100-T

Item	ARTICLES	CLASSES LTL	CLASSES TL	MW
39550	**Cake**, cocoa press, containing not to exceed 15 percent butter fat, in bags:			
Sub 1	Having value only for live stock feed mixtures or for fertilizer purposes	50	35	40
Sub 2	Having value other than for live stock feed mixtures or other than for fertilizer purposes	65	35	36
39560	**Calcite**, roasted, granular form, treated or coated, clinkered and burned to a dead state. LTL. in bags or barrels: TL, loose or in packages	50	35	50
39600	**CAMERA GROUP:** Articles consist of Cameras, Cinema or Photograph Materials, as described in items subject to this grouping.			
39620	**Cameras or Camera Outfits**, see Note, item 39622, in boxes	125	70	15
39622	NOTE—Provisions on outfits only apply when consisting of camera, film, flashholder and reflector, with or without flashbulbs, batteries or carrying case.			
39630	**Cases**, carrying, reel or slide, NOI, in boxes	100	77.5	14
39635	**Cases**, slide carrying or storage, sheet steel, not exceeding 35 united inches, in boxes	85	45	30
39640	**⊙Dry Plates or Films**, unexposed, NOI, in boxes	100	70	30
39650	**Dry Plates**, glass, unexposed, in boxes	85	55	30
39655	**Film**, photographic, self-developing **(Self-Developing Film Packs)**, see Note, item 39656	100	70	24
39656	NOTE—Applies on self-developing film kits or packs consisting of unexposed photographic film, sensitized photographic paper and photographic finishing solution.			
39660	**⊙Films**, photographic, moving picture or other than moving picture, **or Records**, on films; exposed, non-flammable, not exceeding 35 mm, in boxes	200	85	20
39665	**⊙Films**, photographic, moving picture or other than moving picture, **or Records**, on films; exposed, non-flammable, exceeding 35 mm but not exceeding 70 mm, in boxes	300	300	AQ
39670	**Lenses**, camera, in boxes	200	100	10
39675	**Machines**, photographic film developing or processing, NOI, see Note, item 39677, in boxes or crates	92.5	45	30
39677	NOTE—Will also apply on machines for developing or processing X-ray film.			
39680	**Meters**, exposure, photographic, with or without carrying cases, in boxes	200	200	AQ
39690	**Moving Picture Film Cans, Cores, Magazines, Reels or Film Spools**, metal, empty, in boxes	85	37.5	30
39700	**Moving Picture Films, or Films**, other than moving picture; exposed, NOI, in boxes	0	0	
39710	**Outfits**, amateur retouching, in boxes	85	55	30
39720	**Outfits**, amateur printing and developing, in boxes	85	55	30
39730	**Outfits**, motion picture film developing or drying, **or Parts**, in boxes or crates	200	85	20
39740	**Photographers' Materials**, NOI, in boxes, see Note, item 39742	100	70	20
39742	NOTE—Negative flats, used in making lithographic printing plates, may be shipped in fibre tubes with ends securely closed.			
39744	**Photographers' Sinks or Print Washers**, without mechanical or electrical equipment, with or without necessary plumbing fixtures:			
Sub 1	Plastic, with or without bases of same or other materials, subject to Item 170 and having a density in pounds per cubic foot of:			
Sub 2	Less than 6	200	200	AQ
Sub 3	6 or greater	150	100	12
Sub 4	Steel, with or without bases of same or other materials	150	100	12
39746	**Pictures**, stereoscope, consisting of transparencies mounted in fibreboard discs, in boxes	110	55	30
39750	**Projectors**, motion or still picture, see Note, item 39752, in boxes	125	70	20
39752	NOTE—Not to exceed 100 feet of non-flammable ''safety'' film may be accepted with shipments of toy moving picture machines.			
39760	**Screens**, moving picture, NOI, in boxes	125	85	12
39770	**Screens**, projection, portable, roller type, other than motor operated, with or without stands, in boxes or crates	85	55	24
39775	**Screens**, television projection, SU, in boxes	300	300	AQ
39785	**Stands or Tripods**, camera, in boxes or crates:			
Sub 1	SU	200	85	12
Sub 2	KD	100	70	20
39790	**Tanks or Trays**, photographers, cooling or heating, in boxes or crates	100	70	16
39795	**Trays**, photographic slide or transparency, still picture projector, plastic, with or without components of other materials, in boxes	100	70	24
39800	**Candelabra, Candle Holders or Candlesticks**, NOI, other than electric, other than glass and other than gold or silver or gold or silver plated metal, in boxes	100	70	20
39810	**Candles**, NOI, see Note, item 39811, in boxes or Package 2213, subject to Item 170 and having a density in pounds per cubic foot of:			
Sub 1	Less than 1	400	400	AQ
Sub 2	1 but less than 2	300	300	AQ
Sub 3	2 but less than 4	250	250	AQ
Sub 4	4 but less than 6	150	100	12
Sub 5	6 but less than 8	125	85	15
Sub 6	8 but less than 10	100	70	18
Sub 7	10 but less than 12	92.5	65	20
Sub 8	12 but less than 15	85	55	26
Sub 9	15 or greater	70	40	36
39811	NOTE—Also applies on candles contained in or formed in glass or plastic containers; or candles in metal holders with or without shades, other than candelabra or candlesticks.			
39820	**Candles**, tear gas, packed in wooden boxes	150	100	20
39850	**Candlesticks**, wood or molded wood, in boxes	100	55	24

Courtesy: National Motor Freight Classification Committee.

to cause varying degrees of shipper trauma in determining the appropriate tariff to be used. In some cases, several tariffs must be used if the shipment moves between regions.

Assume that you have determined the appropriate tariff. It is now necessary to relate your shipment to a specific origin and destination. Tariffs list origin and destination combinations and assign them "rate basis numbers." In many instances, groupings of origins or destinations are assigned a common rate basis number. Increasingly, those numbers are determined on the basis of zip codes. Figure 9-3 presents a rate basis table from a motor carrier class tariff. As noted earlier, your shipment is moving between Needham, Massachusetts and Hempstead, New York. This rate basis table is based on the first three numbers of the zip codes for origin-destination combinations. The zip code for Needham is 02192 and Hempstead's is 11550. This origin-destination combination is represented by the rate basis number 247. This number is determined by reading across the line 115-116 and down column 020,021,022.

Thus far you have determined the rating, which specifies what is moving, and the rate basis number, which indicates the origin-destination combination. The final step in actually determining the rate is the cross referencing of these two numbers in the tariff section, which specifies "rates in cents per 100 pounds shipped." Figure 9-4 illustrates such a tariff section. Note that rate basis numbers 246, 247, and 248 are grouped in the first column. Weight groups are shown in the second column. The third column represents the class 100 rating. Since this shipment qualified for a class 100 rating, read down the class 100 column to the intersection with the rate basis number grouping 246, 247, and 248. Next, find the appropriate weight group, which in this case is 10,000 pounds, but less than 20,000 pounds. This yields the class rate in cents per 100 pounds shipped. Multiplication of that rate, $10.99, times the 100-pound equivalents in your shipment (100) gives $1,099 in total transportation charges.

As mentioned earlier, due to the significant differences in LTL and TL rates it is often possible to save transportation dollars by sending a shipment that weighs less than the truckload minimum listed in the classification as if it met the truckload minimum weight. In the illustration just completed, the base rate of the LTL shipment is $10.99 per hundred-weight. As illustrated in Figure 9-4, the class rate for the truckload rating of 70 at 24,000 pounds (in the 20,000-29,999 weight group) is $4.79 per hundred weight. To determine when a shipment should be sent "as the truckload minimum weight" instead of at its actual weight, the following simple formula can be used:

FIGURE 9-3

Sample Page from Class Tariff 599-B, Section 2

THE NEW ENGLAND MOTOR RATE BUREAU, INC., AGENT

TARIFF 599-B

SECTION 2

TABLE OF RATE BASIS NUMBERS

(SEE SECTION 2-A FOR APPLICATION OF ZIP CODES WITH DECIMALS)

BETWEEN ZIP CODES (1ST 3 DIGITS)

APPLY RATE BASIS NUMBERS

AND ZIP CODES (1ST 3 DIGITS)	010 011	012	013	014	015 016	017	018	019	020 021 022	023 024	025	026
063	17	27	24	22	18	20	27	28	22	23	327	335
064–066	15	22	22	29	24	28	33	35	31	32	335	342
067	14	19	20	28	23	27	32	35	30	31	335	342
068–069	22	23	28	34	30	33	38	40	36	36	340	347
070–076	232	233	237	243	239	242	247	249	245	245	347	353
088–089	235	236	240	245	242	245	249	251	248	248	350	355
100–104	232	233	237	243	239	242	247	249	245	245	347	353
105–108	228	228	233	239	235	238	243	245	241	241	345	351
110	234	235	239	245	240	243	249	250	247	248	349	355
111–114	232	233	237	243	239	242	247	249	245	245	347	353
115–116	234	235	239	245	240	243	249	250	247	248	349	355
117–118	337	338	342	348	344	347	351	353	349	350	351	359
119	344	345	349	353	350	353	357	358	355	355	357	364

Courtesy: The New England Motor Rate Bureau.

Figure 9-4
Sample Page from Class Tariff 599-B; Section 3

THE NEW ENGLAND MOTOR RATE BUREAU, INC., AGENT

TARIFF 599-B

SECTION 3

(SPECIAL CLASS RATES FOR CLASSES 100, AND LOWER)

RATE BASIS NUMBER	WEIGHT GROUPS	CLASSES RATES IN CENTS PER 100 POUNDS								
		100	92 1/2	85	77 1/2	70	65	60	55	50
	Less than 500 pounds	2924	2721	2545	2412	2223	2090	1959	1842	1710
	500-900 lbs.	2280	2121	1983	1882	1734	1629	1528	1436	1335
	1,000-1,999 lbs.	1718	1599	1494	1384	1281	1202	1125	1057	981
241	2,000-4,999 lbs.	1440	1340	1239	1146	1059	987	917	849	784
242	5,000-9,999 lbs.	1174	1087	998	909	820	763	704	646	588
	10,000-19,999 lbs.	1054	973	895	816	736	684	632	580	526
	20,000-29,999 lbs.	567	549	526	488	454	426	401	396	380
	30,000-39,999 lbs.	429	415	392	352	329	306	288	282	266
	40,000 lbs. or more	406	386	369	331	306	285	269	264	249
	Less than 500 pounds	2946	2742	2564	2431	2241	2107	1974	1856	1725
	500-900 lbs.	2300	2137	2000	1896	1747	1644	1539	1449	1345
	1,000-1,999 lbs.	1736	1613	1510	1397	1293	1216	1135	1067	989
243	2,000-4,999 lbs.	1458	1356	1256	1158	1071	998	925	861	795
	5,000-9,999 lbs.	1187	1097	1009	920	833	771	712	652	592
	10,000-19,999 lbs.	1063	984	901	822	742	691	638	585	533
	20,000-29,999 lbs.	573	558	534	495	460	429	406	400	384
	30,000-39,999 lbs.	437	419	396	357	332	310	291	287	270
	40,000 lbs. or more	414	392	372	335	310	288	272	268	252
	Less than 500 pounds	2972	2764	2585	2452	2258	2124	1990	1872	1738
	500-900 lbs.	2191	2155	2013	1911	1761	1657	1552	1460	1356
	1,000-1,999 lbs.	1749	1626	1525	1409	1304	1226	1147	1075	995
244	2,000-4,999 lbs.	1470	1369	1266	1171	1082	1009	936	869	803
245	5,000-9,999 lbs.	1203	1113	1021	933	843	782	723	663	603
	10,000-19,999 lbs.	1075	993	917	835	753	698	646	591	539
	20,000-29,999 lbs.	581	564	540	500	465	437	414	405	390
	30,000-39,999 lbs.	441	423	399	362	336	313	297	291	273
	40,000 lbs. or more	418	396	376	338	313	293	275	272	255
	Less than 500 pounds	3011	2800	2619	2481	2288	2154	2018	1898	1761
	500-900 lbs.	2350	2185	2045	1938	1786	1681	1575	1482	1374
	1,000-1,999 lbs.	1777	1653	1546	1432	1324	1243	1162	1093	1013
246	2,000-4,999 lbs.	1495	1392	1287	1191	1100	1027	950	885	816
247	5,000-9,999 lbs.	1231	1139	1045	951	861	801	737	677	614
248	10,000-19,999 lbs.	1099	1015	933	851	769	714	660	605	549
	20,000-29,999 lbs.	602	585	562	517	479	452	427	421	401
	30,000-39,999 lbs.	461	442	419	377	349	327	308	305	285
	40,000 lbs. or more	450	427	403	365	338	314	298	293	274
	Less than 500 pounds	3050	2838	2654	2518	2319	2182	2045	1924	1785
	500-900 lbs.	2384	2218	2075	1965	1812	1704	1598	1503	1394
	1,000-1,999 lbs.	1805	1680	1571	1454	1345	1264	1183	1111	1031
249	2,000-4,999 lbs.	1526	1416	1311	1212	1120	1044	967	899	833
	5,000-9,999 lbs.	1259	1162	1068	974	881	817	757	692	629
	10,000-19,999 lbs.	1124	1040	956	873	786	731	675	618	563
	20,000-29,999 lbs.	618	599	574	533	496	464	439	433	415
	30,000-39,999 lbs.	471	453	428	387	359	336	315	312	293
	40,000 lbs. or more	460	437	415	373	344	321	303	299	279

Courtesy: The New England Motor Rate Bureau (modified for use.)

$$TL \text{ rate x } TL \text{ min. wt.} = LTL \text{ rate x } Y$$
$$\$4.79 \text{ x } 24,000 = \$10.99 \text{ x } Y$$
$$114,960 = 10.99YY$$
$$10,460 = Y$$

Therefore, given the prevailing rates on moving self-developing photographic film between Needham, Massachusetts and Hempstead, New York, any shipment weighing more 10,460 pounds should be shipped as 24,000.

According to transportation law, carriers must inform shippers of this "breakeven point" for their freight and should bill the shipper accordingly. However, mistakes are sometimes made in the billing process, and this breakeven formula can be useful to shippers in reviewing carrier charges.

In summary, the basic steps involved in the determination of the applicable rates are as follows: (1) use the classification to look up the commodity being shipped and to determine its rating; (2) select the appropriate tariff and determine the rate basis number that applies to the origin-destination combination of the shipment: (3) cross reference the rating and the rate base number in the section of the tariff that gives class rates in cents per 100 pounds shipped.

Exception Rates. Although development of freight classification systems sought to simplify the rate-quotation process, competitive conditions have compelled carriers to move much of their traffic at rates that differ from normal class rates. As discussed earlier in this chapter, one way to do so is to establish commodity rates. Another is to file "exception" ratings.

An exception rating is essentially an amendment to the classification, which is created to meet competition or to attract a particular type of traffic that the carrier believes will not be attracted by existing class rates. The exception substitutes a lower rating for the normal one. It is still a rating, however, and the class rate applicable to that rating still applies. Frequently, exceptions are published along with rates in a class rate tariff, but some separate exception tariffs do exist.

Other Carrier Charges. The commodity, class and exception tariffs discussed thus far yield rates that cover not only the linehaul movement, but also normal pickup and delivery and terminal processing expenses. However, many accessorial or additional services may be offered by carriers at additional charge. Storage, diversion in transit to an alternative destination, and multiple stops for loading or unloading are but a few of the accessorial services that may be available. The fees for such services are generally contained in special-service tariffs; these fees must be added to the relevant commodity, class or exception rates to determine the total transportation charges for a particular move that requires such special services.

Other Rate Terminology

The jargon pertaining to transportation pricing is extensive. Commodity, contract, class and exception rates have already been discussed. However, several other significant rate terms should be explored.

Transportation rates are sometimes discussed in terms of the manner in which the line-haul journey occurs. The term "local rate" is often applied to a rate which covers a movement that takes place entirely over the lines of one carrier. For example, if a motor carrier picks up a truckload of traffic in New York and carries it to its final destination in Los Angeles, the rate that covers this movement may be referred to as a "local rate." In contrast, if that same shipment is interlined with another trucking company on its way to Los Angeles, the rate that applies to the shipment is often referred to as a "joint rate." In both cases, the terms local and joint refer only to how the traffic moved. The rates are still commodity, class or exception rates and are quoted in the appropriate tariffs.

Two other terms frequently employed in transportation pricing are the "any commodity rate" or the "freight-all-kinds" (FAK) rate. Such rates ignore the commodity being shipped and instead establish flat charges for moving certain volumes between specific points. These rates de-emphasize value as a pricing consideration; they are most extensively utilized in several rail intermodal plans.

"Incentive rates" are rates that encourage shippers to tender very large shipments to carriers. For example, a railroad might offer a base rate that applies to the first 50,000 pounds of a commodity loaded in a rail car and a lower rate on any additional volume loaded in the same car. Incentive rates encourage heavier loading of equipment and hence lead to better utilization of the equipment.

"Multiple car" and "multiple truck" rates are quoted to cover the carrying capacity of more than one transportation vehicle. Such rates are often quoted to offset the capacity advantages enjoyed by competitive forms of carriage. An illustration of such multiple-vehicle rates would be provided by a rate offered by a railroad on the movement of 1,000 tons of coal, even though the capacity of a single hopper car is closer to 100 tons.

The term "transit privilege" has been applied to an agreement in which a carrier establishes a single rate to cover not only the line-haul movement of a commodity, but also any stops enroute for such treatment as milling, fabricating, or refining. Grain movements are often handled under such agreements, which permit grain to be unloaded and milled, then reloaded as flour and moved to its ultimate destination. Transit privileges originated in the 1870s and have been extended to commodities such as lumber, steel, and cotton.

Distance, Weight, and Rate Relationships

As might be expected, freight rates tend to increase as the distance from origin to destination increases. However, rates are only generally related to distance.

Class rates tend to be structured on a distance basis; they typically increase with distance according to "mileage blocks" rather than with each additional mile. These rates do not increase in direct proportion to distance; rather, the increase per mileage block rises less than proportionally as total distance increases. This is known as the "tapering principle" of freight rates. The taper is caused by a variety of factors, including the spreading of terminal costs over longer distances and the perceived lowering of line-haul per-unit costs as distance increases. The tapering distance-rate relationship is illustrated in Figure 9-5. In the illustration it is assumed that a minimum charge is levied on the shipper regardless of shipment distance; hence the curve begins above the origin.

One major departure from this mileage-rate relationship is the group-rate system, which groups points of origin or destination, or both. Such systems and

FIGURE 9-5

Illustration of Rate Taper with Distance

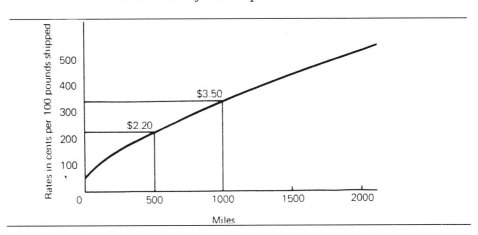

the related rates, which are often called "blanket rates," take two basic forms. Either all points included in the group where traffic originates are assessed the same rate for the same shipments to a specific destination, or all points in a destination group will take the same rate from a specific point of origin. Blanket rates tend to ignore distance, sometimes over broad geographical areas, in assessing transportation charges. In some instances such grouping of origins or destinations have been established largely for the convenience of carriers to simplify rate quotation. In other cases, the desire of shippers to be competitive in distant markets has prompted establishment of group-rate systems. One such blanket rate applied the same rate on lumber shipments for the Pacific Northwest to all destination points in the Northeast.[27] Another levied the same carload charges on dried fruits and vegetables from Fresno, California, to all points outside the Mountain Pacific territory except New York, which receives a lower rate.[28]

Commodity rates, which are influenced by numerous competitive factors and the desire of carriers to generate greater equipment utilization, tend to be less closely related to distance than class rates.

Freight rate levels are also influenced by shipment size. Transportation charges per unit of traffic handled tend to decline as shipment size increases. This weight-rate relationship encourages larger loads and better equipment utilization. Such "weight breaks" lead many shippers to accumulate freight and ship in larger quantities to take advantage of the weight-rate taper.

OTHER RATEMAKING DEVELOPMENTS

During the past several years the pace of ratemaking change and innovation has quickened considerably. Regulatory reform has played a major role in stimulating those changes by giving carriers much greater pricing freedom.

Rate Discounting and Service Guarantees

One manifestation of this increased freedom is a growing emphasis on discounting. Competitive pressures have promoted extensive discounting in air carriage, and discounting has become rampant in the trucking industry. According to one recent study, the median trucking discount, which is generally based on class rates, averaged between 45-49 percent in 1992.[29] While such discounts have become commonplace, many executives in the industry believe that they are eroding the financial stability of the industry. During 1993, Thomas Boswell, Overnite's Chief Executive Officer, referred to discounting as "a self destructive binge that defies logic...we are pricing ourselves out of the business."[30] By mid-1993 several large LTL carriers, including Consolidated Freightways and Yellow Freight System, had begun a program to roll back discounts by a modest two percent. However, even that action was opposed by many shippers who had come to expect such deep discounts.[31]

Many carriers are now linking price and service offers. One such trucking program offered a 40 percent credit on class-rated LTL freight if it was late by more than three days. Other carriers have offered complete refunds if service standards are not met.

Electronic Tariff Filing

As electronic linkages between companies have become more common, the Interstate Commerce Commission has sought to promote electronic tariff filing (ETF) as an alternative to printed tariffs. In 1989 the commission adopted rules authorizing the railroads to engage in ETF. However, according to the agency, the railroads have "taken minimal advantage of their authority to file electronic tariffs."[32] Regulated truckers have not yet been authorized to file tariffs electronically, and the industry has not lobbied aggressively for that authorization.[33]

In a related development, carriers and shippers are increasingly using computer technology and software to enhance managerial decision making. Many shippers use software to analyze various logistics tradeoffs, and with the widespread introduction of personal computers into logistics planning, such applications are expanding rapidly. Further, many firms now routinely exchange purchase orders, invoice transactions, and other business information automatically. The ICC now permits freight bills and loss and damage claims to be transmitted electronically as an alternative to paper bills and claims.

The Undercharge Issue

One of the most controversial carrier ratemaking topics to surface in many years has been the issue of carrier "undercharges." This arose when the trustees of bankrupt motor carriers began sending "balance due" bills to shippers. Prior to declaring bankruptcy those carriers had negotiated discounted rates with shippers, and shippers had paid those rates for service. However, in many instances the discounted rates were never filed with the ICC. Therefore, the trustees argued that the relevant rate was the one which had been filed with the commission, and shippers owed the difference between those rates and the rates which had been previously paid. The ICC responded by allowing shippers to defend themselves against such claims. They could do so by arguing that carriers, by negotiating discounted rates, failing to file those rates with the agency, then filing undercharge claims, were engaging in unreasonable rate practices.[34] However, in its 1990 decision in the Maislin case, the Supreme Court ruled that the ICC did not have the statutory power to declare undercharge claims unreasonable rate practices.[35]

That court ruling led to an avalanche of undercharge bills being sent to thousands of shippers who had done business with motor carriers prior to carrier bankruptcies. The amount of money being sought was staggering. One congressional estimate of potential undercharge liability was $38 billion.[36]

Between 1990 and mid-1993 this issue was extensively debated in Congress. Shippers sought relief from those claims, arguing that they had done business in good faith and that they should not be responsible for the carriers' failure to file the discounted rates with the commission. On the other side of the issue were the trustees of the bankrupt carriers and the Teamsters who saw undercharge payments as the only way to obtain back wages and overdue pension contributions from the bankrupt carriers.[37]

The Senate passed an undercharge bill in June 1993. It not only sought to allow shippers to challenge undercharge claims in federal court, but also provided for a settlement procedure for shippers wishing to end litigation by paying 10-20 percent of the total sought by the estates of the bankrupt carriers.[38] At that time the House version of the bill was still being debated.

RATE NEGOTIATIONS

As the deregulation movement has given carriers more pricing freedom, negotiating skills have become more important to carriers and shippers. Clearly, carriers must understand both the nature of their costs and the nature of demand which exists in the markets they serve if they are to effectively price their services. At the same time, many shippers attempt to estimate the costs incurred by carriers as part of their preparation for negotiations with carriers. They also must establish what various service levels are worth to them.

As discussed extensively in Chapter 2, it is very important that shippers understand what constitutes a good account to a carrier. In some instances, carriers are rather selective with respect to the accounts they pursue.

In many instances, the negotiation process in transportation has become more formalized and professionalized in recent years. This is particularly true with respect to the purchase of transportation services by large companies. Such companies often utilize a rather formal carrier selection process which involves asking carriers to provide proposals concerning how, and at what cost, they would handle the company's traffic in specific markets. This process generates substantial carrier costs in preparing a response to the shipper, and, there is no guarantee that the carrier will be selected by the shipper.

As carrier/shipper negotiations become more common and important in the transportation industries, the issue of negotiating philosophy arises. That is, do the parties to the negotiation see it as a win/lose or a win/win situation?[39] Traditionally, many shippers, particularly those with substantial bargaining leverage, have sought to obtain the lowest possible freight rate, regardless of the impact on the carrier. Negotiations with carriers are often viewed as adversarial contests in which there are clear winners and losers. While this approach minimizes short-term transportation costs, it is unlikely to foster long-term relationships.

In contrast, many manufacturers are increasingly stressing the development of long-term "partnerships" with their suppliers which are beneficial to both parties. While some shippers have adopted this philosophy in negotiating with carriers, it is far from prevalent in the transportation marketplace.

SUMMARY

Traditionally, much of interstate transportation ratemaking took place in a rather constrained environment in which regulatory agencies exerted considerable influence. The regulatory reform movement has eliminated federal pricing controls in air carriage, and significantly lessened them in surface transportation.

Regulatory changes have also affected the collective ratemaking activities of carriers in the rail, truck and domestic water modes. While rate bureaus still exist, they play a far more limited role, and single carrier pricing initiatives dominate the marketplace.

As a result of the broad changes that have been made in transportation's regulatory structure, pricing has become a more significant competitive variable. Ratemaking has increasingly become a function of carrier-shipper negotiation, and less a function of federal regulatory agency procedures.

The rate quotation process in transportation is still complex. While freight classification systems still exist, their relative significance has decreased as competitive considerations have led many carriers to initiate commodity and contract rates. The bulk of intercity rail, motor, and water carrier traffic now moves under such rates.

DISCUSSION QUESTIONS

1. In a ratemaking context, what is an independent action, and what is its importance to you as a shipper?
2. Do you believe that carrier rate bureaus should be allowed to maintain their antitrust exemption? Be specific and discuss the reasoning behind your answer.
3. Compare the carrier ratemaking process in non-regulated transportation markets with that which occurs in regulated transportation markets.
4. What is the reason for the distance taper in the freight rate structure?
5. Discuss the steps involved in the process of determining the appropriate class rate to be applied to a specific shipment.

6.   What are commodity rates and why are they important?

NOTES

1.   Ray Bohman, "A Look at the Latest LTL Rate Hikes," *Traffic Management* (January, 1993), p. 25.

2.   The other modes of domestic transportation did not have collective ratemaking bodies, nor were they granted antitrust exemptions for such activity.

3.   If state based motor carrier rate bureaus are included, there are more than 80 motor carrier bureaus. See Mitchell E. MacDonald, "Rate Bureaus: Is Time Passing Them By?"*Traffic Management* (August, 1992), pp. 46-8.

4.   Robert C. Fellmeth, *The Interstate Commerce Omission* (New York: Grossman Publishers, Inc., 1970), p. 141.

5.   See U.S. Department of Transportation, Office of the Secretary, *Executive Briefing: Transportation Regulatory Modernization and Assistance Legislation* (Washington, D.C.: the Department, 1972), pp. 5-21, 45-50.

6.   U.S. Motor Carrier Ratemaking Study Commission, *Collective Ratemaking in the Trucking Industry* (Washington, D.C.: the Commission, 1983), p. xi.

7.   See "Management Update," *Traffic Management* (September, 1991), p. 1.

8.   Association of American Railroads, *Basic Provisions of Railroad Revitalization and Regulatory Reform Act of 1976* (Washington, D.C.: the Association, 1976), p. 1.

9.   See "Overnite Drops Rate Bureaus, Cites $300,000 Savings," *Traffic Management* (April, 1991), p. 21; also, Mitchell E. MacDonald, "Rate Bureaus: Is Time Passing Them By?" *Traffic Management* (August, 1992), p. 46.

10.   U.S. Interstate Commerce Commission, *1992 Annual Report* (Washington, D.C.: U.S. Government Printing Office, 1993), p. 79.

11.   Ibid.

12.   U.S. Interstate Commerce Commission, *1988 Annual Report* (Washington, D.C.: U.S. Government Printing Office, 1989), p. 33.

13.   Association of American Railroads, "Late-Night Vote Passes Rail Dereg Bill," *Rail News Update* (October 1, 1980), p. 1.

14.   Discussion with Harvey Levine, Association of American Railroads, Washington, D.C., July 16, 1993.

15.   U.S. Interstate Commerce Commission, *1992 Annual Report*, p. 79.

16.   "Disclosing Freight Contracts," *Journal of Commerce*, New York, March 26, 1992, p. 6A.

17. Ex Parte No. 387 (Sub-No.964), *Railroad Transportation Contracts* (not printed), September 3, 1992.

18. See Geoffrey H. Brown, "Shippers Back ICC Plan to End Contract Filing Rule for Rails," *Journal of Commerce*, New York, May 18, 1992, p. 2B; also, "Disclosing Freight Contracts," *Journal of Commerce*, New York, March 26, 1992, p. 6A.

19. Interstate Commerce Commission, *1992 Annual Report*, p. 53.

20. Information provided by trucking industry executives.

21. D. Philip Locklin, *Economics of Transportation*, 7th ed. (Homewood, IL: Richard D. Irwin, Inc., 1972),p. 174.

22. Locklin, p. 175.

23. However, as discussed later in this chapter, exceptions may be filed to modify this rating.

24. Charles A. Taff, *Commercial Motor Transportation*, 4th ed. (Homewood, IL: Richard D. Irwin, Inc., 1969), p. 310.

25. Ray Bohman, "The Distortion in Class Rates," *Traffic Management* (May, 1993), p. 31.

26. *Motor Carrier Rates in New England*, 47 MCC 660, 661 (1948).

27. Stuart Daggett and J.P. Carter, *Structure of Railroad Rates* (Berkeley, CA: University of California Press, 1947), as cited in Dudley F. Pegrum, *Transportation: Economics and Public Policy* (Homewood, IL: Richard D. Irwin, Inc., 1973), p. 225.

28. Roy J. Sampson and Martin T. Farris, *Domestic Transportation: Practice, Theory, and Policy*, 4th ed. (Boston: Houghton Mifflin Company, 1979), pp. 205-6.

29. Ray Bohman, "Discounting: No End in Sight," *Traffic Management* (February, 1993), p. 23.

30. Dane Hamilton, "Freight Rate Discounts Likely to Continue in Truck Industry," *Journal of Commerce*, New York, July 9, 1993, p. 3B.

31. Ibid.

32. U.S. Interstate Commerce Commission, *1991 Annual Report*, p. 73.

33. Ibid.

34. David L. Sparkman, "Rate Undercharge Issue is Focus of Court, ICC Rulings," *Transport Topics* (April 29, 1991, p. 6.

35. Ibid.

36. Gregory S. Johnson, "Shippers Still Smarting Over Undercharge Issue," *Journal of Commerce*, Special Report, New York, November 16, 1992, p. 6A.

37. Geoffrey H. Brown, "Rate Undercharge Rift Narrows, But Teamster Hurdle Remains," *Journal of Commerce*, New York, March 25, 1992, p. 2B.

38. "Trucking Bill Rolling in House," *Journal of Commerce*, New York, July 12, 1993, p. 6A.

39. For an interesting discussion of alternative negotiating philosophies see Roger Fisher and William Ury, *Getting to Yes: Negotiating Agreement without Giving In* (Boston: Houghton Mifflin Company, 1981).

SELECTED REFERENCES

Beier, Frederick J. "Transportation Contracts and the Experience Effect." *Journal of Business Logistics*, Vol. 10, No. 2 (1989), pp. 73-89.

Bohman, Ray. "Discounting: No End in Sight." *TrafficManagement* (February, 1993), p. 23.

Crum, Michael R., and Benjamin J. Allen. "The Changing Nature of the Motor-Carrier Shipper Relationship: Implications for the Trucking Industry." *Transportation Journal*, Vol. 31, No. 2 (Winter, 1991), pp. 41-54.

Davis, Grant M., and Charles S. Sherwood. *Rate Bureaus and Antitrust Conflicts in Transportation*. New York: Praeger Publishers, Inc., 1975.

Harrington, Lisa. "Purchasing and Transportation Get Their Acts Together." *Inbound Logistics* (May, 1992), pp. 20-5.

MacDonald, Mitchell E. "Rate Bureaus: Is Time Passing Them By?" *Traffic Management* (August, 1992), pp. 46-8.

Sacasas, Rene, Paul Munter and George D. Sanders. "Unwanted Assets? Motor Carriers and Auditors in a Post-Maislin World." *Transportation Journal*, Vol. 29, No. 1 (Fall, 1989), pp. 51-7.

Sharp, Jeffrey M., and Robert A. Novack. "Motor Carrier Deregulation and the Filed Rate Doctrine: Catalysts for Conflict." *Transportation Journal*, Vol. 32, No. 2 (Winter, 1992), pp. 46-53.

"Shipper Super Heavyweights." *Traffic Management* (October, 1992), pp. 32-6, 38 and 41.

U.S. Interstate Commerce Commission. *The Impact of the 4R Act: Railroad Ratemaking Provisions*. Washington, D.C.: the Commission, 1978.

U.S. Motor Carrier Ratemaking Study Commission. *Collective Ratemaking in the Trucking Industry*. Washington, D.C.: the Commission, 1983.

Part Four

TRANSPORTATION REGULATION AND PROMOTION

CHAPTER TEN

THE DEVELOPMENT OF TRANSPORTATION REGULATION

Despite the regulatory changes that have occurred in recent years, the transportation system of the United States still operates in a highly regulated environment. The regulatory structure seeks not only to protect the shipping public from potential carrier abuses, but also attempts to facilitate the development of an efficient and economical transportation network that adequately serves national needs.

Understanding of the regulatory structure is important, because that structure determines the guidelines by which shipper, carrier, and governmental interaction occurs. To promote such understanding, this chapter traces the development of the common-carrier concept and reviews the nature of regulation as it evolved between the late 19th Century and the 1940s. Throughout the chapter, attention is given to the forces that led to regulation and the impact that regulation had on the national transportation system.

THE COMMON CARRIER CONCEPT

Since the Middle Ages, transportation has been subjected to various regulatory controls. Such regulations have their roots in early English law, which considered those engaged in the provision of transportation services to the general public to be fulfilling a "common calling." As a result, common carriers were required to serve all customers at reasonable rates and without discrimination. Carriers were also held liable for the safe delivery of goods tendered to them.

The nature and degree of early regulation were influenced by public dependency upon such service and the potential abuses inherent in the carrier-shipper relationship, particularly if the carrier operated as a market monopolist. As a result of this dependency relationship, common carriers were held to be "affected with the public interest."

STATE CONTROL OF EARLY RAILROADS

In the United States, transportation regulation was not applied extensively until the late 19th Century. Prior to that a laissez-faire attitude prevailed as the economy and the nation's transportation system developed.

In the pre-Civil War period, competition among railroads, canals, riverboats, and wagons precluded the need for extensive regulation. This was to change, however, with the growing maturity of the railroad industry.

Although the bulk of the capital that financed the development of the railroads came from the private sector, state and local governments used tax concessions, loans, security guarantees, and land grants to entice the railroads to lay new track. Similarly, massive federal land grants equal to 6.8 percent of the total land area of the United States were extended to a number of railroads to facilitate a transcontinental linkage which was completed in 1869.[1]

These financial inducements not only led to tremendous expansion of the rail network, but also provided an opportunity for financial mismanagement. Many early railroad promoters amassed sizable fortunes by swindling investors in railroad securities. Attempts were made to conceal earnings, worthless stock was issued, and fraudulent bankruptcies were filed. The behavior of the "robber barons" who manipulated the railroad industry during that period played a major role in turning public attitude against the railroads. Such abuses led to calls for railroad regulation.

Following the Civil War, competition in the rail industry grew in intensity. Extensive overbuilding had occurred over many routes, and excess capacity led to price wars between railroads. While prices over competitive routes were depressed, rates to less densely populated areas, which were typically served by a single carrier, rose dramatically. To alleviate the cutthroat nature of competition and to stabilize prices, the railroads established traffic pools which apportioned the traffic of a given route among the carriers. However, the desire of individual carriers to generate additional traffic led to rampant rebates and other collusive agreements between carriers and shippers. The net result of such behavior was the failure of most traffic pool agreements. Discriminatory pricing practices were quite common as large shippers commanded lower rates than their competitors. The railroads, due to overcapacity, were in a poor bargaining position to deal with industrial giants.

THE GRANGE MOVEMENT

While the railroads attempted to cope with excess capacity and cutthroat competition, the agricultural sector also faced critical problems. Agricultural productivity had expanded greatly; however, domestic and foreign demand for grain declined following the Civil War. As a result, farm prices plummeted while inflation increased farm costs. Further, agrarians had invested heavily in the railroads, and they now found many railroad securities to be worthless. Additionally, rail service was poor, rates were high, and discrimination was widespread. In an effort to resolve their common problems (only some of which were railroad related), farmers in the Midwest relied upon a rural group known as the "Grange." This organization was founded in 1867 primarily as an education and social organization for farmers, but it soon became a vehicle for protest and political action against the railroads.[2] The Grange movement was particularly strong in Illinois, Iowa, Minnesota, and Wisconsin. Between 1871 and 1874 the legislatures of these states enacted Granger laws, which regulated various railroad activities. Although there were variations from state to state, the Granger laws were generally quite similar in content. Generally they established maximum-rate controls, attempted to prevent discrimination and limited railroad consolidations because they were viewed as being anti-competitive.

Granger Cases

The railroads argued that they could not function effectively in such a regulated environment, and sought to have the state laws overturned. They claimed that such regulation was unconstitutional, and that even if they could be regulated, they were interstate in nature and thus only subject to federal control.

These contentions led to a series of six Granger cases before the Supreme Court. The most important of the cases was Munn v. Illinois (1877) in which the Supreme Court ruled that the state had the right to regulate an industry "affected with the public interest," and that certain activities had fallen into that category under common law for centuries. Transportation was one such activity. This Supreme Court ruling became the basic foundation upon which transportation regulation was structured in this country.

Two other court findings in Munn v. Illinois were quite important. First, the Court ruled that the decisions of regulatory agencies were final and that once the right to regulate had been established, the role of the courts had been exhausted. However, a short time later this ruling was reversed by the Court, and the right of judicial review was established. Second, the Court ruled that until federal legislation was enacted to regulate interstate commerce, states could regulate such activities even though state action would indirectly affect interstate commerce. This ruling was subsequently reversed by the Court in the landmark Wabash case (1886), which played a major role in establishing federal regulation of transportation.[3] The specifics of the Wabash case are discussed later in this chapter.

Experience Under the Granger Laws

Despite the judicial support accorded to the Granger laws, the success of these statutes in regulating the railroads was limited. Commissions often proved incompetent, and discrimination among various shipping points and among shippers continued.[4] Some railroads worsened the situation by taking full advantage of the maximum-rate schedules prescribed for them.[5]

Railroad arguments against the Granger laws were reinforced by the Panic of 1873 (a short, severe depression), which caused a number of railroad bankruptcies and led to financial problems for many other carriers. The combination of these factors led the Granger states, with the exception of Illinois, to repeal or significantly modify the Granger laws by the late 1870s.

However, the Granger laws were important in several respects. They initiated the idea of the regulatory agency, and they clearly demonstrated the ineffectiveness of highly inflexible laws. More importantly, the Granger cases established the right of the state to formulate controls over businesses that were "affected with the public interest."

MOVEMENT TOWARD FEDERAL REGULATION

While the Granger laws were creating a transportation regulatory structure at the state level, at the national level Congress was also giving increasing attention to the railroads. Monopolistic abuses were being widely publicized, and representatives of agricultural states were joined by groups representing various shipper and merchant interests in calling for federal control of the railroads. Due to the failure of the rail industry's pooling efforts to stabilize prices and earnings, the executives of many railroads also publicly supported federal regulation.[6]

During the 1870s and early 1880s the issue of federal regulation of the railroads attracted increasing congressional attention as various study commissions and lobbyists argued the merits of such action. Finally, in 1886 the Supreme Court decision in the Wabash case made it apparent that effective railroad regulation would necessitate federal intervention. In that case, the Court held that states could not regulate an interstate business regardless of the inactivity of the federal government. This decision, which reversed the Supreme Court ruling on this matter in the Munn v. Illinois case, applied to the nearly three-fourths of the nation's rail traffic that was interstate in nature. Thus such operations were beyond state control. Congress responded to that ruling by passing the Act to Regulate Commerce (commonly known as the Interstate Commerce Act), which was signed into law by President Cleveland on February 4, 1887.

INTERSTATE COMMERCE ACT

The Interstate Commerce Act, which still serves as the cornerstone for transportation regulation in the United States, became effective on April 5, 1887. Its provisions were applicable to all common carriers by railroad engaged in interstate and foreign commerce. Much of the substance of the act was directed at prevention of monopoly abuses and control of discriminatory practices. The desire of Congress to protect the shipping public from such treatment was apparent in the major sections of the act.

The act required that all rates be just and reasonable and stipulated that all unjust and unreasonable rates were unlawful. Congress chose not to define the nature of a reasonable or just charge and, in effect, entrusted the interpretation of these terms to the Interstate Commerce Commission (ICC) which the act also created, and the federal courts. The resulting vagueness of this section was later to cause continuing difficulties for the ICC. The statute also prohibited personal discrimination by making it unlawful for a carrier, by any device (including rebates), to charge one person more than another for like or contemporaneous service under substantially similar circumstances and conditions. By forbidding rebates, the legislation effectively sought to stabilize carrier prices while simultaneously protecting shippers from monopolistic abuses. The law also included a blanket prohibition of undue or unreasonable preference or advantage of any form to any person, place, or kind of traffic. It should be noted that the section did not prohibit preferential or differential treatment, but only limited them to what might be considered just and reasonable. Once again, the directive was vague and subject to commission interpretation. It was unlawful for railroads to enter into any contract, agreement, or combination for the pooling of their freight or earnings. This reflected the prevailing view of Congress that enforced competition was the best regulator of rail rates. The legislation also required that all rates and fares were to be published, made available for public inspection, and filed with the ICC. The public was to be given 10-day notice before prices were raised.

The act also created the Interstate Commerce Commission to administer the new laws. The ICC was to consist of five members, each serving a six-year term. Members were to be appointed by the president, with the advice and consent of the Senate. Later the ICC was expanded to 11 members, and the terms were extended to seven years. There was, and is, no limitation on reappointment. By amendment in 1889, the ICC was ordered to report directly to Congress, thereby assuring the agency an independent status.

EARLY EXPERIENCE WITH THE ACT

Initially, the railroads generally complied with ICC orders, and little controversy arose. However, imperfections in the act soon appeared, and the ICC began to encounter opposition to its orders.

The ICC had to rely upon the courts for enforcement of its orders. Carriers were not required to obey the orders of the ICC during the period of court review, and no preference was given to ICC cases in terms of expediting their hearing in federal courts. As a result, it was not unusual for several years to elapse between the initial ICC cease-and-desist order and the final court ruling on the case. However, the most severe blows to ICC authority were Supreme Court rulings in 1896 and 1897 which made it clear that the ICC did not have the power to prescribe either actual or maximum rates.[7]

Despite its legal setbacks, the Interstate Commerce Act achieved some measure of success in its early years. Rates were being published, and the more blatant forms of discrimination had been eliminated. However, it was apparent that if the ICC was to play an important role in regulating the railroads, additional congressional action would be necessary.

REVITALIZATION OF THE INTERSTATE COMMERCE COMMISSION

Congress responded to the plight of the ICC and to growing national sentiment for stronger federal control of business in general by enacting extensive transportation legislation between 1903 and 1910. During that period the commission was empowered by having its cases given priority over other cases when the attorney general certified that the case was of public importance. The agency was also granted the power to levy fines on both the giver and receiver of rebates. Its jurisdiction was further expanded to include regulation of express companies, sleeping car companies and oil pipelines. The ICC was also given the power to prescribe maximum rates once it had determined that a rate was unjust or unreasonable. Finally, the agency was given authority to suspend rate change proposals for up to 120 days while it addressed the reasonableness of the proposal.

RAIL REGULATION, 1910-20

The statutes that strengthened the ICC led to its emergence as a formidable regulatory body. Given its expanded authority, the ICC actively sought to protect shipper interests in the years immediately preceding World War I. However, the philosophy and actions of the ICC during that period could be easily classified as negative. While the agency sought to eliminate railroad abuses, it showed little concern with protection of carrier interests. Congress had long contended that enforced competition would provide adequate carrier earnings, and the ICC appeared to share this view. However, that position ignored the basic cost structure of the industry, which initially led to regulation.

Armed with its broader authority over carrier ratemaking, the ICC proceeded to suspend, then deny, most railroad rate increase proposals between 1911 and the beginning of World War I.[8] At the same time, the railroads faced rapidly escalating wage and material costs due to inflation.

ICC restraint of railroad rate increases intensified the problems faced by many carriers that were overcapitalized from the earlier expansion period. Financial difficulties caused many railroads to reduce maintenance and equipment outlays, and rail service began to deteriorate. The financial plight of the railroads is illustrated by the fact that by 1916 nearly 10 percent of the industry's trackage was in receivership.[9]

World War I and Nationalization

Traffic expansion following the entrance of the United States into World War I in April 1917 placed heavy demands on the already troubled railroads. Although many railroad executives worked hard to promote effective coordination among the railroads, by the Fall of 1917 it was apparent that the railroads were unable to cope with growing national demands. As a result, the railroads were taken over by proclamation of President Wilson on December 28, 1917.

Congress created a United States Railroad Administration to facilitate federal coordination. During the period of federal control, each railroad was guaranteed profits equal to the average of the three previous years.

Government efforts were primarily concerned with the rapid movement of troops and supplies; profitability was a secondary consideration. Federal control and operation of the railroads lasted until March 1, 1920. While under federal control the national railroad system incurred a deficit of $1.5 billion, nearly $2 million per day.

By controlling the railroads, the federal government sought both to halt an inflationary spiral and to promote movement of needed commodities by holding down rail rates.[10] This was a major cause of the rail system deficit. Despite these measures, inflation continued and railroad wages rose, thereby creating problems that were to plague the railroads following their return to the private sector. Further, although during federal control the government spent more for maintenance than the railroads had during a similar prewar period, inflation led to a decline in actual maintenance work.[11] As a result, the physical plant deteriorated even further during government control.

The rigors of the war effort left many railroads in poor financial condition. Railroad revenues were barely meeting operating expenses, and labor, encouraged by active government promotion of organization efforts during the war, pressed for still higher wages. The possibility of widespread railroad bankruptcies seemed likely, and Congress hesitated to return the railroads to the private sector. Although Congress gave some attention to the concept of permanent railroad nationalization, this alternative was deemed undesirable, and the railroads were returned to the private sector in March 1920. Short-term income guarantees and loans were extended by the federal government to assist the railroads in meeting immediate requirements. However, Congress realized that fundamental problems existed in the regulatory structure, and that revitalization of the railroads would necessitate a more positive approach that gave greater attention to the financial needs of the railroads. Congress attempted to rectify the regulatory imbalance toward negative regulation with passage of the Transportation Act of 1920.

TRANSPORTATION ACT OF 1920

As Congress pondered the plight of the railroads in extensive hearings during 1919 and 1920, it became obvious that, although regulation of the railroads was far from complete, the existing regulation did not appear to be working particularly well. The ICC had not yet been given authority over such important railroad matters as the sale of railroad securities, minimum rates, abandonments or line extensions. At the same time, the dominant philosophy of enforced competition appeared to give too little attention to development of a healthy carrier environment. Consequently, the Transportation Act of 1920, which served as transitional legislation in the transfer of the railroads back to the private sector, both broadened the scope of ICC controls over the railroads and shifted the regulatory philosophy.

Regulatory Changes

With passage of the Transportation Act of 1920, ICC control over railroad rates expanded greatly. The act gave the ICC authority over minimum and actual rates (to prevent ruinous competition), strengthened its role in intrastate ratemaking, and clarified its approach to aggregate industry ratemaking. The commission was directed, in exercising its control over rates, to attempt to allow the railroads as a whole, or in groups to earn a fair return on the fair value of their transportation properties. Congress further broadened ICC rate authority by giving the commission the power to prescribe actual rates once a rate had been found to be unjust or unreasonable. Commission control over rail rates was now complete. The 1920 act also gave the ICC the authority to require intrastate rates to be raised if it considered them to be too low and therefore burdensome to interstate commerce.

During its formative years the railroad industry had suffered from overexpansion and duplication of investment. To reduce the likelihood of imprudent expansion in the future, while also affording some degree of market protection to existing carriers, the 1920 act conferred authority over new railroad construction upon the ICC. Railroads seeking line extensions in the future would have to obtain a certificate of public convenience and necessity from the ICC before undertaking such projects. At the same time, the ICC was granted authority over rail abandonments.

As outlined earlier in this chapter, financial abuses were widespread in the early years of the railroad industry. However, despite many calls for federal control of railroad securities Congress had not acted on this matter prior to 1920.[12] In recognition of this regulatory gap, and undoubtedly influenced by the impaired ability of many railroads to sell securities in the capital markets, Congress gave the ICC exclusive control over the sale of new railroad securities.

Railroad consolidation activity had been slowed considerably after 1900 by Supreme Court interpretation of the Sherman and Clayton Acts, which had established antitrust controls for U.S. industry. However, in drafting the Transportation Act of 1920, Congress sought to create an environment in which rail duplication might be reduced through consolidation of carriers. This was accomplished through inclusion of a provision in the act that permitted the ICC to withdraw any railroad consolidation from operation of the antitrust statutes. This procedure allowed the ICC to approve consolidations that might result in a lessening of competition among rail carriers. This also marked a significant shift in federal policy from enforced intramodal competition to active promotion of rail consolidations that might reduce such competition.

Experience with the 1920 Act

The results of the Transportation Act of 1920 were mixed. Railroad earnings improved following enactment, railroad credit rebounded with ICC control over securities, and service improved with the stabilization of carrier earnings. However, the federal guidelines covering the Commission's expanded rate control authority were rather confusing and this caused continuing interpretational difficulty and numerous court challenges. More importantly, the 1920 legislation failed to recognize the important changes which were taking place in the competitive marketplace. The other modes of carriage, which were not regulated, were emerging as viable competitors for railroad traffic and eroding the industry's traffic base.

Nevertheless, the 1920 act was important in that it marked a dramatic change in regulatory philosophy in its shift toward positive regulation. Public concern with the financial viability of the railroads was to increase in the ensuing years as the economic chaos of the Depression emerged.

INTERMODAL COMPETITION AND THE EXPANSION OF FEDERAL REGULATION

While railroad earnings improved during the 1920s, not all railroads shared the prosperity. Economic fluctuations were frequent and sharp, and they were particularly burdensome on some railroad systems.

The 1920s were marked by increasing federal government promotion of other forms of intercity carriage. Expenditures accelerated in highway building, waterway development, and expansion of the airway system. At the same time, the bulk of airline revenues was being provided by federal airmail contracts. This expanded federal support, coupled with growing state outlays, was to play a major role in the emergence of a truly competitive intermodal transportation network in the 1930s.

With the onset of the Depression, the financial condition of the railroad industry, which was already precarious, deteriorated rapidly. By 1933, 75 class I railroads were in the hands of receivers.[13] Numerous other railroad bankruptcies were averted by loans to railroads through the Reconstruction Finance Corporation. The railroads were also assisted by federal modification of the bankruptcy laws which covered railroad failures. To simplify and accelerate railroad reorganizations, Congress amended the Bankruptcy Act in 1933 by giving only one court jurisdiction over such proceedings. Also, the ICC was empowered to approve reorganization plans and court-appointed trustees.

REGULATION OF MOTOR CARRIAGE

During the 1920s, truck and bus operations emerged as strong competitors for previously captive railroad business. Capital requirements were limited, and the number of motor carrier operations expanded rapidly. Most operations were of small scale, but the sizable profits generated soon led to the emergence of the first large motor carriers. The profit potential attracted numerous operators into motor carriage. Competition was vigorous, but so was economic activity.

Development of State Regulation

As the number of motor vehicles increased and as more truck and bus companies established for-hire operations, there was an increasing outcry for some form of government regulation. Proponents advocated regulation of motor carriage for such diverse reasons as governance of highway use, protection of shippers and passengers from carrier irresponsibility, and protection of the railroads from the inroads of new competitors.

Initial regulation of motor carriage occurred at the state level. Early state regulations were primarily directed at promotion of safety and control of the use of state highways. Individual states established regulatory standards that governed such factors as vehicle speeds, weights, lengths, braking and lighting systems, and driver qualifications. Later, many states enacted regulations that also governed the economic aspects of the industry. Typically, the economic controls provided a state certification process for common carriers, which required a demonstration that the applicant was fit, willing, and able to provide the service and that the service was consistent with the public interest. Rates were also generally regulated, and carriers were required to publish prevailing rates. By 1932, transportation of passengers by motor vehicle was regulated by all states except Delaware, and 39 states had established regulatory controls related to motor carriers of property.[14]

Pressures for Federal Regulation

The financial collapse of the economy during the Depression and the related economic slowdown brought about great changes in transportation. Excess capacity arose in all forms of carriage. This was particularly true in the trucking industry. The industry was overcrowded, and the desire to capture any traffic led to destructive competition among motor carriers and with the railroads.[15] Discriminatory pricing and deteriorating service were typical of the trucking industry, and intensified intermodal competition threatened the solvency of the competitors.

These problems intensified the need for federal regulation of the trucking industry, as state regulations were unable to cope with the chaotic conditions that existed. The railroads and a number of the larger motor carriers, as well as many shippers, alarmed at the rapidly worsening conditions, petitioned Congress to enact legislation that would lead to the regulation of interstate motor carriage.[16]

The Motor Carrier Act

In 1935, after a total of 37 bills requesting motor carrier regulation had been introduced in Congress, the Motor Carrier Act was passed. The act established ICC control over interstate motor carriage and was subsequently incorporated into the Interstate Commerce Act.

The Motor Carrier Act created a comprehensive system of federal controls over motor carriers engaged in carrying passengers and property in interstate and foreign commerce. The federal regulatory structure applied to motor carriage was closely patterned after earlier rail regulation.

Due to the diversity of motor carrier operations, it was clear that a single set of regulations could not be applied to all forms of motor carriage. Consequently, the Motor Carrier Act divided intercity motor carriage into common, contract, exempt, and private carriage, and established a fifth grouping, which consisted of truck brokers.

Common Carriers. Motor carriers who held themselves out to serve the general public were classified as common carriers. The 1935 act established regulation of common carrier entry, ratemaking, consolidations, securities, and safety.

Entry. Common carriers that had begun interstate operations prior to passage of the act were permitted to continue their operations, under a "grandfather clause".[17] Anyone wishing to establish new common carrier operations or to extend existing operations was required to apply to the ICC for a certificate of public convenience and necessity. To obtain a certificate, the applicant was required to demonstrate that he was fit, willing, and able to provide the service, and that the service was required by present and future public necessity. The common carrier certificate specified the geographical operating authority, routes to be followed, and commodities to be carried. In contrast to the strict abandonment controls applied to rail carriage, the ICC was not granted authority over motor carrier abandonment. The competitive nature of the industry and the relatively low financial entry barriers influenced congressional thinking in this matter.

Rates. The Motor Carrier Act closely followed the railroad pattern of regulation with respect to ICC control over common carrier ratemaking. Rates and fares were to be just and reasonable. Unjust and unreasonable preference or prejudice to persons, places, or commodities were forbidden. Rates were to be published and adhered to. Rate changes were to be preceded by 30-day notice, and the ICC was empowered to suspend and investigate such proposals for up to seven months. Upon finding that a rate was unreasonable or unjust, the ICC could prescribe the maximum, minimum, or actual rate.

Consolidation. The provisions of the Interstate Commerce Act that applied to railroad consolidations were extended to motor carriage by the 1935 act. The ICC was given authority over such consolidations and instructed to determine that applications were consistent with the public interest before approving them.

Other Coverage. Securities issued by motor carriers were subjected to the same provisions of the Interstate Commerce Act that applied to railroads. Common carriers were also required to maintain liability insurance and insurance on the goods that they carried. Additionally, the 1935 act charged the ICC with development of rules to govern the maximum hours of operator service, equipment safety standards, and related safety matters.

Contract Carriage. The second category of carriers recognized by the 1935 legislation was contract carriage. Contract carriers were defined as those which transported passengers and property under special and individual contracts or agreements. They generally service a limited number of accounts and do not hold themselves out to the general public.

The grandfather clause of the Motor Carrier Act also applied to contract carriage. However, any party wishing to initiate new contract carrier operations and/or wishing to expand existing operations was required to demonstrate that he was fit, willing, and able, and that the operation was consistent with the public interest. It was generally believed that this was a less significant burden than was the proof of public convenience and necessity required in common carrier certificate cases.

Rates filed with the ICC by contract carriers were subjected to possible suspension and investigation. Following investigation, the ICC was empowered to prescribe the minimum rates of contract carriers, but it could not prescribe their actual rates.

Contract carriers were subjected to the same statutory guidelines as common carriers in such areas as consolidations, securities, and maximum hours of service for employees, and other safety standards.

Until the late 1970s, except under extreme circumstances, the ICC did not permit a single company to conduct "dual operations" as both a common and contract carrier. Congress feared that such operations would provide the opportunity for a carrier to discriminate by hauling goods for favored shippers under lower contract rates.

Exempt Trucking. Motor Carrier Act also contained numerous exemptions, which excluded a variety of classes of for-hire motor vehicles from ICC economic control. By far the most significant of these was the agricultural commodity exemption. Prior to the passage of the Motor Carrier Act, agricultural interests lobbied intensely against the regulation of trucking movement of agricultural goods. They contended that trucking prices would rise rather than fall following regulation. In response to these concerns, Congress exempted vehicles owned and operated by farmers that carry products of farms and supplies (essentially private carriage) and motor vehicles controlled and operated by cooperative associations. More importantly, the act also exempted all motor vehicles carrying livestock, fish, or agricultural commodities. Subsequently horticultural products were included in the agricultural exemption. As a result of these exemptions, regulated motor carriers were permitted to handle agricultural commodities as back-haul traffic and their rates on such movements were not subject to ICC control. However, they were still bound by prevailing safety guidelines.

Another exemption excluded from ICC control the transfer, collection, or delivery services conducted in terminal areas by railroads, water carriers, and freight forwarders. These services were seen as incidental to the line-haul services of other modes. A 1938 amendment to the act also exempted motor vehicles used exclusively in the transportation of passengers or property when incidental to movement by aircraft.

Brokers and Private Trucking. In the early days of trucking enterprises emerged that sold or arranged for transportation by truck. These truck "brokers" were independent of both shippers and carriers and served as intermediaries. Brokers were particularly important to relatively small motor carriers that had limited sales forces. The Motor Carrier Act recognized brokerage as a legitimate and important function in the industry and stipulated that brokers were to be licensed by the ICC. They were also required to furnish bonds or other security to insure their financial responsibility for the services that they performed. Brokers later emerged as important factors in the household goods and agricultural sectors of interstate trucking.

The act also dealt with private motor carriers that transported goods in interstate commerce for themselves and not for-hire. Such operations were not subjected to the economic regulation of the ICC, but were required to abide by safety regulations.

Federal-State Relationships. The Motor Carrier Act of 1935 did not totally displace state regulatory controls. Specifically, the act did not give the ICC jurisdiction over intrastate motor carrier rates, provided that the carrier was operating legally under the jurisdiction of a state regulatory agency.

REGULATION OF AIR CARRIAGE

The next major mode of intercity carriage to be regulated by the federal government in the 1930s was air transportation. Although federal involvement in air transportation dated to the early days of aviation, it accelerated following World War I because of the potential commercial and military applications of aircraft.

Development of Federal Regulation and Promotion

By 1925 the feasibility of airmail service had been demonstrated, and Congress passed the Kelly Act, which permitted the Post Office Department to award airmail contracts to private companies on a competitive-bid basis. These contracts provided a much needed source of steady income for many early airlines and played a major role in promoting further development of the industry.

The following year Congress established the Bureau of Air Commerce within the Department of Commerce and directed it to develop, operate, and maintain all necessary air navigation facilities except airports. The act also conferred upon the Department of Commerce the ability to regulate private and commercial operations with respect to safety. With the precedent set for federal regulation of air safety, the department proceeded to require registration of aircraft, examination of pilots, and establishment of a variety of minimum safety standards.

Even though the airmail contracts provided a steady source of income for the industry, many mail contractors continued to lose money. Passenger fares were too low to be compensatory, but price increases led to reduction in demand.[18] To help stabilize and unify the industry, Congress enacted the McNary-Waters Act of 1930. The statute specified that the postmaster general could award airmail contracts without competitive bidding.[19] The Post Office Department was also granted power to certify routes, control carrier consolidations and extensions, and prescribe a system of accounts for carriers. Thus the precedent for federal economic regulation of the airlines was set.

Early in 1934 a special committee headed by Senator Hugo Black sought and obtained cancellation of all domestic airmail contracts because of suspected collusion between air carriers and Post Office officials.[20] These cancellations resulted in loss of substantial revenues for the airlines and initiated a difficult period in which the army carried the mail.

Congress sought not only to prevent further deterioration of the financial condition of the industry, but also to establish tighter regulatory controls in passing the Air Mail Act of 1934. Under the act and its 1935 amendments, the Post Office Department was empowered to award airmail contracts and to enforce airmail regulations. The ICC was given authority to set airmail rates and was to review these rates periodically. The act also charged the Bureau of Air Commerce with responsibility for air safety and the development and maintenance of the airway system.

Despite congressional action, airline problems persisted. A series of accidents in the winter of 1936-37 eroded public confidence in the industry, and the general business slowdown of early 1938 caused serious financial problems for many airlines.

The Civil Aeronautics Act

In an effort to at least partially remedy the industry's problems, the airline industry itself sponsored the Civil Aeronautics Act, which established federal control of the industry. The act was passed in June 1938. In the act, Congress directed the Civil Aeronautics Authority to "recognize and preserve" the inherent advantages of air transportation, and to promote "adequate, economical and efficient" air service adapted to the "present and future needs" of foreign and domestic commerce.

To administer the economic regulations contained in the 1938 act, Congress created the Civil Aeronautics Authority (CAA) which was renamed the Civil Aeronautics Board (CAB) in 1940. The five members of the board were to be appointed by the president with the advice and consent of the Senate; the term of office was set at six years. There had been considerable debate prior to the enactment of the statute as to whether air regulation should be administered by the ICC. President Roosevelt originally favored extension of ICC authority, but Congress believed that the differences in the industries and the breadth of the ICC's already existing responsibilities necessitated creation of a new agency. However, Congress borrowed liberally from the regulatory structure that it had created for rail and motor carriage in designing airline regulations.

Policy Statement. The Civil Aeronautics Act of 1938 contained a policy statement that directed the newly created regulatory agency to encourage and develop the national air transportation system to meet the present and future needs of our country. No mention was given to other modes of carriage, and Congress clearly intended the CAA to regulate air transportation independently and without regard to the impact of its decisions and policies on other modes. It was also clear from the policy statement that Congress intended air transportation regulation to be promotional as well as remedial.

Entry. The Civil Aeronautics Act contained a grandfather clause. New entry or extension of existing operations could only be obtained by demonstrating to the CAA that the applicant was fit, willing, and able, and that there was a public need for the service. Air carriers were also required to obtain CAA approval before abandoning a route that they had been awarded.

The industry structure inherited by the CAA was much simpler than that of motor carriage, and it involved far fewer carriers. Consequently, through its entry and consolidation decisions, the CAA was able to play a major role in determining the industry structure that eventually emerged.

Rates. The degree of control over carrier rates and fares accorded to the CAA was quite similar to that of the ICC over rail and trucking rates. Airline charges were to be just and reasonable, undue discrimination was prohibited, and rates were to be published and observed. A 30-day notice was required on all rate and fare changes, and the CAA was empowered to suspend and investigate rate proposals for up to 180 days. Following its investigation in rate cases, the CAA could prescribe maximum, minimum, or actual charges.

Miscellaneous Controls. CAA authority also included control over consolidations, mergers, and acquisition of control. It was not, however, granted authority over the securities issued by carriers. The act also gave the CAA the power to exempt any air carrier or class of carriers from economic regulation if it believed that such regulation would place an undue burden on the carriers involved.

Safety. From the time of its creation in 1926 until 1938, the Bureau of Air Commerce administered the airway system and enforced safety regulations pertaining to air transportation. The Civil Aeronautics Act, as amended in 1940, provided for centralized safety regulation and airway operation and regulation under the Civil Aeronautics Administration. Both the Administration and the CAB were placed within the Department of Commerce for budgeting and accounting purposes under a 1940 reorganization plan sponsored by President Roosevelt.

TRANSPORTATION ACT OF 1940

During 1938 and 1939, Congress held extensive hearings on the status of the domestic transportation system. The hearings identified several major areas of concern. Domestic water carriage, particularly the coastal and intercoastal segments, was troubled by rate instability and discriminatory pricing practices.[21] Destructive competition had surfaced. Also, water carriage had become a more effective competitor for previously captive railroad traffic. As a result, congressional concerns about the deteriorating conditions in water carriage were reinforced by railroad calls for regulation of water transportation. The railroads had not completely rebounded from the effects of the Depression. Contributing to the precarious financial position of many railroads were technological advances in the other modes and increased public spending on highways, waterways, and airport-airway development.

It was obvious that the national transportation system was rapidly becoming truly intermodal in nature, and competition among the modes was increasing in intensity. Therefore, Congress sought to draft legislation that would strengthen and stabilize the several modes, while restricting the intensity of intermodal competition. The result was the Transportation Act of 1940. The statute not only established ICC control over domestic water carriage, but also contained a statement of national transportation policy to guide ICC regulation of the several modes. Additionally, the act modified several facets of railroad regulation.

Water Carrier Regulation

Although several earlier statutes had regulated various aspects of domestic water carriage, prior to 1940 water carrier operation over inland rivers and canals was not regulated. Similarly, contract carriage was unregulated except over intercoastal routes. The 1940 act superseded the previous statutes and vested regulatory powers in the ICC.

As originally conceived, the 1940 act was envisioned as a bill to bring all domestic water carriage under ICC control. However, shippers of bulk and liquid commodities and agricultural interests lobbied against the legislation because they feared that it might lead to higher rates. These pressures led to inclusion of several major exemptions in the act that still prevail.

Water Carrier Exemptions. The most important exemption contained in the act was the bulk commodity exemption, which specified that common carriers whose cargo consisted of not more than three bulk commodities in the cargo space of a vessel (or tow) were exempt from the economic controls of the ICC. Liquid commodities carried in bulk in tank vessels were similarly exempted, as were contract carriers that had both specialized vessels and cargo and that did not compete with common carriers. The exemptions also included all private carriers. As a result of these exemptions, only about 10 percent of total intercity ton miles moved by water carriage was subjected to ICC economic controls.[22] Subject to certain operating restrictions, regulated carriers were permitted to haul exempt commodities as back-hauls to regulated movements.

For those carriers subject to ICC controls under the 1940 act, Congress again relied upon a regulatory pattern similar to that which had been applied to other ICC-regulated modes. Regulations pertaining to water carriage were also incorporated into the Interstate Commerce Act.

Entry. Grandfather rights were extended to existing common carriers. Any party wishing to enter the industry or extend its operations after that date was required to secure certificates from the ICC by proving that it was fit, willing, and able to perform the service and that it would serve the public convenience. Contract carriers were required to obtain permits from the ICC before initiating or extending operations. Dual operation as both a common and a contract carrier was forbidden, but the ICC was permitted to grant exceptions to that stipulation.

Rates. Water carrier rates were to be just and reasonable, and they could not be unduly discriminatory. Common carrier rates were to be published and observed. Thirty-day notice was to precede changes in common carrier rates, and these rates could be suspended and investigated by the ICC. Upon finding a common carrier rate unreasonable, the ICC could prescribe maximum, minimum, or actual rates.

Contract carriers were required to file only their minimum rates, and these could be suspended and investigated by the ICC. The rates were also required to meet the standards of reasonableness and discrimination that were applied to common carrier rates.

Miscellaneous Controls. The ICC was also given control over consolidations, mergers, and acquisition of control of common and contract carriers by water. Additionally, through-route and joint-rate arrangements between water carriers could be required by the ICC.

Because of the relative ease of entry into water carriage and the competitive conditions that prevailed at the time of the enactment, Congress did not establish ICC control over water carrier abandonments. Securities issued by water carriers were not subjected to ICC control.

Policy Statement. In the Transportation Act of 1940, Congress attempted, for the first time, to express the national transportation policy of the United States in a simplified format. It was to serve as the preamble to the Interstate Commerce Act. The statement outlined a broad range of considerations to be observed by the ICC in regulating the various modes subject to its jurisdiction. It did not apply to air carriage. The statement of policy read as follows:

> It is hereby declared to be the national transportation policy of the Congress to provide for fair and impartial regulation of all modes of transportation subject to the provisions of the act, so administered as to recognize and preserve the inherent advantages of each; to promote safe, adequate, economical and efficient service and foster sound economic conditions in transportation and among the several carriers; to encourage the establishment and maintenance of reasonable charges for transportation service, without unjust discriminations, undue preferences, or advantages, or unfair or destructive competitive practices; to cooperate with the several States, and the duly authorized officials thereof; and to encourage fair wages and equitable working conditions—all to the end of developing, coordinating, and preserving a national transportation system by water, highway, and rail as well as other means, adequate to meet the needs of the commerce of the United States, of the Postal Service, and of the national defense. All of the provisions of this act shall be administered and enforced with a view to carrying out the above declaration of policy.

Changes in Railroad Regulation. Several provisions of the Transportation Act of 1940 sought to modify existing railroad regulations. The most important of those concerned railroad consolidations and the burden of proof in rate-reduction cases.

The Transportation Act of 1920 had directed the ICC to develop a master consolidation plan to reduce the number of railroad systems in the United States. However, despite considerable effort, the ICC was unable to develop a plan that met with industry approval. Consequently, the 1940 statute stipulated that future railroad consolidations would not have to conform to an ICC master plan. However, the act specified a range of factors to be considered by the ICC in consolidation cases. The specifics of these consolidation guidelines are considered in later chapters.

The act also placed the burden of proof upon the railroads in any rate case. Prior to that time there was no such burden on the carriers in rate-reduction cases. However, this change was generally viewed as a step to strengthen ICC control over competitive intermodal pricing reductions.

REGULATION OF FREIGHT FORWARDING

Following passage of the Transportation Act of 1940, the only major mode of intercity carriage that had not come under federal regulation was freight forwarding. As early as 1930 the ICC had requested that Congress bring freight forwarders under the ICC's jurisdiction. ICC investigations had found that forwarders were routinely departing from published rates, and that rates were quite unstable.[23]. The Commission believed that the business of forwarding companies was in a general state of chaos, and the agency argued that legislation was needed to prevent the practices that had depleted carrier revenues and led to unequal and unjustly discriminatory treatment of shippers.[24]

Finally in 1942 Congress passed the Freight Forwarder Act. The statute established ICC jurisdiction over surface forwarders, and its provisions were incorporated into the Interstate Commerce Act.

Coverage of the Act

The Freight Forwarder Act covered freight forwarders using surface modes in interstate commerce. A grandfather clause allowed continuation of existing forwarding operations. However, as specified by the act, entry into forwarding or extension of existing operations required an ICC permit. Such permits were to be issued to applicants who demonstrated that they were fit, willing, and able to provide the proposed service, and that the service was consistent with the public interest.

Rate regulation of freight forwarders was similar to that of common carriers in other modes. Rates were to be just, reasonable, and not unduly discriminatory. The rates were required to be published and followed. A 30-day notice was required in advance of any rate change, and forwarder rates could be suspended and investigated. The ICC was empowered to prescribe the maximum, minimum, or actual charges of forwarders.

Forwarders were not permitted to own or control railroads, motor carriers, or water carries that were subject to the Interstate Commerce Act. However, such carriers were allowed to own or control freight forwarders.

Although freight forwarders operated as intermediates between carriers and shippers, they were declared to be common carriers in a 1950 amendment to the Interstate Commerce Act.

SUMMARY

Although regulation of transportation originated in the Middle Ages, such controls were not broadly applied in the United States until the late nineteenth century. Prior to that time, an attitude of laissez-faire prevailed, and government was generally supportive of transportation expansion.

However, as railroads came to dominate the transportation marketplace, financial abuses and discrimination became widespread. These conditions led to the passage of the Granger laws in several Midwestern states and eventually necessitated enactment of the Interstate Commerce Act to govern interstate transportation.

Early railroad regulation was primarily concerned with enforcing competition and preventing monopoly abuses. Little concern was given to the financial well-being of the carriers. These negative regulatory controls contributed to financial problems in the industry, which led to passage of the Transportation Act of 1920. That statute sought to create a more balanced approach to regulation that considered both the needs of the shipping public and the carriers. Although the act improved carrier earnings and credit, it did not deal with the major structural changes that were taking place in the national transportation system.

Between 1935 and 1942 federal regulatory controls were extended to trucking, air transportation, water carriage, and freight forwarding. In each instance, passage of the governing statute was at least partially the result of chaotic conditions that had emerged in each particular mode of carriage. Congress was increasingly concerned with regulation of intermodal competition. In regulating these modes of carriage, Congress relied quite heavily upon the regulatory format that had earlier been applied to rail carriage.

Recent years have witnessed widespread criticism of the regulatory framework established during that period. In certain instances these pressures have led to significant changes in federal policy. These developments and their impact on the nature of transportation regulation and promotion are discussed in the next chapter.

DISCUSSION QUESTIONS

1. What were the reasons for the enactment of the Interstate Commerce Act in 1887?
2. Why was the ICC relatively ineffective during its early years?
3. What were the reasons for the failure of the early railroad traffic pools?
4. Compare and contrast federal regulation of the railroads prior to and following passage of the Transportation Act of 1920.
5. Why were grandfather clauses included in the Motor Carrier Act of 1935 and the Civil Aeronautics Act of 1938?
6. Why did Congress believe that it was necessary to regulate the airline industry in 1938?

NOTES

1. John F. Stover, *American Railroads* (Chicago: University of Chicago Press, 1961), p. 88.
2. Hugh S. Norton, *Modern Transportation Economics*, 2nd ed. (Columbus, OH: Charles E. Merrill Publishing Company, 1971), p. 225.
3. Wabash, St. Louis & Pacific Railway Co. v. Illinois, 118 U.S. 557 (1886).
4. Charles F. Phillips, *The Economics of Regulation*, rev. ed. (Homewood, ILL: Richard D. Irwin, Inc., 1969), p. 447.
5. Dudley F. Pegrum, *Transportation: Economics and Public Policy*, 3rd ed. (Homewood, ILL: Richard D. Irwin, Inc., 1973), p. 270.
6. Thomas G. Moore, *Freight Transportation Regulation: Surface Freight and the Interstate Commerce Commission* (Washington, D.C.: American Enterprise Institute for Public Policy Research, 1972), p. 5.
7. Cincinnati, New Orleans and Texas Pacific Railway Company v. Interstate Commerce Commission, 162 U.S. 116 (1896); and Interstate Commerce Commission v. Cincinnati, New Orleans and Texas Pacific Railway Company, 167 U.S. 479 (1897).
8. Marvin L. Fair and Ernest W. Williams, *Economics of Transportation and Logistics* (Dallas, TX: Business Publications, Inc., 1975), p. 388.
9. Moore, p. 18.
10. Walter W. Splawn, *Government Ownership and Operation of Railroads* (New York: MacMillan Publishing Company, Inc., 1928), pp. 375-82.
11. Ibid., p. 381.

12. D. Philip Locklin, *Economics of Transportation*, 7th ed. (Homewood, ILL: Richard D. Irwin, Inc., 1972), p. 241.
13. Phillips, p. 455.
14. Moore, p. 25.
15. Ibid.
16. Ibid.
17. Moore, p. 27.
18. John H. Frederick, *Commercial Air Transportation*, 4th ed.. (Homewood, ILL: Richard D. Irwin, Inc., 1955), p. 81.
19. Ibid.
20. Fair and Williams, p. 139.
21. Pegrum, p. 361.
22. Moore, p. 32.
23. U.S. Interstate Commerce Commission, *44th Annual Report of the Interstate Commerce Commission* (Washington, D.C.: U.S. Government Printing Office, 1939), p. 35.
24. Ibid., p. 82.

SELECTED REFERENCES

Caves, Richard E. *Air Transport and Its Regulators*. Cambridge, MA: Harvard University Press, 1962.

Fair, Marvin L., and John Guandolo. *Transportation Regulation*. 8th ed. Dubuque, IA: William C. Brown Company, 1961.

Fair, Marvin L., and Ernest W. Williams. *Economics of Transportation and Logistics*. rev. ed. Dallas, TX: Business Publications, Inc., 1975. Chapter 19. "Regulation of Transportation: Origin and Scope," pp. 348-85.

Farris, Martin T. "National Transportation Policy: Fact or Fiction?" *Quarterly Review of Economics and Business*, Vol. 10, No. 2 (Summer, 1970), pp. 7-14.

Fogel, Robert W. *Railways and American Economic Growth: Essays in Econometric History*. Baltimore, MD: Johns Hopkins Press, 1964,

Frederick, John H. *Commercial Air Transport*. 5th ed. Homewood, ILL: Richard D. Irwin, Inc., 1965. Chapter 4. "Regulatory Legislation," pp. 107-25.

Friedlaender, Ann F. *The Dilemma of Freight Transport Regulation*. Washington, D.C.: Brookings Institution, 1969. Chapter 2. "The Rationale of Regulation." pp. 7-27.

Fulda, Carl H. *Competition in the Regulated Industries: Transportation*. Boston, MA: Little, Brown and Company, 1961. Chapter 2. "The Regulatory Acts: Their History and Purposes," pp. 7-23.

Kolko, Gabriel. *Railroads and Regulation, 1887-1916*. Princeton, NJ: University Press, 1965.

Lansing, John B. *Transportation and Economic Policy*. New York, Free Press, 1966.

Locklin, D. Philip. *Economics of Transportation*. 7th ed. Homewood, ILL: Richard D. Irwin, Inc., 1972. Chapter 9. "Beginning of Railroad Regulation," pp. 211-21, Chapter 10. "Federal Legislation, 1887-1920," pp. 222-39. Chapter 11. "The Transportation Act of 1920," pp. 240-54.

MacAvoy, Paul W. *The Economic Effects of Regulation: The Trunk Line Railroad Cartels and the Interstate Commerce Commission Before 1900*. Cambridge, MA: The MIT Press, 1965.

Moore, Thomas G. *Freight Transportation Regulation: Surface Freight and the Interstate Commerce Commission*. Washington, D.C.: American Enterprise Institute for Public Policy Research, 1972.

Pegrum, Dudley F. *Transportation: Economics and Public Policy*. 3rd ed. Homewood, ILL: Richard D. Irwin, Inc., 1973. Chapter 13. "Railroad Regulation Since World War I," pp. 290-309. Chapter 14. "Regulation of Motor Transport," pp. 310-35. Chapter 15. "Regulation of Air, Water, and Pipeline Transportation," pp. 336-68.

Phillips, Charles F. *The Economics of Regulation*. rev. ed. Homewood, ILL: Richard D. Irwin, Inc., 1969. Chapter 13. "Regulation of the Transportation Industries," pp. 441-82.

Splawn, Walter W. *Government Ownership and Operation of Railroads*. New York: MacMillan Publishing Company, 1928.

Taff, Charles A. *Commercial Motor Transportation*. 6th ed. Centreville, MD: Cornell Maritime Press, Inc., 1980. Chapter 17. "Regulation and Transport Policy," pp. 403-37.

Boeing 747 *Courtesy of Boeing Co.*

CHAPTER ELEVEN

EVOLUTION OF FEDERAL REGULATION AND PROMOTION

The years preceding World War II were marked by substantial expansion of regulatory controls in intercity transportation, but the postwar period witnessed growing concern about the propriety of existing regulations. This concern was motivated by the continuing financial problems experienced by many intercity carriers and the national need for a viable, efficient transportation system. In an effort to facilitate improvements in the transportation network, the federal government substantially increased its involvement in promotional activities.

This chapter focuses on the re-evaluation of regulatory policies and the major structural and regulatory changes that occurred between the end of World War II and the mid-1970s. The expansion of the federal role in promotion of intercity transportation development is also examined. While federal involvement in urban transportation also expanded dramatically during the period, discussion of that development is deferred to Chapters 18 and 19.

TRANSPORTATION SYSTEM: WORLD WAR II TO 1958

During World War II, intercity traffic volume rose, and for-hire carriers generally experienced higher earnings. The railroads were not nationalized during the conflict, as they had been during World War I, and they carried the great bulk of wartime freight.

Two wartime developments had a decided impact on the national transportation system following the war. First, in 1944 Congress approved in principle the construction of the Interstate Highway System. Approval of this high-speed highway network to link all major metropolitan areas in this country was primarily motivated by military considerations. However, following its funding in 1956, the interstate network was to take on major economic significance in the transportation setting. The system allowed higher effective speeds between cities and lower operating costs to trucks, buses, and private automobiles. As a result, the highway modes were to become even more competitive for freight and passenger movements in intercity markets. Second, the

271

massive movement of military personnel by air during the war clearly demonstrated the passenger-carrying capability of that mode to the general public, and commercial patronage rose rapidly in the postwar years. This development was a contributing factor to the further decline of intercity rail passenger service.

Traffic volume in intercity carriage normalized following the conflict. Economic activity was brisk, and the period bore little resemblance to the chaotic conditions of the 1930s. Little congressional action of regulatory significance occurred during that period. The only exception was passage of the Reed-Bulwinkle Act of 1948, which granted an antitrust exemption to the collective ratemaking activities of ICC-regulated carriers.[1]

Although railroad earnings improved from the late 1940s into the early 1950s, the market share of intercity traffic handled by the railroads declined steadily. Intermodal competition had intensified, and the other modes continued to erode the railroad traffic base. In addition to more intense competition from for-hire carriers, the railroads also faced rapid expansion of private carriage in freight markets and steady growth of the private automobile fleet, which reduced rail passenger volume.

Further complicating matters was the fact that the traffic which the railroads maintained tended to be low in value and, consequently, generated relatively low revenues. At the same time, the railroad passenger deficit rose dramatically in the post-war period and regularly absorbed more than 35 percent of the net operating revenues generated in railroad freight operations.[2]

The aggregate rate of return on net investment of the railroads plummeted between 1955 and 1958, reaching 2.76 percent in 1958.[3] The physical plant of many railroads deteriorated during that period, and refinancing became increasingly difficult. Many railroads faced the threat of bankruptcy.

The deterioration of the railroads had not gone unnoticed at the federal level. Numerous federal studies of the "railroad problem" were conducted during the early 1950s. These studies generally recommended a lessening of railroad regulation and a greater reliance upon market forces in transportation.[4] However, none of the studies prompted congressional action.

Finally, prodded by railroad interests, Congress held extensive hearings on the problems of the railroads in early 1958. As a result of these hearings, Congress enacted the Transportation Act of 1958.[5]

TRANSPORTATION ACT OF 1958

The basic goal of the 1958 statute was to strengthen the financial position of the nation's railroads. The most important provisions of the act were those addressing passenger train discontinuances and loan guarantees for the railroads.

Passenger Train Discontinuances

The passenger service losses being incurred by the railroads were a major concern of Congress. In 1957 those losses exceeded $700 million. The losses absorbed approximately 44 percent of the net operating revenues the industry generated in moving freight during that year.[6]

The ICC was sensitive to the railroad passenger problem, but had never been granted authority over rail passenger service. Consequently, the railroads were generally at the mercy of state regulatory agencies in passenger train discontinuance proceedings. The state agencies were often unreceptive to such railroad petitions.

To remedy this situation, Congress granted the ICC authority over passenger train service. According to the 1958 act, the railroads could issue a 30-day notice of discontinuance on any passenger run that crossed state lines and was subject to any state law or agency. The notice was to be filed with the ICC, and discontinuance would be permitted unless the ICC ruled otherwise. The act also granted the commission the ability to overrule state governments in cases involving purely intrastate rail passenger service.

The passenger train discontinuance provisions of the 1958 statute were quite significant, and between 1958 and 1970 the ICC permitted discontinuance of many intercity passenger trains.[7] These discontinuances partially alleviated the railroad passenger problem, but passenger deficits persisted. In fact, between 1958 and 1970, when Amtrak was established, the aggregate passenger service deficit of the railroads annually ranged between $394 million and $480 million.[8]

Other Changes in Railroad Regulation

Several other provisions of the 1958 act addressed railroad regulatory issues. The ICC was given the power to raise intrastate rail rates when necessary to remove discrimination against interstate commerce. Congress also directed the commission to eliminate its perceived practice of "umbrella ratemaking" which in many instances forced railroads to maintain artificially inflated rates to protect the traffic of competitive modes.[9]

Loan Guarantees

The continuing financial problems of the railroads caused capital access difficulties for the carriers. In many instances, conventional refinancing channels were blocked due to depressed carrier earnings. To partially alleviate this problem, the Transportation Act of 1958 created a loan guarantee program. Under the provisions of the program, the ICC was authorized to guarantee loans by financial institutions to the railroads for the purpose of financing capital outlays or maintenance work. The aggregate amount of ICC loan guarantees outstanding to the railroads at any given time was limited to $500 million by the act. The ICC was only to guarantee such loans if it found that the applicants could not obtain needed funds without the guarantee, and if it further found that there was a reasonable assurance of carrier repayment.

The program, which was originally to expire in March 1961, was later extended to June 1963. During the life of the program nearly $240 million in loan guarantees was authorized by the ICC.[10]

The 1958 loan guarantee program cannot readily be classified as a success.[11] Critics of the program have claimed that it merely postponed bankruptcies. This is borne out by the experience under the act. The five major recipients of the guarantees provided by the act, the Lehigh Valley, the Central of New Jersey, the New Haven, the New York Central, and the Reading, all subsequently declared bankruptcy. These five lines received nearly one-half of the loan guarantee total granted under the act. Several railroad executives contended that the basic problem of the railroads was not obtaining loans, but rather repaying existing debt obligations.[12] They further argued that loan programs failed to address the problems that caused the railroads to have difficulty in meeting outstanding obligations.[13] Loan guarantees were later used in the early 1970s following the collapse of the Penn Central. However, it has become apparent that such programs must be coupled with other substantive changes if they are to do more than simply buy additional time.

FEDERAL AVIATION ACT OF 1958

Until 1958 the Civil Aeronautics Administration remained the dominant federal agency involved in the promotion of air safety. However, several serious accidents in 1958 raised questions concerning the effectiveness of the agency and prompted congressional passage of the Federal Aviation Act of 1958. The statute created the Federal Aviation Agency (FAA) to assume the function of the Civil Aeronautics Administration. The act outlined the following responsibilities for the FAA:

1.   The regulation of air commerce in such a manner as to best promote its development and safety and fulfill the requirements of national defense.

2.   The promotion, encouragement, and development of civil aeronautics.

3.   The control of the use of the navigable airspace of the United States and the regulation of both civil and

military operations in such airspace in the interest of the safety and efficiency of both.

4.   The consolidation of research and development with respect to air navigation facilities as well as the installation and operation thereof.

5.   The development and operation of a common system of air traffic control and navigation for both military and civil aircraft.

Thus the FAA (later renamed the Federal Aviation Administration) was accorded comprehensive authority over air safety and control over airspace.

The Federal Aviation Act also reenacted the economic regulatory structure that had been included in the 1938 act and permitted continuation of CAB control over economic regulation.

PRESIDENTIAL MESSAGES AND CREATION OF THE DOT

The existing regulatory structure continued to be criticized in many circles. In 1961 and 1962 seven major studies of transportation and its regulation were released by various federal agencies and study groups.[14] Although the recommendations of these studies varied, they generally supported relaxation of federal regulations and greater reliance upon market forces.

The Kennedy Transportation Message

In response to the continuing problems of the U.S. transportation system, President Kennedy delivered a special transportation message to Congress on April 5, 1962.[15] In that address, Kennedy criticized the existing regulatory structure as being inconsistent and outdated, and recommended a number of federal regulatory and promotional changes. He proposed more flexible carrier ratemaking and suggested that minimum rate regulation be eliminated on bulk and agricultural movements involving common carriers. He also recommended extension of the agricultural and fishery exemptions to all carriers. His message stressed what he perceived to be inconsistencies in policies of taxation and user charges in transportation. To remedy this situation, he urged repeal of the 10 percent tax on railroad and bus transportation while simultaneously calling for an increase in user charges in air transportation. He also suggested implementation of a waterway user-charge program to recover federal outlays in that area. Additionally, President Kennedy sought to promote more evenhanded treatment of intercity modes by reducing CAB subsidies to local service carriers while abolishing such subsidies to trunk lines.

Obviously, President Kennedy believed that the future viability of the national transportation system required major regulatory and promotional changes in the various modes. His suggestions were subsequently incorporated into legislative proposals and submitted to Congress. As might be expected, in the hearings that followed, many of his recommendations met with strong resistance from those modal interests that were somehow threatened by the proposals. The opposition was strong enough to kill the proposals in committee. Nevertheless, many of President Kennedy's recommendations were reflected in subsequent statutes.

The Johnson Transportation Message

In 1966, President Johnson also chose to deliver a special transportation message to Congress. Departing from the economic regulatory theme of the Kennedy message, President Johnson instead focused more on the need for coordination of the national transportation system, reorganization of transportation planning activities, and active promotion of safety.[16]

In his address, President Johnson contended that the U.S. transportation system lacked true coordination and that this resulted in system inefficiency. He advocated creation of a federal Department of Transportation to promote coordination of existing federal programs and to act as a focal point for future research and development efforts in transportation. The new agency would also become actively involved in transportation policy review and critique, but the economic regulatory functions of the ICC, CAB, and the Federal Maritime Commission were to be unaffected. This was not a new proposal. In fact a cabinet-level transportation agency had first been proposed in 1870.[17]

Another major focus of President Johnson's remarks was transportation safety. He suggested creation of a National Transportation Safety Board to investigate major accidents and to make related recommendations to the appropriate federal bodies. The board was to be placed under the secretary of transportation, yet was to remain independent of DOT operating units. In another safety matter, President Johnson called for establishment of a new highway safety program to be administered by the DOT.

Other recommendations contained in the Johnson message dealt with a broad range of topics, including development of supersonic aircraft, control of aircraft noise, and research and development involving high speed ground transportation.

Creation of the DOT

Congressional hearings were held on several bills involving most of President Johnson's recommendations. Although some opposition was expressed to specific proposals, there was general support for creation of the Department of Transportation. The legislation creating the agency was approved in October 1966.[18] The DOT commenced operations on April 1, 1967; Alan S. Boyd was appointed the first secretary of transportation. Congress also established the independent National Transportation Safety Board which President Johnson had suggested. Its activities are discussed in Chapter 16.

EXPANSION OF FEDERAL PROMOTIONAL ACTIVITIES

Although federal involvement in transportation promotion dates to the early days of our country, it expanded significantly during the 1970s. The promotional expansion was at least partially due to the financial problems incurred by several modes, but it was also motivated by a congressional desire to broaden the capabilities of the national transportation system.

In 1970 the Airport and Airway Development Act established an Airport and Airway Trust Fund, which was to be administered by the secretary of transportation through the Federal Aviation Administration.[19] The fund accumulated revenues from a variety of user charges, ranging from an excise tax on airline passenger tickets and freight bills to registration fees on aircraft. In expanding federal funding of airport-airway development and operation, the 1970 act sought to place the program on a self-financing basis, with users bearing the costs of the system. This same pattern had been applied to building the Interstate Highway System through creation of the Highway Trust Fund in 1956.

Federal funding of urban transportation also expanded dramatically in 1970 with passage of the Urban Mass Transportation Assistance Act.[20] That statute, which was passed in response to congressional concern about the decline of mass transit and the deterioration of air quality in many cities, created a $12 billion funding program for urban transportation projects. The funds were to be administered by the DOT's Urban Mass Transportation Administration (UMTA). The subsequent growth of urban funding programs and their role in the federal effort to revitalize urban transit are examined in detail in Chapters 18 and 19.

The maritime industry also benefitted from expansion of federal promotional programs during the 1970s. The maritime programs, which are administered by the Maritime Administration, provide federal operating and construction subsidies and a variety of other aids such as tax incentives and loan guarantees to ship owners. By the end of the 1970s federal maritime assistance averaged approximately $500 million per year.

The expansion of federal promotional outlays in transportation during the 1970s also included assistance to Amtrak and Conrail. The related rail funding programs are examined in the discussion that follows.

AMTRAK AND CONRAIL

As noted previously, railroad passenger service losses placed a substantial financial burden on U.S. railroads following World War II. Although the situation improved somewhat following passage of the Transportation Act of 1958, which gave the ICC authority to grant passenger train discontinuances, sizable deficits persisted.

Continuing passenger service losses coupled with the June 1970 bankruptcy of the Penn Central, which annually absorbed nearly one-third of the national rail passenger service loss, led to passage of the Rail Passenger Service Act in October 1970.[21] The act established a quasi-public corporation, Amtrak, to manage the national intercity rail passenger service network. Amtrak initiated service in May 1971. Congress provided grants of $40 million and loan guarantees of $100 million to the new organization; the railroads paid $197 million in entry fees to become affiliated with Amtrak. The subsequent operating and financial performance of Amtrak was discussed in detail in Chapter 3.

One of the most significant transportation developments of this century was the Northeast railroad reorganization. Chapter 3 contained a discussion of the factors that led to the collapse of the railroad system of the region in the early 1970s and discussed Conrail's performance. However, the significance of the Northeast railroad crisis and the related reorganization deserves further attention at this point.

The Regional Rail Reorganization Act of 1973 was signed into law by President Ford in January 1974.[22] The bill initiated a transportation planning effort that was unprecedented in scope and complexity. Following the planning process, which lasted nearly two and one-half years, Conrail initiated operations on April 1, 1976. By the time service began, nearly 3,000 miles of lightly used branch lines had been pared from the system, and several thousand additional miles of track were operated under a three-year, joint federal-state subsidy program. In total, the Conrail system included approximately 17,000 miles of track.

The reorganization and rationalization of the Northeast railroads was late in coming. Congress again awaited the emergence of crisis conditions before acting on the problems of the railroads. Earlier congressional action could have precluded at least partially the ultimate deterioration in both the service provided and the financial condition of the railroads.

The collapse of the railroads in the Northeast was not without positive aspects. The reorganization led to substantial reduction in duplicate rail facilities, while moving strongly toward a philosophy that requires those who directly benefit from a particular transportation service to bear its true cost. Further, the collapse focused national attention on the economic significance of the railroads and led to examination of many of the problems that threatened the future viability of the mode.

SUMMARY

Between World War II and the mid-1970s a number of important transportation developments occurred. In the Transportation Act of 1958 Congress attempted to revitalize the national railroad system. Although several provisions of the act brought some relief to the industry, the financial and competitive problems of the railroads persisted.

In 1967 the federal Department of Transportation was established to centralize federal planning and promotion of transportation. The agency was granted considerable power in safety regulation, but its role in economic regulation was basically limited to policy review and critique. Nevertheless, in subsequent years the agency became a leading advocate of regulatory change.

The financial drain of rail passenger service losses and the bankruptcy of the Penn Central led to the creation of Amtrak to operate the intercity rail passenger service network. In 1973, Congress enacted the Regional Rail Reorganization Act, which led to the collective reorganization of seven bankrupt railroads in the Northeast and Midwest and the creation of Conrail. The reorganization was unparalleled in both scope and complexity.

This chapter has emphasized the evolution of federal regulation and promotion between the end of World War II and the mid-1970s; the next chapter focuses on the movement toward regulatory reform that intensified during the late 1970s.

DISCUSSION QUESTIONS _____

1. What are government loan guarantees and how do they differ from traditional loans?
2. What were the major differences between the transportation messages delivered to Congress by Presidents Kennedy and Johnson?
3. Why was the Department of Transportation established?
4. Discuss the factors which led to passage of the Transportation Act of 1958.
5. Why was Amtrak established?

NOTES

1. See Chapter 8 for a more extensive discussion of the Reed-Bulwinkle Act.
2. George W. Hilton, *The Transportation Act of 1958: A Decade of Experience* (Bloomington, IN: Indiana University Press, 1969), p. 13.
3. Association of American Railroads, *Yearbook of Railroad Facts* (Washington, D.C.: the Association, 1968), p. 24.
4. For an excellent summary of the major transportation studies of that period, see Charles F. Phillips, *The Economics of Regulation*, rev. ed. (Homewood, IL: Richard D. Irwin, Inc., 1969), Appendix, Chapter 14, "Selected Bibliography of Postwar Studies of National Transportation Policy," pp. 534-36.
5. *Transportation Act*, Public Law 85-625 (1958).
6. Hilton, p. 36.
7. Ibid., pp. 107-16.
8. Association of American Railroads, *Yearbook of Railroad Facts* (Washington, D.C.: the Association, 1975), p. 21, and several earlier Association reports.
9. It should be noted that interpretation of this directive proved to be a major problem, and the issue was readdressed in the Railroad Revitalization and Regulatory Reform Act of 1976 which is discussed in the next chapter.
10. U.S. Interstate Commerce Commission, *83rd Annual Report of the Interstate Commerce Commission* (Washington, D.C.: U.S. Government Printing Office, 1969), p. 80.
11. For an extensive discussion of those guarantees, see Hilton, pp. 97-154.
12. Statement of George W. Hilton before the Senate Commerce Committee, July 30, 1970, p. 5. (Mimeographed)
13. Ibid.
14. Roy J. Sampson and Martin T. Farris, *Domestic Transportation: Practice, Theory and Policy*, 3rd ed. (Boston: Houghton Mifflin Company, 1975), p. 486.
15. *The Transportation System of Our Nation*, message from the president of the United States, April 5, 1962, House of Representatives, Doc. No. 384, 87th Cong., 2nd Sess. (Washington, D.C.: U.S. Government Printing Office, 1962).
16. *Creating a Department of Transportation*, Hearings, Subcommittee on Government Operations, House of Representatives, 89th Cong., 2nd Sess. (Washington, D.C.: U.S. Government Printing Office, 1966), pp. 36-49.
17. Sampson and Farris, p. 372.

18.   Public Law 89-670 (1966).

19.   *Airport and Airway Development Act*, Public Law 91-258; 84 Stat. 219 (1970).

20.   *Urban Mass Transportation Assistance Act*, Public Law 91-453 (1970).

21.   *Rail Passenger Service Act*, Public Law 91-518; 84 Stat. 1327 (1970).

22.   Public Law 93-236; 45 U.S.C. (1973).

SELECTED REFERENCES

Allen, Bruce W. "ICC Behavior in Rail Abandonments." *ICC Practitioners' Journal*, Vol. 41, No. 5 (July-August, 1974), pp. 553-71.

Douglas, George W., and James C. Miller, "The CAB's Domestic Passenger Fare Investigation." *Bell Journal of Economics*, Vol. 5, No. 1 (Spring, 1974), pp. 205-22.

Fellmeth, Robert. *The Interstate Commerce Omission*. New York: Grossman Publishers, 1970.

Harbeson, Robert W. "Some Policy Implications of Northeastern Railroad Problems." *Transportation Journal*, Vol. 14, No. 1 (Fall, 1974), pp. 5-12.

Harbeson, Robert W. "Toward a More Compensatory Rail Rate Structure." *ICC Practitioners' Journal*, Vol. 40, No. 2 (January-February, 1973), pp. 145-63.

Hilton, George W. *The Transportation Act of 1958: A Decade of Experience*. Bloomington, IN: Indiana University Press, 1969.

Kahn, Fritz. "The Reformation of Railroad Regulation." *ICC Practitioners' Journal*, Vol. 43, No. 4 (May-June, 1976), pp. 509-17.

Moore, Thomas G. *Freight Transportation Regulation: Surface Freight and the Interstate Commerce Commission*. Washington, D.C.: American Enterprise Institute, 1972. Chapter 3. "Development of Multi Modal Regulation, pp. 25-40.

Mulvey, Frank. National Transportation Policy Study Commission. *Amtrak: An Experiment in Rail Service*. NTPSC Special Report No. 2, Washington, D.C. the Commission, 1978.

Spychalski, John C. "Criticisms of Regulated Freight Transport: Do Economists Perceptions Conform with Institutional Realities?" *Transportation Journal*, Vol. 14, No. 3 (Spring, 1975), pp. 5-17.

Task Force on Railroad Productivity. *Improving Railroad Productivity*. Final Report of the National Commission on Productivity and the Council of Economic Advisers. Washington, D.C.: Task Force on Railroad Productivity, 1973.

U.S. Congress, Senate, Committee on Interstate and Foreign Commerce, Special Study Group on Transportation Policies in the United States. *National Transportation Policy* (Doyle Report). 87th Cong., 1st Sess., 1960. Washington, D.C.: U.S. Government Printing Office, 1961.

U.S. Department of Transportation, Office of the Secretary. *The Northeastern Railroad Problem*. A report to Congress. Washington, D.C.: the Department, 1973.

Wilson, George W. "Regulation, Public Policy, and Efficient Provision of Freight Transportation." *Transportation Journal*, Vol. 15, No. 1 (Fall, 1975), pp. 5-20.

CHAPTER TWELVE

REGULATORY REFORM IN TRANSPORTATION

While there had been calls for regulatory reform in transportation for many years, the continuing problems of regulated carriers and concern for the quality of for-hire service reinforced the reform movement in the 1970s and early 1980s. Critics contended that economic regulation protected inefficient operators, promoted unreasonably high rates, and generally fostered a misallocation of transportation resources. Attacks were made on the regulatory structure of each major mode of intercity carriage.

Among the leading advocates of regulatory reform were the president's Council of Economic Advisers and the Federal Department of Transportation. Both called for substantial relaxation of federal economic regulation and a greater reliance upon competitive forces.

This chapter examines the pressures which led to the extensive reevaluation of regulatory policies which began during the 1970s and continues into the 1990s. It also outlines the regulatory changes which have taken place. Special attention is given to the process by which these changes occurred, and the impact of these changes.

RAILROAD REGULATORY REFORM

Beginning in 1971, the DOT annually submitted legislative proposals to Congress to promote substantial changes in the economic regulation of railroads, motor carriers, and airlines. However, although the DOT's initiatives attracted some shipper and consumer group support, Congress showed little interest in the agency's early proposals.

Railroad Revitalization and Regulatory Reform Act

The department's legislative efforts were more successful in 1975. Examination of the problems of the railroads during the Northeast railroad reorganization made it apparent to Congress that at least some of those problems were a function of regulation. Under intense pressure to modify its procedures, the ICC also somewhat reluctantly agreed that some regulatory modification was probably necessary. After conducting extensive hearings on the 1975 DOT railroad proposals, Congress passed the Railroad Revitalization and Regulatory Reform Act, which was signed into law in early 1976.[1] The statute provided some important changes in transportation regulation and made additional federal funding available to revitalize the U.S. railroad system.

Ratemaking. The most important regulatory changes contained in the act pertained to railroad ratemaking. The ICC was given new standards to be applied to railroad rate proposals in determining if the rates were just and reasonable. Rates equal to or exceeding variable cost were not to be found unjust or unreasonable on the basis that they were too low. This provision was a major victory for the railroads, which had advocated the acceptance of variable cost (or out-of-pocket cost) ratemaking for many year. Further, the act provided that no rate was to be declared unjust or unreasonable on the basis that it was too high unless the ICC first determined that the carrier had "market dominance" over the traffic involved. The ICC was also charged with development of market dominance standards.

The 1976 statute also reaffirmed congressional disapproval of "umbrella" ratemaking. It declared that rates should not be held up to a particular level to protect the traffic of any other carrier or mode unless the ICC found that the proposed rates would reduce the going-concern value of the company charging the rates. To further clarify this issue, the act stated that any rate equaling or exceeding variable cost should be considered to be contributing to a company's going-concern value. Once again, the railroad position in intermodal ratemaking appeared to be strengthened.

Some regulatory reform advocates had called for total pricing freedom, but the 1976 act took a more moderate stance and created a gradually expanding zone in which carriers would have pricing freedom. With respect to rate change proposals falling outside that zone, the statute shifted the burden of proof to those protesting the change. Those protesting were to be required to prove that the rate could cause injury and should be found unlawful.

In other rate-related matters, the ICC was given time guidelines to be observed in rate cases involving major capital outlays by carriers, shippers, or receivers, and was charged with development of standards for adequate carrier revenues.

The ratemaking activities of rate bureaus were also addressed by the act. To accelerate bureau processing of rate proposals, the act required bureaus to reach final decisions on all docketed cases within 120 days. Further, bureaus were not permitted to allow agreement or voting on single line rates, and only those carriers participating in the movement were to be permitted to vote on joint line rates.

Other Changes in ICC Duties. Other ICC responsibilities were also modified by the Railroad Revitalization and Regulatory Reform Act of 1976. The ICC was granted the authority to exempt certain railroad activities from regulation if it believed that such regulations were not required by the public interest.

The act also sought to streamline ICC procedures for handling railroad merger and consolidation proposals. The ICC was to rule on any merger or consolidation proposal within two years of its submission to the agency. In the past the commission had often taken much longer than that to rule on such matters.

Concern with the relative role of federal and state government in intrastate ratemaking again surfaced in the 1976 act. The ICC gained exclusive jurisdiction over intrastate rates whenever state agencies failed to rule on such rates within 120 days of carrier filing.

Additionally, the ICC was charged with proposing modernization and revisions to the Interstate Commerce Act within two years.

Railroad Funding. Financing of railroad improvements was also a major aim of the 1976 act. Several of its provisions dealt specifically with that issue. To complete the restructuring of the bankrupt railroads in the Northeast and Midwest, $2.1 billion was made available to Conrail. Funding was generated by granting the new organization authority to issue bonds and stock to the United States Railway Association (the planning and financing agency created by the Regional Rail Reorganization Act of 1973). Additionally, a $600 million government loan program was established to finance railroad rehabilitation of plant and equipment. The act provided loan guarantees of up to $1 billion for railroad purchases of plant and equipment and $1.75 billion for upgrading rail passenger service in the Northeast corridor

Other Provisions. Several other major issues were also addressed by the Railroad Revitalization and Regulatory Reform Act of 1976. These included subsidies for railroad branch line service and discriminatory state taxation of railroads.

With respect to the branch line issue, the act provided $360 million over five years to subsidize unprofitable branch line operations. Under the program the federal share of branch line deficits was set at 100 percent the first year, 90 percent the second, 80 percent the third, and 70 percent for the next two years. Further subsidization was to become a local issue. This provision sought to transfer the economic burden of such operations to state and local government on a gradual basis, thereby allowing these governmental units sufficient time to assess needs and options.

For many years approximately 20 states had maintained property tax systems that were blatantly discriminatory against the railroads.[2] This issue had come before Congress several times, but no action had been taken. Under the 1976 act, states were barred from such practices, and the railroads were permitted to seek relief from state tax discrimination in federal courts. States were also barred from imposing other taxes in lieu of discriminatory property taxes.

Significance to the Reform Movement. Passage of the 1976 Railroad Revitalization and Regulatory Reform Act was significant not only with respect to the direct changes it fostered in railroad regulation, but also because of its indirect impact on the regulatory reform movement in other modes. Its enactment demonstrated a growing congressional willingness to consider statutory changes in transportation regulation. The DOT, bolstered by its success, was to play an even more aggressive role in promoting further regulatory changes.

FURTHER RAILROAD REGULATORY REFORM

While the Railroad Revitalization and Regulatory Reform Act of 1976 initiated a movement toward regulatory changes in the industry, many believed that the statute had not gone far enough in addressing railroad problems.[35] The continuing financial problems of the industry, which ultimately necessitated the liquidation of the Rock Island and substantial cutbacks in the scope of the Milwaukee Road, led to growing pressures toward the end of the decade to reduce the extent of railroad regulation. Calls for such additional changes came not only from the railroads, but also from the DOT and President Carter.

Pre-1980 ICC Administrative Regulatory Reforms

The ICC, which was frequently criticized for its conservative implementation of the provisions of the 1976 statute, showed increasing interest in lessening the railroads' regulatory burden. During 1978-79 many of the agency's administrative actions at the ICC were directed toward that end.

In November 1978 the ICC reversed past policy by voting to allow contract rates between railroads and shippers. Prior to that time, the commission had held that such rates would be anti-competitive and in violation of the Interstate Commerce Act. The 1978 agency ruling asserted that contract volume movements would foster improved car utilization and cost efficiencies.[3] Contract rates were to be considered by the ICC on a case-by-case basis.

In March 1979 the commission voted to stop regulating rates and most other aspects of rail transportation of fresh fruits and vegetables.[4] The railroads had long sought such an exemption to allow them to compete more freely with truckers operating under the agricultural exemption provided under the Motor Carrier Act of 1935.

During 1978-79, the ICC also undertook a number of investigations to determine if specific railroad regulations should be maintained. Among the potential changes reviewed and proposed by the agency were exemption from economic regulation of the trucking portion of intermodal services.

Staggers Rail Act of 1980

While the ICC's administrative actions were important, they were not seen as sufficient by the DOT and President Carter. Consequently, in March 1979, President Carter presented a bill to Congress which sought to make major statutory changes in railroad regulation. In submitting the proposal to Congress the President stated:

> Deregulation presents the only viable option to either massive increases in federal subsidies to the railroads or increased government intervention in their operations -- both of which are highly undesirable.[5]

The Carter proposal addressed such regulatory issues as ratemaking, abandonment of service, entry standards, and mergers. That proposal and other railroad regulatory reform measures were considered by Congress in subsequent months. Ultimately, these efforts produced the Staggers Rail Act, which was signed by President Carter in October 1980.[6]

The statute provided for a major reduction in ICC regulation of railroad ratemaking. The railroad zone of pricing freedom was expanded substantially. The statute initially eliminated ICC control of individual rates that fell below 160 percent of variable cost. That threshold level was scheduled to ultimately float between 170-180 percent of variable cost, depending on ICC cost formula. Beyond that, the railroads were permitted to increase their rates annually by an amount equal to inflation plus 6 percent without ICC suspension or investigation. This guideline applied to the initial four-year period following enactment, and a cumulative ceiling of 18 percent (above inflation) was placed on that freedom. Following the four-year period the standard was to fall to inflation plus 4 percent and was only to apply to carriers that were not earning adequate revenues. General rate increases were to be eliminated by January 1, 1984, and until that time they were to be limited to the annual rate of inflation. Contract rates were also authorized by the act, and were to be filed with the ICC.

The legislation also provided for shorter notice requirements for rate changes, accelerated ICC procedures for handling abandonment and consolidation cases, and substantial expansion of the ICC's authority to exempt commodities from regulation.

In dealing with non-regulatory matters the 1980 legislation provided a $700 million authorization for railroad rehabilitation, granted additional funding to the United States Railroad Association, and extended an emergency authorization of $329 million to Conrail. It also granted employee protection benefits related to the Rock Island and Milwaukee Road problems.[7]

Enactment of the 1980 railroad legislation was an important milestone in President Carter's efforts to promote regulatory reform in each of the three major modes of intercity carriage. As the 1980s began, the regulatory structure of transportation looked dramatically different than it had four years earlier.

Subsequent Administrative Regulatory Reform at the ICC

Since passage of the Staggers Rail Act of 1980 the ICC has continued to aggressively pursue administrative regulatory reforms in rail carriage. Acting under the powers granted to the agency by the Railroad Revitalization and Regulatory Reform Act of 1976 (and broadened by the 1980 legislation), the commission has sought to eliminate regulation whenever it is deemed unnecessary to prevent abuses of market power. The most significant post-1980, rail related administrative actions of the ICC are addressed in the following discussion.

In 1981 the commission exempted from regulation rail and truck services provided by railroads in connection with trailer-on-flatcar and container-on-flatcar operations.[8] The railroads had sought the exemption so that they might broaden their intermodal service offerings. The trucking industry had vehemently opposed the exemption.

The commission, in a January 1983 decision, eliminated the "special circumstances" doctrine, which had generally served to limit railroad participation in trucking to carriage of traffic that had a prior or subsequent movement by rail. In its decision the ICC stated that its action would permit rail-affiliated motor carriers to "offer a full range of services rather than service limited only to that provided as an auxiliary to rail service."[9] This liberalized policy was to be applied not only to railroad applications to institute new motor carrier services, but also to existing railroad-owned trucking operations. This commission decision was also opposed by the trucking industry.

During the past decade the ICC has continued to expand the scope of rail operations which are exempt from its control. The agency has exempted the following types of freight:

1.   coal shipped for export
2.   boxcar traffic[10]

3. frozen foods[11]
4. Lumber, plywood and treated wood products.[12]

The ICC has also sought to limit the reporting requirements of railroads. The most significant action taken in that regard occurred in September 1992 when railroads were exempted from requirements to file contracts, with the exception of contracts covering the movement of agricultural commodities.[13]

This relatively steady stream of ICC administrative actions to deregulation of rail carriage has created a new regulatory climate in the industry. The impact of these changes is discussed later in this chapter.

AIRLINE REGULATORY REFORM

The regulatory policies of the Civil Aeronautics Board also were widely challenged in the mid-1970s. Critics charged that the CAB discouraged airline price competition, thereby promoting expensive service competition. Such competition, which tends to emphasize adding more flights, rapid replacement of equipment, and heavy advertising outlays to create perceived non-price differences between carriers, was alleged to have increased customer costs. Several studies indicated that this orientation resulted in unnecessary costs to the consumer of up to $3.5 billion per year.[14] It was further contended that the agency was overly concerned with protection of regulated carriers and gave inadequate attention to consumer interests. The CAB's impact on airline management was also criticized. It was charged that the board had severely limited managerial prerogatives and that this adversely affected the industry's earnings performance.[15]

The criticism was widespread. Among those advocating deregulation were the president's Council of Economic Advisers, the DOT, Ralph Nader, Common Cause, airline passenger groups, and many academicians. The airlines, however, generally opposed deregulation and argued that it would result in market chaos and further deterioration of the industry's financial condition. During the final stages of the Ford administration, the CAB responded to growing criticism by agreeing that some regulatory reform appeared to be desirable.

A major step toward airline deregulation was taken by President Carter when he appointed Alfred Kahn as Chairman of the Civil Aeronautics Board in June 1977. President Carter was strongly committed to a reduction of federal regulation of transportation, and he had called for regulatory reform in aviation shortly after he assumed office in January 1977. However, Congress responded rather slowly to that request, and Kahn's appointment initiated a major movement toward administrative regulatory reform in aviation. Under Kahn the board quickly and aggressively pursued administrative changes that liberalized fare and entry policies. While these actions drew some criticism from Congress, the board was operating within its legal authority, given the vague nature of the statutory directives contained in the Federal Aviation Act.

Air Cargo Deregulation

During that same period, congressional attention was being given to potential regulatory reform in the cargo sector of the airline industry. After conducting extensive hearings on the topic and undoubtedly influenced by the CAB's administrative actions, Congress passed legislation in November 1977 that effectively deregulated air cargo services.[16]

The statute allowed all scheduled and commuter air carriers that had provided cargo services for the previous year to obtain unlimited operating rights throughout the lower 48 states. Under that provision 74 carriers were granted such authority. Other carriers were permitted to apply for similar authority beginning in November 1978. Fitness was to be the only criterion for denial. It was also stipulated that future rate changes could not be denied unless they were found to be discriminatory or predatory. The CAB issued its final rules to implement the deregulation of air cargo service in November 1978.[17]

Airline Deregulation Act of 1978

Senators Edward Kennedy and Howard Cannon were the primary congressional advocates of airline passenger deregulation. Hearings on this issue had been held sporadically for several years and continued into the Fall of 1978. The Airline Deregulation Act, passed in October 1978, fostered a gradual but extensive reduction in the economic regulation of commercial passenger service.[18] While acknowledging that aviation safety should still be regarded as the highest priority in air commerce, the statute mandated maximum reliance upon competition to promote the development of a variety of adequate, economic, efficient, and low-price services by air carriers. Toward that end, the law prescribed numerous changes in matters such as the status of the CAB, entry and pricing controls, and abandonment of service.

CAB Sunset. The "sunset" provisions of the statute provided for elimination of the CAB and transfer of residual functions to other federal agencies by January 1, 1985.

Entry Controls. In terms of the future structure of the airline industry, probably the most significant provisions of the act pertained to entry controls. The statute provided for gradual relaxation of the CAB's entry policies, culminating with elimination of CAB route authority by December 31, 1981. Until that time the board was directed to issue certificates to applicants that demonstrated they were "fit, willing, and able" to provide the services proposed. Applicants were no longer required to demonstrate that the authority they sought met a public need. When the agency was abolished, the DOT was to assume the responsibility for determining an applicant's "fitness."

Pricing. The 1978 legislation also provided for gradual relaxation of pricing controls, with all control over passenger ratemaking scheduled to end by January 1, 1983.

Abandonment of Service. While Congress sought to promote easier airline exit from noncompensatory markets, there was concern about the potential negative impact on affected communities. To minimize that impact, Congress guaranteed continued air transportation for ten years to all cities that were listed on air carrier certificates on the date of enactment, including cities where certificated carriers had suspended service.

To insure such service, the legislation established a new subsidy program with compensation to be based on the needs of the community and the use of appropriate size aircraft. For each city that was guaranteed service, the CAB was directed to establish a level of "essential air service" (EAS).

Air carriers serving cities that were guaranteed air service were required to give notice before reducing service below the level of essential air transportation. The statute required that when the CAB received such a notice it was to make every effort to arrange for another carrier to provide essential service on a continuing basis. If the board was unable to arrange for such replacement service, it was empowered to require the carriers serving the community to continue to serve the point for additional 30-day intervals. Carriers were entitled to compensation for any losses incurred during the extended period.

When the CAB was eliminated, responsibility for the EAS program were to be shifted to the DOT.

Other Provisions. Several other major issues were addressed by the Airline Deregulation Act of 1978. Among these were expansion of the commuter air carrier exemption, fill-up rights, employee protection guarantees, and mutual aid agreements.

As discussed in Chapter 6, throughout the years commuter airlines operated under an equipment size-related exemption from CAB economic regulation. The 1978 legislation expanded the exemption to cover the operation of aircraft with capacities of less than 60 passengers or 18,000 pounds of cargo.[19] This effectively broadened the markets that could be served by such carriers.

All U.S. certificated carriers engaged in scheduled service between domestic points and points in foreign countries were granted fill-up rights by the statute. These rights permitted the airlines to carry persons, property, and mail between U.S. cities served in the domestic portion of international flights. Granting of this authority was motivated by a congressional desire to foster increases in both load factors and carrier revenues.

The statute also addressed the issue of employee protection. It guaranteed federal financial assistance to airline employees who might be adversely affected by deregulation. This matter is discussed in detail in Chapter 15.

Air Freight Forwarding Deregulation

As noted in Chapter 6, in early 1979 the Civil Aeronautics Board voted to end its economic regulation of the air freight forwarding industry. Consequently, the economic aspects of the industry were no longer subject to federal control.

MOTOR CARRIER REGULATORY REFORM

Criticism of federal regulation of the motor carrier industry also intensified during the 1970s. It was argued that ICC entry policies were too restrictive and were motivated by a commission desire to protect existing carriers.[20] The time consumed and expenses involved in obtaining operating authority from the ICC effectively precluded the entrance of many small businessmen into the industry. Also, the nature of the certificates and permits issued to carriers was attacked in terms of the commodity and route restrictions that they contained. Similarly, growing concentration within the industry, particularly in the general commodity sector, was a matter of concern to many parties, including the DOT and the Department of Justice.[21]

Commission regulation of motor carrier ratemaking was also widely criticized. It was argued that the collective ratemaking of regulated carriers through rate bureaus precluded effective price competition while protecting inefficient carriers. The resulting higher-than-normal prices were seen as yielding excessive profits to many carriers and supporting artificially high wages for organized labor within the industry.

Those advocating regulatory change contended that the prevailing regulatory structure ignored the economic characteristics of the industry, which seemed well suited to reliance upon market forces to determine price/service offerings. Numerous studies of the societal cost of motor carrier regulation were conducted during the 1970s and provided estimates ranging up to $5 billion per year.[22]

Support for regulatory reform in motor carriage was broad based. The DOT, beginning in 1971, annually submitted legislative proposals to Congress to promote substantial changes in the economic regulation of motor carriage. Joining the Department in calling for changes were the Department of Justice, the Federal Trade Commission, the President's Council of Economic Advisers, numerous public interest groups, many academicians, and some congressmen.

However, there was no clear mandate from the shipping public that major regulatory reform should be undertaken in motor carriage. To the contrary, research generally indicated that shippers were well pleased with the quality of motor carrier service.[23] Further, the trucking industry and the Teamsters were adamantly opposed to regulatory changes. The American Trucking Associations argued that liberalization of ICC entry and pricing policies would promote market instability.[24] Supporters of existing regulatory policies argued that in a more liberal regulatory environment the entry of many small businessmen would not only erode the financial position of existing carriers, but would also promote predatory pricing and a decline in service quality. Regulated carriers contended that broad regulatory changes would reduce services to small communities and would result in deterioration of both trucking fuel efficiency and highway safety.[25]

Pre-1980 ICC Administrative Regulatory Reforms

While the ICC acknowledged the criticism of its regulation of motor carriage in the early 1970s, it did little in response. The commission appeared to be awaiting congressional action on the matter. However, that was not readily forthcoming. The DOT's annual submission of motor carrier regulatory reform proposals to Congress had attracted little congressional support.

The situation began to change somewhat during the latter months of the Ford administration when the ICC initiated several internal studies of the need for regulatory change. This growing commission sensitivity to the issue was later reinforced by both President Carter's commitment to regulatory reform and ICC Chairman Daniel O'Neal's agreement with the concept. Despite some internal conflicts between the chairman and several commissioners who continued to advocate maintenance of a conservative regulatory posture, during 1977 the ICC began a decisive movement toward administrative regulatory changes in motor carriage. One sign of the agency's growing interest in such change was provided by the July 1977 release of a Staff Task Report which contained 39 recommendations for regulatory changes in trucking.[26]

Following release of that report, ICC decisions in motor carrier entry cases tended to give more weight to the desires of the shippers supporting the applicants and to the potential benefits of competition in promoting better service at reasonable rates.[27] The perceived liberalization of ICC entry policies contributed to a substantial increase in the number of entry applications received by the commission during 1978 and 1979. The commission's approval rate on such applications also increased steadily, and of those entry cases decided by the ICC during 1979, more than 98 percent were approved.[28] One obvious effect of this policy change was a significant increase in the number of ICC-regulated motor carriers; this reversed a long-term decline in such carriers.

Among other major steps taken by the commission during the 1977-79 period were:

1   release of contract carriers from the "rule of eight,", which had previously limited such carriers to no more than eight accounts

2.   adoption of the "Toto" principle, which allowed private carriers to reach greater levels of efficiency by engaging in for-hire transportation

3.   modification of protest standards to shift the burden of proof for harm to protestants and to restrict protests to carriers actively participating in movements involved in an application

4.   facilitation of the dual operations of carriers as both contract and common carriers to permit both market responsiveness and carrier efficiency[29]

Still further changes were advocated by the commission's Motor Carrier Task Force in a May 1979 report. The Task Force suggested removal of most freight rate and entry controls that applied to 12 different specialized segments of the industry, including those carriers who hauled lumber, building materials metal, and household goods.[30] At approximately the same time, the commission began an investigation of the desirability of granting regulated truckers a pricing zone of reasonableness in which rates might be raised and lowered without ICC approval.

The ICC's movement toward administrative liberalization of motor carrier regulatory policies was not limited to the freight sector of the industry. Policies governing intercity bus operations were also modified substantially. In entry cases the commission began placing primary emphasis on fitness and shifted the burden of proof in such cases to protestants. During the late 1970s the commission annually approved more than 96 percent of the applications it received for intercity bus operating authority.[31] At the same time the agency sought to introduce a greater degree of ratemaking freedom into the industry.

The ICC's administrative policy changes naturally did not go unnoticed by Congress. In fact, on several occasions during 1978 the ICC's authority to make such significant regulatory changes was unofficially challenged by Congress. In each instance, Chairman O'Neal replied that the ICC had not overstepped its authority according to the agency's interpretation of the provisions of the Interstate Commerce Act. However, late in 1979 the commission agreed to take a more gradual approach to further regulatory modification to allow Congress sufficient time to develop a statutory program to promote motor carriage regulatory reform.[32]

The Motor Carrier Act of 1980

As noted earlier in this chapter, Congress did not respond favorably to early DOT motor carrier deregulation proposals. But the inertia of the changes that had already occurred in the airline industry and the ICC's administrative actions prompted serious congressional consideration of that topic in 1978-80. After extensive hearings and debate the Senate and House approved the Motor Carrier Act of 1980, which was signed into law by President Carter in July 1980.[33]

While the movement toward deregulation had been strongly opposed by many trucking industry representatives, the American Trucking Associations supported the final bill. The statute was quite broad, dealing with such issues as the Statement of National Transportation Policy, entry controls, the elimination of operating restrictions, pricing, rate bureau processes, contract and private carriage, and exemptions.

Statement of National Transportation Policy. The act added a paragraph to the Statement of National Transportation Policy which represented a new regulatory philosophy with respect to motor carriage of property. It sought:

> ...to promote competitive and efficient transportation services in order to (A) meet the needs of shippers, receivers, and consumers; (B) allow a variety of quality and price options to meet changing market demands and the diverse requirements of the shipping public; (C) allow the most productive use of equipment and energy resources; (D) enable efficient and well-managed carriers to earn adequate profits, attract capital, and maintain fair wages and working conditions; (E) provide and maintain service to small communities and small shippers; (F) improve and maintain a sound, safe, and competitive privately owned motor carrier system; (G) promote greater participation by minorities in the motor carrier system, and (H) promote intermodal transportation.[34]

Entry Controls. The statute attempted to promote a continued liberalization of motor carrier entry standards. It required entry applicants to be fit, willing, and able and specified that supporting evidence was to demonstrate that the proposed service was responsive to public demand or need. However protestants were to bear the burden of proof in such proceedings and were required to show that the application was inconsistent with the public convenience and necessity. The ICC was directed to consider not only how the application related to the Statement of National Transportation Policy, but also the effect of approval on existing carriers. Traffic diversion from such carriers was not to be considered, in and of itself, to be inconsistent with the public convenience and necessity.

Removal of Operating Restrictions. Congress also sought to eliminate unnecessary operating burdens from regulated motor carriage. The ICC was to remove all gateway restrictions and circuitous route limitations that had been imposed on motor carriers of property. The commission was also required to: act to reasonably broaden categories of commodities a carrier could haul; authorize service to intermediate points on a carrier's routes; authorize round-trip authority where only one-way authority existed; eliminate unreasonable or narrow territorial limitations; remove any unreasonable restriction deemed wasteful of fuel, inefficient, or contrary to the public interest.

Pricing. Motor carrier ratemaking was extensively addressed by the statute. A zone of rate freedom was established which applied to motor carriers and freight forwarders. Rate changes within the zone were not subject to ICC interference. However, it should be noted that the ICC's right to suspend and investigate a proposed rate on the basis that it was discriminatory or predatory was not affected by the legislation.

A rule of ratemaking provision was also included in the Motor Carrier Act of 1980. In proceedings to determine either the reasonableness of rate levels of motor carriers of property or the reasonableness of a territorial rate structure, the ICC was required to authorize revenue levels that were adequate to permit well-managed carriers to cover their operating costs and earn a fair return. While stressing the necessity of considering future cost estimates in such proceedings, the act specifically directed the ICC to consider, among other factors, the effect of the proposed rate on the movement of traffic by that carrier.

Rate Bureaus. Motor carrier rate bureaus were also substantially affected by the legislation. It mandated that beginning January 1, 1981, only those carriers with authority to participate in the services involved would be permitted to vote on a particular rate proposal. This stipulation covered both single and joint line rates. Effective with the passage of the act, carriers were prohibited from discussing or voting on rates proposed under the zone of rate freedom. Beginning in 1984 discussion and voting on single-line rate proposals were to be prohibited. However, carriers were not prohibited from discussing and voting on either general rate increases or decreases or changes in commodity classifications and class tariff structures.

Rate bureaus were also prohibited from interfering with a carrier's right of independent action and forbidden to file a protest or complaint with the ICC against tariff items published by or for any motor carrier of property.

Additionally, the legislation established a Motor Carrier Ratemaking Study Commission to investigate collective ratemaking and the need, if any, for continued antitrust immunity. The commission, which was to be comprised of six members of Congress and four public members, was required to deliver a final report to Congress by January 1, 1983. The final report of the Commission is discussed later in this chapter.

Contract and Private Carriage. In addressing contract carriage, the statute officially eliminated the "rule of eight." Entry procedures were to be streamlined by the ICC and protest guidelines were to be similar to those of common carriage. Contract carrier services were not to be limited to any area or industry. Further, contract carriers were permitted to hold common carrier certificates; common carriers could also obtain contract carriage permits. Persons holding such dual authority were authorized to transport both common and contract traffic in the same vehicle at the same time.

The act dealt with private carriage in terms of the concept of intercorporate hauling. Such hauling was exempted form ICC regulation if the corporate parent involved owned directly or indirectly a 100 percent interest in each of the subsidiaries. However, those engaged in intercorporate hauling were to file notice of such operations with the commission.

Other Exemptions. Congress substantially expanded the number of commodities considered exempt from ICC motor carrier regulation. Livestock and poultry feed as well as agricultural seed and plants were added to the existing agricultural exemptions. Movements of used pallets and used empty containers were also exempted. Further, an exemption was extended to motor carrier movements that were incidental to air carriage.

The statute permitted truckers to carry regulated and exempt commodities in the same vehicle at the same time without affecting the exempt status of the unregulated commodities or the regulated status of non-exempt commodities.

Other Provisions. The Motor Carrier Act of 1980 addressed many other related issues. Foremost among these were motor carrier mergers, insurance requirements, joint rates and through-route regulations, owner-operator problems, and employee assistance.

A time limit was placed on ICC processing of motor carrier merger applications. The agency was given 240 days to conclude its evidentiary proceedings and required to issue its final decision in such cases within 180 days of the conclusion of those proceedings.

Responding to concern about the financial integrity of companies that might enter the industry under more liberal regulatory guidelines, the statute specified insurance requirements. It established a mandatory liability insurance minimum of $750,000 for commercial carries and a $5 million minimum for all carriers transporting hazardous materials. The DOT secretary was directed to study these requirements and empowered to subsequently issue regulations that might reduce the mandated levels.

The statute also addressed the issue of intermodal ratemaking. It authorized the ICC to require establishment of through routes and joint rates between motor carriers and rail and water carriers. Freight forwarders were permitted to enter into contracts with rail and water carriers.

The act assisted owner-operators in several ways. The most significant directive dealt with loading and unloading practices in the trucking industry. Owner-operators long contended that they were often assessed exorbitant loading and/or unloading charges, particularly in servicing facilities employing unionized workers. The statute stipulated that whenever a shipper or receiver required an owner-operator to be assisted in such activities, the shipper or receiver was to be financially responsible for the assistance.

The act also addressed the issue of potential job losses or regulated motor carrier employees related to the regulatory changes. The Secretary of Labor was directed to maintain and publish a list of jobs available with ICC-regulated motor carriers and was to assist those previously employed by such carriers in finding other employment.

An Overview of the Act. Passage of the Motor Carrier Act of 1980 ended three years of extensive congressional deliberation on the matter. It reflected considerable compromise and consequently involved regulatory reform rather than deregulation. In effect the statute acknowledged the legitimacy of many of the ICC's earlier administrative actions. While its passage did not create the "no holds barred" marketplace that many critics of regulatory policy had sought, it did represent a significant step toward promoting greater reliance upon market forces.

The Household Goods Act of 1980

The Motor Carrier Act of 1980 did not directly address the household goods (HHG) sector of the trucking industry. That industry sector was perceived by many members of Congress as being rather different than the rest of trucking not only because of the non-repetitive and personal nature of the services rendered, but also due to the relatively unsophisticated status of the typical consumer of the service.

As a result of this perception, Congress considered separate legislation to address the problems of HHG trucking. These problems were generally thought to be the burden of extensive ICC regulation upon such carriers and the quality of the service provided to shippers. At that time, nearly one-half of the shipper complaints filed with the ICC were related to HHG services. The complaints typically involved the loss or damage of goods and carrier failure to provide the services that previously had been agreed upon. The incidence of such complaints had increased during the late 1970s.

In response to these problems, Congress passed the Household Goods Transportation Act of 1980, which was signed by President Carter in October 1980.[35] The legislation made numerous changes in the relationships between HHG carriers, shippers, and the ICC.[36]

The legislation gave carriers substantially greater pricing freedom, and the ability to offer guaranteed pickup and delivery dates with penalties to be paid to customers for non-performance.

The ICC was also empowered to seek civil penalties against carriers for service deficiencies if harm to shippers could be shown, and was permitted to prohibit specific agents from participating in the industry. New guidelines for claims dispute resolution were also established.

Bus Regulatory Reform Act of 1982

Regulatory reform measures related to interstate bus operations were also considered by Congress in the late 1970s. However, debate on these matters carried over into the Reagan administration, and it was not until November 1982 that the Bus Regulatory Reform Act was signed into law by President Reagan.[37] The most important provisions of the statute addressed the Statement of National Transportation Policy, entry, removal of operating restrictions, abandonment of service, and carrier ratemaking.[38]

Statement of National Transportation Policy. As noted earlier, the Motor Carrier Act of 1980 added a paragraph to the statement of National Transportation Policy. The 1982 legislation added a new section to the Statement that directly addressed bus regulation. It declared that the goals of National Transportation Policy were:

>...in regulating transportation by motor carrier of passengers (A) to cooperate with the States on transportation matters for the purpose of encouraging the States to exercise intrastate regulatory jurisdiction in accordance with the objectives of this subtitle; (B) to provide Federal procedures which ensure that intrastate regulation is exercised in accordance with this subtitle: and (C) to ensure that Federal reform initiatives enacted by the Bus Regulatory Reform Act of 1982 are not nullified by State regulatory actions.

It was therefore clear that Congress intended to redefine the relative distribution of power between the ICC and state governments in regulating the bus industry.

Entry. The Bus Regulatory Reform Act sought to substantially ease federal entry controls. A "public interest" entry standard, which was viewed as considerably less stringent than the earlier "public convenience and necessity" standard, was initiated, and the burden of proof was shifted to protestants.

Even less rigorous "fitness only" guidelines were to be applied to applications involving: (1) services to communities that lacked bus service; (2) proposals to replace discontinued rail or air passenger service; or (3) cases in which the only interstate bus operator serving a particular community had applied to discontinue the service.

Removal of Operating Restrictions. The 1982 statute called for elimination of operating restrictions that placed unnecessary burdens on interstate bus operators. In particular, it directed the ICC to grant round-trip authority to carriers that previously had been limited to one-way authority, and called upon the agency to remove restrictions that prohibited carriers from serving intermediate points along interstate routes.

Exit. While ICC-regulated bus operators historically had been relatively free to reduce schedules or discontinue service in their interstate operations, they often faced major difficulties in attempting to make such adjustments in the intrastate markets that they served. The Bus Regulatory Reform Act provided a mechanism to permit bus operators to make such adjustments despite state objections. It stipulated that if the bus operator had applied to a state and its discontinuance application had been wholly or partially denied, or if the state had failed to act on the application, the operator could petition the ICC for relief. The commission was granted the power to supersede the state decisions and permit a service reduction or a discontinuance of service to the points involved.

Ratemaking. Bus industry ratemaking was also addressed by the 1982 legislation. It provided for gradual reduction of the ICC's control over bus rates, with commission authority to regulate independently set bus rates being eliminated in 1985 (unless rates were deemed predatory or discriminatory). Also, subject to the same limitations, ICC authority over bus rates charged for special or charter services was eliminated effective with the passage of the statute.

The Bus Regulatory Reform Act also addressed collective ratemaking in the industry. Beginning January 1, 1983, it prohibited discussion and voting on single-line rates. Similar prohibitions were to be applied to joint rates proposed by one or more carriers beginning on January 1, 1984. However, carriers were still permitted to discuss and vote upon general rate increases.

Other Provisions. Numerous other aspects of bus industry operations were covered by the legislation. Carrier insurance requirements were increased. States were prohibited from imposing discriminatory taxes on the property of bus operators. The ICC's jurisdiction over the securities issued by bus companies (and truckers) was transferred to the Securities and Exchange Commission, and new guidelines covering the merger of bus properties were given to the commission. In reviewing bus merger proposals, the ICC was to consider the effects on the adequacy of transportation to the public, total fixed charges, and employees. The agency was also to evaluate the effect of rail carriers in the area involved. The statute also stipulated that any bus industry employees who had worked in the industry for at least two years prior to passage of the act were entitled to priority re-employment if they lost their jobs because of the regulatory change.

Report of the Motor Carrier Ratemaking Study Commission

The Motor Carrier Act of 1980 established the Motor Carrier Ratemaking Study Commission and charged it to investigate collective ratemaking in motor carriage and to review the need, if any, for continued antitrust immunity for such activities. In January 1983 the commission made its final report to Congress.[39]In the report the commission concluded that collective ratemaking conflicted with the goals of National Transportation Policy in that it effectively reduced competition. The commission further asserted that such practices resulted in higher rates and prices to the consumer while protecting inefficient carriers. It also rejected the contention that collective ratemaking provided special protection for small shippers. Rather, the commission argued that small shippers were poorly represented in the collective ratemaking process.

The commission recommended a prompt and complete elimination of antitrust immunity for collective ratemaking and related activities in the trucking industry.[40] It urged that all motor carrier ratemaking be subjected to antitrust laws after July 1, 1984. That date had been specified in the Motor Carrier Act of 1980 as the tentative date for elimination of the antitrust exemption covering single-line ratemaking.

As might be expected, the findings of the Motor Carrier Ratemaking Study Commission were strongly opposed by the American Trucking Associations, which continued to support collective ratemaking. In opposing the recommendations, the associations noted that the vote of the commission had been 6-4 in favor of eliminating the antitrust exemption.

Congress did not follow the recommendations of the Study Commission, and the antitrust exemption remained intact. As noted in Chapter 9, the ICC subsequently conducted several internal studies of the issue, but found no compelling reason to eliminate that exemption. Nevertheless, due to the post-regulatory reform nature of the marketplace, collective pricing is far less prevalent today than it was in 1980. This matter is discussed more extensively later in this chapter.

Subsequent Administrative Regulatory Reform at the ICC

The ICC has continued to administratively reduce the regulatory burden of motor carriers. The actions taken by the agency include reduction of reporting requirements and establishment of expedited procedures for handling consolidations of small motor carriers.

Future Motor Carrier Regulatory Reform Prospects

While much progress has been made toward reducing federal regulation of both the interstate trucking and bus industries, there are still extensive statutory guidelines that must be administered by the ICC. Many of those guidelines are imprecise in nature and subject to the varying interpretations of commission members. Consequently, an ICC consisting of a majority of pro-regulation commissioners might be able to slow, if not reverse, progress toward regulatory reform.

Throughout the early 1990s the Department of Transportation continued to submit legislative proposals to Congress to further deregulate motor carriage. Congress has taken no action on those proposals.[41]

THE IMPACT OF REGULATORY REFORM

The regulatory reform measures discussed earlier in this chapter have taken effect. Many of those changes were dramatic in both their suddenness and their scope. While changes of this nature are not easily assimilated in either industrial or governmental settings, many parties have sought to determine whether the regulatory reform movement was a success or a failure. That is not a simple task. The goals articulated by Congress and the regulatory agencies in promoting reforms were quite imprecise; consequently, it is very difficult to measure the extent to which those goals were realized. In fact, it might be argued that the nature of political policy making is such that, whenever possible, clear articulation of legislative and/or administrative goals is avoided. Under these circumstances, it is difficult to hold individuals responsible for problems that might arise in the future.

Further complicating evaluation efforts is the fact the regulatory reforms of such breadth and depth trigger many simultaneous changes. In reviewing related developments, it is unclear what relative weights should be assigned to specific changes. Obviously, an individual's perception of these events will vary considerably according to his or her direct involvement or non-involvement in them.

It must also be recognized that the regulatory changes have not occurred in an industrial vacuum in which everything else remained constant. Recent changes in the transportation industries have been driven not only by regulatory reform measures, but also by prevailing economic conditions (including the worst recession since the Depression and the lingering recession of the early 1990s), and the varying responses of carrier managers to their rapidly changing environment.

The following discussion does not attempt to judge the regulatory reform movement as being either a success or a failure. Clearly, such an effort is far beyond the scope of this book. Rather, it attempts to provide objective observations concerning some of the changes in the air, trucking, and rail modes that may have been at least partially driven by regulatory change.

Structural Changes and Route Realignment

Changes in regulatory policies related to entry, abandonment of service, mergers, and intermodal ownership have contributed to significant structural changes in the transportation industries. These changes have influenced not only the aggregate number and size distribution of carriers in the various modal segments, but also the number of companies operating in specific markets. Further, many carriers have used their new freedoms to significantly alter their route networks.

Air Carriage. The progressive liberalization of aviation entry policies has affected the number of airlines providing scheduled service between large cities. While there were 23 CAB-certificated carriers providing such service in 1978, by early 1984 the total had grown to 46.[42] Since that time, through consolidations and carrier failures, that number has contracted to ten "major" airlines and fourteen "national" airlines.

Most of the new entrant airlines which challenged the more established carriers in the early days of deregulation have disappeared, either through acquisition or failure. Those companies, including People Express and New York Air, were often thinly capitalized and poorly prepared for the intense competition which arose.[43]

Airline failures, including those of long-time industry participants such as Eastern Air Lines and Pan American Airlines, should not have been unexpected. The sizable debt-servicing obligations of some carriers, the cyclical nature of the aviation industry, and elimination of the CAB's protective policies were bound to produce some failures. Other carrier failures should be expected, because an openly competitive marketplace normally will produce both successes and failures. Nevertheless, new companies continue to enter the industry.[44]

The large airlines which participated in the industry prior to the regulatory reform movement have modified their route networks not only by moving into new markets, but also through realignment of routes along "hub and spoke" lines. As discussed in Chapter 6, that concept involves reduction of direct flights and the filtering of feeder traffic through a limited number of major hub airports.

More than 90 percent of the industry's passenger miles are now generated by eight airlines as compared to fifteen in 1984.[45] While some view this development with concern, it should be noted that this does not necessarily imply that the number of carriers serving city pairs has declined. In fact, more than 55 percent of passengers now travel between cities served by more than three carriers. That number was 28 percent in 1979.[46]

As larger carriers have expanded their route networks they have generally eliminated services into smaller communities. Those communities have continued to be served by carriers participating in the "regional" segment of the industry. Small communities which had received scheduled service prior to 1978 were guaranteed continuance of that service until 1988 (later extended to 1998) under the Essential Air Service program. Federal subsidies to regional carriers to support the EAS program were $35.2 million in 1992.[47]

While the number of regional carriers originally expanded as regulatory changes were initiated, there has also been a more recent contraction in their number as a result of consolidations and failures. Between 1981-1992 the number dropped from 246 to 127.[48]

Motor Carriage. Liberalization of ICC entry policies has similarly promoted a major restructuring of interstate trucking. Commission approval of entry applications has exceeded 95 percent since the late 1970s, and the number of ICC-regulated motor carriers increased from approximately 16,000 in 1975 to nearly 50,000 in 1993.[49] Most new entrants have been small and non-unionized. In many market segments these companies have provided strong competition for more established carriers. This has been particularly so in the truckload segment of the business.

Somewhat different dynamics have been operating in the less-than-truckload segment of the industry. In this more liberal regulatory environment, large LTL companies like Yellow Freight System, Consolidated Freightways and Roadway Express have each opened hundreds of new terminals in expanding their route networks. Those carriers have also continued to expand through acquisitions. During the 1990s they have been particularly active in acquiring regional LTL carriers. This trend was illustrated by Yellow's 1993 acquisition of Preston Corporation and Roadway's 1993 purchase of Central Freight Lines.[50] These developments have led to growing concentration in the LTL market with the "Big Three" accounting for approximately 36 percent of aggregate LTL revenues.[51]

The number of motor carrier bankruptcies has increased dramatically since the regulatory reform movement began. The annual failure rate has more than quadrupled, and now exceeds 1,200 per year.[52] However, this should have been expected. Critics of traditional ICC policies often argued that marginal truckers were able to continue operations only through the protective entry and ratemaking policies of the ICC. As those policies have become pro-competitive, many carriers have been unable to adjust to competitive pressures and have failed.

Rail Carriage. The structure of the railroad industry has also changed considerably as regulatory policies have been modified. Streamlined merger procedures and a generally more supportive ICC attitude toward railroad consolidation applications has intensified carrier interest in such combinations (see Chapter 15). Consolidation activity has increased, and end-to-end combinations, which had been effectively prohibited by ICC policies for many year, are becoming far more prevalent. Such combinations reduce costs by eliminating interchange requirements, and will likely improve the quality of rail service by fostering faster through service. Fewer large rail systems have emerged, and in some cases intramodal competition has been reduced. However, much of rail traffic is subject to heavy intermodal competition.

It has become progressively easier to abandon branch line operations, and many carriers are aggressively pursuing system rationalization. Since the Staggers Rail Act was passed in 1980 railroads have abandoned nearly 50,000 miles of rail line, reducing the industry's line mileage by nearly one-third.[53]

In some instances, service along abandoned branch lines has not been eliminated, but has been taken over by "short-line" railroad operators whose lower overhead and operating costs make such service offerings financially viable. Short-lines, whose number has increased substantially since 1980, now generate more than eight percent of the industry's freight traffic.[54]

Intermodal Ownership and Intermodal Alliances. Intermodal ownership has become more common in the transportation industries (see Chapter 15). The relaxation of related federal policies has provided an impetus for integration of the modes within a single corporate entity. However, the effectiveness of the recent wave of voluntary carrier alliances, such as those linking railroads and motor carriers, has led many carriers to move slowly in pursuing intermodal acquisitions.

The Nature of Competition

Regulatory changes have significantly affected the nature of competition in many transportation markets. We continue to evolve from a situation in which the regulatory agencies played a very significant allocative role to one in which individual carriers are increasingly able to respond aggressively to market opportunities.

As the number of carriers participating in many markets has increased, the range of potential actions/reactions which may arise in those markets has broadened. Also, an increasing percentage of intercity freight and passenger traffic now moves at prices which are no longer subject to federal regulation. Carriers have an unprecedented degree of pricing freedom.

There is also considerably less reliance upon collective ratemaking in the railroad and trucking industries. This is due not only to statutory changes limiting such agreements, but also because new entrants in the trucking industry typically have not chosen to participate in them.

More direct carrier-shipper interaction has emerged, and negotiating skills have taken on greater prominence. Results of expanded carrier-shipper interaction and greater pricing freedom include not only more aggressive and innovative pricing behavior, such as railroad contract ratemaking and guaranteed service quality in trucking (see Chapter 9), but also emergence of a broader range of price/service options to be considered by shippers and travelers in many markets. Pricing has become an increasingly important competitive variable, and it is far more responsive to short-term market conditions than it was under tight regulation.

The effects of greater competitive intensity can be shown by examining railroad and airline rates before and after regulatory reform. In 1992 the ICC reported that the average inflation adjusted gross revenue per ton mile for the railroads had fallen by 28.8 percent since 1980.[55] Similarly, in 1991 the inflation adjusted yield per passenger mile in the airline industry was approximately two-thirds what it had been in 1976.[56] Competitive intensity has also held down trucking rates in many markets.[57]

Caution must be used in interpreting such "average" figures. They provide little insight into the pricing dynamics which exist in a specific market. In some markets, particularly those involving small communities, prices have increased substantially.

Impact on the Management Process

A tightly regulated transportation marketplace was more predictable for carriers and shippers than the current marketplace. In the past, carriers were not routinely faced with the threat of new market entrants or competitive price reductions. Similarly, corporate logistics managers could readily predict the nature of carrier rate and service offerings over a moderate time frame. While rates may have been artificially high and service quality questionable, at least logistics managers could count on some constants in their lives. However, the regulatory reform movement has made change the norm.

Regulatory changes have created an environment in which strategic planning is critical to success. From the carrier's standpoint, in a tightly regulated environment many important managerial decisions effectively were made by the regulatory agencies. Now carrier management has more options to assess, and the risks and potential rewards are significantly greater. Management can no longer afford the luxury of reacting to changing conditions after the fact, but rather must anticipate changes and plan for contingencies. Failure to do so can have grave consequences. Nevertheless, experience to date has indicated that individual carriers respond quite differently to the same market freedoms.

Those involved in logistics management are also challenged by this new environment. As discussed in Chapter 2, corporate logistics has become more visible, and increasing attention is being devoted to logistics planning and analysis.

Impact on Labor/Management Relations

During the debate that preceded passage of the regulatory reform statutes, it was often suggested that existing regulations allowed the unions representing transportation workers to obtain higher-than-normal wages and fringe benefits. The argument contended that the protected environment in which regulated companies operated permitted the unions to seek and obtain wages and work rule agreements that could not have been realized in a competitive marketplace. Those supporting regulatory reform believed that changes would force the unions to be more moderate in their demands.

Since that time, many regulatory changes have occurred, and they have had an impact on organized labor in transportation.[58] This has been particularly true in the motor carrier industry. Many of the new firms which have entered the industry employ non-union personnel. As a result, the new entrants have a decidedly lower labor cost structure than many of their more senior competitors, and they are not burdened with the restrictive operating practices and work rules that often plague more established firms. As a result, the newer firms generate substantially greater productivity per labor dollar. Some newer firms in the trucking industry have chosen to reflect this cost advantage in lower prices, and this has fostered vigorous price competition.

A similar pattern had emerged in the late 1970s in the airline industry as new entrant airlines exerted considerable pressure on the more established airlines to reduce costs. That pressure led to unprecedented concessions from airline unions, but the subsequent failure of most of the new entrants allowed the unions to recover those concessions in later rounds of bargaining.

Transportation unions have attempted to organize many of the more successful companies which have entered the industry in the aftermath of the regulatory reform movement. However, the unions have had limited success in doing so. This development appears to reflect not only the more participative design of many of the new companies, but skepticism on the part of workers concerning the potential benefits of union affiliation.[59]

Regulatory Reform and Transportation Safety

Many opponents of regulatory reform in transportation expressed concern that safety would be affected adversely. It was argued that new entrants would be financially unstable and that they would neglect vehicle maintenance thereby jeopardizing public safety. It was also contended that intense price competition would have an adverse impact on established carriers and lead them to downgrade the importance of maintenance expenditures. Others expressed concern that, due to network expansion requirements, carriers would be inclined to employ unqualified operators and their performance would pose a serious safety threat. To date, no evidence has surfaced to substantiate such claims. This issue is examined extensively in Chapter 16.

The Transportation Policy Making Process

Prior to the regulatory reform movement, it was generally assumed that any significant change in transportation regulation would be congressionally sponsored. However, through his selection of regulatory agency personnel, President Carter clearly demonstrated that regulatory agencies do not have to accept a passive role in transportation policy making. In fact, the regulatory reform statutes were enacted following substantial regulatory changes that had already been accomplished administratively by the ICC and CAB. In subsequent years, using its expanded powers to exempt transportation activities from regulation, the ICC continues to reduce the regulatory burden faced by carriers. The agency has also joined the DOT in advocating state deregulation of trucking. Forty-four states still regulate intrastate trucking activities. Those regulations, estimated to cost shippers and carriers $6-8 billion per year, have been the target of DOT attacks for more than a decade.[60]

THE ISSUE OF RE-REGULATION

Since the regulatory reform movement began there have been periodic calls for re-regulation. Those calls have come from such diverse sources as the coal industry, responding to increasing railroad rates, and consumer interest groups protesting growing concentration in the airline industry. To date, such calls have been routinely dismissed by Congress, the DOT and the ICC.[61] They were also rejected by President Clinton's National Commission to Ensure a Strong Competitive Airline Industry in July 1993.[62]

At this time it appears that any significant form of re-regulation is very unlikely. The regulatory reform movement still has inertia, and the federal commitment to increasing reliance upon market forces appears firm. That commitment is broadly supported by the carrier and shipper communities.

EXPANSION OF FEDERAL PROMOTIONAL ACTIVITIES

While the federal government's role in transportation regulation has decreased significantly during the past two decades, its promotional role remains substantial. On an annual basis federal spending for transportation programs is approximately $28 billion. Nearly $23 billion of that amount is recouped through federal transportation user fees and taxes.[63] The modal allocation of those funds and related user fees in intercity transportation were discussed in Chapters 1 through 7. The federal role in urban transportation funding is examined in Chapters 18 and 19.

SUMMARY

The problems experienced by the railroads, airlines, and motor carriers in the early 1970s led to a strong movement toward regulatory reform. Federal policies were widely criticized as not only promoting a misallocation of national resources, but also for stifling innovation and management creativity in the several modes. Since that time the reform movement has fostered unprecedented changes in federal regulatory policies in transportation, not only through statutory changes, but also through numerous administrative actions within the federal regulatory agencies.

The regulatory reform movement has broadly affected the transportation industries. It has fundamentally changed the structure of several modes of carriage, modified the nature of competition in many markets, and has focused carrier and shipper attention on strategic planning. Increased competition from new entrants has exerted considerable pressure not only on the prices charged by more established carriers, but also on the wage and work practices that prevail in those companies. The transportation marketplace has become more dynamic and shippers and carriers are routinely challenged to respond effectively in this rapidly changing environment.

DISCUSSION QUESTIONS

1. While the motor carrier industry opposed movement toward regulatory reform in the late 1970s, the railroads strongly supported the movement. Why did this difference of opinion exist?
2. While promoting regulatory changes, Congress has generally sought to minimize the potential negative effects on various interest groups. Give a specific example of such congressional action and discuss its consequences.
3. Distinguish between administrative and statutory regulatory reforms in transportation.
4. Discuss the impact of the regulatory reform movement on pricing in the transportation industries.
5. Discuss the impact of the regulatory reform movement on the structure of the transportation industries.
6. In your opinion, has the regulatory reform movement been a success? Explain your reasoning.

NOTES

1. *Railroad Revitalization and Regulatory Reform Act*, Public Law 94-210 (1976).
2. U.S. Senate, Committee on Interstate and Foreign Commerce, Special Study Group on Transportation Policies in the United States, *National Transportation Policy* (Doyle Report), 87th Cong., 1st Sess., 1960 (Washington, D.C.: U.S. Government Printing Office, 1961), p. 451.
3. Association of American Railroads, "ICC Changes Past Policy to Allow Contract Rates," *Information Letter* (November 22, 1978), p. 1.
4. In the months immediately following the ruling the railroads experienced a substantial increase in fresh fruit and vegetable traffic. Prior to that, the railroads had witnessed a steady loss of such traffic. See Association of American Railroads, "Railroads Reverse Decline in Fruit, Vegetable Traffic," *Information Letter* (March 28, 1979), pp. 1, 4.
5. Association of American Railroads, "Carter Proposes Rail Deregulation Bill: Deregulation is Called Only Viable Option," *Information Letter* (March 28, 1979), p. 1, 4.

6.	See Association of American Railroads, "Late-Night Vote Passes Rail Dereg Bill," *Rail News Update* (October 1, 1980), pp. 1, 4.

7.	For a discussion of the federal role in such employee protection programs see Chapter 14.

8.	U.S. Interstate Commerce Commission, *1981 Annual Report* (Washington, D.C.: U.S. Government Printing Office, 1981), p. 61.

9.	Association of American Railroads, "Rail-Truck Entry Doctrine Dropped," *Rail News Update* (October 1, 1983), pp. 1, 4.

10.	Association of American Railroads, "Boxcar Deregulation Goes Into Effect," *Rail News Update* (January 11, 1984), p. 1.

11.	American Trucking Associations, "ICC Exempts Rail Transport of Frozen Food from Regulation," *Transport Topics* (December 19, 1983), pp. 1, 28.

12.	U.S. Interstate Commerce Commission, *1991 Annual Report* (Washington, D.C.: U.S. Government Printing Office, 1992), p. 8.

13.	U.S. Interstate Commerce Commission, *1992 Annual Report* (Washington, D.C.: U.S. Government Printing Office, 1993), p. 79.

14.	"The Odds Look Good for Less Airline Regulation," *Business Week* (March 21, 1977), pp. 156, 158.

15.	For a discussion of this issue see William E. Fruhan, *The Fight for Competitive Advantage: A study of the United States Domestic Trunk Air Carriers* (Boston: Division of Research, Graduate School of Business Administration, Harvard University, 1972).

16.	Public Law 95-163 (1977).

17.	"CAB Issues Its Final Rules on Air Cargo Deregulation," *Transport Topics* (November 20, 1978), p. 6.

18.	*Airline Deregulation Act*, Public Law 95-504 (1978).

19.	Prior to this change, the exemption covered aircraft with capacities of less than 30 passengers or 7,500 pounds of cargo.

20.	See John W. Snow, "The Problems of Motor Carrier Regulation and the Ford Administration Proposal for Reform," in *Regulation of Entry and Pricing in Truck Transportation*, Paul W. MacAvoy and John W. Snow, eds. (Washington, D.C.: American Enterprise Institute, 1977), pp. 19-23.

21.	Ibid., p. 20; see also "General Freight Traffic on Many Routes Seen Dominated by a Few Trucking Lines," *Wall Street Journal*, New York, June 25, 1979, p. 5.

22.	Estimate of the Council on Wage and Price Stability as cited by Senator Edward Kennedy in testimony before the Senate Committee on Commerce, Science and Transportation concerning the Trucking Competition and Safety Act of 1979, July 25, 1979.

23. J. Richard Jones, U.S. Department of Transportation, *Industrial Shipper Survey: Plant Level* (Washington, D.C.: the Department, 1979), p. 2.

24. See American Trucking Associations, "Trucking Regulation: In the Public Interest," from an Association Series of Papers on Vital Transportation Issues (Washington, D.C.: the Associations, 1979), p. 2.

25. Ibid., pp. 7-8.

26. For a summary of these recommendations, see U.S. Interstate Commerce Commission, *91st Annual Report* (Washington, D.C.: U.S. Government Printing Office, 1977), pp. 11-12.

27. U.S. Interstate Commerce Commission, Motor Carrier Task Force, *Initial Report of the Motor Carrier Task Force* (Washington, D.C.: the Commission, 1979), p. 6.

28. Information supplied by the Interstate Commerce Commission.

29. Interstate Commerce Commission, Motor Carrier Task Force, p. 7.

30. Ibid., pp. 14-30.

31. American Bus Association, *America's Most Fuel Efficient Passenger Transportation Service* (Washington, D.C.: the Association, 1979), p. 12.

32. "Senator Cannon Warns ICC to Go Cautiously in Deregulation of the Trucking Industry," *Wall Street Journal*, New York, October 23, 1979, p. 7.

33. *Motor Carrier Act*, Public Law 96-296 (1980).

34. Title 49 United States Code, Sec. 4 Section 10101 (a).

35. *Household Goods Transportation Act*, Public Law 96-454 (1980).

36. For an extensive discussion of these changes, see Edward A. Morash, "A Critique of the Household Goods Transportation Act of 1980: Impact and Limitations," *Transportation Journal*, Vol. 20, No. 2 (Winter, 1981), pp. 16-27.

37. *Bus Regulatory Reform Act*, Public Law 97-261 (1982).

38. For a detailed analysis of the provisions of the statute, see Martin T. Farris and Norman E. Daniel, "Bus Regulatory Reform Act of 1982," *Transportation Journal*, Vol. 23, No. 1 (Fall, 1983), pp. 4-15.

39. U.S. Motor Carrier Ratemaking Study Commission, *Collective Ratemaking in the Trucking Industry* (Washington, D.C.: the Commission, 1983).

40. Ibid., p. xv.

41. See Kevin G. Hall, "Taxes, Safety and Truck Deregulation Top Capitol Hill's 92 Agenda," *Traffic World* (January 6, 1992), pp. 10-11.

42. U.S. Civil Aeronautics Board, *Implementation of the Provisions of the Airline Deregulation Act of 1978* (Washington, D.C.: the Board, 1984), p. 15.

43. For an extensive discussion of such issues see U.S. Department of Transportation, Office of the Secretary of Transportation, *Secretary's Task Force on Competition in the U.S. Domestic Airline Industry: Executive Summary* (Washington, D.C.: the Department, 1990).

44. See "Thomas McCarroll, "You Too Can Run An Airline," *Time* (July 19, 1993), p. 54.

45. U.S. Department of Transportation, Office of the Secretary, p. 1.

46. U.S. Department of Transportation, Office of the Secretary, p. 4.

47. U.S. Department of Transportation, Office of the Secretary, "EAS History," (Washington, D.C.: the Department, 1992), Appendix A.

48. Regional Airline Association, *RAA Annual Report-1993* (Washington, D.C: the Association, 1993), p. 16.

49. U.S. Interstate Commerce Commission, *1992 Annual Report*, p. 127.

50. "Yellow Buys Preston, Roadway Acquires Central," *Transportation and Distribution* (January, 1993), p. 13.

51. Standard and Poor's Corporation, Standard and Poor's Industry Surveys, "Trucking Industry Structure," Vol. 2 (October 22, 1992), p. R50.

52. Mitchell E. MacDonald, "It's Still Survival of the Fittest," *Traffic Management* (June, 1991), p. 31.

53. Association of American Railroads, *Railroad Facts*, 1992 ed. (Washington, D.C.: the Association, 1992), p. 44.

54. "The Little Engineers That Could," *Business Week* (July 27, 1992), p. 77.

55. U.S. Interstate Commerce Commission, *1992 Annual Report*, p. 41.

56. Steven A. Morrison and Clifford Winston, "Cleared for Takeoff: The Evolution of the Deregulated Airline Industry," *The American Express Annual Review of Travel*, 1992 ed. (New York: American Express, 1992), p. 79.

57. Mitchell E. MacDonald, "It's Still Survival of the Fittest," *Traffic Management* (June, 1991), pp. 30-3, 35.

58. See Robert C. Lieb and James F. Molloy, "The Major Airlines: Labor Relations in Transition," *Transportation Journal*, Vol. 26, No. 3 (Spring, 1987), pp. 17-29; also, Robert C. Lieb, "The Changing Nature of Labor/Management Relations in Transportation," *Transportation Journal*, Vol. 24, No. 3 (Spring, 1984), pp. 4-14.

59. See Dane Hamilton, "Cardinal Freight's Truckload Drivers Opt Out of the Teamsters Union," *Journal of Commerce*, New York, February 9, 1993, p. 2B.

60. Mitchell E. MacDonald, "ICC, States Move Toward Head-On Collision Over Trucking Regulation," *Traffic Management* (July, 1992), p. 15.

61. "Re-Regulating Trucking," *Journal of Commerce*, New York, August 8, 1992, p. 10A.

62. "The Airline Commission," *Journal of Commerce*, New York, July 21, 1993, p. 8A; also, Peter Passell, "Prescription for Airline Industry: Tinker Just A Bit," *New York Times*, July 21, 1993, pp. D1, D26.
63. Eno Transportation Foundation, Inc. *Transportation in America*, 11th ed. (Lansdowne, VA: the Foundation, 1993), pp. 72-3.

SELECTED REFERENCES

Allen, W. Bruce. "Deregulation and Information Costs." *Transportation Journal*, Vol. 30, No. 2 (Winter, 1990), pp. 58-67.

Allen, W. Bruce, Arayah Preechemetta, Gang Shao and Scott Singer. *The Impact of State Economic Regulation of Motor Carriage on Intrastate and Interstate Commerce*. A report prepared for the U.S. Department of Transportation, Office of the Secretary (Washington, D.C.: the Department, 1990).

Corsi, Thomas M., Curtis M. Grimm, and Jane Feitler. "The Impact of Deregulation on LTL Motor Carriers: Size, Structure, and Organization.' *Transportation Journal*, Vol. 32, No. 2 (Winter, 1992), pp. 24-31.

Douglas, George W., and James C. Miller, *Economic Regulation of Domestic Air Transport: Theory and Policy*. Washington, D.C.: Brookings Institution, 1974.

Farris, Martin T., and Norman E. Daniel. "Bus Regulatory Reform Act of 1980." *Transportation Journal*, Vol. 23, No. 1 (Fall, 1983), pp. 4-15.

Lieb, Robert C. "Promoting Change in Transportation Regulation." *Business Horizons*, Vol. 18, No. 3 (June, 1975), pp. 91-4.

McDonald, Mitchell E. "It's Still Survival of the Fittest." *Traffic Management* (June, 1991), pp. 30-3, 35.

"Ready to Soar Again?" *Business Week* (April 26, 1993), pp. 26-8.

"The Airline Mess." *Business Week* (July 6, 1992), pp. 50-5.

Thomas, Janet M. "Quality Competition and Regulatory Reform: New Evidence of the Impact of the Household Goods Transportation Act of 1980." *Transportation Journal*, Vol. 29, No. 4 (Summer, 1990), pp. 42-51.

U.S. Civil Aeronautics Board. *Implementation of the Provisions of the Airline Deregulation Act of 1978*. Washington, D.C.: the Board, 1984.

U.S. Department of Transportation, Office of the Secretary. "EAS History." (1992) (Mimeographed).

U.S. Department of Transportation, Office of the Secretary. Secretary's Task Force on Competition in the U.S. Domestic Airline Industry. *Executive Summary*. Washington, D.C.: the Department, 1990.

U.S. Department of Transportation, Office of the Secretary. Secretary's Task
      Force on Competition in the U.S. Domestic Airline Industry. *Industry and
      Route Structure*. Washington, D.C.: the Department, 1990.

U.S. Department of Transportation, Office of the Secretary. Secretary's Task
      Force on Competition in the U.S. Domestic Airline Industry. *Pricing:
      Executive Summary*. Washington, D.C.: the Department, 1990.

U.S. Department of Transportation, Office of the Secretary. Secretary's Task
      Force on Competition in the U.S. Domestic Airline Industry. *Regional
      Airline Competition*. Washington, D.C.: the Department, 1990.

U.S. General Accounting Office. *Airline Competition: Effects of Airline Market
      Concentration and Barriers to Entry on Airfares*. Washington, D.C.:
      General Accounting Office, 1991.

U.S. General Accounting Office. *Railroad Regulation: Economic and Financial
      Impacts of the Staggers Rail Act of 1980»* Washington, D.C.: General
      Accounting Office, 1990.

U.S. General Accounting Office. *Surface Transportation: Availability of Intercity
      Bus Service Continues to Decline*. Washington, D.C.: General Accounting
      Office, 1992.

U.S. Interstate Commerce Commission. *The Impact of the 4-R Act Railroad
      Ratemaking Provisions*. Washington, D.C.: the Commission, 1977.

U.S. Motor Carrier Ratemaking Study Commission. *Collective Ratemaking in the
      Trucking Industry*. Washington, D.C.: the Commission, 1983.

Williams, Ernest W. "The National Transportation Policy Study Commission and
      Its Final Report: A Review." *Transportation Journal*, Vol. 19, no. 3
      (Spring, 1980), pp. 5-19.

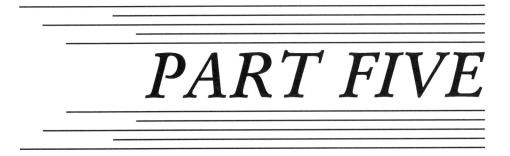

PART FIVE

MANAGEMENT AND PUBLIC POLICY ISSUES IN TRANSPORTATION

CHAPTER THIRTEEN

CARRIER MANAGEMENT

Management in the transportation industries has often been categorized as tradition bound and operations oriented. In the years predating the regulatory reform movement such an orientation would not have been surprising. Major managerial decisions concerning such strategic issues as markets served, services offered and pricing policies were often indirectly made for managers by the regulatory agencies. Managerial creativity was severely constrained by regulation, thus an internal focus was natural. However, such a focus is no longer sufficient if a transportation company is to survive and prosper in the progressively less regulated transportation marketplace which has emerged. Those involved in carrier management have much greater decision making freedom and the responsibilities which accompany that freedom.

This chapter examines carrier management issues, but not in the traditional manner. While it identifies a number of important operational, financial, and marketing issues which must be addressed by carrier managers, its real focus is on how carriers are attempting to differentiate themselves in today's competitive marketplace. While consolidation and labor-management issues are also introduced in this chapter, they are discussed in much greater depth in Chapters 14 and 15.

SYSTEM DESIGN AND OPERATION ISSUES

In any business there is considerable pressure on managers to efficiently use available capital and labor resources while simultaneously satisfying customers and shareholders. This is particularly true in the transportation industries because those capital and labor inputs are very costly. As discussed in earlier chapters several of the modes are quite capital intensive, and transportation workers are among the most highly paid in American industry. To use those resources effectively carrier managers must design a route system, provide the capacity to serve it, and develop procedures by which the system operates.

System Design Issues

Because the resources of a carrier are finite, decisions must be made concerning the routes which a carrier will serve. Route selection decisions are among the most important strategic management decisions faced by carriers and they are discussed in detail later in this chapter.

Having made those route selection decisions, carriers must address capacity management issues (determination of the size and composition of the transportation fleet) and facility planning issues (determination of the location, size, and ownership pattern of facilities used by the company).

When making decisions concerning capacity, managers are clearly influenced by the scope of the markets the company intends to serve, the types of service to be offered, the frequency of service to be offered, and its operating plans, including those projecting equipment utilization rates. A company which efficiently uses its equipment will need less equipment than a competitor which is less efficient. The composition of the fleet is also influenced by many factors including the nature of the markets to be served, operating characteristics of the equipment available, and the potential for equipment interchange between routes. The more standardized the fleet, the easier it is to maintain and interchange between similar routes. The training of operators is also simplified by a standardized fleet. However, the related tradeoff is that the more standardized the equipment, the less suitable it is for use in widely differing markets.

The frequency with which equipment is to be replaced is also influenced by a multitude of factors including government regulations, such as those governing noise levels in commercial aviation, capital availability, utilization levels, and the energy efficiency and operating characteristics of newer generations of equipment.

Long-term capacity planning is one of the most critical and challenging tasks facing carrier management. If too little capacity is available, market opportunities are missed. If too much capacity is available, utilization and productivity levels fall.

The difficulty of effective long-term capacity planning should not be underestimated. That planning process is based on traffic forecasts which are often inaccurate, and that inaccuracy is often beyond the control of management. Business recessions, escalating fuel costs, developments in competitive modes, and military conflicts are but a few of the factors which can cause substantial variation from forecasted volume. Complicating the manager's task is the fact that commitments must be made to equipment suppliers well in advance of delivery date.[1] In commercial aviation, those commitments historically been made several years in advance of delivery of new aircraft. This builds rigidity into the system and often leads to a mismatch of capacity and demand in transportation markets.

Price wars between carriers often result as they attempt to improve equipment utilization rates during periods of overcapacity.[2]

Facility planning issues are also extremely important. Decisions must be made concerning the number, size, location, and ownership pattern of facilities, such as those involved in passenger processing, freight consolidation and distribution, and equipment maintenance. In making such decisions managers must reflect upon a variety of factors including current and projected markets served, the size of those markets, the level of service desired by customers, capital availability, the relationship which exists between facilities, and potential scale economies related to large facilities.

It should be noted that carrier system design should be a continuous process. The route network to be served, the capacity to be offered, and the facility needs of a carrier must be routinely reassessed if the company is to aggressively respond to market shifts.

Operating Issues

Once the system to be served by a carrier has been designed, management must attempt to utilize it efficiently. This involves not only scheduling and dispatching of equipment, facilities and people, but also development of operating procedures. Those operating procedures govern a variety of activities including carriage of passengers and freight between cities, interlining of passengers and freight with other carriers, local pickup and delivery operations, and movements within the company's facilities.

Scheduling of transportation operations is a complex and critically important management task. Scheduling decisions influence not only the competitive presence of a carrier in particular markets, but also the levels of equipment and employee productivity realized by the company. Obviously, the complexity of the scheduling problem increases with the size of the network which the carrier serves and the volume of traffic which it handles. For many years, carrier scheduling was done primarily through experience and intuition. However, increasingly scheduling decisions are made through use of complex computer models which reflect an enormous number of operating constraints such as required maintenance schedules for equipment and regulations governing the number of hours which can be worked by employees.

Decisions concerning operating procedures are no less critical to company success. These decisions must address a broad range of topics such as:

1.   procedures for moving freight from one position to another within a cargo facility

2.   procedures to be followed in loading a transportation vehicle (governing piece-by-piece placement) to maximize usage of the cubic capacity of the vehicle

3.   the routes to be followed by a carrier to minimize distance operated between origin and destination

4.   the speeds at which vehicles are to be operated to optimize fuel efficiency

Again, substantial progress has been made in development of management tools to assist in this decision-making process. Quantitative techniques such as vehicle routing algorithms, queuing theory, and simulation, coupled with industrial engineering analysis, have been very important in improving the operating procedures used by carriers.[3]

FINANCIAL MANAGEMENT ISSUES

Because the size of transportation companies varies substantially, not only across the modes but within modes, so do the financial needs of carriers. At one end of the capital requirements spectrum is the owner-operator in trucking whose fleet may consist of one tractor and one trailer; at the other end of the spectrum are large Class I railroads and truckers and the major airlines whose capital needs may reach billions of dollars. In assessing its capital needs a carrier must consider a variety of alternative sources of capital and evaluate not only its access to those types of funds, but also the implications of reliance upon alternative funding sources.

In terms of working capital, ideally carriers would like to rely exclusively upon current receipts from customers. However, transportation demand often fluctuates with economic conditions, and total reliance upon short-term cash flows could produce a working capital shortfall. To prevent such an occurrence a carrier might seek to establish a line of credit with a financial institution which would allow it to borrow funds to cover short-term needs. Other sources of working capital include retained earnings, if available, borrowing from owners, short-term price cuts to stimulate demand, and in extreme circumstances, borrowing from employees. The last option was used by several airlines which were experiencing extreme financial difficulty in the early 1980s.

Many carriers have focused considerable attention and made substantial investments in attempts to increase the speed of collections from shippers. One example of those efforts is the introduction of hand held computers which are used by the drivers of Federal Express and UPS.[4] Use of that technology allows the billing process to be initiated as soon as the computers are downloaded.

Financing Capital Assets

When considering long-term financing of capital assets carriers basically consider the options of leasing or ownership of those assets. Each of those options is discussed below.

Leasing Equipment. In the transportation industries, leasing of equipment is quite common, particularly in the airline and trucking industries. In aviation, a variety of companies, such as GE Capital Corporation and International Lease Finance Corporation, purchase aircraft and lease them to airlines.[5] This process is attractive to carriers because it limits their capital investment--a Boeing 747-400 sells for more than $125 million. It is also attractive to those leasing equipment to airlines because the assets are mobile and readily marketable, under normal economic conditions, should the carrier default on the lease. However, it should be noted that this process is not without risk to leasing companies. This was demonstrated by the experience of Ryder System, Inc. which began leasing equipment to airlines in 1984. By 1989 the company had leased 47 planes to such carriers as Continental, Midway, and America West. When those three carriers declared bankruptcy and Continental and Midway stopped making lease payments to Ryder, the leasing company began losing $1 million per month. Because of a glut of aircraft on the market at the time, Ryder was unable to sell any of the defaulted equipment. After the leasing company took a $25 million loss in the fourth quarter of 1990, its corporate parent terminated the leasing operations.[6]

Many banks and leasing companies also provide leasing options to motor carriers. Again, under normal circumstances, the equipment is readily marketable if a carrier defaults. Nevertheless, the increased failure rate in the trucking industry has also caused financial problems for truck lessors.

Purchasing Equipment. The way in which carriers purchase equipment varies substantially, not only according to carrier size, but also across the modes. To purchase equipment, small unincorporated carriers generally rely upon the funds made available by owners, depreciation, loans from banks, or financing plans offered by equipment manufacturers. In addition, owner-operators in the trucking industry sometimes buy equipment through fleet purchase plans offered by carriers that they serve on a subcontract basis.

While larger incorporated carriers may also rely upon earnings and depreciation to provide funds for equipment, the magnitude of investment requirements often necessitates consideration of equity versus debt financing to supplement those funding sources. Equity financing, which involves the sale of stock and surrendering an ownership interest to investors, is typically used in the early stages of a carrier's development. As the company matures, additional equity financing and its dilution of ownership interest, often becomes less attractive. In some instances, due to the poor financial performance of the company, it may be impossible to raise additional capital through equity financing. This problem was faced by the railroad industry for several decades following World War II.

Debt financing, which may entail either the sale of corporate bonds, or direct borrowing from financial institutions, with no ownership interest being surrendered, provides another option for carriers. Large railroads, airlines and motor carriers have relied heavily upon debt to finance equipment acquisitions. One interesting form of debt financing, the "equipment trust certificates" is used extensively in the railroad industry. This financial instrument may be used to finance up to 80 percent of the acquisition cost of rolling stock. The railroad pledges the equipment for security, and it may be repossessed by the lessor should the railroad default on the agreement.[7]

Other Major Investments

During the past two decades, large transportation companies have also relied almost exclusively upon debt to finance acquisitions and expansion programs. This has been most pronounced in the airline industry. Further, debt financing has been used by several major airlines in fighting hostile takeover attempts. As this has occurred, the length of time to maturity for bonds has tended to increase. While bonds traditionally had lives of 5-10 years to maturity, many now mature in 20 or more years.

While debt financing increases a carrier's leverage, the carrier is essentially using someone else's money without surrendering an ownership share, it also can cause problems if utilized too extensively. The interest payments on debt obligations continue, regardless of the carrier's current financial situation. That can be a serious problem in a cyclical industry such as the airline industry. Overreliance upon debt financing, coupled with substantial operating losses played an important role in the liquidation of Eastern Air Lines, Pan American Airlines, and Midway Airlines and was also instrumental in the bankruptcies of Continental Airlines and Trans World Airlines.[8]

It should be noted that the railroad industry encountered similar problems in the 1950s-1970s. Those problems contributed to many railroad bankruptcies, including the collapse of most of the railroads serving the Northeast.

MARKETING AND CARRIER DIFFERENTIATION STRATEGIES

Another important task faced by carrier managers is marketing of company services. Managers must define potential markets, estimate demand in those markets, select the markets to be served, and define the appropriate mix of service, price and promotion for specific markets. Many carriers spend enormous amounts on such marketing activities in attempts to differentiate themselves from competitors by creating real or imagined differences in the minds of consumers.

The differentiation strategies used by carriers vary considerably, and they are often used in combination. A number of the most significant differentiation strategies used by carriers are examined in the following discussion. These strategies are typically reflected in a carrier's marketing efforts.

Route Network

The route network served by a carrier is a very important competitive factor. The network strategies followed by carriers range from development of a very focused, limited geographical market niche to that of a global focus. The former strategy is essentially that followed by short-line railroads and some new entrant airlines; the latter has been used by such carriers as Federal Express, UPS, American and United Air Lines, and several large LTL truckers.

Either route network strategy may be appropriate. The smaller carrier doesn't have the financial resources to develop an extensive route network and may be wise to focus its attention on a very limited market. By doing so the carrier may develop close ties with local or regional customers and may establish a solid market niche with strong customer loyalty. Larger carriers, often having access to much greater financial resources, may well choose to offer services in a much broader arena of national or international scope. In this manner, those carriers become attractive to customers who ship or travel on a broad geographical basis. As noted in Chapter 9, there is a decided trend among large shippers to reduce the number of carriers used, and a carrier which serves broad geographical areas has a decided competitive advantage in attracting such accounts. Similarly many travelers prefer not to change carriers during a trip and an airline with a broad route network is likely to look more attractive to such people than another airline which, due to a limited route network, must interchange passengers with other carriers.

It should be noted that a carrier can choose to expand its own operations into new markets, either through new market entry or acquisitions, or it can choose to expand market coverage through strategic alliances. As discussed in Chapters 4 and 6, many truckers and airlines have directly expanded their operations as entry and consolidation policies have liberalized.

In contrast, many railroads and truckers, including Conrail, the Union Pacific, the Burlington Northern, J.B. Hunt and Schneider National have expanded the scope of their intermodal operations through alliances with other carriers.[9] Similarly, several of the major American airlines including Northwest Airlines and USAir have developed alliances with foreign airlines. These alliances effectively broaden market coverage while minimizing capital commitment and risk.

Service Offerings

A carrier must also decide upon the range of services (service mix) it will offer the shipping and traveling public and the frequency with which those services will be offered.

The service mix decision has several components. First, the carrier must decide what "service gradients" will be offered. For example, in cargo operations a carrier must decide what mix of service gradients (same day, next day, second day, etc.) it will offer. While many carriers offer only one service option between origin and destination, companies such as UPS, Federal Express and some trucking companies have followed a multiple service gradient strategy. Such a strategy, which is expensive to implement, recognizes that all shippers do not have the same speed requirements, and that a particular shipper often has different speed requirements for different shipments. Taken to the extreme, carriers following such a strategy attempt to be everything to everybody.

Second, a carrier has to decide if it will offer specialized transportation services such as intermodal services or services specially designed to serve JIT accounts.[10] Those services tend to be more expensive to deliver than traditional services, but increasingly shippers are demanding something other than transportation "business as usual." As will be discussed later in this chapter, a commitment to offer specialized services has significant capital and equipment implications.

Third, a carrier must decide if it should offer something beyond transportation services to customers. As discussed in previous chapters, many cargo carriers, such as Roadway, Consolidated Freightways, Yellow Freight System, UPS and Federal Express, have established third party logistics service subsidiaries to offer a broad range of "value added" logistics services to customers.[11] Airlines have taken similar steps to offer hotel packages and automobile rentals to customers. Such strategies effectively broaden the carrier's product line and can be very attractive to customers seeking "one stop shopping." It also increases the likelihood of potential broad-based partnerships with customers. Again, carriers can choose to either establish their own non-transportation services or develop alliances with other companies who could provide those services for customers. While control is not as extensive, neither is the capital commitment or risk involved.

A carrier can also use scheduling as a differentiating factor. By adding capacity to a particular market a carrier increases the likelihood of meeting the specific needs of the individual traveler or shipper. However, this is a very costly approach to differentiation and one which carries substantial risk of poor equipment and employee utilization if incremental traffic fails to materialize.

Employees

A carrier may also seek to differentiate itself through its employees. In the process of developing an account, handling an order for specific services, delivering that service, handling customer inquiries and billing customers for the service, there are multiple "people" contacts between a carrier and the customer. The interaction of a carrier's employees with customers is critical in maintaining an effective, mutually beneficial relationship. From upper management to the operating level, employees must be recruited, hired, trained, rewarded and hopefully retained, who share the company commitment to customer service. If any link in that interpersonal chain fails, it can do irreparable harm to the carrier's relationship to the customer.

The transportation industries are faced with serious projected shortages of qualified operating and managerial personnel. This means that carriers must compete for talent. As will be discussed in Chapter 14, transportation workers are well paid in comparison with those in other occupational categories. However, high levels of compensation are not sufficient to maintain the human resource base which is critical to a carrier's success. Many carriers still have a militaristic, hierarchial, autocratic management style which places inordinate demands on workers.[12] In many instances the hours worked by managers are very long and working conditions less than desirable. Not surprisingly, management and rank-and-file turnover rates are quite high.[13] Carriers which continue to operate with such antiquated human resource management philosophies will find it increasingly difficult to attract management and operating employees. This is particularly true as the workforce becomes more ethnically and racially diverse. The transportation work environment must become much more "employee friendly" than it is in many companies if those companies are to survive and prosper. Understaffing and the use of negative incentives, though common in many carrier operations, are extremely costly in terms of turnover and absenteeism, and absolutely inappropriate as we approach the 21st Century.

If properly selected, trained and placed in a appropriate working environment, carrier employees can be a major differentiating factor. As such they can play an important role in determining the long-term success of a carrier.

Equipment

The equipment fleet of a carrier can also be used as a differentiating factor. Carrier management must attempt to match the composition of its equipment fleet to the market segments which the carrier serves. By doing so, the carrier not only controls operating costs, but also provides the appropriate equipment for the customer base.

Because of industrial changes, such as those involving manufacturing techniques and materials used in the manufacturing process, the equipment used by a carrier also changes over time. The requirements for canvas-sided trailers to service JIT accounts and completely redesigned rail cars to handle new automobiles are but two examples of such market mandated equipment changes. Such changes are costly, but necessary in a competitive market.

Acquisition of equipment is not the end of the process. The equipment must be well maintained and allocated to appropriate markets to be effectively utilized. Equipment availability is a key carrier selection variable, and well maintained equipment may be used to project an image of a well managed, efficient company.

In a number of instances carriers have been able to limit their capital costs and improve equipment utilization through joint equipment ownership. One illustration of this approach is provided by TTX Corporation, which is jointly owned by the nation's 14 largest railroads. The company owns more than 100,000 pieces of intermodal equipment, and makes it available to railroads on a daily rental basis. Similarly, in many cities Air Cargo, Incorporated, which is collectively owned by scheduled airlines, acts as a common pick up and delivery fleet for the cargo operations of those airlines.[14]

Information Services

During the past decade carriers have spent billions of dollars in developing information capabilities to not only better serve customers, but also to improve the efficiency of their operations. The information applications range from electronic data interchange (EDI) linkages with customers to satellite monitoring of shipments for tracking and tracing. Clearly, carriers have sought to differentiate themselves through information capabilities. Several of the more interesting of these developments have been:

1.   The 1992 introduction by UPS of its $350 million Delivery Information Acquisition Device (DIAD). It is a hand held computer which drivers use to record delivery, pickup and customer signature information. At the end of the day drivers place the DIADs in a rack where the information is downloaded to the company's Delivery Information Automated Lookup System. That system is then accessible to customer service representatives to determine shipment status for more than 60,000 customers who call each day.[15]

2.   Roadway Package Systems use of hand held bar code scanners at delivery points to automate the proof of delivery system. Drivers carry scanners which feed delivery information into the company's central computer system at the end of the day. The system permits the company to offer proof of delivery in two days versus ten days prior to introduction of the system.[16]

3.   The use of Cadec on-board computers on trucks to save fuel and ensure compliance with federal regulations governing driver hours. These units, which monitor such factors as speed, shifting and idle time, also record mileage and hours operated and provide an electronic log for DOT inspectors.[17]

4.   Schneider National's use of satellite communications technology to link its trucks to the company's central dispatch operations. Drivers may be accessed enroute to change delivery times or destinations. Two-way text transmission systems have become common in the industry.[18]

5.   The widespread use of electronic data interchange (EDI) links between shippers and carriers. These can be used by shippers to request service and to update shipment status. Carriers may also use the system to communicate such information as tariffs, changes in delivery schedules, and invoices to customers. More than 350 motor carriers offer EDI linkages to their customers.[19]

6.   The joint effort by American Airlines and CSX Corp. to develop a multi-modal, multi-carrier cargo reservations and tracking system (Encompass).[20]

These, and many similar information systems innovations are not only important in differentiating the services of one carrier from another, but also in promoting operating efficiencies and better equipment utilization.

Quality and Customer Service

While the term "quality" has often been overworked and misunderstood in industry, it is very important in a carrier management context. By specifically defining quality "metrics" concerning such issues as on-time deliveries, loss and damage performance, and response time to customer inquiries, a carrier can monitor system performance and move the company toward continuous improvement. Many carriers, including Conrail, CF MotorFreight, and several airlines have instituted quality programs in conjunction with major accounts and suppliers.[21] In some cases, ongoing communications with customers, worker involvement groups, and sophisticated performance measurement efforts have yielded important quality improvements. Design and implementation of a quality program is not a simple, nor inexpensive effort. It involves "selling" the program to all employees, enlisting their involvement, constant monitoring of results, communication of those results to employees, taking action to correct problems, and intensive communications both within the company and with customers.

In many surveys of transportation customers, respondents have indicated that a variety of service attributes such as consistency of service, dependability and on-time deliveries are often more important to them than price. In recognition of this, carriers often focus on customer service as a differentiating factor. By clearly defining the dimensions of such service attributes and focusing company efforts on improving them, a carrier may attempt to niche itself according to one or more of them. The ability to do so is clearly intertwined with the company's decisions concerning services to be offered, equipment to be utilized, and information technology to be employed.

Price

A carrier may also use pricing strategy as a means to set itself apart from competitors. While pricing was tightly controlled by the ICC and CAB prior to the regulatory reform movement, carriers have considerable pricing freedom in today's marketplace. As a result, price can be used as a competitive variable.

In a particular market a carrier might choose to set its price below competitors, at the competitive level, or above competitors. In setting those prices carriers must be aware that the carrier selection decision is rarely one dimensional. That is, a combination of price and service considerations ultimately determine the carrier which the shipper or traveler chooses. Some potential buyers are very price sensitive, others place more weight on service considerations. The greater a carrier's understanding these dynamics in a particular market, the more likely a viable pricing strategy can be developed.

In developing pricing policies carrier management must be cognizant of the need for effective management of "yields" per revenue passenger mile or freight ton mile. That is, they must make individual pricing decisions in the context of the full range of prices charged by the carrier. Market dynamics differ substantially, hence prices or "yields" will obviously vary from market to market and from trip to trip in the same market. Further, efforts to segment traffic in a particular market will often generate different yields from particular market segments. An illustration of this is provided by the airline industry in which the yields generated by different passengers on the same plane are often dramatically different. Carriers are routinely challenged to find the mix of prices which will optimize the carrier's revenue potential. "Yield management" has become a major carrier focus in the 1990s.

Considerable media attention is given to carrier pricing strategies which entail price reductions. This strategy was used by many of the new entrants in the airline and trucking industries as they attempted to establish market identity, stimulate demand, and gain market share from more established carriers. "No frills" carriers such as People Express and New York Air used such tactics. This prompted major cost cutting efforts by more established carriers so that they might compete on a price basis with the new carriers. The trucking industry has also engaged in widespread "deep discounting" during the past several years as individual carriers have sought to broaden their traffic base. While significant price discounting is often effective in initially attracting traffic, the discounted prices are very likely to be matched by competitors in the longer term. This is particularly true if the carriers involved have similar cost structures, or if carriers threatened by the lower prices have the ability to offset lower yields in some markets through profits generated on other routes. However, if some market participants have substantially lower costs than their competitors, those competitors may be unable to continue operations at that price level. This partially explains the ongoing interest of carrier management in cost reduction potential.[22]

It should be noted that carriers also often use price reductions in attempts to stimulate demand for their services during off-peak periods. Such tactics are widely used in the airline industry to attract business during non-vacation periods such as February-March and October-November of each year.

Clearly, pricing strategy is market specific. In certain markets where competition is intense, prices and margins tend to be lower, unless the carrier offers higher quality services for which the shipping public is willing to pay a premium price. In other markets, where a carrier may have little competition, prices and margins tend to be higher.

SUMMARY

Carrier management has been dramatically affected by the movement toward transportation deregulation. The role of the regulatory agencies in making managerial decisions for carriers has been substantially reduced. As a result, managers have unprecedented freedom to determine such matters as a carrier's route structure, service offerings, and pricing policies.

Many carriers have used this freedom to expand their route networks. They have used a variety of means to do so including new market entry, acquisitions, and alliances with other carriers. However, many carriers have relied quite heavily upon debt to finance such expansion programs and in some cases this has caused serious financial problems.

In the increasingly competitive transportation marketplace carriers naturally seek to differentiate themselves from competitors. Differentiation strategies based on such factors as route networks served, service offerings, and information technology have been widely used by carriers.

DISCUSSION QUESTIONS

1. Discuss briefly how the role of carrier managers has changed as a result of the movement toward transportation deregulation.
2. How has information technology been used by carriers as a means of differentiation?
3. What are the advantages and disadvantages of carrier use of debt financing?
4. What are carrier "alliances" and why are they important?
5. What are the factors which should be considered by carrier management in designing a carrier's equipment fleet?

NOTES

1. For background on the nature of competition between aircraft manufacturers, see Kenneth Labich, "Airbus Takes Off," *Fortune* (June 1, 1992), pp. 102-4, 108.
2. See Air Transport Association, *1993 State of the U.S. Airline Industry* (Washington, D.C.: the Association, 1993), p. 6.
3. For a discussion of such applications see Ronald H. Ballou, "Computer Methods in Transportation-Distribution," *Transportation Journal*, Vol. 16, No. 2 (Winter, 1976), pp. 72-85.
4. See "UPS Opens Information Center; Moves Toward Global Network," *Traffic World* (September 16, 1991), p. 32.
5. See "All The Trouble Isn't in the Sky," *Business Week* (March 11, 1991), p. 84; also, Lawrence H. Kaufman, "Lessors Hit Heavy Turbulence," *Air Commerce*, New York, June 28, 1993, p. 4.
6. "All the Trouble Isn't in The Sky," p. 84.
7. For a discussion of recent railroad equipment purchases see Lawrence H. Kaufman, "Railroads Buying Cars After 12-Year Dry Spell," *Journal of Commerce*, New York, July 28, 1993, pp. 1A, 3A.
8. See "Eastern May Soon Be Forced Into Mothballs," *Business Week* (July 30, 1990), p. 22; also, Paul Page, "Pan Am Ends 64-Year History in Tortured Bankruptcy Proceeding," *Traffic World* (December 9, 1991), p. 11.
9. "Transportation: Key to A "Win-Win" Freight Transportation System," *Defense Transportation Journal* (August, 1992), p. 9.

10. For a discussion of one such industry response to market demand, see Robert C. Lieb and Robert A. Millen, "The Responses of General Commodity Motor Carriers to Just-in-Time Manufacturing Programs," *Transportation Journal*, Vol. 30, No. 1 (Fall, 1990), pp. 5-11.

11. For an extensive discussion of the third party logistics operations of these and other large transportation companies, see Mitchell E. MacDonald, "Who's Who in Third Party Logistics," *Traffic Management* (July, 1993), pp. 34-6, 38-9, 42, 44.

12. For a discussion of this issue, see "Conrail Puts Quality Up Front," *Railway Age* (June, 1992), p. 27.

13. For background information on such issues, see Robert C. Lieb, "The Changing Nature of Labor/Management Relations in Transportation," *Transportation Journal*, Vol. 24, No. 3 (Spring, 1984), pp. 4-14.

14. Peter Tirschwell, "Air Cargo Inc. Delivers for All," *Air Commerce*, New York, January 25, 1993, p. 14.

15. Dennis Livingston, "United Parcel Service Gets a Special Delivery," *Systems Integration* (November, 1991), pp. 54-7.

16. Lou Ann Bell, "Roadway Package's Hand-Held Scanners Improve Delivery Information System," *Traffic World* (May 6, 1991), pp. 19-20.

17. Kevin G. Hall, "Drivers Grumble as Truck Computers Draw Praise from Fleet Managers," *Traffic World* (September 2, 1991), p. 32.

18. See Tony Seidman, "Truckers Need to Capitalize on New Technology, Study Says," *Journal of Commerce*, New York, May 18, 1992, p. 4B.

19. See Robert A. Millen, "Utilization of EDI by Motor Carrier Firms: A Status Report," *Transportation Journal*, Vol. 32, No. 2 (Winter, 1992, pp. 5-13; also, Lisa Harrington, "The ABC's of EDI," *Traffic Management* (August, 1990), pp. 49-52.

20. Mark W. Lyon, "Cargo Net Debate Splits Industry," *Air Commerce* (July 7, 1992), p. 4.

21. "Conrail Puts Quality Up Front," pp. 27-31.

22. See, for example, "Northwest's Sigh of Relief Has Rivals Groaning," *Business Week* (July 26, 1993), p. 84.

SELECTED REFERENCES

Air Transport Association. *1993 State of the U.S. Airline Industry*. Washington, D.C.: the Association, 1993.

Beilock, Richard and Russell B. Capelle, Jr. "Occupational Loyalties Among Truck Drivers." *Transportation Journal*, Vol. 29, No. 3 (Spring, 1990), pp. 20-8.

Coyle, John J., Bardi Edward J., and Joseph L.Cavinato. *Transportation*, 3rd ed. St. Paul, MN: West Publishing Company, 1990. Chapter 19. "Carrier Management," pp. pp. 415-30.

Cunningham, Lawrence F., and Wallace R. Wood. "Diversification in Major U.S. Airlines." *Transportation Journal*, Vol. 22, No. 3 (Spring, 1983), pp. 7-63.

"Joint Ventures Can Pay Off." *Railway Age* (September, 1992), pp. 57-8.

Kaufman, Lawrence H. "Lessors Hit Heavy Turbulence." *Air Commerce*, New York, June 28, 1993, p. 4.

Keenan, Steve. "Bailout by GE Capital Keeps GPA From Crashing." *Air Commerce*, New York, June 28, 1993, p. 5.

Labich, Kenneth. "How Airlines Will Look in the 1990s." *Fortune* (January 1, 1990), pp. 50-1, 54-6.

Lambert, Douglas M., Lewis, M. Christine, and James R. Strock. "Customer-Focused Strategies for Motor Carriers." *Transportation Journal*, Vol. 32, No. 4 (Summer, 1993), pp. 21-8.

Lieb, Robert C., and Robert A. Millen. "The Responses of General Commodity Motor Carriers to Just-In-Time Manufacturing Programs." *Transportation Journal*, Vol. 30, No. 1 (Fall, 1990), pp. 5-11.

Millen, Robert A. "Utilization of EDI by Motor Carrier Firms: A Status Report." *Transportation Journal*, Vol. 32, No. 2 (Winter, 1992), pp. 5-13.

Miller, Luther S. "Big Hopes, Big Spending." *Railway Age* (December, 1992), pp. 24-8.

Murphy, Paul R., Smith, Jonathan E., and James M. Daley. "Environmental Scanning Practices Among LTL Carriers of General Freight." *Transportation Journal*, Vol. 32, No. 1 (Fall, 1992), pp. 51-60.

Rodriguez, Julene and Gene C. Griffin. "The Determinants of Job Satisfaction of Professional Drivers." *Journal of the Transportation Research Forum*, Vol. 30, No. 2 (1990), pp. 453-64.

Seideman, Tony. "Chain of Data Binds Carriers, Manufacturers." in "EDI: Transportation And the Computer" a special report, *Journal of Commerce*, New York, November 18, 1991, p. 9A.

Stephenson, Frederick J., Jr. *Transportation USA*. Reading, MA: Addison-Wesley Publishing Company, 1987. Chapter 15. "Coping with Change: Strategies of Major Domestic Combination Airlines," pp. 398-434.

Taneja, Nawal K. *Airline Planning: Corporate, Financial, and Marketing*. Lexington, MA: Lexington Books, 1982.

Wood, Donald F. and James C. Johnson. *Contemporary Transportation*, 4th ed. New York: Macmillan Publishing Company, 1993. Chapter 15. "Managing Carriers in the Private Sector," pp. 373-407.

Leaseway Transportation "Tautliner Maxi Cube" trailer. There flexible-sided trailers can be opened on both sides to permit rapid loading and unloading of high priority freight. *Courtesy Leaseway Transportation, Cleveland, Ohio*

CHAPTER FOURTEEN

LABOR IN THE TRANSPORTATION INDUSTRIES

One highly publicized and quite important element of the national transportation system is the labor component. We have all read or heard about airline and railroad strikes, and we are periodically apprised by the media of contract negotiations involving U.S. truckers or longshoremen. The attention devoted to labor-management interaction in transportation is quite understandable. Labor compensation is one of the major cost elements of intercity carriers, and therefore is a primary determinant of carrier pricing.

When we read that carrier employees have received a sizable wage increase, it is not superfluous news, because the settlement will result in price increases in many of the commodities and for-hire passenger services that we consume. Other transportation labor contract provisions, such as those related to work rules, are similarly important because they influence the efficiency and health of the transportation industries. Also, transportation strikes can play havoc with the economy not only by retarding the flow of commerce, but also by increasing short-term unemployment among workers in industries that are heavily dependent upon for-hire carriage.

This chapter attempts to provide insight into the nature of existing labor-management relationships in the various modes of intercity carriage.[1] It examines matters such as trends in employment, compensation, and worker productivity. Additionally it reviews industry bargaining patterns and federal mechanisms for dealing with carrier labor disputes. In doing so, the chapter addresses the many important changes in labor-management relations that have taken place in the transportation industries in recent years.

EMPLOYMENT

Employment in the transportation industries comprises approximately 10.2 percent of the total workforce in the United States.[2] That percentage has been steadily declining over the past three decades. It had been 13.5 percent in 1960.[3] Total carrier employment has been influenced by several factors. In many instances technological changes have resulted in the substitution of capital for labor. For example, this has occurred in both the railroad and airline industries with development of equipment with greater load capacities. Another important development that has influenced personnel requirements has been the reduction in service offerings in several modes. Cutbacks in rail passenger and light-density branch-line services provide illustrations of this development. Similarly contributing to the reduced employment base of certain modes has been significant changes in work rules in the transportation industries. Also, as discussed later in this chapter and in Chapter 15, mergers and consolidations of carriers have eliminated many duplicate positions. These work force reductions generally have taken place gradually, due to the employee protection provisions that are often contained in transportation labor agreements.

Two factors have combined to at least partially offset these job-reducing developments. First, as the national economy has grown, the aggregate demand for transportation services also has increased. Second, although many operating positions have been eliminated, the need for managerial talent in the transportation industries has expanded. As the size and market complexity of carriers has increased, there has been a corresponding growth in the need for managerial specialists in many functional areas, such as finance, marketing, and labor relations.

The recessionary pressures of the early 1990s have had a depressing short-term effect on transportation employment. Naturally, as industrial activity declines, the demand for transportation services is reduced and carriers need fewer employees. This sequence of events has led to cutbacks in rail, trucking, and air carrier employment.

Another important shift in the aggregate employment base of the transportation industries has accompanied the regulatory reform movement. Liberalized entry policies in motor and air carriage have led to the market entry of thousands of new trucking companies and several hundred new airlines. In many instances the new entrants have successfully challenged more established carriers and eroded the traffic base of the older firms. As a result, the employees of these new entrants have become an increasingly important component of total employment in transportation. Nearly all new entrants are nonunion companies, and this has fostered a broad substitution of nonunion for union labor inputs. This matter is discussed later in this chapter.

The employment needs of the several modes have varied considerably throughout the years. The factors that have led to both long and short-term variations are identified in the following discussion.

Rail Carriage

The railroad work force declined from 885,000 in 1960 to 259,000 in 1992 (see Table 14-1). This marked an extension of the downward trend in railroad employment that began following World War II. Some factors leading to the long-term decline have been the changing technology of the industry, reductions in passenger operations, consolidations, changes in work rules, and a congressionally sponsored early retirement program that substantially reduced Conrail's employment in the early 1980s. Also, industry efforts to reduce light-density branch-line operations have exerted downward pressure on the work force. Because long-term employees in the railroad industry historically have been granted extensive job protection, most reductions have been accomplished through a process of attrition. Under such an agreement, long-term employees are protected and the work force is reduced by not refilling positions when workers retire or voluntarily leave jobs for other reasons.

TABLE 14-1

Average Number of Employees, Intercity Modes, 1960-1992 (in 000)

Mode	1960	1970	1980	1990	1992
Railroads	885	627	532	285	259
Trucking and Truck Terminals	770	988	1,189	1,534	1,495
Airlines	191	351	453	789	732
Oil Pipelines	23	18	21	20	19
Water Carriers	232	215	213	173	186
Intercity Bus	41	43	38	20	24

SOURCE: Eno Transportation Foundation, Inc., *Transportation in America*, 11th ed. (Lansdowne, VA: the Foundation, 1993), p. 61.

The most important recent development which has led to considerable reduction in the industry's work force has been the wave of "crew consist" agreements signed by the railroads and their major unions between 1988 and 1993. Most major railroads have negotiated reduced crew agreements which stipulate that freight trains can be operated by a crew of two—an engineer and a conductor.[4] A decade ago, that number was typically four.

These crew consist agreements promise to yield major increases in productivity. But, the agreements have been costly. In each instance, the railroad receiving the crew consist concession agreed to make a substantial severance payment to "surplus" crew members. In some cases, these payments were as much as $135,000 per employee.[5]

Motor Carriage

While aggregate intercity motor carrier employment has periodically declined during business slowdowns, the industry has experienced rather steady growth in employment throughout the years. Reflecting this trend, the number of people employed in trucking and trucking terminals increased from 770,000 in 1960 to 1,495,000 in 1992.

There are several major reasons for the long-term growth of trucking employment. These include expansion of the U.S. highway system (particularly the Interstate), the success of the industry in attracting an increasing percentage of intercity freight ton mileage, and emergence of the truck as the dominant form of carriage in short-haul markets.

As noted earlier, the regulatory reform movement has fostered the entry of more than 35,000 new ICC-regulated motor carriers into the marketplace. These companies have had considerable competitive impact, particularly in the truckload segment of the business, and their employees have displaced many Teamsters who formerly worked for the more established motor carriers.

The trucking industry faces a serious problem with respect to hiring and retaining drivers. Turnover rates are extremely high, as are the costs of recruiting and training new drivers.[6] Unless resolved, this problem may constrain the future growth of the industry.

Air Carriage

While the commercial airline industry has exhibited a strong long-term growth pattern in its employment base, industry employment has traditionally been quite vulnerable to economic fluctuations. For example, the recession-induced decline in airline traffic in the early 1980s resulted in significant industry layoffs. Similarly, the reduction in travel which immediately followed the Gulf War led to sizeable cutbacks in both flights and employment. Nevertheless, by 1992 airline employment was 732,000, nearly four times the number working in the industry in 1960.[7]

Industry employment has grown in the aftermath of deregulation. Many new airlines, nearly all non-union companies, have entered the industry. More importantly, the scope of operations of the major airlines has expanded dramatically, leading to many new jobs.

The continued growth of the airline industry may well be constrained by a forecasted shortage of pilots and mechanics. According to a recent study, U.S.

airlines will need to hire 35,000 new pilots and approximately 30,000 new mechanics by the year 2000.[8] There are concerns that military budget cutbacks will reduce the supply of pilots. The military has been the primary supplier of commercial pilots since World War II.[9]

Water Carriage

Domestic water carrier employment has declined slightly in recent years, despite the fact that the traffic volume of that mode has risen. Employment declined from 232,000 in 1960 to 186,000 in 1992. Only about 15,000 of that total were employed by ICC-regulated companies.

Although traffic volume has increased, the introduction of more powerful towboats and the development of barges with greater capacity have reduced employee requirements.

As discussed in Chapter 7, in international water carriage, maritime employment in both seafaring and longshoring job categories has declined substantially in recent years. The most important job-reducing factors have been the growing use of automated loading techniques and containerships in international operations.

Oil Pipelines

Employment in the oil pipeline industry declined from 23,000 to 19,000 between 1960 and 1992. Industry employment requirements have been affected by the growing automation of the industry. This trend may continue as more powerful pumping equipment and larger diameter pipelines become operational. However, if the movement of other commodities, such as coal slurry, through pipelines proves to be economically and politically feasible, such traffic would likely have a positive impact on future industry employment.

COMPENSATION

The significance of worker compensation in transportation is shown by the fact that in one recent year employee compensation equaled 35 percent of the total operating expenses in the railroad industry, 41 percent in the trucking industry, and 35 percent in the airline industry.[10] Consequently, carrier management must be constantly concerned with the efficient utilization of manpower.

As illustrated in Table 14-2, in comparison with U.S. workers in other occupational categories, the transportation workforce generally is well paid. The average total compensation, including fringe benefits, of workers in U.S. industry was $32,812 in 1991.[11] The average total compensation of workers in the three major modes of intercity carriage were as follows: railroads, $56,781; trucking and warehousing, $32,600; and airlines, $42,239.[12] However, it must be realized

TABLE 14-2

Average Annual Earnings and Total Compensation per Full-Time Employee, Transportation and Other Industries, 1991

	Industry Average Wages and Salaries	Average Total Compensation Including Fringe Benefits
Railroads	$42,793	$56,781
Local and Intercity Bus	19,757	23,046
Trucking and Warehousing	26,643	32,600
Water Carriage	34,727	40,244
Airlines	36,827	46,239
Oil Pipelines	46,842	53,053
Manufacturing	30,926	38,137
Communications	39,558	49,721
Finance/Insurance/ Real Estate	33,067	39,752
All Industry Total	27,212	32,812

SOURCE: Eno Transportation Foundation, Inc., *Transportation in America*, 11th ed. (Lansdowne, VA: the Foundation, 1993), p. 60.

that the skill requirements and responsibilities of transportation workers are often greater than those of workers in other occupational categories, and thus some differential may be well justified.

In the early 1980s the worst recession since the Depression and regulatory reforms combined to exert considerable downward pressure on the wages of employees of more established airlines and trucking companies. The economic downturn was accompanied not only by the market entry of many new airlines and trucking firms, but also by the failure of many established companies. Employees of the new airlines worked for substantially lower wage rates than their union counterparts (25-30 percent lower in most cases).[13] Similarly, the typical new motor carrier was a relatively small operator employing non-union labor at roughly 75 percent of prevailing Teamster wage rates.[14] As a result, the new entrants had a decided cost advantage over the older carriers and used that advantage to aggressively seek traffic through lower rates. These developments led to an unprecedented wave of concession bargaining in the airline and trucking industries. The concessions included pay cuts, wage freezes, elimination of automatic cost-of-living adjustments, lower starting salaries for new employees, and variable earnings plans based on company profitability. In return for wage concessions, some carriers agreed to establish profit-sharing programs, others accepted no-layoff plans, and others agreed not to establish non-union subsidiaries.[8] It should be noted that employee stock-ownership and profit-sharing programs were integral parts of the organizational design of many of the new entrants.

As the economy recovered in the mid-1980s many of the unions demanded restoration of previous wage and benefit levels, and that generally occurred. However, the next downward swing in the economy, which began in the late 1980s and continued into the early 1990s, again prompted carriers to ask for concessions.

In many instances the unions complied, but that compliance did not necessarily guarantee carrier survival. Thousands of motor carriers and several major airlines, including Pan American and Eastern Airlines, failed and were liquidated.

Two interesting situations emerged in mid-1993 which provide illustrations of the concession bargaining process and its uncertainty. In the first of these, St. Johnsbury Trucking, New England's largest trucker at the time, asked its Teamster employees to accept a 12 percent wage cut plan and changes in insurance coverage to help the carrier avoid liquidation. The employees refused, the carrier ceased operation and the banks began the liquidation process. The company's president contended that the union's rigidity and failure to recognize financial realities played a major role in the company's demise.[15] One month later, Northwest Airlines convinced its pilots and machinists to accept 15 percent wage cutbacks to save the company from bankruptcy. In return for those concessions the company gave the unions three seats on the board of directors and 37.5 percent of the company's equity to be split among the carrier's six labor unions.[16]

LABOR PRODUCTIVITY

Because the cost of providing transportation services is so substantial, and due to the direct relationship between such costs and prices, there is naturally concern with the measurement of productivity in transportation. Related measurement efforts attempt to determine if the resources devoted to the provision of transportation services are being utilized efficiently.

Simply stated, productivity expresses the relationship between the quantity of labor, capital, land, energy, and other inputs employed and the output of goods and services generated by those inputs. Most parties would agree with this simplified definition of productivity, but this generally is where agreement between management and labor ends concerning the most appropriate means of measuring labor productivity. Similarly, there is little agreement among economists concerning not only how this elusive concept might best be measured, but also the significance of these measurements once they are calculated.

Resolution of these conflicts is beyond the scope of this book. However, it is still possible to comment on productivity trends in several modes of carriage. One of the most frequently used measurements of worker productivity is "output per employee." That measurement, which is calculated annually for more than 90 industries by the Department of Labor's Bureau of Labor Statistics (BLS), relates the output of an industry in a given year to the number of employees in that industry. These measures reflect the combined effects of changes in the efficiency with which labor and capital are used, the amount of capital per employee, and the average quality of labor. However, these measures do not provide insight into the relative contribution of any of the previously mentioned change factors.

Throughout the years, considerable criticism has been leveled at employment practices in transportation. It often has been charged that the transportation unions, particularly those in the railroad industry, have promoted widespread overmanning and featherbedding. However, given the measures of productivity calculated by the BLS, the transportation industries rank quite high in comparison with other industries examined by the BLS (see Table 14-3).

Rail Carriage

On the basis of BLS calculations, the railroads have significantly outpaced the overall level of productivity increase in the private sector over the past four decades. Its short-term performance has been even more impressive. Productivity in the railroad industry grew at a dramatic 9.7 percent per year rate between 1985-1990.[17] There are a number of reasons for the railroad performance. The technology of the industry has changed substantially in recent years. Also, many jobs have been eliminated, thereby realizing economies that were previously prohibited by job protection agreements. Investment per employee has risen substantially, partially due to the contraction of the workforce, and greater capacity equipment has been introduced. In addition, intercity rail passenger and branch line services, which tended to depress aggregate measures of employee productivity, have been substantially reduced. Further railroad productivity gains may be expected in the near future as the previously discussed crew consist agreements take effect.

Intercity Bus

The productivity performance of the intercity bus industry over the past three decades provides some insight into the problems facing the industry. Over that period, output per employee actually declined by an average of -0.4 percent per year. That performance has clearly been affected by not only the long-term decline in intercity bus passenger traffic, but also by the substantial increase in the number of companies participating in the industry as a result of deregulation.

Intercity Trucking

The 2.7 percent annual rate of increase in output per employee registered by intercity trucking (1954-1988) lagged behind the performance of the other major modes. The mediocre performance of the industry may stem from the fact that in recent years trucking industry employment grew more rapidly than traffic volume. Also, the primary burden of providing labor-intensive small shipment

TABLE 14-3

Annual Average Increases in Output per Employee, Total Private Sector and Selected Transportation Industries, 1947-1990

Industry	Average Annual Increase %
Total Private Business Sector	2.2
Railroads[a]	4.6
Intercity Bus[b]	-0.4
Intercity Trucking[c]	2.7
Air Transportation	5.8
Oil Pipelines[d]	4.3

[a]Uses revenue traffic as output. Using car miles as the measure of railroad output yields a 3.1 percent average annual increase between 1947-1990.
[b]Class I and II carriers, 1954-1989.
[c]Class I and II carriers, excluding local carriage, 1954-1989.
[d]1958-1990.

SOURCE: U.S. Department of Labor, Bureau of Labor Statistics, *Productivity Measures for Selected Industries and Government Services* (Washington, D.C.: U.S. Government Printing Office, 1992), pp. 76-9.

service falls upon motor carriers. Much of that traffic, which requires considerable platform and terminal handling, has shifted from rail to motor carriage, thereby tending to reduce motor carrier productivity. However, there are reasons to believe that the industry's performance will improve in the near term. Expanded use of larger vehicles on intercity runs and increased vehicle weight limits should contribute to that improvement.

Air Carriage

In terms of growth in output per employee, the domestic airline industry was one of the leading industries in the United States between 1947 and 1990. It registered an annual average increase of 5.8 percent during that period. Among the factors that contributed to that performance were the tremendous growth in passenger demand, expansion of air cargo volume, improved equipment utilization, and introduction of larger aircraft into major markets.

It should be noted, however, that between 1988-1990 the airline industry experienced a decrease in employee productivity. The Bureau of Labor Statistics asserted that this development was at least partially due to a rapid expansion in industry employment triggered by more stringent inspection guidelines, heightened security and the stress to improve on-time arrivals.[18]

Oil Pipelines

The annual average increase in output per employee registered by the oil pipeline industry between 1958 and 1990 was 4.3 percent. As discussed earlier in this chapter, the application of automated techniques to the industry has increased in scope, and manpower requirements have fallen. While these developments have occurred, the volume handled by the industry has risen steadily.

Labor Productivity: An Overview

Although the productivity gains registered by several modes of intercity carriage appear impressive, they must be viewed with caution. Productivity measurement is a complex concept that involves the interaction of a number of variables. Attempts to measure and interpret productivity in transportation often have led to disputes between management and labor. Consequently, productivity figures have played a rather limited role in transportation contract negotiations.

UNION STRUCTURE AND BARGAINING PATTERNS

The labor force in transportation is highly unionized. While approximately 16 percent of the U.S. workforce is unionized, the percentage is considerably higher in each major mode of carriage.[19] However, as noted earlier in this chapter, since the movement toward deregulation began, non-union companies have become increasingly important market factors, particularly in the trucking industry.

As union membership in transportation has contracted, it appears that the political clout of those labor unions has also diminished. Nevertheless, extensive unionization still has an important impact on the nature of bargaining in transportation.

Union Structure

Although there has been a long-term reduction in the number of unions that represent transportation employees, there is still a proliferation of labor organizations in transportation. The sheer number of bargaining units in several modes of carriage tends to promote difficulty in reaching agreements.

The union structure in transportation has a craft orientation. That is, different unions represent specific crafts within an industry. The railroad industry provides an illustration of that craft union orientation. Despite considerable union consolidation during the past two decades, there are still 13 major railroad unions.[20]

In contrast, a number of "industrial unions" have emerged whose membership is open to all workers in a particular industry, regardless of their occupational categories. The Brotherhood of Teamsters, Chauffeurs, and Warehousemen (Teamsters) is an example of such an industrial union. It represents more than 160,000 motor carrier employees, down from 240,000 in 1980.[21]

Bargaining Patterns

The bargaining patterns employed in the major modes of carriage (rail, truck, and air) vary substantially. By the mid-1960s a pattern of national contract negotiations had emerged in the trucking and railroad industries. Carriers that chose to participate in such negotiations were represented collectively by industry bargaining units. That bargaining format produced increased uniformity in carrier wage/benefit settlements and eliminated many of the regional differences that had existed. While that bargaining format still exists, the economic and regulatory changes of the past decade have raised serious questions concerning the future viability of this approach to labor negotiations in those two modes.

In the railroad industry, the National Railway Labor conference (NRLC) which was established in 1963, serves as a bargaining arm for the railroads in national negotiations concerning wages and benefits. Work rule issues are generally negotiated on a railroad-by-railroad basis.

If they choose to do so, individual railroads have the right to bargain independently of the NRLC. In recent rounds of contract negotiations, carriers such as the Burlington Northern and CSX have chosen to conduct their negotiations independently. The union counterpart of the NRLC is the National Railway Labor Executives Association, and it bargains with the NRLC.

Every three years since 1964 the Teamsters and the industry's bargaining organization (originally Trucking Employers, Inc., and now Transportation Management, Inc.) have produced a National Master Freight Agreement. By the early 1970s nearly 500 large motor carriers, which employed nearly 400,000 Teamsters, had chosen to participate in the national agreement. In contrast, by 1991 the number of companies participating in the national agreement fell to 26, almost all of which were large less-than-truckload carriers.[22]

Executives of many of the companies that have withdrawn from the agreement contend that the national format no longer represents the best interests of many trucking operations. In fact, they view it as a real threat to their existence. They argue that the national format produces compensation levels that fail to reflect significant local and regional differences. Having withdrawn from the National Master Freight Agreement, many companies now reach local or regional agreements that include rates of pay and benefit levels that they deem more appropriate than those of the national settlement.

The airline industry does not participate in industry-wide bargaining, but rather bargains on a carrier-by-carrier, union-by-union basis. However, out of competitive necessity carriers closely monitor the settlements of their major competitors and are clearly influenced by the settlements of those companies.

THE FEDERAL GOVERNMENT AND TRANSPORTATION LABOR DISPUTES

Because of the importance of the transportation system to the realization of national goals, the federal government has developed a variety of legislative mechanisms for dealing with labor disputes in transportation. Federal concern with transportation work stoppages originated during the nineteenth century as the railroads emerged as the nation's first big business, and as the confrontations between management and labor became increasingly violent. The importance of the railroads to the economy had become apparent, and any possibility of a work stoppage in the industry was regarded as a threat to national well-being. Therefore, throughout the latter part of the century and into the first quarter of the Twentieth Century, Congress enacted several statutes that sought to improve labor relations in the railroad industry.[23] While those legislative efforts had limited success in resolving railroad labor disputes, they nevertheless established precedents for such practices as mediation, voluntary and binding arbitration, grievance procedures, and the eight-hour day. Such practices later became common throughout American industry.

The Railway Labor Act

During World War I the railroads operated under direct federal control, and throughout that period railroad unions made considerable progress in establishing collective bargaining powers. They also gained acceptance of standardized national operating practices. The unions were aided in their efforts by active federal government promotion of the expansion of the organized labor movement in the industry.

In view of these developments, new federal mechanisms were needed to deal with railroad labor issues in the postwar period. Congress sought to provide such mechanisms in several labor-related provisions of the Transportation Act of 1920. The statute defined procedures for establishment of labor adjustment boards to intervene in cases involving grievances and working condition disputes. It also established a Railroad Labor Board, which was given exclusive jurisdiction over wage controversies. However, the law did not provide any means of enforcing the decisions of the board, nor did it include any antistrike provisions. As a result, it was not too surprising that the legislation failed to achieve its principal objectives.[24] Labor disputes continued, and several major strikes occurred during the next few years. The dissatisfaction of both labor and management with the provisions of the 1920 legislation led to their active cooperation in supporting the Railway Labor Act of 1926.

The 1926 legislation (and the creation of the National Railway Adjustment Board in 1934) established the procedures that still govern labor disputes in the railroad industry. The act replaced all previous legislation dealing with railroad labor disputes; its provisions apply to all railroad employees. It relies heavily upon collective bargaining and conciliation or mediation as the basic means of solving labor-management disputes. If such voluntary procedures fail to generate a settlement, federal intervention may follow.

Minor Disputes. The Railway Labor Act provided that bipartisan adjustment boards were to be created through agreement between carriers and unions to settle "minor" disputes which were defined as those involving interpretation of existing contracts. However, difficulties arose in establishing the boards. As a result, the National Railroad Adjustment Board was created in 1934. The board consists of 36 members, 18 selected by carriers and 18 chosen by the unions. The board has jurisdiction over disputes arising out of grievances or out of interpretation of agreements concerning rates of pay, rules, or working conditions. Decisions of the board are final and binding on both parties.

Major Disputes. There is no similar procedure for solving "major" disputes in the railroad industry. These disputes arise out of new contract negotiations. If collective bargaining fails to generate a mutually agreeable pact, no procedure requires binding arbitration, short of direct congressional action.

The National Mediation Board (NMB) was created in 1934 to facilitate settlement of major disputes. The board consists of three presidentially appointed members, each serving three-year terms. The board has jurisdiction over disputes involving rates of pay or changes in rules and working conditions in those instances in which the parties to an agreement have been unable to reach a settlement.

When either party to a railroad labor contract desires a major modification, they are required to issue a "Section 6 notice." This is a written notice filed at least 30 days before intended action concerning the contract. If the desired changes cannot be settled through collective bargaining, either party may request the services of the NMB, or the board may intervene without request.

Initially, the board attempts to promote a settlement through mediation. If this fails, the board seeks to have the parties agree to binding arbitration. If arbitration is refused, the NMB notifies the parties that its mediatory efforts have failed, and for 30 days thereafter, unless the parties agree to arbitration in the interim or an emergency board is created, no change shall be made in the conditions that prevailed at the time the dispute arose. At that point, if in the NMB's opinion a strike could lead to a national emergency, it is required to notify the president, who may create an emergency board, which has 30 days to investigate the dispute. For that period and for a 30-day period following the report of the emergency board, the parties to the dispute must maintain the status quo.

Following its study, the emergency board reports its findings to the president. The recommendations of the emergency board are not enforceable, but they have been accepted in a number of instances. However, in recent years this seldom has been the case. Faced with a potential strike due to the failure of the parties to accept the findings of the emergency board (which may lead to a national emergency), the president can either allow the strike to occur or ask Congress for emergency legislation to prevent it. The latter course of action has been taken quite frequently in recent years, including four times between 1989-1992.[25]

Air Carrier Coverage. The provisions of the Railway Labor Act were broadened in 1936 to cover employees of air carriers engaged in interstate commerce. The coverage and procedures of the act are the same for airline disputes as for similar disputes in the railroad industry. The act authorizes the creation of a National Air Transport Adjustment Board, but no such board has ever been established.[26] However, carriers and unions have formed "system boards of adjustment," and these have been reasonably successful in settling minor disputes concerning grievances and contract interpretation.[27] The National Mediation Board functions in the same manner in airline disputes as it does in railroad conflicts.

Labor Disputes in Other Modes

Although the impact of strikes in other forms of carriage can also have quite negative effects on the U.S. economy, there are no special legislative procedures to prevent such strikes. Work stoppages in motor carriage, domestic water carriage, or the maritime industry are handled like disputes in any other industry (excluding rail and air carriage). Overall industry guidelines have, however, come about through enactment of the National Labor Relations Act of 1935 (the Wagner Act), the Fair Labor Standards Act of 1938, and the Labor-Management Relations Act of 1947 (better known as the Taft-Hartley Act).

The 1935 statute recognized the right of collective bargaining throughout U.S. industry and required management to bargain with unions that were duly certified by the National Labor Relations Board. The act also gave the board the power to deal with unfair labor practices. In conjunction with this law, the Fair Labor Standards Act of 1938 provided standards for minimum wages and maximum hours in interstate commerce.

In 1947 the Taft-Hartley Act added a list of unfair employee practices to the list of unfair employer practices contained in the 1935 act. Among those practices forbidden by the law were the coercion of employers or employees and charging excessive initiation fees. The law also established a "cooling off" period that could be utilized to gain additional time to settle disputes which might lead to strikes that threatened national health or safety. Accordingly, a 60-day notice must be given by a party wishing to change or terminate prevailing conditions of employment. During the following 60 days, the Federal Mediation and Conciliation Service (created by the act) attempts to bring the two parties to agreement. If an agreement has not been reached by the expiration of the 60-day period, the unions are free to strike. At that point, if the conflict has national significance, the president may appoint a board of inquiry to investigate the dispute. At the same time, if the president believes that the strike poses a threat to national well-being, he has the power to direct the attorney general to request an injunction

(Taft-Hartley injunction) from a federal court. If the attorney general obtains the injunction, workers must return to work for 80 days. During the 80-day period, efforts are made to settle the disputes. However, if an agreement is not reached during that time span, the legislative procedures have been exhausted, and only direct congressional action can prevent the strike.

Another labor statute, the Labor-Management Disclosure Act of 1959, was enacted in response to conditions in the transportation industries. In particular, alleged mismanagement of Teamster pension funds by union officers led directly to passage of that statute, which made mandatory the reporting and disclosure of certain transactions of labor organizations and employers.

It should be noted that the Teamsters continue to have legal difficulties. In 1989 the union reached an agreement with the Justice Department to settle a massive racketeering suit alleging union ties with organized crime. Among the reforms agreed to by the union was a shift to election of the union's president by the rank-and-file members of the union. That took place in 1991 and resulted in the election of Ron Carey as president of the union.[28]

Experience under Federal Labor Dispute Guidelines

The procedures provided in the Railway Labor Act for handling major railroad disputes have been used frequently since their inception. Since 1926 hundreds of railroad emergency boards have been created, following the failure of the NMB to promote labor-management agreement on contract issues. However, recommendations of the emergency boards have been accepted infrequently by the parties, and strikes have often resulted. As previously noted, in a number of instances, direct congressional action has been required to settle the disputes. This experience has raised questions concerning the adequacy of the Railway Labor Act guidelines. It has been argued that the existence of these procedures effectively postpones the need for any hard bargaining until the emergency board study period is nearly expired.[29] It has also been contended that the NMB and its procedures are basically redundant to those of the Federal Mediation and Conciliation Service, and that railroads and airlines should be brought under the provisions of the Taft-Hartley Act.[30]

There have also been periodic calls for establishment of a "final offer selection" process to be applied to major labor disputes in transportation. This mechanism, which was given considerable congressional attention during the Nixon administration, would establish a procedure by which the parties to a dispute would each submit a final offer to an impartial third party. That party would then choose one of the final offers, without modification, and that would constitute the settlement. Calls for establishment of such a procedure have been quite controversial, and there appears to be little current congressional interest in the topic.

Public Sector Strikes

The early 1980s witnessed a change in governmental policies concerning transportation employee strikes in the public sector. While the federal government and nearly all states prohibit strikes by public employees, many such strikes have occurred. Prior to the 1981 walkout by its members, the Professional Air Traffic Controllers Organization (PATCO) had engaged in illegal job actions in 1970 and 1978. Numerous illegal transit union strikes had also taken place despite existing no-strike laws. It appeared that these laws were not taken seriously; the likelihood of strong countermeasures was remote, and work stoppages often seemed to further the desired ends of the unions through public pressures to resume service.

The Reagan Administration's handling of the August 1981 PATCO strike seems to have changed that perception. The federal government reacted to the controllers' illegal strike in a decisive manner, firing the striking controllers, and gave notice that such actions would not be tolerated. In the aftermath of those firings and the decertification of the union, similar strong stands have been taken against illegal transit strikes in several cities. However, in mid-1993 President Clinton blurred this issue by welcoming the controllers who had been fired by the Reagan administration to reapply for their former jobs.

The debate concerning the right to strike for public employees is both complex and emotional. It is clearly beyond the scope of this book to address the propriety of no-strike laws.[31]

Federal Role in Job Guarantees

The role of the federal government in transportation labor has not been limited to establishment of procedures for strike resolution. Congress has also played an active role in promoting job protection in the railroad industry. Congressional concern for worker security in cases of railroad mergers and consolidations was reflected in the Transportation Act of 1940. In part the act specified that:

> as a condition of its approval (of a merger or consolidation)...the Commission shall require a fair and equitable arrangement to protect the interests of the railroad employees affected. In its order of approval the Commission shall include terms and conditions providing that during the period of four years from the effective date of such order such transaction will not result in

employees of the carrier or carriers by railroad affected by such order being in a worse position with respect to their employment, except that the protection afforded to any employee pursuant to this sentence shall not be required to continue for a longer period, following the effective date of such order, than the period during which such employee was in the employ of such carrier or carriers prior to the effective date of such order.[32]

In cases that have come before the ICC, these provisions have been considered to constitute minimum coverage of employees, and broader protections have been given to employees in a number of instances.[33] Generally attrition programs are relied upon to eliminate jobs. The agreements also typically stipulate that workers can be transferred throughout the resulting system. If workers are unwilling to move, cash settlements are made. As might be expected, such extensive employee protection has been costly to the carriers involved.[34]

In 1970, Congress applied the same basic pattern of employee protection to railroad workers affected by the creation of Amtrak and extended the period of coverage to six years.[35] Congressional concern for employee protection also surfaced during hearings on the Northeast Railroad Reorganization. The line reductions discussed in these hearings implied major cutbacks in railroad employment in the region. Although Congress wished to extend employee protections as it had in the past, it was clear that the seven bankrupt railroads being reorganized were not financially strong enough to make such guarantees. Consequently, in 1973 Congress established a $250 million federally financed protection plan, which contained the standard range of guarantees. The railroad unions were then expected to renegotiate all outstanding contracts with Conrail.

Congressional concern for the welfare of railroad employees is laudable. There is limited job potential for many long-term railroad employees who do not have readily transferable skills. However, experience with the guarantees accorded under the 1973 agreement illustrates that such guarantees can also be counterproductive. In return for its guarantees, Congress should have required substantial work rule and operating practice changes from the railroad unions. Those changes were not voluntarily forthcoming. The reorganization provided an unprecedented opportunity to improve worker productivity in the region (which had been the lowest in the industry prior to the reorganization). This would have been a decisive movement toward establishment of a viable railroad system in the region. Modification of long-standing work rules and practices in Conrail could have served as a pattern for future negotiations on a national basis. Unfortunately, the opportunity was mishandled by Congress, and the costs have been significant. In fact, the $250 million employee protection fund established by Congress, which was to last to the year 2021, was depleted by 1979.[36] During the next two years Congress provided supplemental appropriations to finance the protection fund shortfall. However, in June 1981 Congress enacted the Northeast Rail Services Act, which not only reduced the level of benefits paid to affected Conrail employees, but also reduced the length of the Conrail guarantee to three years from the date of that statute's passage.[37] The reduction and ultimate elimination of those guarantees in 1984 played an important role in promoting Conrail's financial turnaround.

Congressional concern with potential negative job-market impacts on transportation employees has not been limited to the railroad industry. The Airline Deregulation Act of 1978 addressed similar concerns. Employees with at least four years of service were to be protected against potential job loss and erosion of earnings. In part, the statute specified that employees who were adversely affected would be eligible for job protection payments for up to 72 months after such payments began. While the Civil Aeronautics Board was initially empowered to evaluate applications for coverage under the law, that authority was transferred to the DOT in 1985. To date, no benefits have been paid under that program.[38]

As discussed in Chapter 12, Congress did not provide extensive employee guarantees in the post-1978 regulatory reform statutes. Hopefully, the experience with the Conrail guarantees will continue to influence related congressional actions.

FELA and the Railroads

The railroad industry is troubled by another form of federal labor regulation which does not apply to any other industry. Railroad employees are covered by the provisions of the Federal Employers' Liability Act (FELA) which was established by Congress in 1908. The law predated workers' compensation laws, and reflected the widespread belief that state courts were controlled by the railroads and offered little recourse for rail workers injured on the job. FELA provided railroad workers access to the federal courts.

Despite the fact that all states now have workers' compensation laws that cover all other workers, railroad workers are still covered by FELA. The law places the employer and employee in an adversarial position. To be compensated for job-related injuries, railroaders must sue their employers in federal court, and must prove carrier negligence to collect.

Railroad payments on FELA claims have risen dramatically in recent years and exceed $1 billion annually.[39] The nation's railroads believe that FELA creates significant competitive problems for them. Railroads estimate that their injury-related costs are 155 percent higher per employee than those of the long-distance truckers who are their major competitors.[40] The Association of American Railroads, which is the industry's major trade association, sees "no reason why claims shouldn't be covered by state laws which cover virtually all other workers."[41] The railroads have lobbied aggressively for repeal of FELA, but Congress has shown little interest in the issue.

SUMMARY

The significance of the labor component in transportation cannot be overstated. Employee compensation comprises a major portion of the cost structure of the industry and, consequently, has a decided impact on carrier prices. Work rules and job descriptions contained in labor contracts are major determinants of worker efficiency. Further, work stoppages can have a quite negative impact on the flow of commerce in the United States.

The employment picture in transportation is mixed. A variety of factors, including technological changes, mergers, and abandonment of services in several modes, have combined to exert downward pressures on carrier employment. However, these pressures have been partially offset by the growth of aggregate demand for transportation services that have accompanied U.S. economic expansion. Transportation workers are well paid in comparison with workers in other occupational categories. Employee compensation has risen steadily and thus contributed to higher rates and fares. The productivity of transportation workers has tended to outpace that of workers in the aggregate private sector. However, the significance of these productivity figures is the subject of considerable debate; they must therefore be viewed with caution.

While the transportation work force is highly unionized, as a result of regulatory changes non-union companies have become increasingly important, particularly in the trucking industry. During the last decade their market presence and recessionary pressures have combined to displace many union members, and fostered widespread concession bargaining in transportation. Competitive and economic pressures have also led many of the more established, unionized companies to withdraw from national bargaining agreements.

Due to public dependency upon continued transportation service and the negative impact of strikes, the federal government has established guidelines under the Railway Labor Act and the Taft-Hartley Act for postponing or preventing major transportation strikes. However, experience under these acts has led to serious questions concerning their adequacy.

In an attempt to mitigate potential negative job-market impacts on the transportation workforce, during the 1970s Congress became increasingly involved in establishment of employee protection programs. While these programs were well intentioned, they were also extremely costly and contributed to emergence of an artificial bargaining climate in which organized labor often had little incentive to bargain creatively with management. Congress appears to have recognized this problem and has scaled back its commitment to such protection programs.

DISCUSSION QUESTIONS _____

1.   Why have carriers formed collective bargaining units such as the National Railway Labor Conference?
2.   Do you believe that a "final offer selection" process should be established to cover major transportation labor disputes? Explain your reasoning.
3.   Discuss the factors that can influence the productivity figures registered by workers in the transportation industries.
4.   Why would a union choose a strategy of bargaining a national contract?
5.   What are the most important factors which have led to the long-term contraction of railroad employment?
6.   Distinguish between a craft and an industrial union.

NOTES _____

1.   Transit labor is examined in Chapters 18 and 19.
2.   Eno Transportation Foundation, Inc., *Transportation in America*, 11th ed. (Lansdowne, VA: the Foundation, 1993), p. 23.
3.   Ibid.
4.   See "Santa Fe, UTU Agree on Crew Reduction," *On Track* (September 30, 1992), p. 3.
5.   "UTU Okays Crew Pact with CSX," *On Track* (August 5, 1992), p. 3.
6.   See G. Stephen Taylor, "Using Performance Appraisals of Dispatchers to Reduce Driver Turnover," *Transportation Journal*, Vol. 30, No. 4 (Summer, 1991), pp. 49-55.
7.   Eno Transportation Foundation, p. 61.
8.   Mark B. Solomon, "Shortage of Pilots, Mechanics May Send Airlines into Turbulence," *Journal of Commerce*, New York, May 13, 1992, p. 3B.
9.   Ibid.
10. Standard and Poor's, "Air Transport Outlook," *Industry Surveys*, Vol. 160, No. 26, Sec.1 (June 25, 1992), p. A35.
11. Eno Transportation Foundation, Inc.p. 60.
12. Ibid.
13. See Robert J. Joedicke, *The Goose That Laid Gold Eggs* (New York: Lehman Brothers Kuhn Loeb Research, February, 1983), pp. 10, 14, 56.
14. U.S. Government Accounting Office, *Effects of Regulatory Reform on Unemployment in the Trucking Industry* (Washington, D.C.: U.S. Government Accounting Office, 1982), p. 14.

15. Dane Hamilton, "St. Johnsbury President Says Failure Largely Union's Fault," *Journal of Commerce*, New York, June 24, 1993, pp. 1A-2A.
16. "Northwest's Sigh of Relief Has Rivals Groaning," *Business Week* (July 26, 1993), p. 84.
17. U.S. Department of Labor, Bureau of Labor Statistics, *Productivity Measures for Selected Industries and Government Services* (Washington, D.C.: U.S. Government Printing Office, 1992), p. 4.
18. U.S. Department of Labor, Bureau of Labor Statistics, p. 3.
19. "Labor Pains," *Journal of Commerce*, New York, September 3, 1991, p. 1A.
20. For an extensive discussion of this and related matters see Robert C. Lieb, *Background Paper on Railroad Labor Issues*, prepared for the Transportation Research Board (Boston, MA: Northeastern University, 1990), p. 5.
21. "Labor Pains," p. 3B.
22. "Teamster Members Ratify New 3-year National Freight Contract," *Traffic World* (May 6, 1991), p. 22.
23. These included the Arbitration Act (1884), the Erdman Act of 1898, the Newlands Act of 1913, and the Transportation Act of 1920.
24. Dudley F. Pegrum, *Transportation: Economics and Public Policy*, rev. ed. (Homewood, IL: Richard D. Irwin, Inc., 1968), p. 507.
25. See Lawrence M. Lesser, "Settling Transportation Disputes," *Journal of Commerce*, New York, August 25, 1992, 8A.
26. Ibid.
27. Ibid.
28. See "Teamsters Reborn," *Journal of Commerce*, New York, December 16, 1991, p. 6A.
29. John Hoerr and Stephen H. Wildstrom, "Ripe for Oblivion: The Railway Labor Act," *Business Week* (December 15, 1975), p. 27.
30. Ibid.
31. For an extensive discussion of this issue see Grace Sterrett and Antone Aboud, *The Right to Strike in Public Employment* (Ithaca, NY: ILR Press, 1982).
32. *Transportation Act of 1940*, 49 U.S.C. Sec. 5 (2) (f) (1940).
33. It should be noted that railroad workers historically have not been protected from job loss due to technological changes or reorganizations within a single railroad.
34. For example, the total cost of the job protection provisions incorporated into the Penn Central consolidation was $78 million.
35. U.S. Department of Labor, Office of Information, "Rail Worker Protection Plan Certified by Hodgson," April 16, 1971. (News release)

36. Joseph Rosenbloom, "The Conrail Layoff Plan," *The Boston Globe*, May 12, 1978, p. 35.
37. *Northeast Rail Services Act*, Public Law 97-35 (1981).
38. Starr B. McMullen, "Employee Protection After Airline Deregulation," *Transportation Journal*, Vol. 25, No. 3 (Spring, 1986), pp. 20-4.
39. "Is This Liability Law A Gravy Train?" *Business Week*, November 6, 1989, p. 93.
40. Association of American Railroads, "Antique Compensation System Impairs Railroad Competitiveness," Washington, D.C., November 16, 1989, p. 2.
41. "Quoteline," *On Track*, November 1, 1989, p. 1.

SELECTED REFERENCES

Behar, Richard. "How Hoffa Haunts the Teamsters." *Time* (December 21, 1992), pp. 60-1.

Beilock, Richard, and Russell B. Capelle, Jr. "Occupational Loyalties Among Truck Drivers." *Transportation Journal*, Vol. 29, No. 3 (Spring, 1990), pp. 20-8.

Breskin, Ira. "Teamsters Hold Direct Election." *Air Commerce*, New York, May 28, 1991, p. 4.

Bernstein, Aaron. *Grounded: Frank Lorenzo and the Destruction of Eastern Airlines*. (New York: Simon and Schuster, 1990).

Jennings, Kenneth. "Eastern's Final Days: Labor Relations Lessons for Managers in Other Organizations." *Transportation Journal*, Vol. 31, No. 3 (Spring, 1992), pp. 27-38.

Jennings, Kenneth. "Peripheral Collective Bargaining at Eastern Airlines." *Transportation Journal*, Vol. 29, No. 3 (Spring, 1990), pp. 4-19.

Lawrence, Martha B., and Richard G. Sharp. "Freight Transportation Productivity in the 1980s: A Retrospective." *Journal of the Transportation Research Forum*, Vol. 32, No. 1 (1991), pp. 158-71.

Lieb, Robert C. *Background Paper on Railroad Labor Issues*. Prepared for the Transportation Research Board. Boston, MA: Northeastern University, 1990.

Lieb, Robert C. "The Changing Nature of Labor/Management Relations in Transportation." *Transportation Journal*, Vol. 24, No. 3 (Spring, 1984), pp. 4-14.

Lieb, Robert C., and James F. Molloy. "The Major Airlines: Labor Relations in Transition." *Transportation Journal*, Vol. 26, No. 3 (Spring, 1987), pp. 17-29.

McMullen, B. Starr. "Employee Protection After Airline Deregulation." *Transportation Journal*, Vol. 25, No. 3 (Spring, 1986), pp. 20-4.

Murphy, Paul R., and Richard F. Poist. "Managing the Human Side of Public Warehousing: An Overview of Modern Practices." *Transportation Journal*, Vol. 31, No. 3 (Spring, 1992), pp. 54-62.

"Northwest's Sigh of Relief Has Rivals Groaning." *Business Week* (July 26, 1993), p. 84.

Solomon, Mark B. "Layoffs in Aviation Skyrocket." *Air Commerce*, New York, March 29, 1993, pp. 3, 10-11.

Taylor, G. Steven. "Using Performance Appraisals of Dispatchers to Reduce Driver Turnover." *Transportation Journal*, Vol. 30, No. 4 (Summer, 1991), pp. 49-55.

U.S. Department of Transportation. Office of the Secretary. *Labor Relations and Labor Costs in the Airline Industry: Contemporary Issues*. (Washington, D.C.: the Department, 1992.

Welty, Gus. "Are Times Really Changing?" *Railway Age* (June, 1992), pp. 36-8.

CHAPTER FIFTEEN

CONSOLIDATIONS, INTERMODAL OWNERSHIP AND CARRIER DIVERSIFICATION

The structure of an industry, including characteristics such as its competitive intensity and the size and diversity of market participants, is a major determinant of how business is conducted in the industry. In turn, that influences the economic performance of the industry. As a result, legislators and regulators have long been concerned with factors that might affect the structure of the transportation industries. One manifestation of this concern has been the establishment of federal policies governing carrier consolidations, intermodal ownership, and carrier diversification.

As used in this chapter, "consolidation" refers to any combination of two or more carriers of the same mode that results in their being managed as a unit.[1] In contrast, "intermodal ownership" involves combinations of carriers engaged in different forms of transportation, such as a railroad acquiring a motor carrier. "Diversification" in transportation involves the movement of a transportation enterprise into a non-transportation activity.

Each of these diverse approaches to altering carrier structure has attracted increasing attention as transportation policies have come under closer scrutiny. Because of the significance of federal policies related to these structural issues, this chapter examines the motives that have led carriers to consider such actions. It also explores the factors that have influenced federal policy formulation concerning carrier consolidations, intermodal ownership and carrier diversification. Attention is also given to the impact that carrier restructuring has had on the transportation industries.

CONSOLIDATION

The following discussion examines not only the major factors that have led carriers to consider consolidation opportunities, but also the extent of consolidation activity by mode.

Consolidation Motives

Many factors have influenced the degree of carrier interest in consolidations. The most important have been cost-reduction possibilities, financial considerations, and competitive implications.

Cost Reduction Possibilities. Consolidation may make it possible for carriers to substantially reduce the overhead burden that was previously borne by individual companies. Intramodal combinations may provide a means of reducing the number of employees involved in clerical, statistical, and accounting operations. Similar cost reductions might also be realized through elimination of duplicate facilities, such as field sales offices, terminals, switching yards, and pickup and delivery operations. Operating cost savings may also be possible. If terminals and shops can be consolidated, some reduction in the number of operating personnel might be envisioned. However, as discussed in Chapter 14, employee cutbacks of this nature are generally subject to regulatory agency review.

Abandonment of duplicate routes can also generate cost savings. When the consolidation involves carriers with parallel route structures, it is often both feasible and desirable to eliminate certain routes and runs. Traffic may be rerouted over more economical and less circuitous routes. This has been an important consideration in a number of rail consolidation applications. By eliminating duplicate runs, it may be possible to generate greater traffic density while utilizing less equipment. This might permit more efficient use of equipment while allowing elimination of excess capacity. Proposals of this nature, however, are carefully scrutinized by the regulatory agencies, which seek to protect shipper interests against service deterioration. End-to-end consolidations may eliminate costly and time-consuming interchanges of traffic on multiple-line hauls. The reduction of traffic interchange might also lead to lower damage claims due to less handling.

Consolidations might also promote realization of economies of scale. Increasing size may have a positive effect on average costs. Economies may be realized either through management or machine specialization as firm size increases. Management specialists may be hired and this may have a positive effect on productivity. Similarly, as the scale of an enterprise is expanded, specialization in machinery becomes a distinct possibility, and productivity benefits may follow. Scale economies may also be realized in purchasing through quantity discounts on machinery and supplies, and in financial operations. The nature of scale economies and their incidence in the various modes were discussed in Chapter 8.

Financial Considerations. Elimination of duplicate terminals, yards, and other transport-related facilities, which may be possible because of carrier consolidations, might provide capital gains through the sale of property. Such sales could produce considerable capital for carriers, particularly railroads, which have substantial property holdings in many major cities. Property taxes also would be reduced if such sales took place. Consolidation also may offer a means of survival to carriers experiencing financial difficulties. In many instances, troubled carriers have sought financially stable consolidation partners to offset their financial woes. Properly conceived and implemented consolidations may assist the troubled carrier in establishing a sounder financial base, which is essential in attracting needed investment capital.

Competitive Considerations. Carriers also may seek consolidations to improve their competitive positions. To that end, consolidations may reduce the pressures of intramodal competition. However, these competitive reductions are among the major factors to be considered by the Interstate Commerce Commission, the Department of Transportation, and the Department of Justice in evaluating consolidation proposals.

End-to-end consolidations may broaden the territories served by the carrier and also may allow the provision of through services to improve the carrier's competitive position. These considerations have played a major role in promoting a number of consolidations in both rail and motor carriage. Motor carriers often have utilized consolidations as a means of broadening territories served and to increase the range of commodities that they might carry.[2]

Railroad Consolidations

The discussions of Chapters 10 through 12 noted that federal regulatory policy concerning railroad consolidations has changed significantly over time. Consequently, the intensity of railroad consolidation activity also has varied considerably throughout the years.

Early Railroad Consolidations. Most early rail lines were local and served quite limited areas. However, as population grew and dispersed and industrialization decentralized, it became apparent that many rail lines were interdependent. As interline traffic expanded, railroad owners sought to consolidate local lines to improve efficiency in handling such traffic. This early consolidation movement was hindered somewhat by restrictive state charters and laws, but congressional pressures and the potential economic benefits of carrier consolidation combined to effectively eliminate most of these barriers by the mid-1860s.[3]

Railroad Consolidations and Antitrust Laws. Although the Sherman Antitrust Act was passed in 1890, there was a prevailing attitude that its provisions did not apply to railroad consolidations.[4] However, several court cases, the most important of which was the Northern Securities Company case of 1904, brought rail consolidations within the domain of the antitrust laws.[5] These court rulings, coupled with passage of the Clayton Act in 1914, which strengthened the antitrust statutes, effectively prohibited further railroad consolidations until after World War I.

Consolidations and the Transportation Act of 1920. American involvement in World War I placed considerable strain on the national railroad system; when the system failed to meet government performance expectations, the railroads were placed under direct federal control and operation in 1917. As discussed in Chapter 10, the rigors of the war effort left many railroads in precarious financial and physical condition. In an effort to prevent the financial collapse of the railroads, Congress passed the Transportation Act of 1920. The most important provision of that statute, in terms of the present discussion, was a directive to the ICC to formulate a plan to consolidate the U.S. railroads into a limited number of systems. Weak and strong roads in various regions were to be combined to create railroads that were balanced in terms of earning power. All future consolidations were required to conform to the plan that the ICC was to formulate. The act also empowered the ICC to withdraw any railroad consolidation from the operation of the antitrust statutes. Thus the ICC could approve consolidations that might result in reduced rail competition. Federal policy concerning railroad consolidations therefore shifted from enforced intramodal competition and a prohibition of consolidations to active promotion of consolidations that might reduce such competition.

The ICC struggled with the master plan concept for nearly a decade, and several times during that period the commission petitioned Congress to relieve it of the burden. However, Congress did not respond to those requests. In 1929 the ICC adopted a "final" consolidation plan, which consisted of 21 systems. However, lack of agreement between carriers and Congress concerning the propriety of the plan, the fact that the carriers were not compelled to consolidate, and the Depression all combined to render the plan inoperable. It was not until 1940 that Congress abandoned the master plan concept and declared that the initiative in future railroad consolidation proposals should come from the carriers. The ICC was relieved of its responsibility of preparing a consolidation plan, and its role in future consolidation proposals was defined as determining if the proposals met the standards of the Interstate Commerce Act. In such cases the ICC was given the statutory charge to consider the impact of the proposed consolidation upon the following:

1. the public need for adequate transportation service
2. other carriers
3. the fixed charges of the railroads involved
4. employees.[6]

Subsequent Railroad Consolidations. Between 1940 and 1958 relatively few consolidations were proposed by the railroads. However, between 1958 and 1968 the ICC was deluged with consolidation applications involving many major U.S. railroads. Rapidly escalating operating costs and the increasing intensity of intermodal competition provided the major impetus for this wave of applications, which generally sought to eliminate duplicate operations.

Many of these applications, which were reviewed according to the ICC's case-by-case approach, met the standards prescribed by the ICC and were approved. Major railroad consolidations approved during that period created the Penn Central, the Burlington Northern, and the Baltimore and Ohio-Chesapeake and Ohio systems, among others. Many of these consolidation cases were quite time consuming. For example, the proposal that sought to link the Pennsylvania and New York Central railroads into the Penn Central was originally submitted to the ICC in 1962, but was not finally decided by the commission until 1966.[7] Such delays resulted in widespread criticism of ICC procedures in handling consolidation cases.

The railroad consolidation movement slowed somewhat following the June 1970 bankruptcy of the Penn Central. Some congressmen blamed the collapse of the Penn Central on the consolidation, but it soon became apparent that the railroad's problems were the result of many factors. Among these were the changing economic conditions of the region, forced continuance of unprofitable services, and managerial infighting. As a result, the unofficial moratorium on railroad consolidations was rather short-lived. In fact, as discussed in Chapter 3, Congress subsequently became actively involved in the creation of Conrail through a massive consolidation of seven bankrupt railroads in the Northeast and Midwest.

Further railroad consolidations were supported by the DOT beginning in 1975. The department called for a new wave of consolidations, particularly of an end-to-end nature, to promote a more efficient U.S. railroad system.[8] Also, the Railroad Revitalization and Regulatory Reform Act of 1976 contained provisions to accelerate ICC consideration of railroad consolidation applications. Under the provisions of the act, the ICC was given a 24-month time limit for processing such applications and rendering a final decision.[9]

The prospect of more rapid processing of consolidation proposals has led to a number of consolidation applications being filed with the ICC. Among the major consolidations which have subsequently been approved have been:

1.   The joining of the Chessie System and Family Lines to create a 26,000-mile system under CSX Transportation.

2.   The consolidation of the Norfolk & Western with the Southern Railway into the Norfolk Southern Corporation, which serves 21 states over nearly 18,000 miles of track.

3.   The combination of the Union Pacific, Missouri Pacific, and Western Pacific to produce a 22,000-mile system under the Union Pacific Corporation.

Effects of Railroad Consolidations. The many railroad consolidations approved by the ICC have had a decided impact on the structure of the railroad industry. They have led to emergence of a limited number of major systems and have promoted a much needed reduction of duplication within the industry.

Motor Carrier Consolidations

The Motor Carrier Act of 1935 established ICC jurisdiction over consolidations involving regulated motor carrier. In the ensuing years the rather restrictive entry policies of the ICC (prior to the deregulation movement) provided a major incentive for motor carrier consolidations. Often the certificates granted were quite limited, particularly in terms of territories to be served. To expand the base of their operations, carriers could either request new operating authority from the ICC, or seek to consolidate with a company that had complementary operating authority. Carriers often perceived it as being easier to obtain ICC approval of a consolidation proposal than new operating authority. Under those circumstances, in a typical year the ICC approved hundreds of motor carrier consolidations. The majority of those were end-to-end in nature. Many of the largest motor carriers which exist today essentially built their systems through acquisitions.

As ICC entry policies have liberalized, the route authority desired by motor carriers generally has become readily available through the commission. Consequently, there is less incentive for motor carriers to seek consolidations. Nevertheless, consolidations are still attractive to carriers seeking an immediate presence in a new market and the ability to capitalize on the goodwill previously generated by the carrier to be acquired.

Effects of Motor Carrier Consolidations. Motor carrier consolidations have contributed to some concentration of intercity trucking activities, particularly in the less-than-truckload sector of the industry. The large LTL carriers which emerged through consolidations, and have expanded their networks by entering new markets under the ICC's more liberal entry policies, have become formidable competitors. Potential new entrants typically lack the capital to establish effective competitive networks. While liberal consolidation policies have also helped shape the truckload sector of the business, the more limited capital requirements of that sector of the industry promote more effective competition between large numbers of carriers.

Water Carrier, Pipeline and Forwarder Consolidations

There has been relatively little consolidation activity involving water carriers that are subject to ICC jurisdiction. Most consolidations that have occurred have been of an end-to-end nature.

The Federal Energy Regulatory Commission has no jurisdiction over pipeline consolidations. Although a limited number of pipeline consolidations have occurred in recent years, the structure of the industry was primarily defined by a series of consolidations that occurred in the latter part of the nineteenth century.

Consolidations involving surface freight forwarders are not subject to ICC control. Many consolidations have occurred, leading to a significant concentration of forwarding activities. Air freight forwarder consolidations were historically subject to CAB approval. However, in 1979 the CAB ended its regulation of air freight forwarding, and consolidations are no longer regulated.

Airline Consolidations

The Civil Aeronautics Act of 1938 brought airline consolidations within the jurisdiction of the CAB. Subsequently, the board attempted to protect competition whenever possible, and denied several large-scale consolidation proposals because it believed the potential negative impact on competition outweighed the prospective carrier benefits.

Over the next four decades, nine of the 19 domestic trunk lines that were granted "grandfather" rights were consolidated into other airlines. The board also generally permitted consolidations of local service carriers when evidence indicated that the transaction would lead to development of a stronger local carrier.[10] However, the CAB sought to maintain a separation between local service and trunk line carriers and therefore did not look favorably upon trunk line proposals to acquire local service carriers.

Board decisions on consolidation applications often seemed to be highly influenced by the financial conditions of the applicant airlines. In a number of instances the Board approved consolidation applications which linked a strong carrier with another that was having serious financial problems.[11]

The Airline Deregulation Act of 1978 triggered a new wave of interest in consolidations. This was accompanied by what appeared to be a liberalization of the CAB's policies toward consolidations and a number of large-scale consolidations were approved before the agency was eliminated in 1985. At that time, the Department of Transportation assumed regulatory responsibility for airline consolidations, and it also exhibited a rather liberal attitude toward such transactions. That continued until regulatory responsibility was transferred to the Department of Justice in 1989.

As shown in Figure 15-1, over the last fifteen years airline consolidations have had a substantial impact on the structure of the industry. As a result of 11 mergers and 16 acquisitions, 90 percent of the industry's passenger miles are now generated by eight major airlines.[12] While these consolidations have clearly yielded operating efficiencies, they have also raised questions concerning their impact on airline competitiveness.

INTERMODAL OWNERSHIP

Intermodal ownership provides carriers engaged in one mode of carriage with the ability, either through direct ownership or security control, to operate or influence the operations of a carrier engaged in another mode. Until the late 1970s, transportation policies generally restricted the extent of intermodal ownership in the United States. That situation has changed significantly since that time. The following discussion examines the evolution of federal intermodal ownership policy.

Federal Policy

Until the deregulation movement began, federal policies governing intermodal ownership seemed to reflect a belief that intermodal ownership was undesirable. However, no single statute or policy reflected the federal position concerning this matter.[13] Rather, this important regulatory issue was governed by the provisions of several statutes, including the Panama Canal Act of 1912, the Motor Carrier Act of 1935, the Civil Aeronautics Act of 1938, and the Freight Forwarder Act of 1942. The provisions of these statutes were subsequently incorporated into either the Interstate Commerce Act or the Federal Aviation Act.

Each of the previously mentioned statutes was formulated during a period of extreme financial difficulty for the mode involved. The overriding intent of Congress seemed to be the protection of the newer, developing modes from the domination of carriers engaged in the more established forms of transportation. Typically, the governing provisions did not constitute a definite prohibition of intermodal ownership.[14] However, in many instances the legislative barriers were substantial obstacles to integration efforts. The governing provisions often were inconsistent with respect to the various modes and modal combinations, and several contained special provisions that had to be met only by railroads.[15] The

FIGURE 15-1
Airline Consolidations and Failures, 1978-1992

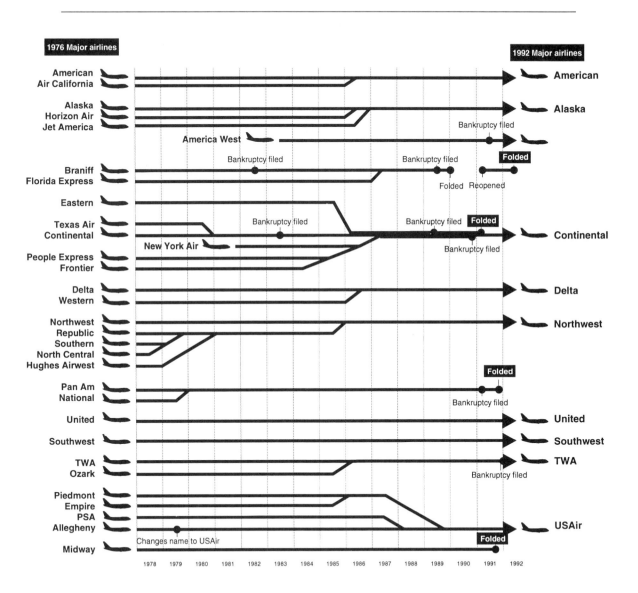

SOURCE: Kurt Eichenwald, "Airline Stocks Climb As Jobs Nose Dive," *Syracuse Herald American*, January 10, 1993, p. C1. The exhibit cited Airline Economics, Inc., Air Transport Association, Global Aviation and Associates, Traffic World, and airline companies as sources, with the research conducted by Wendy Govier.

vagueness of the provisions also caused continuing interpretative difficulties for the regulatory agencies.

Since the late 1970s there have been a number of important changes in federal policies related to intermodal ownership. These changes, which have permitted a significant increase in the extent of intermodal ownership, are examined in the following modal discussions.

Evolution of Intermodal Ownership

Despite the history of restrictive legislative and regulatory agency policies that governed intermodal ownership, there are a number of instances in which such integration has occurred. Typically, a company that controls several modes of transportation operates the separate modes as distinct operating subsidiaries.

Intermodal combinations have come about through a variety of circumstances. First, the statutes related to the ownership of certain forms of transportation, such as pipelines, have never contained provisions that limited intermodal ownership. Second, several legislative provisions that govern certain forms of transportation integration were accompanied by grandfather clauses, which permitted operations that predated the legislation to be continued. This explains, for instance, the extensive participation of rail carriers in motor carriage. Third, integration has been accomplished through the process of applying to the proper regulatory agency and subsequently meeting the provisions of the relevant statute. As previously mentioned, in most instances the governing statute does not constitute a definite prohibition of such ownership, and the applicant may be successful in substantiating the public benefit of the proposed transaction. In such cases, shipper support has generally been quite important.

Water Carriage. The Panama Canal Act of 1912 sought to prevent railroad domination of water carriers that operated through the newly opened canal. However, the ICC interpreted the rather vague provisions of the act quite strictly, and the commission's decisions in the 1915 Lake Lines cases practically eliminated the participation of the railroads in domestic water carriage.[16] That restrictive attitude continued into the 1980s when the commission liberalized its policies and began to approve water carrier acquisitions by carriers in other modes. To date, the most important acquisition has been that of American Commercial Barge Lines, which was the largest inland barge operator in the United States, by CSX Corporation, parent of one of the nation's largest railroads.[17] CSX subsequently acquired Sea-Land Services, the country's largest international maritime operator, giving it both domestic and international water carriage capabilities.

Pipeline Operations. Several federally regulated oil pipeline companies are either owned or controlled by railroads, among them the Southern Pacific, and the Union Pacific. This form of intermodal ownership has been possible because such combinations are not subject to federal regulation. In a number of instances rail-pipeline integration has provided a means of handling petroleum products more efficiently and economically.

Motor Carriage. The ownership or control of motor carrier operations by carriers primarily engaged in other modes is rather extensive. An interest in trucking activities has been established by a number of rail, water, and air carriers, as well as by freight forwarders. This is not surprising, because the truck is the most important vehicle involved in the promotion and coordination of intermodal service offerings. Most forms of coordinated transportation rely upon motor carriage at least for pickup and delivery activities, if not for performance of part of the linehaul movement itself.

Of the other modes of transportation, the railroads, by far, have the most extensive interest in trucking operations. Most class I railroads have controlling interest in at least one motor carrier operation. Prior to the regulatory reform movement, railroad involvement in trucking was generally limited to operations which had a prior or subsequent movement by rail. However, some railroads conducted unrestricted trucking operations which had predated the Motor Carrier Act of 1935 and were thus "grandfathered."

While the railroad industry continued to argue against limitations on their involvement in trucking, it was not until the regulatory reform movement began that policies began to change significantly. In particular, railroad involvement in trucking has increased broadly since the ICC not only exempted from regulation all rail and truck service provided in connection with piggybacking service, but also eliminated any bias against railroad applicants seeking unrestricted trucking authority.[18] The most important trucking acquisition by a railroad which has occurred following those policy changes was Union Pacific Corporation's acquisition of Overnite Transportation, one of the country's largest motor carriers.[19]

Several air cargo companies have also aggressively moved into interstate trucking during the past decade. Tiger International, which was acquired by Federal Express in 1989, had previously purchased several ICC-regulated motor carriers. More recently, TNT North America has embarked on a program to build a network of independent regional motor carriers through acquisitions.[20]

Air Carriage. The provisions of the Federal Aviation Act that governed surface carrier involvement in airline passenger transportation were strictly interpreted by the CAB. In fact, not once during its existence did the board permit a surface carrier to enter that field.

However, there were instances of such involvement prior to federal regulation of the industry. For example, the Boston and Maine and Maine Central railroads partially financed the development of Northeast Airlines. The airline was originally incorporated in 1931 as Boston-Maine Airways. This rail-air relationship predated the Civil Aeronautics Act of 1938 and was thus protected under grandfather rights. However, the CAB ruled that the railroads would not be permitted to increase their control of the airline, and the original interest was eventually liquidated.[21] During that same time period, the Pennsylvania Railroad also became involved in airline passenger service. In 1938 the railroad purchased a 20 percent equity interest in Transcontinental Air Transport, which later became part of Trans World Airlines. Through this interest in air carriage, the railroad sought to develop coordinated passenger service, which would rely upon rail service during the night and air service during the day. However, after a series of administrative difficulties with the CAB following regulation, the railroad relinquished its interest in the airline.[22]

There would appear to be few current barriers to prevent surface carriers from moving into airline passenger operations. Neither the DOT, which must rule on the "fitness" of new entrants, nor the Department of Justice, which regulates airline acquisitions, appear to have any bias against surface carriers in such cases.

For many years the CAB opposed surface carrier involvement in air freight forwarding. However, in 1969 the board reversed its policy and began granting forwarding authorizations to many surface carriers. Air cargo and air forwarding were subsequently deregulated. Many air forwarders are now owned or controlled by surface carriers. The most extensive example of this form of intermodal relationship is provided by the ownership of Emery Worldwide by Consolidated Freightways. Consolidated, which already had an air freight forwarding subsidiary, acquired Emery in 1989 to dramatically expand its involvement in domestic and international air cargo services.[23]

Experience with Intermodal Ownership

The arguments typically posed against intermodal ownership have not been validated by experience with the concept. Where intermodal ownership has been permitted, it has promoted a more rational assignment of transportation functions to the modes that are best suited economically to provide such services. Examples may be found in railroads channeling various types of traffic to pipeline, motor carrier, and water carrier subsidiaries. Railroad expansion of single company intermodal services provides another illustration of more efficient traffic allocation.

Intermodal ownership has not resulted in any significant disruption of competition and has shown no tendency to create a monopolistic situation in the transportation marketplace. Limited financial and regulatory entry barriers in several modes of carriage would prevent that from happening.

Intermodal ownership has become widespread, and a substantial number of multi-modal companies such as CSX Transportation, Union Pacific Corporation, Consolidated Freightways and TNT North America have emerged. A major challenge facing the management of such companies is development of an organization structure that will allow the benefits of transportation integration to be realized by shippers and carriers alike.

CARRIER DIVERSIFICATION

Many carriers have sought to diversify their operations by expanding into non-transportation activities. Carriers have done so for several reasons.

First, as noted in earlier chapters, the rate of return offered by many industries is substantially higher than that which has been generated in certain forms of transportation. A rate of return that compares favorably with the rest of U.S. industry is necessary to obtain the investment capital required for modernization and expansion of transportation activities. Second, by diversifying into non-transportation activities, carriers may find it possible to combine different profit cycles, which might improve their cash flow positions. Third, diversification might improve the carriers' likelihood of survival in case of a business decline in a particular segment of its traffic. Fourth, the tax credits that many carriers have accumulated may be used to offset profits in other operations.

Federal Policy

For many years the federal government attempted to limit railroad involvement in non-transportation activities. During the late nineteenth and early twentieth centuries, a number of railroads diversified into businesses such as lumber production and coal mining. In some cases the railroads would transport their own commodities, which were directly competitive with similar items produced by shippers who also used the railroads for transportation. By charging competitive shippers high rates, or by charging themselves artificially low rates to ship the same products, railroads were able to create an insurmountable competitive advantage for their own products. The "commodities clause" of the Hepburn Act of 1906 sought to eliminate this discrimination, by preventing railroads from transporting articles that they had produced, or had an interest in, over interstate routes.[24] The act forced many railroads to divest themselves of non-transportation interests. The commodities clause applied only to railroads and was not extended to the other modes.

Federal control over carrier diversification was further tightened by the Transportation Act of 1920, which established ICC control over the sale of railroad securities. This was significant, because the railroads had often used the proceeds of security sales to acquire other companies.

Those laws restricted railroad diversification efforts until the railroads discovered a legal loophole which allowed them to form parent holding companies which were not subject to ICC control. Those holding companies were then used as the vehicle for railroad diversification.

Carrier Diversification Efforts

Many railroads, truckers and airlines have participated in the diversification movement. Carriers have diversified into a wide range of businesses, including real estate development, manufacturing, food processing, and financial services. The most interesting and extensive diversification development of the past decade has been the establishment of third party logistics subsidiaries or divisions by large transportation companies. As discussed in Chapter 2, third party logistics companies offer a broad range of logistics services to customers. Carriers which establish such operations are able to offer shippers not only transportation services, but also a variety of "value added" services. Table 15-1 provides a list of large transportation companies which have established third party logistics enterprises.

SUMMARY

Federal policies governing carrier consolidations have varied considerably over time and with respect to the various modes. However, in the aftermath of regulatory reform, major consolidations in the railroad, trucking and airline industries have led to a significant restructuring of those industries.

Until the late 1970s Congress generally followed a restrictive policy toward intermodal ownership. Federal policies concerning the integration of the modes were vague and inconsistent with respect to different modal combinations. However, those policies have changed, and multimodal transportation companies have become far more prevalent in the marketplace.

Many carriers, attracted by higher rates of return in non-transportation industries, have pursued diversification into those industries. During the past decade, the most significant form of carrier diversification has been the movement of large transportation companies into the field of third party logistics.

TABLE 15-1

Third Party Logistics Operations of Large Carriers

Third Party Logistics Company	*Carrier Parent*
Airborne Express Logistics Services	Airborne Express
Bekins Logistics	Bekins Van Lines
Burnham Services Corp.	Burnham Moving and Storage
Business Logistics Services	Federal Express Corp.
Customized Logistics Services	North American Van Lines
Customized Transportation, Inc.	CSX Corp.
Innovative Logistics, Inc.	Carolina Freight Corp.
Menlo Logistics	Consolidated Freightways
Roadway Logistics Systems	Roadway Services, Inc.
Ryder Dedicated Logistics	Ryder System
Schneider Logistics	Schneider National
Skyway Freight System, Inc.	Union Pacific Corp.
TNT Contract Logistics	TNT Freightways Corp.
UPS Worldwide Logistics	United Parcel Service
Yellow Logistics Services, Inc.	Yellow Freight System

SOURCE: Mitchell E. MacDonald, "Who's Who in Third Party Logistics," *Traffic Management* (July, 1993), pp. 34-6, 38-9, 42, 44.

DISCUSSION QUESTIONS

1. What have been the basic motivating factors in most recent railroad consolidations?
2. What are the benefits of intermodal ownership?
3. Why have many carriers sought to diversify into non-transportation activities?
4. What factors should be considered by a regulatory agency in judging the merits of a consolidation application?
5. Why did the federal government choose to limit intermodal ownership for many years?
6. Railroad workers have historically been accorded comprehensive job guarantees in carrier consolidations. Do you believe that such guarantees are appropriate? Explain your reasoning.

NOTES _____

1. The terms "consolidation" and merger are often used interchangeably. However, there is a significant difference in the financial implications of the two terms. In a consolidation, two or more firms combine to form a new company. A merger occurs when one company is absorbed into another, and the absorbed company ceases to exist.

2. Nadreen A. Burnie, ed., *Transportation Mergers and Acquisitions* (Evanston, Il: Transportation Center, Northwestern University, 1962), p. 27.

3. U.S. Congress, Senate, Committee on Interstate and Foreign Commerce, Special Study Group on Transportation Policies in the United States, *National Transportation Policy* (Doyle Report), 87th Cong., 1st Sess., 1960 (Washington, D.C.: U.S. Government Printing Office, 1961), p. 230.

4. Burnie, p. 34.

5. *Northern Securities Company v. United States*, 193 U.S. 197 (1904).

6. *Interstate Commerce Act*, Sec. 5(6)(c) (1969).

7. *Pennsylvania Railroad Company-Merger-New York Central Railroad Company*, 327 ICC 475 (1966).

8. "Fewer but Stronger Airlines, Railroads Is Goal of New Transportation Secretary," *Wall Street Journal*, New York, April 9, 1975, p. 2.

9. The lengthiest and probably most complex railroad consolidation case ever considered by the ICC was the *Rock Island Merger Case*, 347 ICC 556 (1974). The case was before the ICC for nearly 10 years. Ironically, soon after the ICC gave its approval to the consolidation the Rock Island declared bankruptcy and the consolidation was never consummated.

10. *West Coast Case*, 8 CAB 636, 639 (1947).

11. See "Subsidies for Pan Am and TWA Rejected, but CAB Will Study Pan Am Situation," *Wall Street Journal*, New York, September 19, 1974, p. 4.

12. U.S. Department of Transportation, Office of the Secretary, *Secretary's Task Force on Competition in the U.S. Domestic Airline Industry*, Executive Summary (Washington, D.C.: the Department, 1990), p. 1.

13. Robert C. Lieb, "Intermodal Ownership: Experience and Evaluation," *ICC Practitioners' Journal*, Vol. 38, No. 5 (July-August, 1971), p. 746.

14. Byron Nupp, "Regulatory Standards in Common Ownership in Transportation," *ICC Practitioners' Journal*, Vol. 34, No. 1 (November-December, 1966), p. 21.

15. Ibid., p. 35.

16. *Lake Lines Applications Under the Panama Canal Act*, 33 ICC 699 (1915).

17.   "A Green Light for Rails to Hook onto Barges," *Business Week* (August 6, 1984), p. 25.

18.   Association of American Railroads, "Rail-Truck Entry Doctrine Dropped," *Rail News Update* (January 12, 1983), pp. 1, 4.

19.   Mitchell E. MacDonald, "Total Transportation: An Unreachable Goal?" *Traffic Management* (December, 1989), p. 36.

20.   Ibid., pp. 36-7.

21.   *Boston and Maine and Maine Central Railroads Control Northeast Airlines, Inc.*, 4 CAB 379 (1943).

22.   Robert C. Lieb, *Freight Transportation: A Study of Federal Intermodal Ownership Policy* (New York: Praeger Publishers, Inc., 1972), p. 121.

23.   Mark B. Solomon, "Emery Rises Up From the Ashes," *Air Commerce*, New York, February 23, 1993, pp. 4, 13.

24.   See Roy J. Sampson and Martin T. Farris, *Domestic Transportation: Practice, Theory and Policy*, 4th ed. (Boston: Houghton Mifflin Company, 1979), p. 323.

SELECTED REFERENCES

Dennis, Scott M. "Acquisition of Truckload Motor Carriers by Railroads: An Antitrust Analysis."*Transportation Journal*, Vol. 30, No. 3 (Spring, 1991), pp. 57-63.

Harper, Donald V., and Philip T. Evers. "Competitive Issues in Intermodal Railroad-Truck Service."*Transportation Journal*, Vol. 32, No. 3 (Spring, 1993), pp. 31-45.

Healy, Kent T. "The Merger Movement in Transportation."*American Economic Review*, Vol. 52, No. 2 (May, 1962), pp. 436-44.

Johnson, James C. *Trucking Mergers*. Lexington, MA: D.C. Heath and Company, 1973.

Jordan, William A. "Problems Stemming from Airline Mergers and Acquisitions."*Transportation Journal*, Vol. 27, No. 4 (Summer, 1988), pp. 9-30.

Kaufman, Lawrence H. "Transportation Supermarket Was Ahead of Curve."*Air Commerce*. New York, February 22, 1993, pp. 4, 6.

Lieb, Robert C. *Freight Transportation: A Study of Federal Intermodal Ownership Policy*. New York: Praeger Publishers, Inc., 1972.

Lieb, Robert C. "Intermodal Ownership: The Perspective of Railroad Chief Executives."*Transportation Journal*, Vol. 21, No. 3 (Spring, 1982), pp. 70-5.

MacDonald, Mitchell E. "The New Intermodal Alliances."*Traffic Management* (October, 1992), pp. 60-2.

MacDonald, Mitchell E. "Total Transportation: An Unreachable Goal?" *Traffic Management* (December, 1989), pp. 35-7, 39.

MacDonald, Mitchell E. "Who's Who in Third Party Logistics."*Traffic Management* (July, 1993), pp. 34-6, 38-9, 42, 44, 46.

Richardson, Helen L. "A Warming Trend in Intermodal Relationships." *Transportation and Distribution* (May, 1991), pp. 29-31, 34.

Richardson, Helen L. "Economy Spurs Growth in Outsourcing."*Transportation and Distribution* (March, 1993), pp. 45-7.

Solomon, Mark B. "Emery Rises Up From the Ashes." *Air Commerce*. New York, February 22, 1993, pp. 4, 13.

U.S. Department of Transportation. Office of the Secretary. *Secretary's Task Force on Competition in the U.S. Domestic Airline Industry*. Executive Summary. Washington, D.C.: the Department, 1990.

U.S. Interstate Commerce Commission. *Railroad Conglomerates and Other Corporate Structure*. Washington, D.C.: U.S. Government Printing Office, 1977.

Whitehurst, Clinton H., ed. *Forming Multimodal Transportation Companies: Barriers, Benefits, and Problems*. Washington, D.C.: American Enterprise Institute, 1978.

CHAPTER SIXTEEN

TRANSPORTATION SAFETY

The United States has the most extensive and modern transportation system in the world. It provides our population with unparalleled mobility and a variety of modal options for most trips. Thus the transportation system yields tremendous societal benefits. However, the related mobility of our population and increasing vehicle speeds have combined to pose a major threat to national safety. In a typical year more than 43,000 Americans die and four million more are injured in transportation-related accidents.[1] This chapter focuses on the impact of transportation on national safety and reviews government, manufacturer, carrier, union, and employee efforts to minimize societal costs.

The promotion of transportation safety has long been a public concern. As discussed in earlier chapters, safety considerations played a major role in the early development of transportation regulation in this country. It is fitting that the promotion of transportation safety is accorded a high national priority. Approximately one-half of all accidental deaths in this country are transportation related.[2] Further, the economic cost of transportation accidents is enormous. In the highway modes alone, traffic deaths, injuries, and property damage have been estimated at nearly $138 billion annually, or more than 2 percent of Gross Domestic Product.[3] To put these figures in proper perspective, it must be realized that they do not, and cannot, adequately reflect the cost of human suffering related to such accidents.

Many significant steps have been taken in recent years to foster transportation safety. Improvement in infrastructure, and efforts to prevent accidents and increase the likelihood of survival in accidents have been made in several modes. However, it must be realized that such measures generate sizable costs that are borne either directly or indirectly by the general public. Inclusion of safety features in new automobiles gives added protection, but also adds substantially to vehicle prices. Other government directives, such as those requiring improved braking systems on intercity trucks, generate additional carrier costs, which are ultimately reflected in freight rates.

Thus the government and the general public are faced with a massive transportation safety cost-benefit analysis. The results of such calculations are unclear not only because of the number of variables included in the analysis, but also due to the difficulty in quantifying certain cost and benefit elements. What is the true cost of a human life? There are no simple answers to such questions, so debate is inevitable each time new safety measures are proposed. At what point should modifications be suspended? In terms of cost-benefit analysis, one might assert that modifications should continue until potential costs offset potential benefits. However, as noted, there are serious questions concerning the quality of such estimates. Resolution of this problem is clearly beyond the scope of this book, but this dilemma will continue to be a significant decision-making issue in future transportation safety programs.

SAFETY PROMOTION AND REGULATION

Many parties, including government agencies, equipment manufacturers, carriers, unions, and the general public are involved in the promotion and regulation of transportation safety. In the aggregate they have played an important role in dramatically reducing the number of fatalities from transportation accidents. As shown in Table 16-1 that number fell from 54,719 in 1980 to 43,707 in 1991.

Role of Government

In attempting to protect the public interest, government plays a major role in the promotion and regulation of transportation safety. Early regulation and promotion emerged at the state level, but the federal government now dominates such activities.

Department of Transportation. Previous chapters outlined the development of safety regulation by mode and noted that federal promotion and regulation of transportation safety was centralized within the Department of Transportation on April 1, 1967. State involvement in transportation safety has remained vested in a variety of state agencies and commissions. However, federal and state transportation safety programs are often interdependent. In many instances, the DOT must rely upon state agencies to enforce federal safety standards if the standards are to be effective. At the same time, a substantial portion of the funds utilized by states in efforts such as upgrading highway facilities and rehabilitating convicted drunk drivers is supplied under DOT grant programs.

In some instances, federal and state officials disagree on transportation safety matters. For example, the Surface Transportation Act of 1983, which was supported by the federal DOT, required states to permit tandem trailer trucks to operate on interstate highways and other major roads. Prior to passage of that

TABLE 16-1

Transportation Fatalities and Accidental Deaths, 1970-1991

	1970	1975	1980	1985	1987	1988[a]	1989[a]	1990[d]	1991[d]
Motor Vehicles	54,633	44,525	51,091	43,825	46,390	47,093	45,555	44,529[b]	41,150
Auto occcupants	41,170	25,929	27,455	23,214	25,132	25,808	25,046	24,092[b]	22,347
Truck occupants[b]		5,477	8,748	7,666	8,910	9,217	9,402	9,306[b]	9,039
Motorcycle riders	2,330	3,189	5,144	4,564	4,036	3,662	3,143	3,224[b]	2,808
Pedestrians/Others[c]	11,133	9,930	9,744	8,381	8,312	8,406	7,964	7,907	6,956
Railroad	852	608	666	469	575	529	568	640[b]	647
Intercity/commuter	785	575	584	454	541	510	523	599[b]	583
Urban transit	67	33	82	15	34	19	45	51[b]	64
Aircraft	1,456	1,473	1,382	1,590[b]	1,163[b]	1,153[b]	1,151[b]	838[b]	942
Large air carriers	146	124	1	526	232	285	278	39	50
Commuter		28	37	37	59	21	31	4	77
Air Taxi		6?	105	76	65	58	83	50[b]	69
General aviation	1,310	1,252	1,239	951[b]	807[b]	789[b]	759[b]	745[b]	746
Water Vessels	1,596	1,709	1,566	1,247	1,155	1,027	992	919[b]	954
Commercial	178	243	206	131	119	81	96	54[b]	30
Recreational	1,418	1,466	1,360	1,116	1,036	946	896	865[b]	924
Pipeline	26	21	14	31	12	20	39	8[b]	14
Gas	22	14	11	26	9	18	36	5	14
Liquid	4	7	3	5	3	2	3	3	0
Total Transport	58,563	48,336	54,719	47,161	49,299	49,814	48,305	46,934[b]	43,707
Total Accidental Deaths	114,638	103,030	105,718	93,457	95,020	96,500	94,500	93,500	88,000
% Transport of Total	51.1%	46.9%	51.8%	50.5%	51.9%	51.6%	51.1%	50.2%[b]	49.7%

a. Breakdown:
		1975	1980	1985	1987	1988	1989	1990	1991
Large Trucks:		717	976	820	727	786	729	571[b]	544
Other Trucks:		4,760	7,772	6,846	8,183	8,431	8,673	8,735[b]	8,495

b. Revised.

c. Includes intercity buses: 59   42   62[b]   89[b]   64[b]   74   55   36

d. Preliminary.

SOURCE: Eno Transportation Foundation, Inc. *Transportation in America*, 11th ed., December supplement (Lansdowne, VA: the Foundation, 1993), p. 75.

legislation, 13 states prohibited such operations. Despite enactment of the federal statute, highway officials in Connecticut did not comply with the mandate and challenged the law in federal court. The state contended that it had the constitutional power to police its highways and protect its residents. It argued that the tandem trailer operations posed a safety hazard. The case ultimately went to the Supreme Court, which ruled that the state had to comply with the provisions of the federal statute.[5] Similar federal-state conflicts arose later in the decade when several states sought to raise speed limits above those mandated by the DOT.

Federal involvement in transportation safety is multidimensional. Through its numerous funding programs, the DOT finances expansion and upgrading of transportation facilities, such as highways, airports, and air navigation facilities, which promote transportation safety. The department also plays a major regulatory role in developing and enforcing operating procedures, qualification standards for operators, and equipment standards. Additionally, the agency finances extensive research into safety-related issues and technology and then disseminates information to equipment manufacturers, other government agencies, carriers, and the general public. Specific DOT safety activities are outlined later in this chapter.

National Transportation Safety Board. In 1966 Congress established the National Transportation Safety Board (NTSB) as an independent agency within the DOT. Eight years later Congress completely separated the agency from the Department to avoid potential conflict of interest between the NTSB and the various modal administrations of the DOT.

The NTSB has no authority to regulate, fund or be directly involved in the operation of any mode of transportation. However, it is charged with determination of the probable cause of transportation accidents. It promotes transportation safety through its investigation of accidents and its subsequent recommendations to government agencies, manufacturers, carriers, and other organizations which might implement those recommendations. Between 1966 and the end of 1991 the agency made 8,713 safety recommendations, and more than 81 percent of them had been, or were in the process of being implemented.[4] Each year the agency publishes its "Most Wanted" list of changes it would like to see implemented. In recent years that list has included calls for such actions as identifying airline pilots with a history of substance abuse, making automobile seat belt use mandatory in all states, and increasing penalties for boating while intoxicated.[5]

Role of Equipment Manufacturers

Equipment failure can lead to serious transportation accidents. Obviously, no manufacturer strives to develop faulty transportation equipment. However, manufacturers are sensitive to the impact that improved safety systems will have on equipment prices. Consequently, unless all manufacturers adopt similar safety features, there tends to be a lag in the introduction of new safety features because they reduce a company's price competitiveness. As a result, the DOT often finances research into new safety features for transportation equipment and establishes equipment standards that must be met by all manufacturers.

A slightly different situation exists in the market for private automobiles. In recent years manufacturers have sought to "sell" safety features to the consumer as a differentiating factor. For example, many of the advertising appeals used by automobile manufacturers stress the safety features of their products, including airbags and antilock brakes. The advertising attention focused on airbags is somewhat ironic in view of the fact that those companies fought against inclusion of airbags in their products for nearly 20 years. This matter is discussed later in this chapter.

Role of Carriers, Unions, and Employees

Carrier management, unions, and carrier employees also influence transportation safety. A company's efforts in the selection and training of operating personnel will have an impact on the safety performance of the carrier. Similarly, management views, both official and unofficial, concerning matters such as compliance with federal and state safety standards will be reflected by operating personnel. Carriers also can seek to influence equipment manufacturers in terms of future vehicle designs and modifications of existing systems that pose safety hazards. Organized labor also has played an important role in promoting transportation safety. For instance, in their contract negotiations, the Teamsters have long influenced industry policies on equipment adoption and operating practices, and the objections of the Airline Pilots Association to the carriage of hazardous materials on commercial flights ultimately led to more stringent handling requirements and the diversion of a large volume of hazardous traffic to all-cargo flights.[6] Such active union involvement is quite desirable because of the familiarity of operating personnel with potential hazards that might not be readily apparent to management.

The individual employee, often operating without direct management supervision, is ultimately responsible for safe operation of transportation vehicles. Their training, willingness to obey safety directives, and concern with public safety are therefore critical in promoting transportation safety.

Role of the Public

For many years the general public played a limited role in the promotion of transportation safety, except through individual efforts as operators of transportation vehicles. That role was still very important because driver and pilot errors are major causes of accidents involving automobiles, trucks and general aviation.

However, the public role in promoting transportation safety has expanded considerably in recent years. Organizations such as Mothers Against Drunken Driving (MADD), the Automobile Association of America, and those representing airline and railroad passengers have become increasingly visible and vocal. Such organizations play an important role in determining and expressing public opinion and have broadly influenced public policy making in such areas as drunken driving penalties and highway speed limits.

MODAL DEVELOPMENTS

Governmental desire to further facilitate transportation safety has led to a steady expansion of public sector involvement in that realm. Given the breadth and depth of federal, state, and local government involvement in promotion and regulation of transportation safety, it is beyond the scope of this book to recount all relevant developments. However, the following discussion highlights those recent developments that have had the most significant impact on the safety performance of the major modes of intercity carriage.

Highway Safety

As the national highway system has expanded in scope and vehicle registrations and average speeds have risen, potential safety hazards have increased. Reflecting the dominance of the automobile in passenger transportation, nearly 90 percent of the fatal accidents in transportation involve automobiles.[7] Motor vehicle accidents account for nearly 47 percent of all accidental deaths in America and are the leading cause of death among those 15-34 years of age.[8] The severity of the highway safety problem is illustrated by the fact that nearly two million Americans have lost their lives on our country's highways.[9] That number of deaths exceeds the total combat fatalities experienced by the United States in all wars.[10] Further, as noted earlier in this chapter, the economic and social costs of highway accidents are staggering. As shown in Table 16 2, the National Highway Traffic Safety Administration has estimated that each highway fatality costs the nation more than $700,000 in expenses and economic losses.

TABLE 16-2

Cost of Each Highway Fatality, Expenses and Economic Losses, 1990

Lost wages, benefits	$458,606
Value of household work	101,658
Medical expenses	3,705
Funeral costs	2,988
Police, fire and ambulance	930
Administering insurance	48,336
Legal, court costs	70,934
Workplace costs	6,679
Property damage	8,058
Traffic delay	387
Total	$702,281

SOURCE: U.S. Department of Transportation, National Highway Traffic Safety Administration, as cited in "The Costs of Fatalities," *USA Today*, October 9, 1992, p. 3A.

The Nature of Government Involvement. In response to this national problem, a number of steps have been taken at both the federal and state level to further promote highway safety, and these actions have had an effect. The number of highway deaths recorded in 1992 was the lowest in 30 years.[11]

Establishment of the Department of Transportation in 1967 led to centralization of federal highway safety activities within the department. Several organizational components of the DOT are actively involved in highway safety matters. Safety of vehicles, drivers, passengers, and pedestrians is the responsibility of the National Highway Traffic Safety Administration (NHTSA), which organizationally is housed in the office of the secretary. Also, two bureaus of the department's Federal Highway Administration (FHA) manage certain highway safety activities. The Bureau of Public Roads oversees construction and highway design safety; the Bureau of Motor Vehicle Safety is charged with responsibility for commercial motor carrier safety.

The centralization of these highway safety activities within the DOT has provided a consistency and continuity that did not exist prior to the agency's creation. Several federal agencies, including the ICC and the Department of Commerce, formerly had played fragmented roles in highway safety. DOT leadership in this field is illustrated by the fact that now all states have comprehensive highway safety programs based on national highway safety standards established by the department.

The effectiveness of DOT efforts is partially a function of two 1966 statutes that gave the DOT substantial highway safety powers beyond those that previously had been administered by other federal agencies. The National Traffic and Motor Vehicle Safety Act authorized the Secretary of Transportation to issue federal performance standards for new and used motor vehicles and their equipment. That act has led to the development of numerous DOT standards pertaining to matters such as motor vehicle tire strength and braking systems. The Highway Safety Act authorized the secretary to issue federal safety performance standards for various state highway programs to which the states must conform, provided federal grants-in-aid are given to assist in implementation of the standards. Since that time, numerous federal standards have been issued covering such state programs as periodic vehicle inspection; driver education; highway design, construction, and maintenance; and traffic control devices.[16] Some of the most important DOT initiatives in the field of highway safety are discussed below.

Drunk Driving. The DOT has focused considerable attention on highway accident prevention, and one of its major targets has been the drunk driver. Extensive use of alcohol is the single largest factor contributing to serious crashes on U.S. highways. Nearly half of all highway fatalities are caused by driving under the influence (DUI).[12] In responding to this problem, the DOT has initiated a number of programs, including grants made to state and local government agencies for special patrol units to detect drunk drivers before they cause accidents. Funds also are made available for special education programs for convicted drunken drivers. Congress has used its funding leverage as a means of convincing states to raise the legal drinking age to 21; in July 1984 President Reagan signed into law legislation that would reduce federal highway assistance to states which failed to do so. By 1988 all states had done so.[13]

States have also responded directly to growing public concern with the drunk driving problem. During the 1980s forty states tightened their drunk driving laws and 39 states enacted laws that mandated jail terms for repeat drunk driving offenders.[14] States have also increased their efforts to detect drunk drivers, and in recent years the number of DUI arrests have averaged more 1.8 million per year.[15]

While alcohol-related traffic fatalities have dropped nearly 30 percent since 1980, DUI is still a major problem. During 1991, 19,900 people died in alcohol related crashes and 318,000 were injured.[16] Forty-one states and the District of Columbia still have a blood alcohol content (BAC) standard of .10 as the legal measure of drunk driving. The NTSB the DOT have advocated a national reduction to .08, but the states have moved slowly on their recommendations.[17] Similarly, several states have considered installing ignition interlock systems with breath analysis devices in the automobiles of convicted drunken drivers, but have not employed them on a broad basis.[18]

Pedestrian Safety. In attempting to prevent highway accidents, the DOT also has focused attention on pedestrian safety and driver education. As shown in Table 16-1, pedestrian fatalities account for nearly 17 percent of all highway deaths. The DOT therefore has mounted a broad public information effort, particularly aimed at children, concerning matters such as proper usage of street crossings and bicycle operation. Federal outlays for driver education efforts also recognize that many accidents are the result of driver error. Therefore, these programs stress such factors as vehicle braking distances and proper signaling.

Vehicle Design. With the volume of traffic handled by the contemporary highway system, some accidents are inevitable. Consequently, the DOT also has devoted attention to accident survival. Extensive testing of vehicles and safety features is conducted by the agency. Major changes in construction standards for doors, roofs, and bumpers have been mandated by DOT in recent years. NHTSA has also issued guidelines regarding crash protection which include such features as sun visor padding, head restraints, strong seat anchors, and steering columns which collapse in a crash.

Seat Belt Use. During the late 1970s and early 1980s research clearly indicated that seat belts were effective in reducing highway deaths and injuries; however, many motorists did not use them. In fact, one DOT study showed that they were used only 20 percent of the time by front-seat occupants, and that more than 90 percent of those killed in automobile accidents were not wearing seat belts at the time of the crash.[19] Such statistics led the DOT to advocate mandatory seat belt use laws at the state level. That proposal was quite controversial. Strong opposition was voiced by those who believed that such laws constituted infringements on personal liberty. Nevertheless, by 1992 thirty-eight states and the District of Columbia had enacted mandatory seat belt usage laws.[20] Those laws have led to increased usage rates. NHTSA estimated the national usage rate to be 59 percent in 1991.[21] Increased usage has yielded impressive benefits. The NTSB estimated that of the more than 19,300 lives saved by seat belt use between 1984-1989, 14,200 resulted from mandatory use laws.[22]

Airbags and Other Passive Restraints. Because many automobile occupants traditionally failed to use active safety restraint systems (those which the individual activates, such as conventional seat belts), the DOT conducted extensive research into a variety of "passive" restraint systems. The two systems ultimately endorsed by the department were "airbags" and "automatic seat belts." Airbags are fabric cushions that automatically inflate upon impact to protect passengers. Automatic seat belts are similar to ordinary seat belt systems, but they automatically fasten around occupants when they enter the vehicle and close the doors.

Although Congress mandated inclusion of passive restraint systems in all new automobiles by 1977, disputes between the DOT and equipment manufacturers concerning system reliability led to a series of postponements. The department eventually ruled that every automobile sold in the United States was to have automatic crash protection (airbags or automatic seat belts) by model year 1984. But, in October 1981, the department rescinded that mandate. At that time, the DOT was being criticized widely for what appeared to be an extension of the deregulation philosophy into the area of safety. The agency's decision was challenged in the courts, and in June 1983 the Supreme Court ruled that the DOT had acted in an arbitrary and capricious manner and directed the department to reconsider the matter.[24]

In July 1984 Secretary of Transportation Elizabeth Dole announced the DOT's revised guidelines on passive restraints. According to those standards, beginning with the 1987 model year, a steadily increasing percentage of new automobiles were required to be equipped with airbags or automatic seat belts. Ten percent of 1987 models were required to be so equipped, and the percentage was scheduled to increase to 25, 40, and 100 for the 1988, 1989, and 1990 model years, respectively. While several manufacturers moved slowly in embracing the airbag and opted to include automatic seat belts in their models, consumers soon showed a preference for the airbag. As noted earlier in this chapter, the automobile manufacturers responded to this development by making airbags a focal point of automobile advertising. They also de-emphasized automatic seat belts and began to include airbags in more models. As a result, it has been estimated that by 1995 18 percent of all cars on the road will have airbags (up from 1.8 percent in 1990).[23] NHTSA has estimated that airbags will save approximately 2,400 lives between 1990 and 1995.[24] Research has also indicated that use of airbags in conjunction with lap and shoulder belts reduces the chance of fatal injury by 23 percent and severe injury by 68 percent.[25] To promote further safety improvements, Congress, in the 1991 Intermodal Surface Transportation Efficiency Act, specified that all new passenger automobiles would have to be equipped with driver and front passenger airbags by 1998. The legislation also required airbags in vans, pickups, and sport utility vehicles within the same time frame.

55 Miles Per Hour Speed Limit. In reaction to the 1973-74 oil embargo, Congress mandated a national 55-miles-per-hour speed limit and subsequently required state enforcement of that standard as a prerequisite for federal highway funding. While the initial purpose of that action was to promote energy conservation, many believe that the reduced speed limit has also contributed to safety improvements. Nevertheless, as the energy crisis subsequently lessened in intensity, many states sought to have speed limits increased on the Interstate highway system. After nearly a decade of debate, in 1987 the DOT permitted states to increase the speed limit to 65-miles-per-hour on rural sections of the Interstate. Thirty-eight states did so. Following those changes, the fatality rates on the highways with increased speed limits substantially surpassed those of highways which retained the lower speed limits.[26] As a result, the debate concerning appropriate speed limits continues.

Intelligent Highways and Vehicles. In its attempt to further improve highway safety, the DOT has focused increased attention on the highway system and its potential linkage to the drivers and vehicles using it. The agency has sought to promote development of "smart highways." Such highways would incorporate a variety of technologies and potentially include such features as a network of roadway sensors, vehicle-to-vehicle radar, electronic warning signs, microwave collision avoidance systems, "smart" traffic lights to regulate traffic flow, and satellite tracking of vehicles.[27] Research into these and related changes is being conducted under the Intelligent Vehicle Highway Systems (IVHS) program of the department. Between 1991-93 NHTSA spent approximately $17 million on IVHS projects.[28] While the payoff on many of these potential innovations is long-term, it appears quite likely that the benefits will be substantial.[29]

Aviation Safety.

The tremendous growth that has occurred in both commercial and general aviation during the past decade has led to growing national emphasis on aviation safety. Such concern for aviation safety is not new. Deteriorating airline safety conditions during the mid-1930s was one major reason for passage of the Civil Aeronautics Act of 1938.

Prior to 1966 the independent Federal Aviation Administration and the Civil Aeronautics Board were charged with promotion and regulation of air safety. When the DOT was established, the FAA became an operating administration of the department and was given control over all aspects of aviation safety except accident investigation, which was transferred to the National Transportation Safety Board. As a result, the FAA has become the dominant force in both promoting air safety and enforcing safety regulations.

FAA Activities. The FAA's involvement in air safety takes many forms. Its most significant task involves funding and operation of the national airway system. According to the FAA:

The Nation's airway system is managed by the close integration of the terminal air traffic control, enroute air traffic control, and flight service systems. The terminal and enroute systems provide for separation of aircraft, flow control (temporary limitation of traffic into congested airspace), navigation and approach guidance, and information service to airway users. The flight service system provides weather and other preflight information service and inflight information assistance, and accepts flight-related inputs from airmen.[30]

The FAA also funds airport expansion and safety improvements. Under existing funding programs, the FAA extends grants to airports for construction of runways and taxiways, lighting, approach aids, emergency vehicles, and many other safety-related improvements.

Responsibilities of the agency also include the testing and certification of airmen. As might be expected, quite rigid medical and skill standards are applied to such personnel. Airports that serve certified air carriers must themselves be certified by the FAA or they must discontinue such operations. This requirement is intended to ensure that those airports are equipped adequately to provide safe air transportation.

The FAA is also responsible for certification of new equipment before it is introduced into use, and the agency issues minimum performance standards for aircraft equipment. In recent years the FAA has issued new or updated standards on equipment such as altimeters, flight data recorders, distance-measuring equipment, and fire detectors. Safety rules and regulations are also administered by the FAA. Some matters receiving FAA attention have been development of standards requiring the use of nontoxic and nonflammable materials in aircraft passenger compartments, the establishment of improved operator training, and refinement of procedures for aircraft emergency evacuations.

Safety Performance and Problem Areas. The FAA activities outlined in the preceding discussion and the combined efforts of the commercial airlines and equipment manufacturers have led to a marked improvement in commercial aviation safety. Since the first comprehensive airline safety records were compiled in 1949, the domestic air carrier fatality rate has declined by more than 90 percent.[29]

However, there are several significant areas of concern in aviation safety. Predominant among these are concerns with the adequacy of the air traffic control system, the relationship between deregulation and airline safety, and the accident and fatality rates of regional airlines.

The illegal August 1981 strike by the Professional Air Traffic Controllers Organization (PATCO) against the federal government gave considerable visibility to the nation's air traffic control (ATC) system. It ultimately led to the dismissal of more than 11,000 controllers and the decertification of the union. As a result of the firings, the air traffic control system operated during the next several years with less than a full complement of controllers. Although temporary limits were placed on flight operations at major airports to ease the burden on the air traffic control system, critics argued that conditions were still unsafe. However, that contention was not validated by safety performance data. Nevertheless, the PATCO strike appeared to increase congressional interest in further automation of the air traffic control system. Congress responded with passage of an $11 billion air traffic control modernization bill, which was to bring state-of-the-art technology to the system.[31] While that legislation led to a decade of system improvements including a new landing-guidance system and computerized collision-avoidance warnings for pilots, there is still considerable concern that the system is dated and inadequate. The Air Transport Association has estimated that ATC delays cost airlines and their customers more than $3 billion per year.[32] That organization, which believes the system is antiquated, has called on Congress to substantially modernize and upgrade the ATC system.[33] The NTSB has also called for improvements in the ATC system.

During the debate that preceded passage of the Airline Deregulation Act of 1978, some opponents of the legislation asserted that increased competition would lead to a deterioration of commercial airline safety. They argued that intense price competition would cause marginal carriers to compromise maintenance standards. However, despite consumer concerns, in the 1978-93 period no evidence surfaced to substantiate those claims.[34] In fact, according to traditional measurements of airline safety performance, safety has actually improved since deregulation, particularly among major airlines.[35] This development is particularly interesting in view of the fact that the average age of the U.S. commercial aviation fleet (13 years) has increased substantially since economic deregulation.[36] The increasing age of the commercial fleet has led the FAA to tighten maintenance schedules and inspection procedures.

The safety performance of regional airlines continues to be a matter of public concern. Despite long-term improvements in their safety performance, regional airlines, shown as commuter and air taxi operators in Table 16-1, had their worst safety year in history in 1991. That year 145 people lost their lives in crashes involving regional airlines. Those crashes, which resulted from a number of causes including human error, wind-shear, and equipment failure, led to calls for tighter safety regulation of regional airlines.

While the FAA viewed general aviation as a major safety problem area for many years, that sector's safety performance has improved substantially in recent years. The number of general aviation fatalities declined by approximately 40 percent between 1980-91. Contributing to that improvement were FAA development of educational and training materials for private pilots, and establishment of more stringent crashworthiness standards for small planes. Also of importance was a significant increase in the number of pilots participating in professional training, both initially and on a recurring basis.[37]

FAA-Industry Interaction. The FAA's relationship with the commercial airlines has long been controversial. Critics have charged that the agency has been reluctant to require equipment modifications that involve substantial carrier costs. The intensity of these allegations has periodically increased following commercial crashes. Prior to several of those crashes the FAA had recommended, but not required, modification of equipment units that were directly implicated in the crashes.

The difficulty of the FAA's dual task of promoting the aviation industry and regulating airline safety should not be minimized. In some cases, these tasks seem to be in direct conflict. Such conflicts may exert a sizable public cost. In an industry that is changing as rapidly as commercial aviation, this dual role may be untenable. Congressional reconsideration of the basic mission of the FAA would seem to be appropriate.

Railroad Safety

Prior to creation of the DOT, several federal bodies, including the ICC, the Department of Commerce, and the Department of the Interior, were involved in railroad safety enforcement. When the DOT was established, its organization structure included the Federal Railroad Administration (FRA), which assumed federal control over railroad safety. The authority of the FRA subsequently was expanded with the passage of the Rail Safety Act of 1970, which gave the agency broader powers in matters such as establishment of track and equipment safety standards.

FRA safety programs are administered by its Bureau of Railroad Safety. The primary programs enforced by the bureau are locomotive inspection, equipment inspection, and investigation of accidents. Other safety-related activities of the FRA include development of track and equipment standards, development of operating procedures, and investigation of complaints. The agency also conducts extensive research into railroad safety matters.

The National Transportation Safety Board has primary responsibility for railroad accident investigation. It investigates approximately 100 railroad accidents each year.[38]

The railroad industry has compiled an excellent safety record. In fact, 1992 was safest year in modern railroad history. The 4,900 accidents, 575 deaths, and 1,969 injuries were the lowest figures ever recorded.[39]

Throughout the years the industry's most significant safety problem has been related to grade crossing accidents. However, between 1982-92 the number of grade crossing accidents fell by 42 percent. Contributing to that improvement were Operation Lifesaver and the Federal Crossing Improvement Program. The former involves public information, driver education and traffic law enforcement initiatives; the latter, dedicated funding which was renewed in the Intermodal Surface Transportation Efficiency Act of 1991.[40]

The industry's performance with respect to freight train derailment has also improved. This is clearly related to upgraded track conditions which have been fostered by improved railroad earnings, and federal grants, loans, and loan guarantees provided under several programs to improve track conditions.

Oil Pipeline and Waterway Safety

Promotion of safety in both commercial and recreational boating is the responsibility of the U.S. Coast Guard, which is a component of the Department of Transportation. The safety-related activities of the Coast Guard are quite varied.

Under the provisions of the Boat Safety Act of 1971, the agency was empowered to regulate the design, manufacture, and use of boats. Subsequently, the agency has played a major role in this area. This has been true particularly with respect to development of construction standards aimed at preventing the swamping or capsizing of small boats. That statute also provided the Coast Guard with authority to extend grants to public and private interests to promote boating safety.

Coast Guard involvement in boating safety also increased with passage of the 1972 Port and Waterway Safety Act. The provisions of the act have led to Coast Guard establishment of vessel traffic systems for areas of heavy marine-traffic concentration and have also promoted improvements of navigational aids for the waterway system.

Other Coast Guard safety activities include search and rescue efforts, certification of marine vessels, vessel inspection through its marine inspection units, and training of state and local law enforcement officers. Responsibility for investigation of serious marine accidents rests with the National Transportation Safety Board.

The Department of Transportation's Office of Pipeline Safety maintains regulatory responsibilities over liquid pipeline systems operated by carriers engaged in interstate commerce. Although this mode handles no passengers and poses little direct threat to human life, the hazardous nature of many of the commodities handled poses an indirect threat. Nevertheless, the oil pipeline industry has compiled an outstanding safety record.

Congress has granted the DOT broad powers in regulating pipeline safety. The Office of Pipeline Safety has been given authority to develop standards for design, construction, operation, and maintenance of pipeline systems. Additional activities of the office have included pipeline inspection, the issuance of periodic information bulletins, and the offering of safety seminars for state and local regulatory officials.

HAZARDOUS MATERIALS TRANSPORTATION

The movement and handling of hazardous materials (HAZMAT) has attracted substantial attention during the past two decades. This attention is justified in view of the volume of hazardous materials which moves. About four billion tons of regulated hazardous materials are shipped each year, with more than 250,000 shipments of such materials moving in the U.S. transportation network each day.[41]

The DOT's modal administrations, the agency's Research and Special Programs Administration, and state government units share responsibility for regulation, inspection, and enforcement of hazardous materials handling guidelines. Those agencies have combined to develop an extensive set of guidelines for classification of hazardous materials, handling and marking of those materials, documentation, and reporting of spills and packaging. The Hazardous Materials Transportation Uniform Safety Act of 1990 established new training guidelines for all employees who handle hazardous materials transportation as part of their jobs.[42] The legislation gave companies until October 1993 to have all employees trained according to those guidelines.

Federal and state agencies involved in HAZMAT regulation have also been granted power to enforce those regulations, and the agencies have been very aggressive in using those powers. For example, during 1991 the Federal Aviation Administration fined air cargo shippers and carriers a record $937,000 for HAZMAT violations. That marked approximately a fourfold increase in fines over the previous year.[43]

Such stringent regulation of the handling and transportation of hazardous materials is not only important in promoting personal safety, but also in preventing environmental degradation. That issue is discussed extensively in Chapter 17.

ALCOHOL AND DRUG TESTING FOR TRANSPORTATION WORKERS

In response to several major transportation accidents involving drug or alcohol-impaired operators the Department of Transportation has moved aggressively to institute broad drug and alcohol testing programs in the several modes of carriage. These rules, which have withstood numerous court challenges on the basis of alleged infringement of privacy rights, require employers to conduct pre-employment, random, reasonable-suspicion, post-accident, return-to-duty, and follow-up tests.[44] While debate continues concerning the frequency and timing of such testing, opinion polls indicate that the public supports worker testing.[45] Gradual refinement of testing policies and procedures should enhance the safety performance of the national transportation system.

SUMMARY

While the national transportation system produces enormous societal benefits, it also poses a threat to the safety of the general public. Many steps have been to minimize safety hazards, and the safety performance of the national transportation system has improved significantly. However, safety controls are generally quite expensive. Therefore, government and the general public must carefully weigh the costs and potential benefits of policy alternatives. Such calculations are rather complex, not only because of the number of variables included in the analysis, but also because it is difficult to quantify many safety considerations.

Significant strides have been taken in recent years to improve transportation safety. However, there is much room for improvement, which can only be accomplished through the active cooperation of government, equipment manufacturers, carriers, union, employees, and the general public.

DISCUSSION QUESTIONS

1. Discuss the interaction between federal and state government units in promoting highway safety.
2. Has the movement toward transportation deregulation adversely affected the safety performance of the national transportation system?
3. Discuss the role of carrier employees in promoting transportation safety.
4. Should automobile seat belt use be mandatory? Explain your reasoning.
5. Do you support random alcohol and drug testing of transportation industry employees? Explain your reasoning.

NOTES

1. Eno Transportation Foundation, Inc., *Transportation in America*, 11th ed., December supplement (Lansdowne, VA: the Foundation, 1993, p. 75.
2. Ibid.
3. Lori Sharn and James R. Healey, "Cost of Vehicle Crashes Staggering," *USA Today*, October 9-11, 1992, 1A.
4. U.S. National Transportation Safety Board, *Annual Report to Congress, 1991* (Washington, D.C.: the Board, 1992), p. 13.

5.   Ibid., pp. 14-15.
6.   For a discussion of the steps taken by the FAA to lessen this hazard see U.S. Department of Transportation, *Eighth Annual Report* (Washington, D.C.: U.S. Government Printing Office, 1975), p. 21.
7.   Eno Transportation Foundation, p. 75.
8.   Ibid; also, Betsy A. Lehman, "Fatalities Down But Speed Still Kills," *The Boston Globe*, August 9, 1993, pp. 25, 29.
9.   U.S. Congress, House, *Message from the President of the United States Transmitting a Proposal for a Cabinet-Level Department of Transportation Consolidating Various Existing Transportation Agencies*, House Doc. 399, 89th Cong., 2nd Sess., p. 54. (Updated)
10.   Ibid.
11.   "Traffic Deaths Fall to A 31-Year Low," *The Boston Globe*, August 12, 1993, p. 1.
12.   Lehman, p. 29.
13.   James H. Rubin, "Curfew Is Urged to Limit Youth Drinking and Driving," *The Boston Globe*, March 31, 1993, p. 3.
14.   "Drunk Drivers Turn to the Bar," *Time* (January 16, 1984), p. 62.
15.   "Drunken-Driving Arrests," *USA Today*, April 26, 1990, p. 1A.
16.   "92 Fatalities Projected to be Record Low," *MADD In Action*, Vol. 12, No. 1 (Winter, 1993), p. 1; also, "Georgia Activist Hired As Public Policy Director," *MADD In Action*, Vol. 12, No. 1 (Winter, 1993), p. 2.
17.   "DOT Study Recommends States Adopt .08 Blood Alcohol Level," *MADD In Action*, Vol. 12, No. 1 (Winter, 1993), p. 4.
18.   Peter J. Howe, "Weld Kills Drunk Driver Bill," *The Boston Globe*, January 8, 1993, p. 1.
19.   U.S. Department of Transportation, *Eleventh Annual Report* (Washington, D.C.: U.S. Government Printing Office, 1978), p. 39.
20.   National Transportation Safety Board, p. 61.
21.   Data supplied by the National Highway Traffic Safety Administration, 1993.
22.   National Transportation Safety Board, p. 61.
23.   "How Many Lives Have Airbags Saved?" *Parade Magazine* (June 20, 1993), p. 10.
24.   Ibid.
25.   Ibid.
26.   Lehman, p. 29.
27.   "Safety First," a special advertising section, *Business Week* (November 2, 1992), pp. 37-8.
28.   Ibid.

29. U.S. Department of Transportation, *Moving America: New Directions, New Opportunities-A Statement of National Transportation Policy, Strategies for Action* (Washington, D.C: the Department, 1990), p. 84.

30. U.S. Department of Transportation, *1974 National Transportation Report* (Washington, D.C.: U.S. Government Printing Office, 1974), p. 316.

31. "Can We Keep The Skies Safe?" *Newsweek* (January 30, 1984), p. 31.

32. Air Transport Association, *1993 State of the U.S. Airline Industry* (Washington, D.C.: the Association, 1993), p. 11.

33. Ibid.

34. John Greenwald, "Tarnished Wings," *Time* (March 13, 1989), p. 40. In a Time/CNN survey cited in the article nearly two-thirds of respondents believe that commercial airplanes were less safe than they had been five years earlier.

35. Eno Transportation Foundation, p. 75; also, Steven A. Morrison and Clifford Winston, "Cleared for Takeoff: The Evolution of the Deregulated Airline Industry," *The Annual Review of Travel*, 1992 ed. (New York: American Express, 1992), p. 85.

36. Greenwald, p. 40.

37. "U.S. Says Air Crashes Dipped," *New York Times*, January 19, 1991, p.

38. National Transportation Safety Board, p. 85.

39. William DiBenedetto, "Rail, Highway Safety Improved Last Year, House Panels Told," *Journal of Commerce*, New York, May 6, 1993, p. 3B.

40. "Crossing Accidents Continue to Decline," *Railway Age* (December, 1992), p. 15.

41. National Transportation Safety Board, p. 101.

42. Mitchell E. MacDonald, "Will You Meet the Hazmat Training Deadline?" *Traffic Management* (December, 1992), pp. 32-4.

43. Tony Seideman, "Crackdown Yields Fourfold Increase in Hazardous Air Shipment Fines," *Journal of Commerce*, New York, March 26, 1992, p. 1A.

44. See "Here Come the Specimen Jars," *Time* (January 29, 1990), p. 60; also, "Safe and Sober," *Traffic World* (December 21, 1992), p. 4.

45. "Here Come the Specimen Jars," p. 60.

SELECTED REFERENCES

Andel, Tom. "Are Your Hazmat People Trained? Prove It! "*Transportation and Distribution* (October, 1992), pp. 28-30.

Best, Annie. "Lack of Hazmat Training Could Prove Costly."*Air Commerce*. New York, June 26, 1993, pp. 7, 13.

Browning, Lisa M. and Jonathan M. Korn. "Spot Your Hazmat Training Problems." *Transportation and Distribution* (June, 1993), pp. 26-9.

Bruning, Edward R. "The Relationship Between Profitability and Safety Performance in Trucking Firms." *Transportation Journal*, Vol. 28, No. 3 (Spring, 1989), pp. 40-9.

Helmick, John S. and Nicholas A. Glaskowsky Jr. "State and Federal Regulation of Pilots, Piloting, and Pilotage: A Study in Contrasts and Conflict." *Transportation Journal*, Vol. 31, No. 4 (Summer, 1992), pp. 47-59.

Henriksson, Lennart E. "Meeting the Challenges of Alcohol and Other Drug Abuse: Advice for Transportation Managers."*Transportation Journal*, Vol. 32, No. 2 (Winter, 1992), pp. 33-7.

MacDonald, Mitchell E. "Will You Meet the Hazmat Training Deadline?" *Traffic Management* (December, 1992), pp. 32-4.

Oster, Clinton V.,Jr. and John S. Strong. "Risk Tiers and Safety Mismatches in International Aviation." *Journal of the Transportation Research Forum*, Vol. 32, No. 1 (1991), pp. 73-85.

Reagan, Frank. "Drivers and Drugs: An Industry Responds."*Inbound Logistics* (December, 1991), pp. 20-3. "Safety First." A special advertising section, *Business Week* (November 2, 1992), 43 pp.

Sharp, Jeffrey M., Novack, Robert A., and Michael A. Anderson. "Purchasing Hazardous Waste Transportation Service: Federal Legal Considerations." *Transportation Journal*, Vol. 31, No. 2 (Winte, 1991), pp. 4-14. *Transportation Deregulation and Safety*. Summary reports on a conference. Evanston, IL: Northwestern University, Transportation Center, 1987), 54 pp. U.S. National Transportation Safety Board. *Annual Report to Congress, 1991*. Washington, D.C.: the Board, 1992.

CHAPTER SEVENTEEN

ENERGY AND ENVIRONMENTAL ISSUES IN TRANSPORTATION

With less than 6 percent of the world's population, the United States annually accounts for approximately 30 percent of the world's energy consumption.[1] Until the early 1970s, the country benefited from seemingly endless supplies of relatively low-cost energy. In fact, prior to the 1973-74 Arab oil embargo, U.S. gasoline prices had been declining in real terms for many years.[2] That embargo abruptly exposed us to the realities of soaring energy prices, dwindling supplies of gasoline and heating oil, and long lines at service stations.

In the years immediately following that embargo, the public was bombarded by various appeals for energy conservation and promotion of national energy self-sufficiency. Government officials, the general public, carriers, and vehicle manufacturers became sensitized to the significance of the transportation/energy interface. Development of that sensitivity was long overdue. In subsequent years considerable energy-related legislation has been enacted, but many question the adequacy of those legislative steps. Oil imports still represent the largest component of our nation's trade imbalance. Forty-four billion of the nation's $66 billion trade deficit in 1991 was attributable to oil imports.[3]

We have also witnessed growing concerns about other environmental issues linked to transportation. Transportation activities clearly impact on such environmental issues as air quality in our cities, the noise levels which surround us, and our water resources. The 1989 Exxon Valdez disaster clearly illustrated these linkages.

This chapter focuses on the significance of energy and environmental issues in transportation. Attention is given to the impact of energy and environmental problems on carriers and other users of the national transportation system. The actions of public policy makers and vehicle manufacturers are also explored.

TRANSPORTATION AS AN ENERGY CONSUMER

As shown in Table 17-1, transportation as an end-use sector accounts for more than 27 percent of total U.S. consumption of energy resources. Only the electric utility sector accounts for a greater percentage of total energy usage. While the transportation sector's energy consumption has increased steadily in absolute terms since 1950, its percentage of total energy consumption has remained in the 23-28 percent range.

Table 17-2 specifies transportation's consumption of various energy resources. Its consumption of petroleum products, as measured in barrels of petroleum, remained relatively stable between 1987-1991, despite national increases in passenger and freight movements. This reflects the steady introduction of more fuel efficient vehicles into the marketplace. Nevertheless, transportation still accounts for more than 65 percent of national consumption of refined petroleum products.[4] That percentage expanded from 55.6 percent in 1980 to 65.4 percent in 1991.[5] The modal share of annual petroleum consumption is approximately as follows: highway modes, 81 percent; water carriage, 6 percent; rail, 2 percent, and air carriage, 10 percent.[6]

RELATIVE MODAL ENERGY EFFICIENCY

Recent years have witnessed continuing interest in determining the relative fuel efficiencies of the various modes. Clarification of such efficiencies could be of importance to public policy makers in assessing possible actions to improve modal fuel efficiency or to channel traffic to more fuel-efficient modes through regulatory or promotional steps. Of course, there could be considerable debate concerning whether such actions are appropriate for government agencies. This is particularly true in view of the movement toward less government intervention and greater reliance upon market forces in the economy of the United States.

Numerous studies have attempted to evaluate the several modes in terms of energy consumption per various output units. Such research has been hindered somewhat because of the many factors that can affect the fuel-efficiency pattern of a particular mode. Among those are the following:

1. technological characteristics of the mode and related fuel consumption patterns
2. operating conditions under which the mode functions (topography, trip length, operating speed, etc.)
3. passenger or freight-carrying capacity of the vehicle involved

TABLE 17-1

Consumption of Energy by End-Use Sector (Quadrillion BTU), 1955-1991

Year	Residential and Commercial[1]	% of Total	Industrial[1]	% of Total	Transportation[1]	% of Total	Electric Utilities	% of Total	Total Energy Consumption
1955	7.39	19.0	15.42	39.7	9.48	24.4	6.50	16.7	38.82
1960	8.75	20.0	16.26	37.1	10.56	24.1	8.19	18.7	43.80
1965	10.00	19.0	19.24	36.5	12.40	23.5	11.01	20.9	52.68
1970	12.14	18.3	21.92	33.0	16.06	24.2	16.27	24.5	66.43
1971	12.35	18.2	21.66	31.9	16.69	24.6	17.15	25.3	67.89
1972	12.64	17.8	22.39	31.4	17.68	24.8	18.52	26.0	71.26
1973	12.27	16.5	23.54	31.7	18.58	25.0	19.85	26.7	74.28
1974	11.77	16.2	22.62	31.2	18.09	24.9	20.02	27.6	72.54
1975	11.60	16.5	20.36	28.9	18.21	25.8	20.35	28.9	70.55
1976	12.25	16.5	21.44	28.8	19.07	25.6	21.57	29.0	74.36
1977	11.87	15.6	21.88	28.7	19.78	25.9	22.71	30.1	76.29
1978	11.91	15.3	21.84	28.0	20.58	26.4	23.72	30.4	78.09
1979	11.53	14.6	22.77	28.9	20.44	25.9	24.13	30.6	78.90
1980	10.72	14.1	21.04	27.7	19.66	25.9	24.51	32.3	75.96
1981	10.04	13.6	19.68	26.6	19.47	26.3	24.76	33.5	73.99
1982	10.06	14.2	17.45	24.6	19.03	26.9	24.27	34.3	70.85
1983	9.72	13.8	16.72	23.7	19.10	27.1	24.96	35.4	70.52
1984	10.04	13.5	18.29	24.7	19.76	26.7	25.98	35.1	74.10
1985	9.78	13.2	17.63	23.8	20.02	27.1	26.48	35.8	73.95
1986	9.56	12.9	17.24	23.2	20.77	28.0	26.64	35.9	74.24
1987	9.71	12.6	18.15	23.6	21.40	27.8	27.55	35.9	76.84
1988	10.29	12.8	18.99	23.7	22.26	27.8	28.63	35.7	80.20
1989	10.41	12.8	19.10	23.5	22.51	27.7	29.29	36.0	81.35
1990r	9.62	11.8	19.55	24.0	22.48	27.7	29.60	36.4	81.29
1991	9.90	12.1r	19.43	23.8	22.24	27.3	29.90	36.7	81.51

r = revised.
[1] Includes only those fossil fuels consumed directly in the sector.
Note: Sum of components may not equal total due to independent rounding.

SOURCE: U.S. Department of Transportation, Research and Special Programs Administration, *National Transportation Statistics* (Washington, D.C.: U.S. Government Printing Office, 1992), p. 112.

TABLE 17-2

U.S. Energy Consumption by the Transportation Sector, 1955-1991

Year	Petroleum Million Barrels	Petroleum Trillion[4] Btu	Natural Gas[1] Trillion Cubic Feet	Natural Gas[1] Trillion[4] Btu	Total Fossil Fuels[2] Trillion Btu	Sales of Electricity[3] Million Kilowatt-Hours	Sales of Electricity[3] Trillion[4] Btu	Total Transportation Consumption Trillion[5] Btu	Total Transportation Consumption % of Total Gross Energy Consumption	Total Gross Energy Consumption Quadrillion Btu
1955	1,627.9	8,804	0.25	259	9,063	4,563	15.6	9,079	23.4	38.82
1960	1,881.2	10,136	0.35	362	10,498	4,770	16.3	10,514	24.0	43.80
1965	2,204.6	11,876	0.50	516	12,392	4,652	15.9	12,408	23.6	52.68
1970	2,839.7	15,315	0.72	742	16,057	4,633	15.8	16,073	24.3	66.43
1971	2,952.9	15,913	0.74	763	16,676	4,537	15.5	16,692	24.6	67.89
1972	3,136.6	16,900	0.77	791	17,691	4,440	15.1	17,706	24.8	71.26
1973	3,305.0	17,831	0.73	745	18,576	4,186	14.3	18,590	25.0	74.28
1974	3,225.6	17,399	0.67	686	18,085	4,258	14.5	18,100	25.0	72.54
1975	3,266.7	17,614	0.58	592	18,206	4,273	14.6	18,221	25.8	70.55
1976	3,430.2	18,506	0.55	560	19,066	4,338	14.8	19,081	25.7	74.36
1977	3,563.1	19,241	0.53	540	19,781	4,212	14.4	19,795	25.9	76.29
1978	3,708.5	20,041	0.53	538	20,579	4,336	14.8	20,594	26.4	78.09
1979	3,652.3	19,825	0.60	611	20,436	4,256	14.5	20,451	25.9	78.90
1980	3,494.1	19,008	0.63	645	19,653	4,275	14.6	19,668	25.9	75.96
1981	3,463.0	18,811	0.64	657	19,468	4,206	14.4	19,482	26.3	73.99
1982	3,397.0	18,420	0.60	616	19,036	4,288	14.6	19,051	26.9	70.85
1983	3,433.6	18,593	0.49	505	19,098	4,300	14.7	19,113	27.1	70.52
1984	3,544.1	19,216	0.53	546	19,762	4,483	15.3	19,777	26.7	74.10
1985	3,596.5	19,504	0.50	516	20,020	4,704	16.1	20,036	27.1	73.95
1986	3,734.8	20,269	0.49	504	20,773	4,714	16.1	20,789	28.0	74.24
1987	3,842.9	20,867	0.52	536	21,403	4,878	16.6	21,420	27.9	76.85
1988	3,979.4	21,624	0.61	628	22,252	5,110	17.4	22,269	27.8	80.20
1989r	4,018.6	21,861	0.63	649	22,510	5,294	17.7	22,528	27.7	81.35
1990	4,004.4	21,804	0.66	680	22,484	5,297	18.1	22,502	27.7	81.27
1991p	3,936.2	21,413	0.80	825	22,238	5,398	18.4	22,256	27.3	81.50

r = revised.
p = preliminary.
[1] Pipeline fuel. [2] Sum of Petroleum and Natural Gas. [3] Includes only energy used by Railroads and Railways. [4] Btu's derived by multiplying by conversion factors in Table A3 for Petroleum in Transportation, Table A4 for Natural Gas Consumption by Non-Utility, and Table A7 for Electricity Consumption, U.S. DOE/EIA, *Monthly Energy Review*, April 1992. [5] Sum of Total Fossil Fuels and Sales of Electricity.

SOURCE: U.S. Department of Transportation, Research and Special Programs, *National Transportation Statistics* (Washington, D.C.: U.S. Government Printing Office, 1992, p. 113.

4.   demand pattern for the service—strongly influenced by the options available to potential users

5.   load factor realized (percentage of cargo or passenger carrying capacity which is utilized)

6.   time period examined.

Consequently, many assumptions must be made in conducting such research, and this contributes to the difficulty in comparing research findings. Not surprisingly, there have been many studies of the topic but no consensus has emerged. Clearly, it is beyond the scope of this book to address the intricacies of such a complex research topic. However, Table 17-3 contains a DOT summary of estimated fuel efficiencies of the passenger modes. In terms of the freight modes, the DOT has estimated that the railroads consumed 418 BTUs to move a ton-mile in 1990. That represented an improvement of nearly 30 percent between 1980-1990.[7] DOT estimates of the relative fuel efficiencies of the other freight modes were not available; however, one source has estimated that the railroads produce 2.5 times the ton-miles generated by trucks per gallon of fuel.[8]

TABLE 17-3
Relative Fuel Efficiencies, Passenger Modes, 1990

Mode	*British Thermal Unit (BTU) per Passenger Mile*
Class I Intercity Bus	994
Motorcycles	1,821
Amtrak	2,071
Passenger Automobiles	3,688
Local Transit Bus	3,729
Certified Air Carriers	5,049
General Aviation	10,726

SOURCE: U.S. Department of Transportation, Research and Special Programs Administration, *National Transportation Statistics* (Washington, D.C.: U.S. Government Printing Office, 1992), pp. 130-6.

As implied earlier, caution must be used in interpreting such data. The data are quite aggregate in nature and are not market specific. Further, they are based on many limiting assumptions. Extensive work must be done in refining not only the energy data base, but also the methodological approaches to measuring relative modal fuel efficiencies. Given such refinements, the results might be used effectively as guidelines for public policy development.

ENERGY PROBLEMS: IMPACTS AND RESPONSES

Fuel consumption patterns and conservation possibilities differ substantially across the modes. Further, changing fuel prices and periodic shortages impact differently on the several modes. Such differences have fostered varying responses to transportation/energy problems from legislators, regulators, carriers, other users, and vehicle manufacturers. The following discussion examines these impacts and responses related to the automobile, intercity rail and bus operations, trucking, and air carriage.

The Automobile

The automobile dominates short-haul passenger movements and accounts for 81 percent of intercity passenger miles. It is also the nation's largest consumer of petroleum products, accounting for nearly 45 percent of the total.[9] Automobiles have become an integral component of America's lifestyle, but the mobility they offer is costly. Automobile-oriented expenses account for approximately 13 percent of consumers' annual disposable income.[10]

The number of automobiles registered in the United States grew steadily between 1980-1991 as did automobile miles traveled. Average miles traveled per gallon also increased significantly (See Table 17-4). That gain reflects the improved fuel efficiency of new automobiles entering the national automotive fleet. This matter is discussed more extensively later in this chapter.

Despite efficiency improvements, the automobile, due to the magnitude of its continuing energy requirements, will continue to be viewed as the major area for potential energy conservation in transportation.

Congressional Actions. Congress has taken a number of steps to promote improved automobile fuel efficiency. Reacting to the 1973-74 oil embargo, Congress mandated a national 55-miles-per-hour speed limit and subsequently required state enforcement of that standard as a prerequisite for federal highway funding. Another significant policy directive was included in the Energy Policy and Conservation Act of 1975.[11] The statute stipulated that the new passenger car fleet of each manufacturer was to meet an average fuel economy standard of 18 miles per gallon (mpg) by 1978, and that standard was to increase incrementally in subsequent model years. Table 17-4 examines the progress which has been made in improving new automobile fuel efficiency. Federal legislation has mandated continuing increases in the Corporate Average Fuel Economy (CAFE)

TABLE 17-4

Average Fuel Efficiency of U.S. Passenger Cars, 1955-1992

Year	Average U.S. Passenger Car Fuel Efficiency, (mpg) (Calendar Year Basis)	New Car Fuel Efficiency, (mpg)[1] (Model Year Basis)	
		Domestic Cars	Domestic and Imported Cars
1955	14.53	16.0	16.1
1960	14.28	15.5	16.1
1965	14.27	15.4	15.9
1970	13.52	14.1	15.2
1971	13.54	13.7	14.7
1972	13.40	13.6	14.4
1973	13.30	13.3	14.2
1974	13.42	12.8	13.7
1975	13.52	15.1	16.2
1976	13.53	16.5	17.4
1977	13.80	17.6	18.8
1978	14.04	18.7	19.9
1979	14.41	19.3	20.3
1980	15.46	22.6	24.3
1981	15.94	24.2	25.9
1982	16.65	25.0	26.6
1983	17.14	24.4	26.4
1984	17.83	25.5	26.9
1985	18.20	26.3	27.6
1986	18.27	26.9	28.2
1987	19.20	27.0	28.5
1988	19.87	27.4	28.8
1989	20.31	27.2	28.4
1990	20.92	26.9	28.0
1991	n/a	27.4	28.3
1992	n/a	26.9	27.8

n/a   = not available.
[1]   55% city, 45% highway miles sales weighted harmonic average.

SOURCE: U.S. Department of Transportation, Research and Special Programs Administration, *National Transportation Statistics* (Washington, D.C.: U.S. Government Printing Office, 1992), p. 127.

standard for automobile manufacturers, and by 1993 the standard was 27.5 mpg. The Clinton administration has called for CAFE standards of 40-45 mpg.[12]

Several other legislative initiatives have addressed automotive fuel issues. These include the Alternative Motor Fuels Act of 1988, the Clean Air Act of 1990, the Intermodal Surface Transportation Efficiency Act of 1991, and the Comprehensive National Energy Policy Act of 1992. These legislative initiatives have sought to increase the use of alternative fuels by automobiles not only to reduce petroleum consumption in transportation, but also to improve air quality. The air quality provisions of these statutes are examined later in this chapter.

Congress has also attempted to make for-hire passenger modes look more attractive as a means of reducing national reliance upon the automobile. Chapters 3 and 4 discussed the specific steps taken by Congress to revitalize Amtrak and intercity bus passenger services; efforts to improve and expand urban mass transportation systems are examined in Chapters 18 and 19.

Additionally, Congress has given attention not only to the potential use of negative incentives, such as further increases in gasoline excise taxes to restrict demand, but also to the need for development of standby gasoline rationing programs for use during emergency periods. While several increases in gasoline excise taxes have been legislated during the past decade, those increases have not been viewed as efforts to restrict demand. Rather, they have been used as a means of either increasing funds available for highway and transit improvement, or reducing the budget deficit. The most recent of those increases was the 4.3 cent per gallon increase included in President Clinton's budget proposal which was approved by Congress in August 1993. That increase took effect in October 1993 and the proceeds are being used to reduce the federal deficit.[13]

As shown in Table 17-5, despite the increases in highway use taxes, by 1991 the average retail prices of highway fuels were well below their highest levels in the 1980s. Further, fuel prices increased much more slowly than the prices of other consumer goods and services between 1980 and 1991.[14]

Other Governmental Efforts. The Department of Transportation, the Department of Energy (DOE), and the Environmental Protection Agency (EPA) have initiated numerous programs to reduce automotive energy consumption. One collaborative effort involving the DOT and DOE seeks to promote greater fuel efficiency in the use of the existing national automobile fleet. It promotes improvements in such areas as vehicle maintenance, vehicle diagnostics, inspection procedures and driver education. The DOT has also played an important role in distributing related research findings to the media, community groups, automobile manufacturers, and schools. To conserve energy, the department also promoted national acceptance of the right-turn-on-red-signal rule, which has reduced highway vehicle idling time.

The Department of Energy has become increasingly involved in automobile-related programs in its efforts to foster transportation conservation. Its Electric And Hybrid Vehicle Research and Development Program includes research, development, and demonstration of current and advanced vehicles and provides incentives to users and manufacturers of propulsion systems and vehicles. DOE's Vehicle Propulsion Technology Research and Development Program, which places special emphasis on the automobile, seeks to promote fuel efficiency through development of alternative propulsion systems. Further, its

TABLE 17-5

Average Retail Price of Transportation Fuel, 1980-1991

(cents per gallon)

| Year | Aviation Fuels | | Highway Fuels | | | | Railroad Fuel |
	Aviation Gasoline	Jet Fuel Kerosene	Motor Gasoline Leaded Regular	Motor Gasoline Unleaded Premium	Motor Gasoline Unleaded Regular	Truck No. 2 Diesel	Diesel
1980	108.4	86.8	119.1	128.1	124.5	81.8	83.0
1981	130.3	102.4	131.1	147.0	137.8	99.5	100.2
1982	131.2	96.3	122.2	141.5	129.6	94.2	95.4
1983	125.5	87.8	115.7	138.3	124.1	82.6	83.1
1984	123.4	84.2	112.9	136.6	121.2	82.3	82.6
1985	120.1	79.6	111.5	134.0	120.2	78.9	78.3
1986	101.1	52.9	85.7	108.5	92.7	47.8	49.2
1987	90.7	54.3	89.7	109.3	94.8	55.1	53.8
1988	89.1	51.3	89.9	110.7	94.6	50.0	49.2
1989	99.5	59.2	99.8	119.7	102.1	58.5	56.3
1990	112.0	76.6	114.9	134.9	116.4	72.5	69.2
1991	104.7	65.3	n/a	132.1	114.0	64.8	n/a

n/a = not available.

SOURCE: U.S. Department of Transportation, Research and Special Programs Administration, *National Transportation Statistics* (Washington, D.C.: U.S. Government Printing Office, 1992), p. 124.

Alternative Fuels Utilization Program is concerned with reducing and eventually replacing highway vehicle dependence upon petroleum products. The agency sought $464 million from Congress to support transportation conservation research during FY 1993.[15] While the DOE's efforts have promoted important developments related to the use of electricity and solar energy to power automobiles, in the short-term neither technology appears to have broad market applicability.

Automobile Manufacturer Actions. Faced not only with federal mandates to improve fuel efficiency, but also with intense competition from foreign producers, U.S. automobile manufacturers have endeavored to improve fuel efficiency through a variety of changes. These have included the following:

1.   vehicle weight reductions
2.   engine improvements and alternative engines
3.   improved transmissions
4.   other technological advances, such as better aerodynamics
5.   cutting back on production of models with poor fuel economy
6.   reduced acceleration performance.

Given federal guidelines, U.S. auto makers have placed greater emphasis in new model lines on lighter weight, smaller, more fuel-efficient vehicles. As discussed earlier in this chapter, their progress in such efforts has been impressive. American manufacturers also participate in several joint ventures with foreign producers, which in some cases have enabled them to add foreign-produced compact and subcompact automobiles to their product lines with little lead time and reduced capital requirements.

While these and related developments have promoted energy conservation, they also have raised serious questions concerning the crash-worthiness of smaller automobiles. As might be expected, federal research has indicated that passengers in smaller automobiles are considerably more vulnerable to serious injury or death in case of an accident than are passengers in larger automobiles. However, as indicated in Chapter 16, improvements in vehicle design, the introduction of airbags and other safety equipment, and tougher drunk driving laws have combined to lower fatality rates even as automobiles have become smaller.

Trucks and Buses

Trucks and buses account for approximately 36 percent of petroleum consumption by transportation.[16] Consequently, as energy concerns have mounted, the role of trucks and buses in both intercity and local markets has come under increasing government scrutiny. As previously shown in Table 17-5, for-hire carriers have experienced rather wide swings in diesel fuel prices during the past decade, and they have also been exposed to periodic fuel shortages.

Carrier Actions. The responses of for-hire motor carriers of freight and passengers to energy problems have been quite varied. They have included not only internal fleet management efforts, but also participation in cooperative programs with the federal government, and lobbying efforts directed at various federal agencies.

Among the internal steps taken by many carriers have been closer monitoring of tire pressure, filter change intervals, alignment requirements, and tune-up schedules. Many carriers have also participated in voluntary programs sponsored by the DOT, DOE and the EPA. These programs which have attracted the participation of motor carriers, vehicle and engine manufacturers, trade associations, and labor groups, have fostered numerous improvements including:

1.   reduced aerodynamic drag through use of wind deflectors and other devices
2.   reduced rolling resistance by a change to radial tires
3.   modification of the power train and reduction of the demand for horsepower
4.   improved driving practices, such as shutting off the engine instead of idling
5.   more efficient dispatching, freight loading, and routing, especially in urban areas
6.   speed controls by use of governors and/or driver motivation efforts.[17]

Acting individually a number of motor carriers have established programs to increase fuel efficiency and/or use alternative fuels. For example, many truckers have installed on-board computers to establish the relationship between operating speeds and fuel consumption. In another interesting application, United Parcel Service has experimented with the use of compressed natural gas in some pickup and delivery vehicles in Washington, D.C. and New York City. The company claims that the fuel emits substantially less pollutants than gasoline and that the performance of vehicles powered by the alternative fuel has not been significantly different than those vehicles using gasoline.[18] Daily maintenance costs of the experimental fleet have actually been lower than those of the company's gasoline powered vehicles.[19] Roadway Express has also begun experimentation with a number of super-cooled, liquid natural gas pickup and delivery vehicles.[20]

Government Actions. The cooperative and individual efforts of the DOT, DOE and EPA in promoting improved fuel efficiency in the highway modes have already been discussed. The research efforts of those agencies continue to yield valuable insights into truck and bus fuel economy.

Congress has continued to enact energy legislation which impacts on the trucking and bus industries. One of the most important of those legislative initiatives was contained in the Clean Air Act of 1990. The statute mandated that beginning in model year 1998 half of all new trucks operating in urban areas that have been designated as having severe air-quality problems must be powered by an alternative fuel. Trucks with gross vehicle weights between 8,501 and 26,000 pounds that are centrally garaged and fueled will be covered by those guidelines. Hundreds of trucking companies and private fleets will be affected by those requirements. Companies operating less than 10 trucks will be exempt from those statutory guidelines.[21] While those guidelines were primarily directed at improving air quality in designated urban areas, they will also effectively reduce the trucking industry's dependence upon petroleum products.

Truck and Bus Manufacturer Actions. As previously noted, many vehicle and engine manufacturers participate in voluntary truck and bus fuel economy programs. Their participation has primarily involved efforts to modify power train components and vehicle aerodynamics.

One major truck manufacturer, Detroit Diesel Corporation, has developed methanol truck engines. The company is also involved in testing of bus and truck engines powered by such alternative fuels as ethanol, and natural gas.[22]

Railroads

Fuel expenses consume approximately seven cents of each revenue dollar earned by the nation's freight railroads.[23] Despite the fact that the volume of freight carried by the railroads has grown steadily, the industry's consumption of diesel fuel declined by nearly one-quarter between 1980 and 1991.[24] Throughout that period the price of diesel fuel fluctuated considerably, ranging from a low of 49 to a high of 95 cents per gallon.[25]

Carrier Actions. Railroads have reacted in several ways to energy concerns. Operational changes have been widely employed. These have included less frequent runs of longer trains, reduced locomotive idling time, use of automatic fueling devices to reduce spillage, and more widespread use of equipment with greater cargo-carrying capacity. Some railroads also have sought to promote expansion of services that are perceived as being more fuel efficient, such as unit train and intermodal operations. Further, during the past decade railroads have dramatically reduced light-density branch line operations which historically consumed a disproportionate share of the industry's energy resources.

Government Actions. Expansion of federal railroad research activities has been at least partially motivated by energy conservation considerations. Also, federal funding of the upgrading of Amtrak's track and facilities has promoted more efficient operations and hence better fuel-consumption patterns. In addition, the DOT has become increasingly involved in programs to improve railroad fuel efficiency. The agency's efforts have included programs to reduce empty mileage through better freight car management, working with equipment manufacturers on potential design improvements, and evaluation of the feasibility of changes such as potential expansion of railroad electrification. The Department of Energy has also been involved in testing of alternative fuels for railroad diesel engines.

Equipment Manufacturer Actions. Rail car and engine manufacturers have also responded to energy concerns. This has involved not only the introduction of a more fuel-efficient diesel engines, but also experimentation with the use of lighter weight materials in car and engine design.

In many instances manufacturers have substituted aluminum for steel in construction of rail equipment. The use of high strength plastics, weighing less than half the materials they have replaced, has also increased significantly. The Union Pacific's S.M.A.R.T. cars, which are used for containerized movement of motor vehicles, use containers made of such materials.[26] The newest generation of locomotives produced by General Electric for Amtrak also are also lighter and more fuel-efficient than the equipment to be replaced.[27]

Development of Road-Railer and double-stack container technologies was similarly motivated by energy considerations. Both types of equipment weigh substantially less than the equipment they replaced, yielding greater energy efficiency.

Airlines

During the past two decades commercial airline operations have been dramatically affected by the volatility of jet fuel prices. While jet fuel cost approximately 12 cents per gallon in 1973, it exceeded 60 cents per gallon in 1993.[28] It had been as high as $1.40 per gallon during the Gulf War. The industry attributed most of its record loss of $4 billion in 1990 to the doubling of fuel costs which occurred during the fourth quarter of that year.[29]

The industry accounts for approximately 11 percent of transportation's petroleum consumption.[30] On an annual basis fuel costs comprise 15-20 of the industry's operating costs. It has been estimated that each one-cent increase in fuel costs adds approximately $150 million to the industry's operating costs.[31]

Carrier Actions. The airlines have initiated numerous changes in operating practices to conserve fuel. These changes have ranged from reduction in cruising speeds to removal of exterior paint from planes to reduce aerodynamic drag.

As might be expected, the airlines have also devoted considerable attention to reassessment of their fleet characteristics. Fuel efficiency is now a far more significant selection criterion for new equipment than it was when jet fuel was relatively inexpensive.

As discussed in Chapter 13, many carriers have ordered new, more fuel efficient aircraft, and have substituted smaller aircraft in lighter density markets. The airlines have also initiated joint efforts with the National Aeronautics and Space Administration (NASA) to foster development of more efficient engines.

Government Actions. The DOT's Federal Aviation Administration (FAA), the DOE, and the National Aeronautics and Space Administration (NASA) have all actively responded to concerns about airline fuel efficiency. For example, the FAA has revised takeoff and landing procedures so that traffic does not build up and thereby cause delays. "Gatehold" procedures have also been modified. It takeoff delay is projected at longer than five minutes, aircraft are held at the gate and do not start their engines. Fuel savings related to adoption of such operational changes have been estimated at 600 million gallons per year.[32] Additionally, the DOE continues to conduct research and development activities related to potential improvements in fuel efficiency which might result from changes in aeronautics and the air traffic control system.[33] NASA's participation in this area has primarily focused on its Aircraft Energy Efficiency program which analyzes aircraft engines and structures and develop design alternatives.

Aircraft Manufacturer Actions. Aircraft manufacturers continue to develop more fuel-efficient planes. For example, in the early 1980s, Boeing introduced its 757/767 family of jets which used 30-40 percent less fuel than the previous generation of jets. During that period Boeing's major competitors also made progress in reducing energy consumption. As the 1990s began a new generation of more fuel efficient aircraft was being introduced by Boeing, McDonnell Douglas, and Europe's Airbus Industrie.[34] One of the new planes, Boeing's 747-400 freighter which was introduced in March 1993, was promoted as using 10 percent less fuel than competitive planes.[35]

As discussed later in this chapter, the desire for improved fuel efficiency is not the only factor which will lead to major changes in the fleets of domestic airlines in the 1990s. Federal noise level regulations will also play a major role.

MOVEMENT OF ENERGY RESOURCES

Energy commodities are important sources of traffic for the intercity modes. For example, coal accounts for approximately 27 percent of railroad carloadings.[36] Energy traffic also represents more than 23 percent of the annual tonnage handled by class I motor carriers of freight and comprises in excess of 60 percent of all waterborne commerce moving in the United States.[37] In many instances there is considerable intermodal competition for energy traffic. Even crude and refined petroleum is not "captive" to the pipeline industry. While pipelines annually handle approximately 52 percent of crude and refined petroleum tonnage, water carriage (22 percent) and trucking (24 percent) provide substantial competition.[38]

FUTURE DIRECTIONS OF TRANSPORTATION/ENERGY POLICY

For many years the American public and federal policy makers did not perceive transportation/energy interrelationships as matters of concern. The nation benefited from the unparalleled mobility fostered by the easy availability of low-priced petroleum. While this mobility had real economic and social value, it also contributed to depletion of energy resources and increasing reliance upon foreign energy sources.

The 1973-74 energy crisis shocked not only the American public, but also federal policy makers. As a result of that rather sobering experience, numerous legislative and administrative initiatives related to energy concerns were enacted between 1975 and 1980.

However, by the early 1980s energy considerations seemed to command far less attention in Washington. A number of factors, including conservation efforts, improved automobile fuel efficiency, and stabilization of gasoline prices contributed to that situation. Consequently, little congressional attention was devoted to energy issues, and federal commitment to energy programs appeared to wane. In fact, President Reagan advocated elimination of the Department of Energy because he believed that most energy problems should be left to the marketplace for resolution.[39]

Toward the end of the decade concern with environmental issues led Congress to again address transportation/energy issues. The Alternative Motor Fuels Act of 1988 and the Clean Air Act of 1990 emphasized the desirability of increasing the use of alternative fuels in vehicles not only to improve air quality but to reduce oil consumption. The previously mentioned Comprehensive National Energy Policy Act of 1992 followed, prompted by the Iraqi invasion of Kuwait which resulted in oil prices reaching $30 per barrel. Many believed that the increased oil prices led the American economy into recession.[40]

The energy-related legislative initiatives of the late-1980s and early-1990s were notable in that they not only acknowledged the significance of the relationship between transportation and energy, but also outlined broad energy policies to address such issues. While it is too early to assess the impact of those policies, their development constituted an important step in dealing with national energy issues on a realistic basis.

OTHER ENVIRONMENTAL CONCERNS

The impact of the national transportation system on the environment is not limited to consumption of scarce energy resources. Rather it is multidimensional in nature and often involves negative effects on the physical environment.

The energy conversion process utilized in the various modes (primarily the internal combustion engine) historically has been responsible for approximately one-half of total pollutants emitted into the atmosphere. In one recent year it was estimated that transportation accounted for 43 percent of the nitrogen oxide, 39 percent of volatile organic compounds, 64 percent of carbon monoxide, 11 percent of hydrocarbons, and 73 percent of the lead emissions in the air.[41] Those pollutants have generated sizeable societal costs including respiratory problems for many people and the deterioration of property. The operation of transportation vehicles has tended to be rather noisy, and this has contributed to noise-level problems. Further, transportation facilities, such as highways, airports, and terminals, have consumed tremendous parcels of land and in the process have led to social problems related to population dislocations.

Those extensive transportation-environment interactions have led to increasing governmental efforts to minimize the harmful effects of transportation progress. Such efforts have occurred at the federal, state, and local levels and have often involved the active cooperation of several governmental units. At the federal level, environmental protection efforts related to transportation have been primarily conducted by the DOT and the Environmental Protection Agency.

Within the DOT development and enforcement of specific environmental standards has been delegated to the modal administrations, such as the Federal Aviation Administration. Because of the important role that the DOT plays in financing transportation infrastructure, it must necessarily be sensitive to the potential environmental impact of such outlays. Therefore, the DOT requires quite detailed environmental impact statements on all major projects before work can begin.

When the EPA was established by Congress in 1970, it was given broad responsibilities and powers to foster environmental protection. Two basic charges were improvement of air quality and reduction of noise levels in our cities. EPA efforts in these areas naturally have had a heavy transportation orientation. As a result, the EPA and the DOT have actively cooperated on numerous projects.

Modal Developments

Due to unique operating characteristics, each mode has had a different impact on the environment, and the modes have thus attracted a varying degree of governmental attention. The major environmental developments of recent years related to the intercity modes are traced in the following discussion.

Highway Modes. The combined efforts of the DOT and the EPA have contributed to a significant reduction of the negative environmental impact of the highway modes. The EPA is empowered to establish automobile emission standards and its efforts have fostered major improvements in air quality. As a result of the agency's efforts, since 1970 automobile emissions of hydrocarbons and carbon monoxide have been reduced by more than 90 percent.[42]

Many of the congressional clean air guidelines have been incorporated in the Clean Air Act, first passed in 1963, and its subsequent amendments. The 1990 Clean Air Act amendments made many important changes. Among the most important of those were:

1. establishment of more stringent tailpipe emission standards beginning in 1994
2. a mandated increase in the oxygen content of fuels by 1992
3. a requirement that all vehicles produced in the 1996 model year be able to demonstrate a 15 percent reduction in their polluting emissions
4. a requirement that beginning in model year 1998 half of all new trucks operating in urban areas faced with severe air quality problems be powered by alternative fuels—as noted earlier in this chapter, this requirement applies only to vehicles weighing between 8,501 and 26,000 pounds and fleets with 10 or more vehicles.[43]

In 1992 the EPA also imposed tougher vehicle inspection and maintenance requirements for 181 metropolitan areas. Those requirements, which were scheduled to take effect in 1994, were aimed at reducing smog-causing emissions by 28 percent and carbon monoxide emissions by 31 percent.[44]

Highway noise pollution has also been a target of the DOT and EPA. Noise level standards have been issued for use in planning and designing federally assisted highways, and quantitative models have been developed to estimate air and noise pollution levels associated with specific highway project proposals. Additionally, the two federal agencies have jointly developed noise level standards that have been applied to motor carriers.

Aviation. To date the major federal concern with the environmental impact of aviation has involved noise pollution. Recognition of the significance of that problem led Congress, in 1968, to provide the Federal Aviation Administration with statutory authority to prescribe rules and regulations for the control and abatement of aircraft noise and sonic booms. The FAA's subsequent efforts have included development of programs to reduce aircraft engine noise and the establishment of takeoff and landing procedures to minimize airport-vicinity noise levels. Additionally, the agency has actively cooperated with state and local authorities on matters such as sound-proofing programs for homes, schools, and hospitals in airport zones and the establishment of property buffer zones around airports.

In terms of aircraft noise reduction, the most important legislative initiative of the past decade was the Airport Noise and Capacity Act of 1990. That legislation specified that by January 1, 2000 every airliner operating within the U.S. must meet "Stage 3" noise specifications. To meet those requirements airlines must either re-engine, install "hush kits", or replace older aircraft. "Stage 2" jets comprised approximately 54 percent of U.S. carriers' fleets in the early 1990s, and cost of compliance with "Stage 3" guidelines has been estimated to range between $2 billion and $5 billion, depending upon whether planes are modified or replaced.[45] Clearly, this places another financial burden on an industry which is already troubled.

Aviation air pollution also has received the attention of both the FAA and the EPA. Their combined efforts have led to major reductions in engine emissions, which have been primarily accomplished through retrofit programs. Also, in-flight fuel dumping, which was a standard aviation practice, has been discontinued due to its adverse impact on air quality.

The Clean Air Act amendments of 1990 also affected the airlines. Congress tightened its ambient air quality standards and directed states to modify their plans and enforcement procedures for such stationary points as airports.[46]

Rail Carriage. Railroad diesel engines contribute relatively little to air pollution compared with the internal combustion engines on U.S. highways, and they are not as noisy as many types of jet aircraft. Therefore, it is not surprising that the railroads have not received as much environmental attention as the highway and air modes. However, the Federal Railroad Administration has issued operating and equipment standards that have reduced railroad noise and emission levels.

Water Carriage. In the marine environment the Coast Guard is the primary agency responsible for enforcement of federal antipollution laws and treaties. Thus far, the major threat to the marine environment has been oil spills.

Traditionally the Coast Guard has tended to emphasize development of adequate clean-up capability for removing oil and hazardous materials from the water. To facilitate such efforts, the Coast Guard maintains a National Response Center, which coordinates clean-up activities, and oil spill "strike teams" to participate in those activities.[47] More recently Coast Guard emphasis has shifted to prevention of spills through regulation of vessel construction and operation and oil transfer facilities. The Coast Guard has also worked toward development of separated sea lanes to offer improved protection against spills caused by collisions and groundings.

In addition to these activities, the Coast Guard also conducts extensive research into the potential causes of water pollution and prevention techniques. The agency also is responsible for environmental impact studies related to specific waterway projects and provides technical assistance on pollution control techniques to various domestic and international organizations.

The Exxon Valdez oil spill in Alaska's Prince William Sound in 1989 focused public attention on the enormity of environmental damage which can occur through spills, and prompted passage of the Oil Pollution Act of 1990. The law requires most existing single-hulled tankers operating in U.S. waters to be refitted with double hulls by 2010. The cost of compliance has been estimated at $7 billion by 2015.[48] It also established a $1 billion oil spill cleanup fund which is financed by a five cent per barrel oil tax. Additionally, the act increased shipowner liability related to oil spills to $1,200 per gross registered vessel ton (up from $150) or $10 million, whichever is greater, for vessels weighing in escess of 3,000 gross tons. The federal liability for smaller tankers was set at $2 million.[49] However, the 1990 legislation also permitted states to establish their own carrier liability limits, and some states have unlimited liability guidelines.[50]

Oil Pipelines. Potential oil pipeline malfunctions also pose environmental threats. However, the industry and the DOT's Office of Pipeline Safety have worked closely to develop elaborate shut-off and safety systems to minimize potential environmental hazards. Rigid standards also have been developed for materials and construction procedures to be used in pipeline systems.

The Alaskan pipeline project posed a series of environmental threats. In addition to the threat of system malfunctions resulting in oil spills, there were also potential threats to Alaska's delicate permafrost, because the oil was to be heated as it moved through the pipeline. Further, above-ground segments of the pipeline threatened to impede the migratory patterns of arctic animals. The resolution of these environmental concerns delayed the construction of the Alaskan pipeline for nearly five years. Although the delay was quite costly, it did result in a tremendous reduction of the potential environmental threat posed by the project.

SUMMARY

The transportation system is a major consumer of energy resources, and also a major source of environmental pollutants. As energy and environmental problems have intensified, carriers and other users have had to cope with volatile fuel prices, periodic shortages, and increasing government regulations. Through their actions public policy makers and vehicle manufacturers have sought to promote greater fuel efficiency and improved air quality. The Clean Air Act of 1990, the Oil Pollution Act of 1990 and the Comprehensive National Energy Policy Act of 1992 provide clear illustrations of growing congressional sensitivity to energy and environmental issues.

During the past two decades the United States has made considerable progress in addressing critical energy and environmental problems. However, the problems which remain will require decisive national action and a commitment by carriers, manufacturers, and users to work together toward their resolution.

DISCUSSION QUESTIONS _____

1. You have just been appointed the President's special adviser on the transportation/energy interface. Realizing that private and for-hire transportation consume enormous quantities of petroleum, the President has asked you to develop a five-year plan to reduce energy consumption by transportation activities. What would be the components of your program? Why did you select the various components, and what would their impact be?

2. Discuss the steps which have been taken to improve automobile fuel-efficiency.

3. Discuss the relative roles of the Department of Transportation and the Department of Energy in promoting energy conservation in transportation.

4. What are CAFE standards and what is their significance?

5. Discuss the steps taken by manufacturers to improve the fuel efficiency of transportation vehicles.

NOTES _____

1. Ford Foundation Energy Policy Project, *A Time to Choose: Energy Future* (Cambridge, MA: Ballinger Publishing Company, 1974), p. 5.

2. B. Bruce-Briggs, "Gasoline Prices and the Suburban Way of Life," *The Public Interest* (Fall, 1974), pp. 131-36.

3. American Gas Association, Alliance to Save Energy, and the Solar Energy Industries Association, as cited by Richard H. Rosenzweig, "The Energy Bill," *Public Utilities Fortnightly* (January 1, 1993), p. 16.

4. U.S. Department of Transportation, Research and Special Programs Administration, *National Transportation Statistics* (Washington, D.C.: U.S. Government Printing Office, 1992), p. 149.

5. Ibid.

6. Eno Transportation Foundation, Inc., *Transportation in America*, 11th ed. (Lansdowne, VA: the Foundation, 1993), p. 57. The total does not equal 100 percent due to rounding.

7. *National Transportation Statistics*, p. 135.

8. Gus Welty, "Railroads and the Environment," *Railway Age* (February, 1993), p. 27.
    Transportation in America, p. 56. It should be noted that this number includes petroleum consumption by taxis.

10. U.S. Department of Commerce, *Statistical Abstract of the United States, 1991* (Washington, D.C.: U.S. Government Printing Office, 1991), p. 448.

11. *Energy Policy and Conservation Act*, Public Law 94-163 (1975).

12. Lori A. Burkhart, "Fine-Tuning the Act," *Public Utilities Fortnightly* (January 1, 1993), p. 28.

13. See Thomas M. Strah, "Fuel Tax Increase Passes Congress," *Transport Topics* (August 16, 1993), pp. 1, 26.

14. *National Transportation Statistics*, p. 126.

15. U.S. Department of Transportation, Federal Transit Administration, Office of Technical Assistance and Safety, *Clean Air Program*, Technical Assistance Brief, Bulletin No. 3 (April, 1992), p. 5.

16. *Transportation in America*, p. 56.

17. U.S. Department of Transportation, *Energy Conservation in Transportation* (Washington, D.C.: the Department, 1979).

18. Information provided by United Parcel Service, Atlanta, Georgia.

19. Mitchell E. MacDonald, "What's New at the Pump?" *Traffic Management* (February, 1992), pp. 49-50.

20. Ibid.

21. Ibid., p. 48.

22. "Innovative Engines Burn New Types of Fuel," *Traffic Mangement* (August, 1992), pp. 33-4.

23. Association of American Railroads, *Railroad Facts* (Washington, D.C.: the Association, 1992), p. 11.

24. Ibid., p. 60.

25. Ibid.

26. Gus Welty, "Rolling Stock for the 90s," *Railway Age* (September, 1992), pp. 49-50.

27. Robert Roberts, "New Directions for Amtrak," *Railway Age* (July, 1991), p. 63.

28. Air Transport Association, *1993 State of the U.S. Airline Industry* (Washington, D.C.: the Association, 1993), p. 7.

29. Air Transport Association, *Air Transport, 1991* (WAshington, D.C.: the Association, 1991), p. 2.

30. *Transportation in America*, p. 57.

31. Air Transport Association, *1993 State of the U.S. Airline Industry*, p. 7.

32. U.S. Department of Transportation, *Energy Conservation in Transportation*, p. 5.

33. U.S. Department of Transportation, Federal Transit Administration, *Clean Air Program*, Technical Assistance Brief, Bulletin No. 3 (April, 1992), p.

34. James Ott, "New Technology Key to Airline Cost Cuts," *Aviation Week and Space Technology* (November 23, 1992), p. 42.

35. Maria Hong and Annie Best, "Manufacturers Try to Ride Out Downturn," *Air Commerce*, New York, September 28, 1992, p. 12.

36. *Railroad Facts*, p. 25.

37. U.S. Department of Transportation, Transportation Systems Center, *National Transportation Statistics* (Washington, D.C.: U.S. Government Printing Office, 1979), pp. 18-21.

38. *Transportation in America*, p. 59.

39. Alan Murray, "Energy," *1982 Congressional Quarterly Almanac* (Washington, D.C.: Congressional Quarterly, Inc., 1983), p. 298.

40. Rosenzweig, p. 16.

41. U.S Environmental Protection Agency, Office of Mobile Sources, "Transportation Control Measure Information Documents," (October, 1991), p. 6.

42. For an extensive discussion of governmental efforts to control air pollution, see Alan Altshuler, with James P. Womack and John R. Pucher, *The Urban Transportation System: Politics and Policy Innovation* (Cambridge, MA: the M.I.T. Press, 1981), Chapter 6 "Air Quality," pp. 172-209.

43. Richard Szathmary, "The Alternative-Fuel Alternative," *Sales and Marketing Management* (April, 1992), 80-2, 84-5.

44. H. Josef Hebert, "Tougher Standards for Car Emissions Set,: *The Boston Globe*, November 6, 1992, p. 3.

45. U.S. General Accounting Office, *Aviation Noise: Costs of Phasing Out Noisy Aircraft* (Washington, D.C.: General Accounting Office, 1991), pp. 2-3.

46. Graham Martin, "How to Meet the Next Generation of Environmental Regulations," *Airline Executive International* (September, 1991), p. 18.
47. Patrick Crow, "Oil Spill Overkill," *Oil and Gas Journal* (December 2, 1991), p. 29.
48. "The Risks of Oil Spills," *Risk Management* (December, 1992), p. 54.
49. Robin Buckner Price, "U.S. Oil Spill Law to Cause Growing Tanker Problem," *Oil and Gas Journal* (September 30, 1991), p. 21.
50. Elizabeth Canna, "Will Oil-Spill Bill Invite Abusers?" *American Shipper* (October, 1990), p. 78.

SELECTED REFERENCES

"Honk If You Hate the EPA." *Business Week* (July 27, 1993),p . 37.

"Innovative Engines Burn New Types of Fuel." *Traffic Management* (August, 1992), pp. 33-4.

MacDonald, Mitchell E. "What's New at the Pump?" *Traffic Management* (February, 1992), pp. 48-50, 52-3.

Nelms, Douglas W. "The Coming Quiet." *Air Transport World* (February, 1993), pp. 47-8, 50-2.

"New Regs Mean New Rigs." *Traffic Management* (May, 1991), pp. 55-7.

Rosenzweig, Richard H. "The Energy Bill." *Public Utilities Fortnightly* (January 1, 1993), pp. 16-17, 52-5.

Szathmary, Richard. "The Alternative Fuel Alternative." *Sales and Marketing Management* (April, 1992), 80-2, 84, 85.

"Tanker Owners Cope with OPA, but..." *Oil and Gas Journal* (July 27, 1992), pp. 38, 41, 42.

U.S. Department of Transportation, Federal Transit Administration. *Clean Air Program.* Technical Assistance Brief, Bulletin No. 3 (April, 1992), 11 pp.

U.S. Department of Transportation, Federal Transit Administration. *Clean Air Program: Overview.* Technical Assistance Brief, Bulletin No. 4 (Fall, 1992), 11 pp.

U.S. Department of Transportation, Research and Special Programs Administration. *National Transportation Statistics.* Washington, D.C.: U.S. Government Printing Office, 1992.

U.S. Department of Transportation and U.S. Department of Energy. *National Energy Transportation Study.* Washington, D.C.: the Departments, 1980.

U.S. General Accounting Office. *Aviation Noise: Costs of Phasing Out Noisy Aircraft.* Washington, D.C.: General Accounting Office, 1991.

Warren, William J. "Cargo Owners Must Learn to Live with OPA." *Amercian Shipper* (August, 1991), pp. 70, 72.

Welty, Gus. "Railroads and the Environment." *Railway Age* (February, 1993), pp. 27-9.

Welty, Gus. "Rolling Stock for the 90s." *Railway Age* (September, 1992), pp. 49-50, 52-3.

Part Six

METROPOLITAN TRANSPORTATION

CHAPTER EIGHTEEN

PROBLEMS OF METROPOLITAN TRANSPORTATION

Some of the most pressing national transportation problems exist in our cities and their surrounding metropolitan areas. Among these problems are the pollution and congestion caused by extensive automobile usage and the long-term financial difficulties of the transit industry.[1] These and related problems have posed serious threats to the quality of urban life.

This chapter outlines and examines the major transportation problems that exist in the metropolitan areas. It stresses the interrelationship between transportation and other matters of metropolitan concern, such as population shifts, land use patterns, and air quality. The chapter also addresses the importance of freight movements in metropolitan traffic flows and identifies the interface that exists between metropolitan and intercity transportation. Chapter 19 then explores the efforts that have been made to remedy metropolitan transportation problems.

METROPOLITAN INTERRELATIONSHIPS INVOLVING TRANSPORTATION

The transportation system of a metropolitan area is closely interrelated with the area's development pattern and its economic dynamics. An understanding of these interrelationships is extremely important to those engaged in metropolitan area planning. Several of the more important of these interrelationships are examined in the following discussion.

Population Trends

The U.S. population has become increasingly urban as a steady population shift has taken place from rural to urban locations. In 1900 the Census Bureau considered only 40 percent of the population to be urbanized.[2] By the early 1990s more than 77 percent of the population resided in urban areas.[3]

In recent years a related population shift has occurred. It has involved the dispersion of urban population over wider metropolitan areas. This development, often referred to as suburbanization, has fostered lower population densities in many of our central cities. Suburbanization has been both a function of transportation availability and a cause of serious metropolitan transportation problems.

Before the development of large-scale public transportation in urban areas, it generally was necessary for workers to reside close to their places of employment. That situation, coupled with the early clustering of industrial activities in our central cities, led to high urban population density. However, as public transportation became available, it was possible for workers to live apart from their job locations, and commutation emerged. The related population dispersal was reinforced by the development of the automobile; today, widespread automobile ownership and the advanced highway system make it possible for people to live many miles from their jobs. Transportation improvements therefore have increased population mobility, which in turn has promoted suburbanization.

Unfortunately, the suburbanization process has also created several serious transportation problems. As population disperses more widely from the central city, it becomes increasingly less likely that it can be adequately served by transit systems. Density diminishes, and the potential number of origin-destination pairs becomes too great. Consequently, more people rely upon the automobile for commutation, and transit patronage and revenues decline. This pattern has been observed in many of our major metropolitan areas. Besides contributing to the decline of transit, increased automobile commutation has led to serious pollution, congestion, and energy consumption problems. It has also promoted higher automobile accident and insurance rates in our cities. Despite substantial improvements in transit operations, it has been estimated that nearly 89 percent of commuters use private automobiles to get to work.[4]

Land Use Patterns

Transportation development and land use patterns in metropolitan areas are closely intertwined. The mobility created by transportation improvements has significantly increased land values in suburban areas as "bedroom communities" have emerged. However, there are several related problems. Transportation facilities have become major consumers of metropolitan land. In most cities, approximately one-third of all land is devoted to streets, railroad yards, terminals, airports, and parking facilities.[5] Consequently, the amount of unused land and open space has seriously diminished in many cities. Properties that are adjacent to transportation facilities often have become blighted, which has lowered property values and has had a negative impact on the quality of urban life.

Tax Base Considerations

Transportation development has also influenced the tax base of our cities. New transportation facilities have oten displaced residents and businesses, thereby eroding the tax base. This has aggravated an existing problem, because many cities already had high concentrations of tax-exempt properties such as churches and schools.[6]

Further, the commuting mobility of the middle and upper income classes has left our cities with major concentrations of the elderly and the poor. These people depend quite heavily upon social services, but cannot afford to underwrite them through taxes. These same core dwellers tend to be quite dependent upon transit to meet their transportation needs. Unfortunately, rising transit deficits have often led to service cutbacks, which have further impaired the ability of these people to reach work locations. This problem has intensified with the relocation of many industrial activities to the suburbs. These developments have combined to economically trap the poor in our cities and have contributed to increasing public assistance needs.

Environmental Considerations

Transportation has also contributed to air and noise pollution and congestion problems in our metropolitan areas. The street systems of many of our large cities were not designed to handle the volume of contemporary traffic flows. Nor do they effectively separate vehicle and pedestrian flows. The resulting congestion increases travel time and vehicle fuel consumption rates. As congestion worsens, exhaust fumes increase and pollution problems intensify. Traffic congestion often results in average automobile operating speeds of less than 20 miles-per-hour (mph) in many U.S. cities. Transit buses, which must share the street system with other vehicle classes, run much slower. One study estimated that buses average 5.2 mph in central business districts and 10 mph in overall city travel.[7]

As discussed in Chapter 17, the severity of urban pollution problems has prompted considerable congressional action. The specific congressional responses are examined in detail in Chapter 19.

The obvious linkage between increased urban automobile usage and a variety of socioeconomic and environmental problems that exist in metropolitan areas has prompted federal, state, and local officials to reassess transit's role in metropolitan transportation. However, the transit industry also has experienced serious problems.

STATUS OF THE TRANSIT INDUSTRY

While public interest in transit operations has increased dramatically in recent years, the industry has experienced a variety of problems that continue to threaten the viability of transit service in many cities. Among the problems faced by the industry have been the long-term decline in ridership, steadily increasing operating losses, rapidly escalating costs, and the heavy concentration of demand during peak hours. The industry has also suffered due to stringent local regulation and the long-term highway orientation of government transportation spending programs.

The U.S. transit industry consists of more than 5,000 systems. Of those, approximately 2,700 provide bus service, 3,900 operate demand response service (non-fixed route service using vans or buses--passengers are serviced at pre-arranged times and locations), and 100 operate other modes. About 1,500 systems operate more than one mode.[8] The U.S. transit fleet consists of about 94,000 vehicles, including 60,000 buses, 16,000 demand response vehicles, 10,400 heavy rail cars, and 4,400 commuter rail cars.[9]

Ridership and Earnings

Mass-transit ridership declined by more than 60 percent between 1950 and 1970. Several factors contributed to the long-term decline in transit patronage. Among these were the trend toward low-density development, growing affluence, increasing highway spending programs, and heavy utilization of the automobile. In all but a few cities the automobile had emerged as the dominant mode of urban passenger movement. However, as shown in Table 18-1, transit ridership has grown considerably since 1970, thus reversing the long-term downtrend in ridership. During 1991 approximately 8.6 billion trips were taken on transit. That total consisted of 5.7 billion bus trips, 2.7 billion trips on the various rail modes, and the balance on other road and water modes.[10] Fifty-four percent of those trips were work-related.[11] The reasons for the growth in transit ridership during the past two decades are examined in Chapter 19.

The transit industry has incurred steadily growing deficits (see Table 18-2 which contains industry operating deficit data). The aggregate operating loss for the industry was nearly $9.8 billion in 1991.[12] Federal, state, and local government operating assistance provided approximately $9.8 billion to help offset that loss. Because of continuing financial problems, many transit properties have declared bankruptcy, and some medium-size communities have lost transit service completely. One major cause of the industry deficit has been a rapidly rising cost spiral.

TABLE 18-1
Transit Passenger Trips, 1970-1991

CALENDAR YEAR	RAILWAY			TROLLEY BUS	MOTOR BUS	DEMAND RESPONSE	OTHER	TOTAL PASSENGER RIDES/TRIPS(b)
	LIGHT RAIL	HEAVY RAIL	COMMUTER RAIL					
	(MILLIONS)	(MILLIONS)	(MILLIONS)	(MILLIONS)	(MILLIONS)	(MILLIONS)	(MILLIONS)	(MILLIONS)
1970	235	1,881	--	182	5,034	--	--	7,332
1975	124	1,673	260	78	5,084	--	65	7,284
1976	112	1,632	260	75	5,247	--	67	7,393
1977	103	1,610	265	70	5,488	--	67	7,603
1978	104	1,706	267	70	5,721	--	67	7,935
1979	107	1,777	279	75	6,156	--	67	8,461
1980	133	2,108	280	142	5,837	--	67	8,567
1981	123	2,094	268	138	5,594	--	67	8,284
1982	136	2,115	259	151	5,324	--	67	8,052
1983	137	2,167	262	160	5,422	--	55	8,203
1984	135	2,231	267	165	5,908	62	61	8,829
1985	132	2,290	275	142	5,675	59	63	8,636
1986	130	2,333	306	139	5,753	63	53	8,777
1987	133	2,402	311	141	5,614	64	70	8,735
1988	154	2,308	325	136	5,590	73	80	8,666
1989	162	2,542	330	130	5,620	70	77	8,931
1990	175	2,346	328	126	5,677	68	79	8,799
P 1991	186	2,167	324	125	5,686	72	83	8,643

P = Preliminary   -- Data not available

(a) Total Passenger Rides from 1960 through 1979 based on individual transit data collection procedures. Unlinked Transit Passenger Trips beginning in 1980 based on data collection procedures defined by Federal Transit Act, Section 15. Prior to 1984, excludes demand response and most rural and smaller systems. Series not continuous between 1983 and 1984.

(b) Excludes commuter railroad, cable car, inclined plane, automated guideway, and urban ferry boat prior to 1975.

SOURCE: American Public Transit Association, *1992 Transit Fact Book* (Washington, D.C.: the Association, 1992), p. 64.

TABLE 18-2

Transit Industry Operating Deficit 1970-1991

Year	Deficit (000)[a]
1970	(288,212)
1971	(411,400)
1972	(513,126)
1973	(738,499)
1974	(1,299,673)
1975	(1,703,526)
1976	(1,859,808)
1977	(2,024,791)
1978	(2,330,966)
1979	(2,707,497)
1980	(3,583,800)
1981	(4,240,576)
1982	(4,410,889)
1983	(4,451,900)
1984	(6,345,800)
1985	(7,104,400)
1986	(7,599,100)
1987	(8,040,300)
1988	(8,647,500)
1989	(8,715,700)
1990	(9,295,800)
1991	(9,767,200)

[a]Calculated by subtracting Total Operating Expenses from Total Operating Revenues. Depreciation, amortization, and other reconciling items are not reflected. If they were, the industry's annual deficit would be considerably greater.

SOURCE: American Public Transit Association, *1992 Transit Fact Book* (Washington, D.C.: the Association, 1992), pp. 46, 51, and earlier editions.

Industry Costs

Transit industry costs have escalated steadily in recent years. Equipment and supply cost increases have been significant, but rising labor costs have been far more important. Labor compensation is the major operating cost element in most transit activities, comprising nearly 69 percent of industry operating expenses.[13] The importance of the magnitude of labor compensation is illustrated by the fact that in several of the largest U.S. transit systems, employee compensation exceeds operating revenues. Average annual compensation, including fringe benefits, of transit workers was approximately $41,000 during 1991.[14] In 1991 the industry employed approximately 265,000 employees, compared to 138,000 in 1970.[15]

Labor Costs and Productivity

Although the impact of wage increases can often be reduced through increased productivity, for many years the transit industry experienced constant or declining worker productivity.[16] However, that trend has been reversed in recent years, with the industry registering significant improvements in a variety of productivity measurements including vehicle miles/employee and vehicle hours/employee.[17]

One important factor leading to such productivity improvements has been the growing use of part-time employees. They are particularly useful in meeting peak-hour demands (discussed later in this chapter). Part-time agreements now exist in more than 180 cities, including Seattle, Boston, Baltimore, and the District of Columbia.[18] The agreements typically limit part-time employees to a specified percentage of the total workforce, and incorporate some form of employment guarantee for full-time workers. In a related development, more transit companies are turning to contracting out of certain functions such as vehicle maintenance and cleaning when they can be performed less expensively by outside contractors.

Peak Hour Problems

The transit industry is troubled by peak-hour problems. Although in the long-term transit ridership has fallen dramatically in many cities, service still tends to be quite heavily used during the peak commutation periods of 7 to 9 a.m. and 4 to 6 p.m. In most major cities, transit facilities are used to capacity during those periods, but ridership falls off precipitously during off-peak hours. It is not uncommon for 60-70 percent of normal weekday volume to be handled during the four peak hours.[19] Consequently, transit systems must still meet the manpower and equipment levels dictated by peak demands, but are then faced with the prospect of under-utilized personnel and equipment during off-peak periods.

As noted earlier, many transit companies have turned to the use of part-time employees to cope with this problem. Other companies now use buses for charter services during slack periods, and in some cities transit unions have agreed to work split shifts so that a single group of workers can handle both the morning and evening rushes.

Some cities have experimented with lower off-peak fares as a means of both limiting peak demand and stimulating off-peak utilization. However, the results of such pricing schemes have been mixed.

Transit Regulations

The transit industry also has been troubled by rather stringent local regulations. When the transit industry emerged during the late nineteenth century, it was primarily financed and operated by private companies. In most instances those companies were granted charters by the local government. Under the provisions of the charters, the rates charged and services offered generally were controlled by public authorities. In subsequent years the charter stipulations caused serious difficulties for many private transit companies. Rates often were held at rather low levels despite increasing costs, and the companies often forced to continue noncompensatory services. These regulatory controls contributed heavily to the many bankruptcies that occurred in the transit industry, and they accelerated the movement toward public ownership of transit properties.

Regulation of transit fares and services generally has continued following the private-to-public ownership transition. If anything, the public systems are under even greater political pressures than their private predecessors to maintain fare levels. This has contributed to the revenue deficiencies experienced by many publicly owned transit systems. These and related fare issues are discussed in Chapter 19.

Highway Spending and Transit

Government spending programs in transportation historically have been skewed toward the highway modes. This has been particularly true of expenditures at the federal level. Substantial federal aid has been available for urban highway programs for many years, but federal outlays for transit were minuscule prior to 1970. Transit tended to be viewed as a local matter. Due to these funding inequities, state and local transportation planners gravitated toward highway solutions to metropolitan transportation problems. As improved urban highway systems attracted more riders from transit operations, the automobile often became a superior alternative to transit systems that were underfunded and deteriorating in service quality. The highway orientation of metropolitan transportation programs, particularly after World War II, contributed heavily to the problems of the transit industry.

Future Role of Transit

It has become increasingly obvious that metropolitan commutation needs can no longer be satisfied through increased reliance upon the automobile. The societal costs of the continued pursuit of the traditional "highway solution" are too great. As a result, the federal government has dramatically expanded its funding role in an effort to revitalize transit. The nature of the federal commitment and its interaction with state and local programs are explored extensively in Chapter 19.

METROPOLITAN FREIGHT MOVEMENTS

No examination of the transportation problems of U.S. metropolitan areas would be complete without reference to the movement of freight. Freight movements have a decided impact on traffic flows and environmental issues.

Historically, cities have served as freight transportation hubs in which outbound traffic was consolidated for movement to other cities and inbound freight was sorted for local delivery. Therefore, the terminal facilities of both intercity modes and local cartage companies tended to cluster near the center city to facilitate traffic interchange. This led to considerable mixing of passenger and freight vehicles in the metropolitan traffic flow.

The decentralization of industry and urban highway expansion has fostered a shift of many freight terminals to suburban locations. This development has reduced freight traffic volume within cities, but it cannot possibly eliminate such traffic. Retail establishments still require replenishment of inventory and customer deliveries. Supplies of food must still be delivered to stores that service urban residents. Parcels and documents must flow between businesses.

There is a heavy concentration of trucks in urban areas to serve such needs. Nearly two-thirds of all trucks registered in the United States are operated locally in urban areas.[20] Although more than one-half of all urban truck trips involve freight pickup and delivery, trucks are also engaged in such diverse urban activities as construction, mail delivery, and the provision of maintenance services.

Most city streets were not designed to cope with truck movements. They are often narrow, and off-street loading and unloading facilities are frequently inadequate. Consequently, many local pickup and delivery vehicles obstruct traffic flows each time they stop. One study estimated that a typical truck pickup and delivery stop of 12 minutes duration can cause as much as 17 vehicle hours of delay to other vehicles if the truck blocks one lane of traffic.[21] This greatly contributes to the congestion and air quality problems experienced in central business districts. Aggravating the situation still further is the fact that many of those trucks carry partial loads.

Public officials in some cities have considered modification of freight pickup and delivery patterns to combat congestion problems. Suggestions have been made to establish joint terminals where the pickup and delivery functions of the line-haul and local carriers could be coordinated. However, coordination of those carriers is a massive undertaking, and little progress has been made in implementing this concept. Proposals to restrict local truck services to periods before and after the normal business day have also been considered in several cities. Such restrictions would reduce congestion and pollution problems during the day. However, such restrictions have been opposed strongly by both merchants and local truckers. Merchants contend that their operating hours and employment needs would be affected adversely by such arrangements; truckers oppose the change in their work patterns that the restrictions would necessitate. Consequently, such plans have not been implemented.

METROPOLITAN-INTERCITY TRANSPORTATION INTERFACE

Metropolitan transportation problems cannot be addressed in isolation because of the complex interrelationship that exists with intercity freight and passenger movements. The bulk of pickup and delivery activities of intercity truckers occurs within metropolitan areas. Local traffic congestion increases carrier running time and costs and reduces worker productivity. Further, the ability of intercity carriers to meet freight delivery schedules is quite dependent upon ease of local movement. Therefore, congestion problems that appear to be local transportation issues can lead to cost and service difficulties for intercity carriers.

Similarly, those intercity travelers who use for-hire modes must generally enter the metropolitan traffic stream. Unfortunately, intercity passenger services, particularly airline operations, also experience heavy peak-hour demands, which coincide with the peaking of local commutation traffic. This often creates serious traffic congestion problems near intercity passenger terminals, which inconveniences both intercity and local travelers who must share common highway facilities. Further, many intercity passengers reaching destination terminals are quite dependent upon local transit and taxi services to complete their trips.

The freight and passenger terminals of intercity carriers also consume major parcels of metropolitan land, thereby contributing to the land use and blight problems discussed earlier in this chapter. Metropolitan operations of intercity carriers are also a significant cause of noise and air pollution problems.

In view of the degree and importance of the interaction of metropolitan and intercity transportation systems, increasing attention has been devoted to comprehensive transportation planning at the federal, state, and local levels. These planning efforts are discussed in detail in the next chapter.

SUMMARY

A strong interrelationship exists between the passenger and freight transportation systems of a metropolitan area and such issues as population trends and land use patterns. Additionally, the space demands of the transportation network can lead to erosion of the area's tax base, while vehicle operations contribute to pollution, congestion, and energy consumption problems. Consequently, it is not surprising that metropolitan transportation has attracted growing national attention in recent years.

In most metropolitan areas the automobile has emerged as the dominant form of passenger carriage. Besides intensifying environmental difficulties, this development also has led to major declines in transit ridership and revenues. The combination of automobile competition, rising costs, and stringent regulation has threatened the viability of the transit industry.

Although given little planning emphasis in the past, freight movements within metropolitan areas are quite important. They are necessary to supply business and consumers, but they also cause difficulties, because our central cities were not designed to accommodate major flows of truck traffic.

An important interface exists between metropolitan and intercity transportation. An intercity carrier's service and cost performance are significantly influenced by the nature of local transportation facilities and the degree of congestion encountered when making local pickup and delivery stops. At the same time, the presence of intercity vehicles in the metropolitan traffic stream contributes to congestion and pollution.

These metropolitan transportation problems and interrelationships have created a need for integrated transportation planning involving local, state, and federal officials. These planning efforts and the funding programs established to promote metropolitan transportation development are the major topics of discussion in Chapter 19.

DISCUSSION QUESTIONS

1. Discuss the factors that have influenced transit patronage in the post-World War II period.
2. What is the "peak-hour" problem in the transit industry?
3. Why has the transit industry increasingly relied upon part-time labor and contracting out?
4. How has transportation affected land use patterns in metropolitan areas?
5. What have been the major causes of the transit industry's long-term financial problems?

NOTES

1. This chapter uses the American Public Transit Association's definition of transit which includes all multiple-occupancy-vehicle passenger services of a local and regional nature provided for general public use. This includes public and private bus, rail, and water services, Amtrak and Greyhound service under contract to transit systems, vanpools operated under contract to transit systems, taxi services under similar contracts, and non-profit agency transportation for the aged, disabled, and disadvantages.
2. George M. Smerk, *Urban Mass Transportation: A Dozen Years of Federal Policy* (Bloomington, IN: Indiana University Press, 1974), p. 5.
3. U.S. Bureau of the Census, *Statistical Abstract of the United States, 1991* (Washington, D.C.: U.S. Government Printing Office, 1991, Table 32, p. 27.
4. Data supplied by the Highway Users Federation.
5. Wilfred Owen, *The Metropolitan Transportation Problem*, rev. ed. (Washington, D.C.: the Brookings Institution, 1966), p. 190.
6. Ibid., pp. 151-53.
7. Herbert S. Levinson, "Analyzing Tranist Time Performance," *Transportation Research Record*, No. 915 (1983) as cited in U.S. Department of Transportation, Federal Transit Administration. *Characteristics of Urban Transportation Systems*, rev. ed. (Washington, D.C.: the Department, 1992), Table 3-1 (pages not numbered).
8. American Public Transit Association, *1992 Transit Fact Book* (Washington, D.C.: the Association, 1992), p. 11.
9. Ibid., p. 11.
10. Ibid., p. 11.
11. Ibid.
12. Ibid., pp. 42-3.

13. Ibid., p. 45.
14. Ibid., p. 97.
15. Ibid., p. 90; plus earlier editions.
16. See Robert C. Lieb, U.S. Department of Transportation, *Labor in the Transit Industry* (Washington, D.C.: U.S. Government Printing Office, 1976), pp. 46-57; also Darold T. Barnum, *From Private to Public; Labor Relations in Urban Mass Transit* (Lubbock, TX: College of Business Administration, Texas Tech University, 1977), pp. 157-8.
17. Ibid., p. 24.
18. U.S. Department of Transportation, Urban Mass Transportation Administration, *Fiscal and Organizational Impacts of Part-Time Labor in Public Transit* (Washington, D.C.: the Department, 1985), p. 11.
19. John R. Meyer, John F. Kain, and Martin Wohl, *The Urban Transportation Problem* (Cambridge, MA: Harvard University Press, 1965), p. 95.
20. For an interesting discussion of related matters, see Alan Altshuler with James P. Womack and John R. Pucher, *The Urban Transportation System: Politics and Policy Innovation* (Cambridge, MA: the M.I.T. Press, 1981), Appendix A, "Urban Freight Transportation, pp. 472-74.
21. Ken Ogden, "Urban Freight Policy," *ITS Review* (August, 1992), p. 3.

SELECTED REFERENCES

American Public Transit Association. *1992 Transit Fact Book*. Washington, D.C.: the Association, 1992.

Altshuler, Alan, with James P. Womack and John R. Pucher. *The Urban Transportation System: Politics and Policy Innovation*. Cambridge, MA: The M.I.T. Press, 1981.

Buel, Ronald A. *Dead End: The Automobile in Mass Transportation*. Englewood Cliffs, NJ: Prentice-Hall, Inc., 1972.

Gakenheimer, Ralph, ed. *The Automobile and the Environment: An International Perspective*. Cambridge, MA: The M.I.T. Press, 1978.

Meyer, John R., and Jose A. Gomez-Ibanez. *Autos, Transit and Cities*. Cambridge, MA: Harvard University Press, 1981.

Meyer, John R., John F. Kain, and Martin Wohl. *The Urban Transportation Problem*. Cambridge, MA: Harvard University Press, 1965.

Owen, Wilfred. *The Accessible City*. Washington, D.C.: the Brookings Institution, 1972.

Owen, Wilfred. *The Metropolitan Transportation Problem*, rev. ed. Washington, D.C.: the Brookings Institution, 1966.

Shen, David L., and Jer-Wei Wu. U.S. Department of Transportation, Federal Transit Administration. *Commuter Rail: A Study of Current Systems.* Washington, D.C.: the Department, 1992.

Smerk, George M. *The Federal Role in Urban Mass Transportation.* Bloomington, IN: Indiana University Press, 1991.

Smerk, George M. *Urban Mass Transportation: A Dozen Years of Federal Policy.* Bloomington, IN: Indiana University Press, 1974.

Smerk, George M. "Urban Mass Transportation: From Private to Public to Privatization." *Transportation Journal*, Vol. 26, No. 1 (Fall, 1986), pp. 83-91.

Smerk, George M. *Urban Transportation: The Federal Role.* Bloomington, IN: Indiana University Press, 1965.

U.S. Department of Transportation, Federal Transit Administration. *Characteristics of Urban Transportation Systems.* Washington, D.C.: the Department, 1992.

U.S. Department of Transportation, Urban Mass Transportation Administration. *Fiscal and Organizational Impacts of Part-Time Labor in Public Transit.* Washington, D.C.: the Department, 1985.

Weiner, Edward. U.S. Department of Transportation, Office of the Secretary. *Urban Transportation Planning in the United States: An Historical Overview*, rev. ed. (Washington, D.C.: the Department, 1992.

CHAPTER NINETEEN

SOLVING METROPOLITAN TRANSPORTATION PROBLEMS

Chapter 18 stressed the significance and problems of metropolitan transportation, and this chapter traces the responses of local, state, and federal government units to those problems. Attention is devoted not only to those programs that have sought to revitalize transit but also those that have promoted integration of the highway modes into metropolitan planning. Additionally, the impact of those programs is reviewed, and the movement toward coordinated transportation planning in metropolitan areas is explored.

LOCAL AND STATE ROLE IN TRANSIT

During the formative years of the transit industry, the involvement of local government in transit was limited primarily to chartering private companies to provide the services and to regulation of their activities. However, the financial problems experienced by many private transit companies and community desire to promote continuity of service necessitated a growing local government involvement in transit financing.

Bankruptcies of private transit systems led to public acquisition of transit facilities in many of our large cities, including New York, Chicago, Detroit, Boston, Pittsburgh, and San Francisco. Approximately one-third of all U.S. transit systems are publicly owned, but public systems generate 94 percent of the industry's passenger trips.[1]

In addition to its ownership and operation role in transit, local government has become extensively involved in subsidizing public and private transit system deficits. It has become increasingly difficult for transit systems to be self-sufficient through fare box revenues. To offset rising costs, transit systems often have resorted to fare increases. As a result, the average transit fare in the United States rose from 10.0 cents in 1950 to 70.2 cents in 1991.[2] Although fare increases yield greater revenue per rider, they also tend to further erode transit's ridership base. One study conducted by the American Public Transit Association indicated that on average a 10 percent increase in bus fares leads to a 4 percent decline in ridership.³Additionally, transit fare hikes tend to be rather regressive and place a disproportionate burden on lower income groups, which rely quite heavily upon transit services. In view of the negative ramifications of fare increases, officials in many cities have opted to establish or increase public subsidies to transit systems rather than to continue to raise fares.

The subsidy programs have been financed by various means. Among the financial arrangements used have been tax assessments to the communities served, local sales tax levies earmarked for transit subsides, and transit taxes on automobiles registered in metropolitan areas. Such arrangements have provided a means of preserving transit system operations, but they have not supplied adequate funding for significant improvements in transit service.The competition for local tax dollars has been intense, and transit upgrading necessarily has been weighed against increased taxes. Nevertheless, as shown in Table 19-1, each year local governments still provide approximately 57 percent of the total operating subsidies given to transit operators. As a result of continuing financial pressures, local officials have increasingly turned to state and federal government units for transit assistance.

State government has progressively been drawn into the mass transit issue. Most states have enacted legislation to preserve public transportation systems in metropolitan areas. Nearly half of the states provide direct financial subsidies to those systems, and state subsidies annually comprise slightly more than one-third of all operating assistance received by the transit industry.⁴

The form of subsidization varies widely, and the subsidies draw upon a broad range of tax programs. For example, California utilizes a combination of real estate taxes and a sales tax to finance transit projects; Oregon uses payroll taxes for the same purpose. Such state assistance has been useful, but it has not provided the capital infusion necessary to revitalize transit. That burden has fallen increasingly upon the federal government.

FEDERAL ROLE IN TRANSIT

Prior to 1960 there was little federal involvement in transit affairs. While billions of dollars were spent on highway, airport-airway, and waterway projects, federal transit funding was nonexistent. The prevailing attitude in Washington appeared to be that transit was a local matter. This situation has changed significantly since 1960. The federal government now plays a major role, not only by providing capital grants to cities but also by contributing funds to partially offset operating deficits. The evolution of the federal role in transit is examined in the following discussion.

TABLE 19-1

Sources of Transit Industry Revenues (Dollars)

CALENDAR YEAR	OPERATING REVENUE			OPERATING ASSISTANCE				TOTAL REVENUE
	PASSENGER(a)	OTHER	TOTAL	LOCAL & STATE		FEDERAL	TOTAL	
	(MILLIONS)	(MILLIONS)	(MILLIONS)	(MILLIONS)		(MILLIONS)	(MILLIONS)	(MILLIONS)
1976	$2,025.6	$210.5	$2,236.1	$1,224.5		$ 442.9	$1,647.3	$3,883.4
1977	2,157.1	196.5	2,353.6	1,319.5		584.5	1,904.1	4,257.7
1978	2,271.0	178.9	2,449.9	1,542.1		689.5	2,231.7	4,681.5
1979	2,436.3	211.5	2,647.8	2,054.6		855.8	2,910.4	5,558.2
1980	2,556.8	248.3	2,805.1	2,611.2		1,093.9	3,705.1	6,510.2
1981	2,701.4	343.8	3,045.2	3,225.7		1,095.1	4,320.8	7,366.0
1982	3,077.0	380.0	3,457.0	3,582.0		1,005.4	4,587.4	8,044.3
1983	3,171.6	332.5	3,504.1	4,194.6		827.0	5,021.6	8,525.7
1984	4,447.7	780.5	5,228.2	5,399.1		995.8	6,394.9	11,623.1
1985	4,574.7	701.8	5,276.5	5,978.5		939.6	6,918.1	12,194.6

CALENDAR YEAR	OPERATING REVENUE			OPERATING ASSISTANCE				TOTAL REVENUE
	PASSENGER(a)	OTHER	TOTAL	LOCAL	STATE	FEDERAL	TOTAL	
	(MILLIONS)	(MILLIONS)	(MILLIONS)			(MILLIONS)	(MILLIONS)	(MILLIONS)
1986	5,113.1	737.3	5,850.4	4,244.5	2,305.6	941.2	7,491.3	13,341.7
1987	5,114.1	776.6	5,890.6	4,680.6	2,564.6	955.1	8,200.3	14,091.0
1988	5,224.6	840.7	6,065.3	4,893.1	2,677.1	901.1	8,471.3	14,536.6
1989	5,419.9	836.7	6,256.6	4,995.4	2,796.3	936.6	8,728.3	14,984.9
1990	5,890.8	895.0	6,785.8	5,326.8	2,970.6	970.0	9,267.4	16,053.2
P 1991	6,064.0	954.3	7,018.3	5,605.1	3,241.8	945.0	9,791.9	16,810.2

P = Preliminary

*Excludes commuter railroad, automated guideway, urban ferry boat, demand response and most rural and smaller systems prior to 1984. Series not continuous between 1983 and 1984.

(a) Beginning 1984 includes fare revenue retained by contractors.

(b) Local operating assistance includes taxes levied directly by transit system and other subsidies from local government such as bridge and tunnel tolls and non-transit parking lot revenue.

SOURCE: American Public Transit Association, *1992 Transit Fact Book* (Washington, D.C.: the Association, 1992), p. 51.

Housing Act of 1961

The late 1950s and early 1960s were marked by a growing awareness of the problems of our cities. The deterioration of the quality of urban life was apparent. This led to a substantial expansion of the federal role in urban affairs. Numerous programs were established to channel federal funds into urban areas. With increasing attention being devoted to the urban setting, the role of transit in achieving urban objectives began to attract congressional attention. A coalition of urban interest groups, transit officials, and local politicians intensified their lobbying efforts for federal transit funding. These efforts were reinforced by two major federal reports on transportation issues, which were released in 1960.[5] Both studies called for increased federal involvement in solving the commutation problems of our cities.

In response to these developments, Congress took several steps to create transit support in the Housing Act of 1961. The transit-related provisions of that statute were as follows:

1. Twenty-five million dollars was authorized for mass-transit demonstration grants. The federal share of demonstration projects was to be two-thirds of project cost, with the balance to be funded by local and state government.
2. Cities were directed to include mass-transportation planning as an integral part of comprehensive urban planning under the act's planning grants program.
3. Fifty million dollars in low-interest loans were made available to the transit industry.[6]

The amount of money committed to transit under the act was modest, but it marked a major victory for transit supporters in that an initial federal funding commitment to transit had been made. A number of small-scale demonstration grants were awarded. Among the projects funded under the program were improvements in the bus system of Detroit, the operation of low-fare commuter rail services in the Philadelphia area, and minibus operations in the central business district of Washington, D.C. However, both the absolute amount of federal money available and the nature of the projects funded indicated that the 1961 act was concerned primarily with limited experimentation, rather than large-scale improvements in transit systems.

Urban Mass Transportation Act of 1964

Encouraged by their success in 1961, transit advocates continued to press for expanded federal funding. They found a strong ally in President John F. Kennedy who supported expansion of the federal commitment to transit.[7]

Initial efforts to obtain congressional support for these measures were unsuccessful. Further, the assassination of the president in November 1963 and the period of political transition that followed lowered the priority accorded to transit matters by the White House. However, by mid-1964 transit legislation was again being promoted actively by the White House. This time Congress responded favorably to the legislative proposal, and on July 9 the Urban Mass Transportation Act of 1964 was signed into law by President Johnson.[8] The act sought not only to provide improvement and development aid to mass transit systems, but also to encourage integrated transportation planning. The statute became the basic foundation of future federal transit involvement.

The demonstration and loan programs established in 1961 were continued. More importantly, the 1964 act established a capital grant program that provided federal transit funds on a two-thirds federal, one-third state and local funding basis. The funds could be used for practically any transit-related project. All capital grants were to be made to public agencies, but private interests were encouraged to work with the agencies in jointly securing funds. The act further stipulated that no state was to receive more than 12.5 percent of the total funds disbursed during a given year.

The act provided $375 million in capital grant funds over a three-year period and established relocation allowances for businesses and residents that might be displaced by transit projects. Also of major importance was Section 13 of the statue, which provided job protection guarantees to transit workers who might be adversely affected by federal grants. These worker protection guidelines continue to generate controversy; they are examined later in this chapter.

The importance of the Urban Mass Transportation Act's capital grant provisions should not be underestimated. The transit industry had suffered from capital shortages for many years, and funds had not been available to upgrade and expand transit facilities. The new federal capital grants program made such efforts possible, providing that local and state interests could raise their one-third share of project costs. Subsequent expansion of the federal capital grants program has been of major importance in promoting revitalization of the transit industry.

Federal Developments, 1964-1969

The next several years witnessed a number of significant legislative developments that were to influence the future federal role in transit. Although the concept of federal participation in transit financing had been firmly established in 1964, the absolute amount of funding provided under the Urban Mass Transportation Act was still quite modest in comparison with transit needs. In 1966, Congress addressed this issue by making several modifications in the 1964 act. Capital grants provided under the act were extended at the rate of $150 million per year in fiscal 1967, 1968, and 1969. Increases in demonstration project funding were also approved, and federal funds were made available for planning, engineering, and designing mass transit projects. The latter appropriations marked a congressional response to the cities which contended that they could not finance the extensive planning process, which was a prerequisite for funding applications.

The next significant development occurred the following year when the DOT commenced operations. One year later, in 1968, the transit funding program was transferred from HUD to the DOT. The Urban Mass Transportation Administration (UMTA) was then established within the DOT to administer federal transit programs. The scope of UMTA's operations has expanded substantially since that time, and the agency (renamed the Federal Transit Administration in 1991) has become increasingly involved in formulation of DOT policies related to all forms of metropolitan transportation development.

Also of importance was the National Environmental Policy Act in 1969. The act, mirroring growing national concern with environmental issues, established strict prerequisites on urban transportation construction for protection and enhancement of the environment. It also required preparation of environmental impact statements for all major federally funded projects.[9] Although this stipulation generally has resulted in longer and more expensive planning efforts in metropolitan transportation projects, it also has led to greater sensitivity to the possible adverse effects of such projects.

Urban Mass Transportation Assistance Act of 1970

Transit advocates were pleased that federal outlays for transit were increasing, but they believed that the federal commitments were too short-term. Representatives of urban areas contended that establishment of a long-term federal commitment to transit would make it much easier to raise local transit funds. Some suggested creation of a transit trust fund similar to the existing Highway Trust Fund; others proposed yearly appropriations from the Highway Trust Fund for transit projects. Both proposals met with strong opposition. The Bureau of the Budget (now the Office of Management and Budget) adamantly objected to the creation of a transit fund because of the rigidity of such spending programs, and highway interests fought to protect existing highway expenditure programs.[10]

Although President Nixon opposed establishment of a special transit fund, he supported a substantial increase in transit funding. Consequently, in 1969 he announced his intention to support a $10 billion, 12-year program of transit assistance. The proposal quickly attracted support of transit and urban interest groups, including the U.S. Conference of Mayors and the National League of Cities. Further, highway interests were persuaded to support the proposal in return for the support of the urban interest group coalition when the Highway Trust Fund came up for renewal in 1972.[11] Given that solid block of support, the Urban Mass Transportation Assistance Act of 1970 proceeded through Congress and was signed into law by President Nixon on October 15, 1970.[12]

In the bill, which modified many provisions of the 1964 statute, Congress responded to requests for long-term transit funding by authorizing $10 billion for transit over the next 12 years. The initial $3.1 billion of that amount was appropriated by the act to be awarded during fiscal 1971.

In addition to providing a major increase in federal transit funding, the act also reflected growing congressional concern with the side effects of transportation projects. Applicants for capital grants were directed to hold public hearings on the economic, social, and environmental impacts of proposed transit projects. These considerations were to be weighed in final project deliberations. Further, the secretary of transportation was directed to consult with the heads of other federal agencies with regard to projects affecting the environment to assure that federal transit commitments were prudent.

Highway Act of 1973

The mass transit lobby had succeeded in obtaining a sizable long-term commitment from Congress in 1970, but it still had two other major goals. The first was establishment of a program of operating subsidies for transit, and the second was diversion of Highway Trust Fund monies to major transit projects.[13]

The administration strongly opposed transit operating subsidies, because it was feared that such payments would reinforce inefficiency in transit operations. However, it favored diversion of some highway money to transit projects. These issues were debated extensively in Congress and on August 13, 1973, finally were settled legislatively with the passage of the Federal Highway Act of 1973.

The act contained several important transit provisions. In dealing with the existing transit funding program, Congress appropriated $3 billion more from the $10 billion program initiated in 1970. Also, the federal share of transit project funding was increased from two-thirds to 80 percent.[14] To facilitate improved transit planning, the act gave the secretary of transportation the power to fund transit planning up to 100 percent of planning costs.

In terms of new programs, the act permitted certain highway authorizations (Highway Trust Fund allocations to the Federal-Aid Urban System) to be used for either highway or public mass transit projects. If used for transit purposes, the funds could be used to finance either transit-related facilities or purchase of buses or rail transit rolling stock. The total amount of discretionary funding available was set at $780 million in fiscal 1974, and $800 million for each of the next two fiscal years. Another provision of the 1973 act permitted substitution of transit projects for proposed Interstate Highway segments, if the segments were withdrawn from the interstate system.

Congress did not approve transit operating subsidies in 1973. However, the issue was to arise again during the following year.

National Mass Transportation Assistance Act of 1974

Growing energy concerns, prompted by the Arab oil embargo, and steadily increasing transit deficits prompted further congressional transit action. It took the form of the National Mass Transportation Assistance Act of 1974.[15]

The act significantly increased federal transit funding by authorizing $11.8 billion over a six-year period. Of that total, $7.3 billion was to be made available for capital assistance to transit systems, and $500 million was earmarked for rural mass transportation projects. The remaining $4 billion was to be allocated to urban areas according to a formula based on population and population density. These funds could be used for either capital or operating assistance. Thus federal transit operating assistance became a reality.

Surface Transportation Assistance Act of 1978

In the years immediately following passage of the 1974 legislation, growing federal attention was devoted to energy conservation and the potential role that transit might play in meeting national energy goals. During that time the transit industry lobbied aggressively for a further increase in the level of federal capital commitments to transit.[16] Congress addressed these matters in the Surface Transportation Assistance Act of 1978.[17]

The statute provided $15.2 billion in federal assistance for fiscal years 1979 through 1983. Of that total, $6.5 billion was to be allocated on the basis of formula grants and $7.5 billion was to be utilized as discretionary capital grant funds. The balance was to fund a variety of programs including expanded educational training programs for transit managers and increased assistance to nonurban and rural areas.

The new program of aid for nonurban and rural areas was one of the major changes fostered by the act.[18] It provided a formula grant program for such areas that was similar to that initiated in 1974 for urbanized areas. Further, federal assistance to these areas was expanded to cover not only capital grants, but also operating assistance.

Surface Transportation Act of 1982

The 1978 legislation expanded the level of federal transit funding and continued it into the early 1980s. However, as the 1970s ended, transit advocates were again seeking legislation to further expand federal transit funding. During that period that nation was in the grips of an inflationary spiral that put severe pressures on many transit systems as the cost of supplies, equipment, and labor costs rose dramatically.

While the Carter administration had been generally perceived as having an antitransit bias during its first two years, the gasoline shortages and rising prices of 1979 seemed to change that posture. Nevertheless, there still was substantial opposition to any further increase in transit funding. Numerous questions had been raised about transit's ability to solve any of our nation's major urban transportation problems, and many congressmen saw transit funding as an attractive possibility for severe funding cuts in pursuing a balanced federal budget. Despite extensive hearings on transit funding in 1979-80, Congress neither passed new transit funding legislation nor slashed federal transit appropriations.[19]

During the early months of the Reagan administration there were mixed signals concerning the administration's views concerning mass transit funding. While Budget Director David Stockman called for major cutbacks in transit funding, Drew Lewis, Secretary of Transportation, appeared to be a strong transit advocate.

During 1982 Lewis played a strong leadership role in seeking congressional acceptance of legislation that sought to simultaneously address transit's future funding needs and the nation's serious highway and bridge maintenance problems. Lewis and a broad group of supporters, including highway and transit interests, most major labor organizations, nearly all governors, most big city mayors, and the Chamber of Commerce, sought to finance the expansion of federal funding through an increase in the federal gasoline excise tax. That concept was strongly opposed by the American Trucking Associations, oil companies, and congressional conservatives who opposed any tax increase during a recession.

Congressional deliberations produced the Surface Transportation Act of 1982 which included a 5 cents per gallon increase in the federal gasoline excise tax.[20] The related highway funding provisions of the act were discussed in detail in Chapter 4. Transit issues were addressed in Title 3 of the act, which was known as the Federal Public Transportation Act of 1982. Among the major provisions of Title 3 were:

1.   the largest transit funding authorization in history--$17.74 billion over the 1983-1986 period

2.   establishment of a new Highway Trust Fund mass transit account, which would accumulate one cent per gallon of the new excise tax levy that would be used for mass transit; this was expected to generate approximately $5.5 billion by late 1985

3.   restructuring of federal aid to transit through creation of a new block grant program that allowed expenditures for planning, capital, and operating items. State and local government units were given substantial discretion in choosing projects to be funded with block grants. The block grants were to be distributed on the basis of population, and within population groups, funds were to be apportioned by several formulas that reflected such things as population and route miles of transit service.

Federal Mass Transportation Act of 1987

As a result of the 1978 and 1982 statutes, federal transit assistance had become quite comprehensive. It included a multi-year, multibillion dollar commitment of funds, not only for urban areas, but also for nonurban and rural areas. Funds were available through direct congressional appropriations and through limited diversion from the Highway Trust Fund. The metamorphosis that the federal transit role had undergone following passage of the Housing Act of 1961 had been dramatic, and it profoundly influenced the industry.

Nineteen eighty-four marked the twentieth anniversary of federal involvement in transit funding. Over that period more than $30 billion had been provided to transit through 7,000 capital and operating assistance grants. Those funds helped purchase more than 54,000 buses, almost 6,500 rail vehicles, 18 ferry boats, 35 people mover vehicles, and approximately 13,500 vans for transportation for elderly and handicapped.[21]

That year marked the beginning of both the legislative process to develop new mass transit funding and President Reagan's second term in office. It soon became apparent that as the federal deficit mounted, the White House commitment to the federal transit program lessened. The administration sought to scale back transit appropriations in fiscal year 1984.[22] However, the congressional commitment to transit was quite firm, and cutback attempts were rebuffed.

Increasingly the administration called for less federal involvement in "local" matters, greater local financial responsibility, heavier reliance upon user charges, and "privatization" whenever possible. In a transit context privatization could take many forms such as provision of competitive transit services, subcontracting with a public transit authority, or service contracts for a private management company to run a public transit agency.[23]

Between 1984 and 1987 Congress considered numerous transit funding bills. Throughout that period the President sought to reduce the federal commitment to transit. Operating assistance to transit properties appeared to be particularly offensive to the White House which called for their elimination. As transit interests sought to offset the White House pressure the House and Senate worked to reconcile their often widely different highway and transit bills. Finally, in March 1987 both houses agreed on a compromise version of the highway and transit legislation and it was passed overwhelmingly in both the House and the Senate.[24]

However, President Reagan, calling the five year $88 billion legislation ($18 billion for transit) a "budget buster", vetoed the legislation. One week later Congress responded by overriding the Presidential veto and the legislation, which included the Federal Mass Transportation Act of 1987, was enacted.[25] Among the most important provisions of the law were:

1. continuation of federal transit programs for five years through fiscal year 1991 ($17.8 billion)
2. a requirement that UMTA develop "new start" criteria which would be primarily applied to proposed new rail systems--this appeared to be a response to critics who argued that such costly systems were funded without adequate consideration of alternatives or their cost effectiveness
3. an increase in the "Buy American" requirement for transit equipment from 50 percent to 60 percent after 1991
4. a tightening of local planning requirements to qualify for federal transit funds--a strategic financial plan was to be developed to assure that sufficient funds from all sources would be available to complete and operate proposed projects.[26]

The 1987 transit legislation was important not only because it provided funding for transit programs for the next five years, but also because it demonstrated that Congress was strongly committed to the programs. That commitment was broad based and bipartisan, and it had a dramatic impact on transit. During the 1980s federal transit funding not only assisted the transit industry with funding for equipment, facility improvement, and operating subsidies, but also stimulated a wave of new rail starts. Among the cities initiating new rail programs or extending existing systems were Pittsburgh, Buffalo, Miami, San Diego, Portland, Sacramento, Seattle and Los Angeles.[27]

Americans with Disabilities Act of 1990

While the transportation rights of the handicapped had been legislatively addressed as early as 1970, the most comprehensive approach to guaranteeing accessibility was contained in the Americans with Disabilities Act of 1990.[28] Prior to its passage, local officials had effectively been given the choice of providing handicapped accessibility through lift-equipped fixed route service, paratransit service, or a combination of the two. The 1990 statute, which guaranteed accessibility to the 43 million Americans with disabilities, provided more specific guidelines. The act mandated that all transit buses and rail cars purchased subsequent to its enactment were required to be handicapped accessible. When the act was passed approximately 35 percent of the industry's bus fleet was accessible to handicapped individuals.[29] The legislation also stipulated that over a five year period every transit train was to have at least one car that would be accessible to a person in a wheelchair. Systems offering fixed-route service were also required to offer comparable paratransit service in accordance with DOT guidelines. Any new facilities were to be accessible and existing facilities were to be modified to provide handicapped accessibility, when possible.

Intermodal Surface Transportation Act of 1991 (ISTEA)

As the 1990s began Congress again was faced with a number of transit issues. Should the federal transit funding program continue? Should operating assistance be terminated? What degree of autonomy should be given to state and local governments in deciding how to use federal highway and transit funds? What steps should be taken to relieve congestion and improve air quality in the country's metropolitan areas? Should federal highway and transit funding programs be dramatically reduced to help control the federal deficit?

After extensive debate on these issues Congress produced the largest highway and transit bill in history. The Intermodal Surface Transportation Efficiency Act of 1991, which was signed into law on December 18, 1991, provided $151 billion dollars for highway and transit programs over the subsequent six years. The details of the highway funding provisions of the act were discussed in Chapter 4; transit was to receive a record $31.5 billion. Transit funding authorization levels for fiscal years 1992-1996 are detailed in Table 19-2.

The legislation contained numerous metropolitan transportation and transit provisions. Among the most important of these were:

1.   establishment of a new block grant program, the Surface Transportation Program, which made funds available for a wide range of highway, transit, safety and environmental efforts.

2.   creation of a new Congestion Mitigation and Air Quality Improvement Program to be applied in urban areas which had not achieved ozone and carbon monoxide containment targets.

3.   development of a Congestion Pricing Pilot Program to establish five projects to examine the use of pricing to alleviate metropolitan congestion

4.   changing the name of the Urban Mass Transportation Administration to the Federal Transit Administration

5.   a requirement that states develop statewide transportation improvement programs which were subject to federal approval at least every two years.[30]

Transit supporters saw the ISTEA legislation as a major victory. Congress, faced with the enormous federal deficit and a soft economy, still authorized record levels of federal transit support through fiscal year 1996.

TABLE 19-2

Intermodal Surface Transportation Efficiency Act of 1991
Transit Funding Authorization Levels, By Fiscal Year
(in millions of dollars)

Category	1992	1993	1994	1995	1996	1997	Total
Discretionary	1,342	2,030	2,050	2,050	2,050	2,900	12,422
Formula	1,823	2,604	2,643	2,643	2,643	3,741	16,096
Rural	106	152	154	154	154	218	937
I Substitutions	160	165	0	0	0	0	325
Elderly & Disabled	55	70	69	69	69	97	428
Plan & Research	120	164	161	161	161	224	987
Administration	37	50	49	49	49	70	304
Total	3,643	5,235	5,125	5,125	5,125	7,250	31,499

SOURCE: Edward Weiner, U.S. Department of Transportation, Office of the Secretary, *Urban Transportation Planning in the United States: An Historical Overview*, rev. ed. (Washington, D.C.: the Department, 1992), p. 241.

IMPACT OF FEDERAL TRANSIT PROGRAMS

The expansion of the federal role in transit since 1961 has influenced the transit industry in many ways. It has provided funds to modernize and expand transit services in our cities, to begin a number of new rail transit systems, to partially offset operating losses, and to experiment with alternative forms of transit service. Federal aid has also sponsored management development in the industry. Additionally, the federal transit statutes have influenced intergovernmental relationships and accorded extensive job protection to transit workers who might be affected adversely by federal grants.

Modernization and Expansion Funds

Since 1961, federal transit funding programs have provided billions of dollars to an industry that had suffered from chronic capital shortages. These funds have allowed many cities to modernize existing transit facilities and others to expand transit capability. As a result of this growing support, the industry's vehicle fleet and service offerings have expanded. Service improvements have clearly contributed to the industry's reversal of the declining ridership pattern that it experienced in the post-World War II period.

The increasing availability of federal funds has led to a resurgence of interest in subways and other rail-oriented transit options. As noted earlier in this chapter, this has led to new rail starts in many cities including Pittsburgh, Buffalo, Miami, Portland, Seattle, and Los Angeles.

Transit Experimentation

Since its creation, FTA has financed experimentation with new forms of transit technology, such as moving sidewalks, people-moving systems, and high-speed rail technology. Such experimentation has attracted considerable public attention, but has often been criticized as being impractical. Increasingly the FTA has given higher priority to programs involving less exotic technology such as development of exclusive busways and implementation of paratransit services.

Exclusive busways, which separate commuter bus operations from the normal traffic flow, have been federally supported in a number of metropolitan areas, including Boston, San Francisco, Milwaukee, Seattle, and Washington, D.C. Generally, these projects have stimulated increases in bus ridership by improving the effective speed of buses that operate over exclusive rights-of-way on limited routes.

FTA also has become heavily involved in promotion of paratransit services, which involve organized ride-sharing activities ranging from private automobiles to conventional transit modes. Paratransit services operate directly in response to demand without fixed schedules or routes, except where they are prearranged, as in subscription and charter bus operations. The most significant forms of paratransit are daily and short-term car rental, taxicabs, dial-a-ride systems, jitneys, carpools, and subscription and charter bus systems. In promoting paratransit services, FTA has not envisioned these services as a substitute for mass transit. Rather, paratransit has been seen as a means of meeting demands that are not easily accommodated by mass transit. Numerous paratransit programs have been funded by FTA, and they have played a particularly important role in meeting the mobility needs of the elderly and handicapped. The future role of many paratransit services is unclear at this time due to the provisions of the Americans with Disabilities Act of 1990, which mandated greater handicapped accessibility to traditional fixed route transit services.

Management Development

Federal funding also has been used in an attempt to upgrade management skills in the transit industry. If transit is to be revitalized and expanded, the industry will have to attract and hold talented managers. However, most transit systems historically have devoted little attention to these matters. Management recruiting and training expenditures often have been viewed as unnecessary outlays. To fill managerial positions, the industry has relied quite heavily upon promotion from within; consequently, many transit managers have lacked adequate educational backgrounds and functional skills to perform effectively. In responding to this problem FTA sponsors and funds continuing education programs for transit industry managers.

Federal, Local and State Government Interaction

The extension of federal transit funds to our cities has necessitated extensive interaction between UMTA and local government officials. In some instances this interaction has led to disputes concerning the relative roles to be played by each in transit planning. The basic conflict has involved resolution of FTA's desire to play a strong leadership role in transit development and the desire of local government for self-determination. During FTA's (then UMTA) early years this conflict manifested itself in the agency's views concerning fixed-rail transit proposals. Officials of several major cities believed that their transit needs could be best served by fixed-rail rapid transit systems, but FTA was strongly opposed to funding such systems, due to the magnitude of their cost and their inflexibility. As a result, the agency generally refused to grant funds to new rail projects and concentrated its funding on projects involving bus service. The agency's position infuriated officials of cities that were denied rail transit funding.

However, as noted earlier in this chapter, the frequency and intensity of such disputes have lessened. Federal transit funding programs have moved decidedly toward greater local self determination. The increasing importance of block and formula grants exemplifies this philosophical change.

As previously noted the 1991 ISTEA legislation also mandated a continuous statewide transportation planning process. All modes, including transit, are to be covered in the state planning effort, and it is to be coordinated with planning efforts carried out in the state's metropolitan areas.

Labor Protection

Federal involvement in transit has also affected industry labor relations. Prior to passage of the 1964 transit statute, Congress was concerned that federal capital grants to transit might lead to substitution of capital for labor in the industry, thereby exerting further downward pressure on transit employment.[31] In response to that potential problem, Congress included Section 13(c) in the Urban Mass Transportation Act.Under its provisions, transit workers were guaranteed continuation of their bargaining rights, compensation levels, and working conditions. They were also given priority for employment or reemployment. Training or retraining would be provided if necessary. These benefits were patterned after those previously included under Section 5 of the Interstate Commerce Act, which governed railroad consolidations.

Whereas the benefits that Section 13(c) accords to labor are obvious, transit management has been quite critical of the guidelines. Before a transit system can obtain a capital grant or operating assistance from FTA, it must sign a 13(c) agreement with its union or unions. Management has contended that this stipulation effectively gives labor the power to veto FTA grants and forces transit systems to agree to steadily escalating 13(c) benefits.[32] However, the transit systems have failed to document the specific costs of the 13(c) guidelines, and very few transit grants have been denied because of the failure of management and labor to reach a 13(c) accord. Congress has demonstrated little interest in changing the labor protection guidelines and is unlikely to do so unless transit system officials can clearly document the cost inefficiencies caused by Section 13(c).[33]

COPING WITH THE AUTOMOBILE

Despite steady transit improvements, the automobile will continue to dominate metropolitan passenger movements in the foreseeable future unless public policy restricts automobile usage or petroleum supplies are reduced. Transit cannot match the flexibility of the automobile and many systems do not possess the physical capacity to handle large-scale increases in patronage, particularly during peak hours. Therefore, the relevant public policy issues related to future metropolitan automobile usage involve better integration of the automobile into metropolitan transportation planning and minimization of its harmful effects on the environment.

Highway Expansion

It appears likely that urban planners will rely less heavily upon new highway projects in meeting future metropolitan transportation needs. Growing emphasis on environmental issues, enormous highway and bridge maintenance funding needs, and increased availability of federal transit funding should combine to slow new highway construction in these areas. These developments have reinforced the "freeway revolt" of the early 1970s, which consisted of intense lobbying activities by urban interest groups that opposed highway expansion due to its adverse social and environmental impact. As a result of the intensity of this community resistance, many highway projects were canceled, and some cities instituted moratoriums on highway building.

Such community activism was a relatively new phenomenon in the early 1970s, but in the 1990s it issan established force in the public policy making process. The growing participation of citizen interest groups in metropolitan transportation planning efforts is likely to lead to increased use of discretionary federal transportation funds for transit rather than highway projects. Consequently, a major concern in the coming years will be better maintenance and utilization of existing highway facilities.

Utilizing Metropolitan Highway Capacity

Efforts to increase the effective capacity of existing metropolitan highways and streets have taken several forms. In many cities, on-street parking has been banned on major commuting arteries during rush hours. Demand-responsive traffic signaling systems have also been utilized. High occupancy vehicle lanes have become common in urban areas.

Carpooling and vanpooling also offer substantial potential for improving highway utilization. The automobile is the dominant vehicle in the metropolitan traffic flow, and its capacity generally has been underutilized. Improved automobile occupancy rates would not only tend to lessen congestion problems, but also contribute to improved environmental conditions. As a result, the DOT and the Environmental Protection Agency have worked with many communities in promoting carpool programs. Computer matching services are now available in many cities. The DOT contends that the potential for carpooling is the greatest:

> where trip origins and destinations are concentrated in small areas separated by a relatively long trip, and where there is some disincentive to private automobile travel such as long, time consuming trips, severe highway congestion, high parking charges or restrictions, or limited access to a private automobile.[34]

To increase the attractiveness of carpooling, some cities have extended special parking privileges to high-occupancy vehicles, and on some urban expressways carpools have been given access to express lanes. Increasing attention also is being given to the concept of differential tolls for carpools versus single-occupant automobiles on urban expressways.

Parking Facilities

The availability of parking spaces within a city naturally influences the commuter's modal choice decision. Consequently, city officials must develop a strategy related to parking, and it must be treated as a major component of local transportation planning. This entails decision making related not only to the management of the supply of parking spaces, but also to the level of parking fees.

Any increase in the supply of parking spaces gives the commuter an added incentive to drive. As a result, public officials in many cities have advocated limiting the number of new parking spaces approved for their cities. Although this action would increase the relative attractiveness of transit, it must be realized that such proposals encounter stiff opposition. Several groups that generally have opposed plans to restrict parking expansion are businesses located within the city, urban residents, and construction interests. Collectively, these groups can and have mounted substantial political pressure against such action.

Therefore, public officials have found it quite difficult to place a ceiling on urban parking spaces. However, they have increasingly turned to tighter controls over illegal parking. In most cities illegal parking spaces comprise a sizable portion of the available parking space. For example, several studies conducted in Boston have indicated that nearly one-fourth of parking spaces in use during business hours are illegal.[35] In response to this situation, officials in several cities have significantly increased parking fines and promoted more aggressive vehicle-towing campaigns. Over an extended period, as drivers become more selective in parking their vehicles, those actions can effectively reduce the number of available parking spaces.

Given the existing supply of parking spaces in a city, public officials can make driving less attractive by raising parking fees in public parking facilities. Major increases can significantly influence the total cost of driving. In the past, proposed parking fee increases often have been opposed strongly by retailers, who fear a related contraction of business, and organizations with many employees who drive to work. As a result, parking fee increases typically have been quite gradual.

In many cities emphasis seems to be shifting to suburban parking facilities which provide linkages with regular route transit operations. However, convincing suburban communities to allow large parking facilities to be developed within their boundaries is often quite difficult.

In any event, public decisions concerning parking facilities will continue to exert an influence on urban modal selection. The direction of future parking policies is likely to be a function of the intensity of environmental and energy problems and related federal programs.

Air Quality and the Automobile

As discussed in Chapter 17 considerable governmental attention has been devoted to reducing the negative effects of the automobile on urban life. Legislative actions such as those contained in the 1990 Clean Air Act amendments and the Comprehensive National Energy Policy Act of 1992, coupled with administrative mandates of the EPA, have substantially reduced automobile emission levels. Nevertheless, by 1992 181 metropolitan areas had failed to achieve compliance with federal ozone and carbon monoxide levels.[36] At the same time transit vehicles contribute far less pollution to the air than automobiles.[37] As a result, further governmental action to restrict automobile use or improve automobile maintenance are quite likely.

Automobile Disincentives

As discussed earlier in this chapter, transit ridership in the United States has increased during the past two decades.[38] Nevertheless, in many large cities traffic congestion continues to grow, and in a number of instances has spread into the suburbs. These development have raised questions concerning the commuting public's long-term willingness to switch to improved transit services.

If the public is reluctant to voluntarily forsake the automobile for commutation, and if environmental and energy considerations require more limited automobile usage, it may be necessary to rely upon disincentives. Such disincentives, which would be aimed at decreasing the relative attractiveness of the automobile, might take many forms. Steps could be taken to increase the cost of automobile usage through increased tolls on urban expressways, bridges, and tunnels (particularly during rush hours), higher parking fees, or increased excise taxes on gasoline. Other actions might be aimed at decreasing the automobile's access to the city. Cutbacks in parking facilities, creation of auto-free zones, and outright bans on automobile usage would increase the relative attractiveness of transit. Such policy decisions would be unpopular politically, but they may be necessary if national goals necessitate a major shift in commutation patterns from the automobile to transit.

NEED FOR INTEGRATED PLANNING

Attempts to solve metropolitan transportation problems historically have been troubled by organizational difficulties. Typically, several local and state agencies have controlled the various components of the metropolitan transportation system. This has increased the difficulty of developing a multimodal planning posture that attempts to meet metropolitan transportation needs efficiently. Further complicating the situation has been the multiplicity of political jurisdictions within a given metropolitan area. The intensity of this problem is illustrated by the fact that more than 18,000 political and administrative jurisdictions are represented in the 212 metropolitan areas recognized by the Department of Commerce.[39] It has been extremely difficult to coordinate these governmental units in a transportation-planning framework. This problem is even more complicated in the many metropolitan areas that extend across one or more state lines. Similarly, the growing involvement of the federal government in metropolitan transportation funding has necessitated even greater intergovernmental coordination. At the same time, it must be recognized that transportation planning must be integrated with other metropolitan community planning efforts.

As discussed earlier in this chapter, the federal government has used its funding leverage to promote metropolitan (and statewide) transportation planning that is not only multimodal in nature, but also geographically comprehensive and related to other planning efforts. The resulting coordination of planning efforts should play an important role in preparing our metropolitan areas to meet their mobility and environmental goals in the 21st Century.

SUMMARY

For many years the transportation problems of our metropolitan areas were treated as strictly local matters. This placed considerable pressure on local officials, who lacked sufficient funds to bolster failing transit systems. At the same time, they found it difficult to cope with the urban highway system's voracious appetite for property and its related pollution and congestion problems.

However, beginning in the early 1960s, congressional efforts to improve the quality of urban life led to a substantial increase in federal assistance to our cities. In recognition of the important role that transit can play in supporting local objectives, Congress began limited funding of transit projects in 1961. Since that time, growing national concerns with both improvement of environmental quality and energy conservation have prompted a tremendous expansion of federal transit funding. At the same time, the Department of Transportation has used the federal funding of transit and urban highway projects for leverage in promoting integrated metropolitan and statewide transportation planning.

The cooperative efforts of federal, state, and local government units have partially alleviated several major metropolitan transportation problems. Air pollution levels have been reduced substantially in many of our cities, and federal funds have promoted major improvements in transit services. Further, the long-term downtrend in transit ridership has been reversed. However, much remains to be done, and it can only be accomplished through continued cooperative efforts and long-term federal funding commitments.

DISCUSSION QUESTIONS

1. Do you believe that further increases in transit ridership can be achieved through continued system improvements? If you are not a regular transit patron, what would it take to make such service attractive to you?

2. Given that major transit properties invariably incur operating deficits, why aren't fares raised to make the services self-supporting?

3. As mayor of a large northeastern city, you have been approached by the members of the city council with a suggestion to ban automobile traffic in the central business district. You are scheduled to meet with the council tomorrow to inform them of your reaction. Discuss the benefits that such a program might foster and the problems that it might cause. Be complete in your discussion and include all relevant factors. Further, crafty politician that you are, you begin to weigh the matter in terms of votes. Who would provide support for an automobile ban? Who would oppose you if you decided to support the proposal?

4.   As chairperson of the Transportation Advisory Committee of a midwestern metropolitan area of approximately one million residents (core plus suburbs), you must make a report to the rest of the committee and the mayor concerning selection of the future transit system of your city. Your presentation essentially involves the choice of the most appropriate technology—rail versus bus operations. What factors will you consider in formulating your recommendations?

NOTES

1.   American Public Transit Association, *1992 Transit Fact Book* (Washington, D.C.: the Association, 1992), p. 33.
2.   Ibid., p. 56.
3.   Ibid., p. 13.
4.   Ibid., p. 51.
5.   See James M. Landis, *Report on Regulatory Agencies to the President-Elect*, submitted by the Chairman of the Subcommittee on Administrative Practice and Procedure to the Committee on the Judiciary of the U.S. Senate, 86th Cong., 2nd Sess., 1960 (Washington, D.C.: U.S. Government Printing Office); also, U.S. Senate, Committee on Interstate and Foreign Commerce, Special Study Group on Transportation Policies in the United States, *National Transportation Policy* (Doyle Report), 87th Cong., 1st Sess., 1960 (Washington, D.C.: U.S. Government Printing Office, 1961), pp. 552-635.
6.   George M. Smerk, *Urban Mass Transportation: A Dozen Years of Federal Policy* (Bloomington, IN: Indiana University Press, 1974), pp. 48-9.
7.   *The Transportation System of Our Nation*, message from the President of the United States, April 5, 1962, House of Representatives, Doc. No. 384, 87th Cong., 2nd Sess. (Washington, D.C.: U.S. Government Printing Office, 1962).
8.   *Urban Mass Transportation Act*, Public Law 88-365 (1964).
9.   U.S. Department of Transportation, *1974 National Transportation Report* (Washington, D.C.: U.S. Government Printing Office, 1975), p. 155.
10.   Smerk, *Urban Mass Transportation*, p. 76.
11.   Ibid.
12.   *Urban Mass Transportation Assistance Act*, Public Law 91-453 (1970).
13.   U.S. Department of Transportation, *1974 National Transportation Report*, p. 155.

14.   The Federal-Aid Highway Acts of 1968 and 1970 permitted the states to divert some of the funds they received from the Highway Trust Fund to transit-related projects, such as exclusive or preferential bus lanes, parking facilities, or bus stops. However, the funds could not be used for major capital projects.

15.   *National Mass Transportation Assistance Act* Public Law 93-503 (1974).

16.   George M. Smerk, "Update on Federal Mass Transportation Policy: The Surface Transportation Act of 1978," *Transportation Journal*, Vol. 18, NO. 3 (Spring, 1979), pp. 16-19.

17.   *Surface Transportation Assistance Act*, Public Law 05-599 (1978).

18.   U.S. Department of Transportation, Office of the Secretary, *Implementing Transportation Policy* (Washington, D.C.: the Department, 1973), pp. 14-15.

19.   For a discussion of the congressional debate concerning these issues, see George M. Smerk, "The Transit Act That Never Was: Public Transportation Legislation, 1979-1980," *Transportation Journal*, Vol. 20, No. 4 (Summer, 1981), pp. 29-53.

20.   *Surface Transportation Act*, Public Law 97-424 (1982).

21.   George M. Smerk, *The Federal Role in Urban Mass Transportation* (Bloomington, IN: Indiana University Press, 1991), p. 219.

22.   For a discussion of the Reagan proposals, see C. Carroll Carter, "Editorial," *Mass Transit*, Vol. 10, No. 7 (July, 1983), p. 5; also, C. Carroll Carter, "Editorial," *Mass Transit*, Vol. 11, No. 4 (April, 1984), p. 5.

23.   For discussions of privatization see George M. Smerk, "Urban Mass Transportation: From Private to Public to Privatization," *Transportation Journal*, Vol. 26, No. 1 (Fall, 1986), pp. 83-91; also, Mark S. Donovan, "Partnerships," *Mass Transit* (April, 1990), pp. 30-1.

24.   Smerk, *The Federal Role in Urban Mass Transportation*, p. 253.

25.   *Federal Mass Transportation Act of 1987*, Public Law 100-17.

26.   Smerk, *The Federal Role in Urban Mass Transportation*, pp. 256-7.

27.   Ibid., p. 241.

28.   *Americans with Disabilities Act*, Public Law 101-336 (1990).

29.   Dick Thornburgh, "The Americans with Disabilities Act: What It Means to All Americans," *Labor Law Journal* (December, 1990), p. 806.

30.   For an extensive discussion of the ISTEA legislation, see Edward Weiner, U.S. Department of Transportation, Office of the Secretary, *Urban Transportation Planning in the United States: An Historical Overview*, rev. ed. (Washington, D.C.: the Department, 1992), particularly Chapter 12. "Strategic Planning,", pp. 213-58.

31.   Robert C. Lieb, U.S. Department of Transportation, Office of the Secretary, *Labor in the Transit Industry* (Washington, D.C.: U.S. Government Printing Office, 1976), p. 6.

32.   See Thomas Crosby, "Section 13(c): to Grant or Not to Grant," *Mass Transit* (May, 1977), pp. 10-13.

33.   Frederick B. Siskind and Ernst W. Stromdorfer, *The Economic Cost Impact of the Labor Protection Provisions of Section 13(c) of the Urban Mass Transportation Act of 1964*, Part I (Springfield, VA: National Technical Information Service, 1978), pp. xiii.

34.   U.S. Department of Transportation, *1974 National Transportation Report*, p. 148.

35.   Data supplied by the Office of the Parking Commissioner, Boston, MA.

36.   Richard Szathmary, "The Alternative-Fuel Alternative," *Sales and Marketing Management* (April, 1992), pp. 80-2, 84-5.

37.   American Public Transit Association, p. 21.

38.   Ibid., p. 65.

39.   Information supplied by the U.S. Department of Commerce.

SELECTED REFERENCES

"A Gridlock Buster for the 21st Century?" *Business Week* (August 27, 1990), p. 84.

American Public Transit Association. *1992 Transit Fact Book*. Washington, D.C.: the Association, 1992.

Brucato, Patricia S. "Safety First." *Mass Transit* (May-June, 1991), pp. 18-20.

Cavinato, Joseph L., and Martha L. Cuckovich. "Transportation and Tourism for the Disabled: An Assessment." *Transportation Journal*, Vol. 31 No. 3 (Spring, 1992), pp. 46-53.

"GM Drives the Electric Car Closer to Reality." *Business Week* (May 14, 1990), pp. 60-1.

Larson, Thomas D. "Metropolitan Congestion: Towards A Tolerable Accommodation." *Transportation Quarterly*, Vol. 42, No. 4 (October, 1988), pp. 489-98.

Middleton, William D. "The New Age of Light Rail Vehicles."*Railway Age* (February, 1993), pp. 33-4, 36-38B, 42, 44, 46-50.

Miller, Luther S. "The Clinton Years: Will the Good Times *Railway Age* (January, 1993), pp. 40-2.

Rafter, David, and Joel Alter. "Local Government Involvement in Metropolitan Transit Planning." *Transportation Quarterly* Vol. 45, No. 2 (April, 1991), pp. 233-42.

Smerk, George M. *The Federal Role in Urban Mass Transportation*. Bloomington, IN: Indiana University Press, 1991.

Smith, Mary F., Nabil Y. Razzouk, and Scott A. Richardson. "The Role of Marketing in Mass Transit: An Empirical Investigation." *Transportation Journal*, Vol. 30, No. 1 (Fall, 1990), pp. 20-9.

Strandberg, Keith W. "ADA: The Intent, Impact and Implementation." *Mass Transit* (July-August, 1990), pp. 24, 26-31.

U.S. Department of Transportation, Federal Highway Administration and Urban Mass Transportation Administration. *Private Sector Involvement in Urban Transportation: Case Studies*. Washington, D.C.: the Department, 1986.

U.S. Department of Transportation, Urban Mass Transportation Administration. *Strategic Plan*. Washington, D.C.: the Department, 1991.

U.S. General Accounting Office. *Mass Transit: Effects of Tax Changes on Commuter Behavior*. Washington, D.C.: General Accounting Office, 1992.

Weiner, Edward. U.S. Department of Transportation, Office of the Secretary. *Urban Transportation Planning in the United States: An Historical Overview*, rev. ed. (Washington, D.C.: the Department, 1992.

MBTA Green Line Service, Boston *Courtesy Massachusetts Bay Transportation Authority*

Index